6th International Metrology Conference (CAFMET 2016)

AA005619

Dakar, Senegal
21 - 24 March 2016

ISBN: 978-1-5108-3074-5

Printed from e-media with permission by:

Curran Associates, Inc.
57 Morehouse Lane
Red Hook, NY 12571

Some format issues inherent in the e-media version may also appear in this print version.

Printed by Curran Associates, Inc. (2016)

Comite African de Metrologie (CAFMET)
62 av. Notre Dame du Lac
49000 Angers
France

Phone: 33 (0) 6 73 62 32 62
Fax: 33 (0) 2 41 88 84 21

contact@cafmet.com

Additional copies of this publication are available from:

Curran Associates, Inc.
57 Morehouse Lane
Red Hook, NY 12571 USA
Phone: 845-758-0400
Fax: 845-758-2633
Email: curran@proceedings.com
Web: www.proceedings.com

Summury

Sommaire

Measuring simultaneously the surface tension and the contact angle using the meniscus on a sphere

S. Champmartin[1,a], A. Ambari[1], A. Charki[2] and J.Y. Le Pommelec[1]

[1]ENSAM Angers, LAMPA, 2 bd. du Ronceray, 49035 Angers, France
[2]University of Angers, ISTIA-LASQUO, 62 av. Notre Dame du Lac, 49000 Angers, France

Received:

Abstract. This paper proposes a new technique to simultaneously measure the static contact angle and the surface tension of a liquid using a spherical geometry. Unlike the other existing methods, the knowledge of one of both previous parameters is not mandatory. The technique is based on the measurement of two simple physical quantities: the height of the meniscus formed on a spherical surface and the resulting vertical force exerted on this object. The meniscus height at equilibrium, which has no exact analytical expression, is often estimated with an approximate 2D model, valid only for very large spheres compared to the capillary length. We develop instead another simplified solution of the Young-Laplace equation based on the work of Ferguson for the meniscus on a cylinder and adapted for the spherical shape. This alternative method, which is less restrictive in terms of the sphere size, is successfully compared to numerical solutions of the complete Young-Laplace equation. It appears to be accurate for sphere radii larger than only two capillary lengths. Finally the feasibility of the method is experimentally tested and validated for three common liquids and two "small" steel spheres. This technique is easy to implement and as accurate as the existing techniques.

Keywords: surface tension, contact angle, Young-Laplace equation, tensionetry

1 Introduction

The interactions between a liquid and a solid surface are met among the most common phenomena in Nature (ground water, oil reservoirs…) as well as in many industrial processes (coating, imbibition…). One of the key parameters [1-4] in such interactions is the contact angle θ defined as the angle between the tangents of the liquid-vapor and solid-liquid interfaces where the three phases join (triple line). According to the classical Young's equation [5], θ depends only on the interfacial energies:

$$\cos\theta = \frac{\sigma_{sv} - \sigma_{sl}}{\sigma} \quad (1)$$

with σ the liquid-vapor surface energy (commonly called the surface tension), σ_{sv} and σ_{sl} respectively the solid-vapor and solid-liquid surface energies. From the viewpoint of thermodynamics, these energies represent the works to produce a unit surface of interface at constant temperature, pressure and chemical potential. The value of θ gives a good indication of how well a liquid and a solid interact: low-energy solids such as polymers are generally poorly wetted by liquids which form droplets with a high contact angle value ($\theta \geq 90°$); high-energy solids such as metals and glass are surfaces on which most liquids wet spontaneously forming puddles with a low value of the contact angle ($\theta \leq 90°$). The knowledge of θ is also necessary to predict the invasion of liquids in porous media or in solid surface finishing. Experimentally it is very hard to measure a unique value of θ because the contact angle at equilibrium is subject to a hysteresis [6,7] of at least $10°$. This phenomenon is the result of the surface structural heterogeneities (slight roughness, spatial inhomogeneities) and chemical contamination. The simplest means to obtain θ consists in using a goniometer to measure the contact angle at the triple line of a sessile drop on a solid plane surface [8]. This technique is known to be inaccurate and sensitive to the surface cleanliness. Most alternative techniques are based on the measurement of the force exerted by a meniscus on solid surfaces of various shapes and the knowledge of the surface tension σ is prerequisite [9]. The techniques to measure σ are also numerous and described in details in many textbooks [4,10,11]: capillary rise method, pendant drop method, stalagnometric method, maximum pressure bubble method, Wilhelmy or Du Noüy methods, capillary waves method [12,13]… In most of these techniques, the knowledge of the contact angle is necessary beforehand or estimated to be zero. In this work, we propose a simple technique to simultaneously

a)Author to whom correspondence should be addressed. Electronic mail: stephane.champmartin@ensam.eu.

determine θ and σ. This new technique is based on the measurement of two accessible physical quantities: the capillary force on a solid surface, which can be directly given by a microbalance and the height of the formed meniscus which can be easily obtained by image analysis. Note that contrary to the other classical methods, any assumptions about the value of these parameters are required. We use in this work a solid spherical surface because this simple shape presents several advantages: the meniscus is axisymmetric, stable14 and free of discontinuities or end effects (unlike the plate in the method of Wilhelmy) allowing an easy optical inspection of its height; the axisymmetric shape of the meniscus makes the numerical and/or semi-analytical resolution of the Young-Laplace equation relatively easier; there is only one meniscus (unlike the ring in the method of Du Noüy); in the plate and ring methods, the spatial positioning of the solid is much more critical than for a sphere (the sphere touches the liquid bath at only one point whereas the base of the ring or of the plate must be perfectly parallel to the liquid level); the spherical shape is compact and has naturally the smallest surface-to-volume ratio, reducing the potential surface contamination; finally the experimental results show a noticeable reproducibility. On the other hand the height of the meniscus must be numerically calculated in this case. In the following, we study the vertical force exerted by the capillary bridge on the sphere. This force depends on the height of the meniscus and two simplified models are proposed and discussed by comparing them to a numerical solution. Finally the method is successfully validated experimentally.

2 Theoretical and numerical analysis

Fig. 1 below presents the sketch of the problem below. As soon as the sphere of radius b contacts the liquid, the latter rises onto the solid surface and forms at equilibrium an axisymmetric meniscus with a height z_0 above the level of the liquid bath. The triple line radius r_0 is related to the sphere radius b and to z_0 by a simple geometrical relation:

$$r_0 = \sqrt{z_0(2b - z_0)} \qquad (2)$$

At the triple line, the tangent to the meniscus and to the vertical direction form an angle β_0. This virtual contact angle is related to the actual contact angle θ by:

$$\beta_0 = \theta - \alpha \qquad (3)$$

α is the angle between the vertical direction and the tangent to the sphere at the triple line. This angle is a function of the meniscus height z_0 and of the sphere radius b:

$$\tan\alpha = \frac{b - z_0}{\sqrt{z_0(2b - z_0)}} \qquad (4)$$

The vertical component of the capillary force on the sphere is:

$$p = 2\pi r_0 \sigma \cos\beta_0 + \rho g \pi z_0^2 \left(b - \frac{2z_0}{3}\right) \qquad (5)$$

This force is composed of two parts: the first one $2\pi r_0 \sigma \cos\beta_0$ is the vertical projection of the capillary force with the virtual contact angle β_0. This contribution is also equal to the weight of the liquid contained in the outer part of the meniscus for $r > r_0$. The second contribution $\rho g \pi z_0^2 \left(b - \frac{2z_0}{3}\right)$ is the weight of the liquid volume in the inner part of the meniscus for $r < r_0$. This volume is the cylinder of radius r_0 and height z_0 reduced by the volume of the spherical cap of base radius r_0 and height z_0. If the contact angle θ is given, the measurement of the force p and of the height z_0 and the use of Eq. (5) give a direct way to determining the surface tension σ.

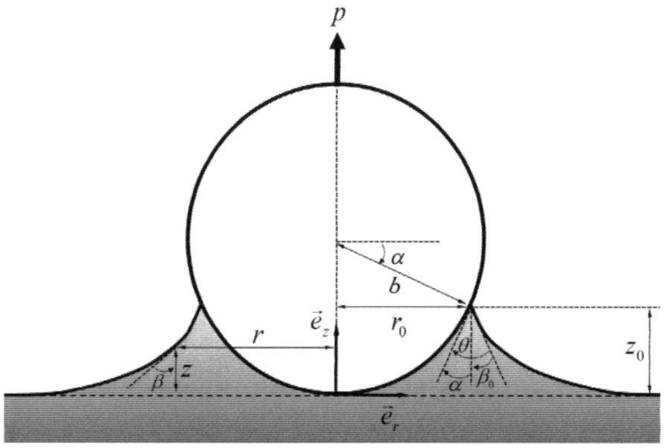

Fig. 1. Schematic representation of the meniscus on a sphere and notations.

Likewise if the surface tension is known, the measurement of p and z_0 give access to the contact angle θ. In order to determine one of the parameters, the knowledge of the other one is needed as in the classical tensiometry techniques described in the introduction. In order to overcome this dependence, another relation between z_0 and θ is required. This missing relation is obtained determining the height of the meniscus. This type of problems belongs to a class of mathematical issues studied by many authors15-17. The profile of the meniscus is a solution of the Young-Laplace equation:

$$\sigma\left(\frac{1}{r_1} + \frac{1}{r_2}\right) = \rho g z \qquad (6)$$

with r_1 and r_2 the principal radii of curvature, ρ the liquid density, g the gravity constant and z the vertical coordinate. In the present situation the meniscus is axisymmetric and the previous equation in cylindrical coordinates becomes:

$$\frac{\ddot{r}}{[1+\dot{r}^2]^{\frac{3}{2}}} - \frac{1}{r[1+\dot{r}^2]^{\frac{1}{2}}} = \frac{z}{a^2} \qquad (7)$$

with $a = \sqrt{\frac{\sigma}{\rho g}}$ the capillary length (the typical length above which the gravity effects prevail over the capillary effects, typically around a few millimeters for most liquids), $\dot{r} = \frac{dr}{dz}$

and $\ddot{r} = \frac{d^2r}{dz^2}$. The boundary conditions are:

$$\begin{cases} \text{for } r \to \infty:\ z = 0, \dot{r} \to -\infty & (8a) \\ \text{for } r = r_0:\ z = z_0, \dot{r}_0 = -\tan\beta_0 & (8b) \end{cases}$$

Eq. (7) has no analytical solution with the boundary conditions (8a,b). However it is possible to obtain approximate solutions by means of some simplifications.

First approximation: 2D

When the sphere is large compared to the capillary length ($b \gg a$, large Bond or Eötvös numbers), the second term on the left-hand side of Eq. (7) is negligible. Indeed close to the triple line, we have $z_0 \sim a$, $r_1 \sim \sqrt{ab}$ and $r_2 \sim b$ implying that $\frac{1}{r_2} \ll \frac{1}{r_1}$. Then the Young-Laplace equation reduces to:

$$\frac{\ddot{r}}{[1+\dot{r}^2]^{\frac{3}{2}}} = \frac{z}{a^2} \qquad (9)$$

This equation is valid when the axisymmetric curvature is negligible compared to the in-plane curvature. We can integrate Eq. (9) and using the boundary condition (8a), it gives:

$$\frac{\dot{r}}{[1+\dot{r}^2]^{\frac{1}{2}}} = \frac{z^2}{2a^2} - 1 \qquad (10)$$

The meniscus height z_0 of the triple line at equilibrium is found using the second boundary condition (8b):

$$\frac{z_0^2}{2a^2} - 1 + \sin\beta_0 = 0 \qquad (11)$$

This is of course the same relation as the one obtained for the capillary rise on a vertical plane or on a very large vertical cylinder when the real contact angle is replaced by the virtual contact angle β_0. This 2D model is often used in the literature because of its simplicity but because the second curvature $\frac{1}{r_2}$ is completely neglected in this model, the solution (11) is expected to be accurate only for large spheres as we will confirm later.

Second approximation: Ferguson

In the case of the meniscus formed on a vertical cylinder, Ferguson18 proposed to partially take into account the second curvature $\frac{1}{r_2}$. We adapt here his analysis in the case of the spherical surface, considering the latter as a stack of cylindrical slices. The term $\frac{1}{[1+\dot{r}^2]^{\frac{1}{2}}}$ in the second term on the left hand side of Eq. (7) is replaced using Eq. (10) of the previous 2D approximation:

$$\frac{1}{[1+\dot{r}^2]^{\frac{1}{2}}} = \frac{1}{\dot{r}}\left(\frac{z^2}{2a^2} - 1\right) \qquad (12)$$

$\dot{r}$ is the slope of the profile of the meniscus at a given height z and is simply:

$$\dot{r} = -\tan\beta = \frac{\sin\beta}{\sqrt{1-\sin^2\beta}} \qquad (13)$$

Using Eq. (11) we obtain:

$$\dot{r} = -\frac{1 - \frac{z^2}{2a^2}}{\frac{z}{a}\sqrt{1 - \frac{z^2}{4a^2}}} \qquad (14)$$

Putting (14) into (12) gives:

$$\frac{1}{[1+\dot{r}^2]^{\frac{1}{2}}} = \frac{z}{a}\sqrt{1 - \frac{z^2}{4a^2}} \qquad (15)$$

The approximate Young-Laplace equation now writes:

$$\frac{\ddot{r}}{[1+\dot{r}^2]^{\frac{3}{2}}} = \frac{z}{a^2} + \frac{z}{ra}\sqrt{1 - \frac{z^2}{4a^2}} \qquad (16)$$

Supposing that the meniscus radius r is of the order of the triple line radius r_0, we obtain:

$$\frac{\ddot{r}}{[1+\dot{r}^2]^{\frac{3}{2}}} = \frac{z}{a^2} + \frac{z}{r_0 a}\sqrt{1 - \frac{z^2}{4a^2}} \qquad (17)$$

This equation can be integrated, and using the boundary condition (8a), it gives:

$$\frac{\dot{r}}{[1+\dot{r}^2]^{\frac{1}{2}}} = \frac{z^2}{2a^2} - 1 - \frac{4a}{3r_0}\left[\left(1 - \frac{z^2}{4a^2}\right)^{\frac{3}{2}} - 1\right] \qquad (18)$$

The height z_0 of the triple line is obtained again using the second boundary condition (8b):

$$\frac{z_0^2}{2a^2} - 1 + \sin\beta_0 = \frac{4a}{3r_0}\left[\left(1 - \frac{z_0^2}{4a^2}\right)^{\frac{3}{2}} - 1\right] \qquad (19)$$

The right hand side term in (19) is negative and corrects downwards the previous 2D approximation (11). In order to evaluate the accuracy of these approximate solutions, we now perform a numerical resolution of the Young-Laplace equation.

Numerical resolution

Eq. (7) was first normalized using the capillary length as the length scale ($Z = \frac{z}{a}$ and $R = \frac{r}{a}$) and split into two first order equations:

$$\begin{cases} F = \dot{R} & (20a) \\ \dot{F} = Z[1+F^2]^{\frac{3}{2}} + \frac{1+F^2}{R} & (20b) \end{cases}$$

Starting from an initial value of the height of the triple line $Z_{0,1}$ and for a given contact angle θ, we calculate an initial value of the radius of the triple line $R_{0,1} = \sqrt{Z_{0,1}(2B - Z_{0,1})}$ with $B = \frac{b}{a}$, of the angle $\beta_{0,1}$ using Eqs. (3-4) and of the slope of the meniscus $\dot{R}_{0,1} = -\tan\beta_{0,1}$ at the same place. The values of $R(Z + dZ)$ and $\dot{R}(Z + dZ)$ are calculated using a first order development. In order to converge rapidly, we chose for $Z_{0,1}$ the solution of Eq. (19) (Ferguson approximation) which slightly overestimates the real solution. Consequently, the asymptotic solution of Z when $R \rightarrow \infty$ is positive and the matching at the level of the liquid bath is not achieved. The algorithm is repeated with a decreased value $Z_{0,2} < Z_{0,1}$ and repeated until an acceptable solution is found at the horizontal liquid bath level. In practice we consider that the initial guess of Z_0 is accurate enough when the following conditions are met:

$$\text{for } R = 10\ ,\ |\dot{R}| > 1000 \text{ and } |Z| < 10^{-3}$$

This procedure was programmed in FORTRAN on a standard personal computer and converged in a few seconds.

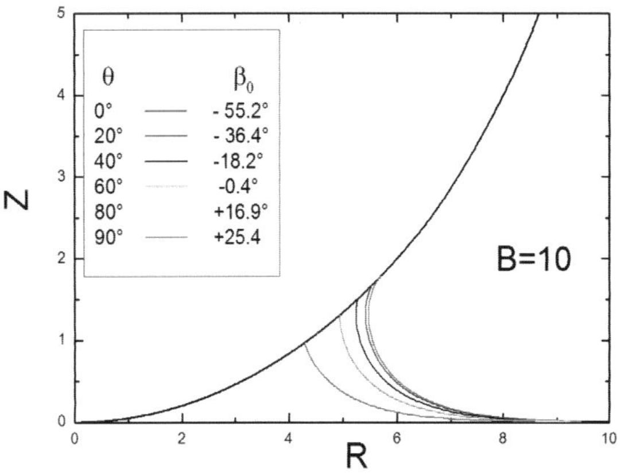

Fig. 2. Numerical meniscus profiles for $B = 10$ and $0° \leq \theta \leq 90°$ ($-55.2° \leq \beta_0 \leq 25.4°$)

To illustrate the numerical method, we display in Fig. 2 the calculated profiles of the meniscus in the case $B = 10$ and for contact angles in the range $0° \leq \theta \leq 90°$ corresponding to $-55.2° \leq \beta_0 \leq 25.4°$. In this figure we note that the sign of the slope of the meniscus profile can change when the liquid is wetting the solid surface (low θ values). In those cases, the meniscus presents a minimal radius smaller than the triple line radius. For non-wetting conditions (high θ values), the slope of the meniscus is always negative and the triple radius is the minimal radial extension of the meniscus. We now turn our attention to the determination of the height of the meniscus. In Fig. 3 below we display the normalized height $Z_0 = \frac{z_0}{a}$ as a function of the normalized sphere radius $B = \frac{b}{a}$ for two contact angles $\theta = 20°$ (partially wetting material) and $\theta = 100°$ (non-wetting material).

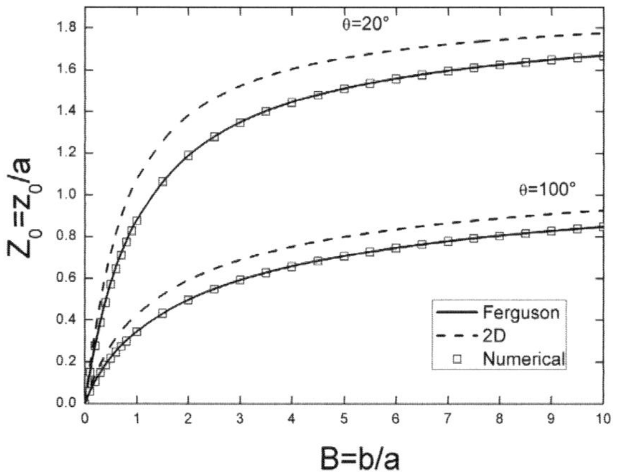

Fig.3. Z_0 vs. B for $\theta = 20°$ and $\theta = 100°$.

We can see that the 2D approximation noticeably overestimates the numerical solution, whereas that of Ferguson appears to be in good agreement with the numerical solution. This is confirmed in Fig. 4 and 5 where the relative difference between the numerical solution and the solutions based on the 2D and the Ferguson approximations are given as a function of B for contact angles between $20° \leq \theta \leq 130°$. For the 2D approximation (Fig. 4), the relative difference is large, slowly decreases and strongly depends on the value the value of θ . For the Ferguson approximation (Fig. 5), the relative difference rapidly decreases as B increases and seems to be relatively insensitive to the value of θ . As soon as $B > 2$, the solution of Ferguson (19) differs from the numerical one by less than 1% for all the contact angles less than $130°$. Experimentally there is no smooth unpatterned surface on which such a high value of the contact angle can be found. For instance for water and low energy hydrophobic smooth surfaces, the contact angles peak around 120° to 130° [19]. We conclude that the 2D approximation is too rough to accurately estimate the height of the meniscus (unless very large spheres are used: for instance for $\theta = 130°$, the solutions are the same within 1% for $B > 1500$) and that the approximate solution of Ferguson is precise enough as soon as the sphere radius is only at least twice the capillary length.

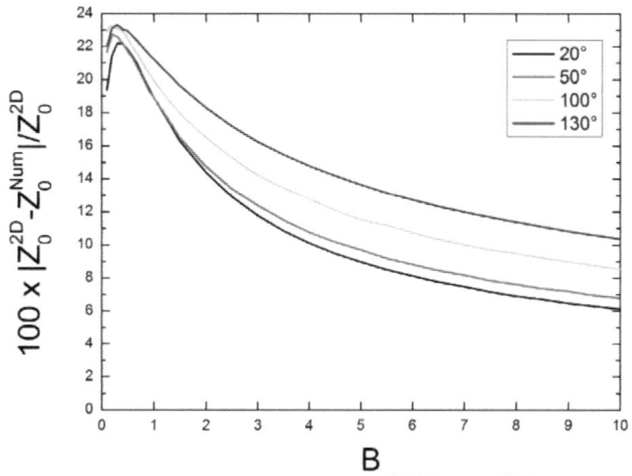

Fig. 4. Relative difference between z_0^{Num} and z_0^{2D} vs. B .

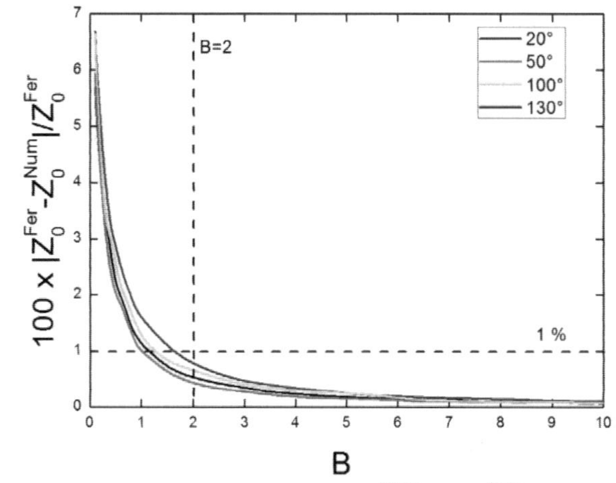

Fig. 5 Relative difference between z_0^{Num} and z_0^{Fer} vs. B .

The latter being of the order of 2 millimeters for most liquids, the Ferguson approximation is sufficient for spheres of radii of the order of 4 millimeters. In the following, we use the Ferguson approximate equation (19) to calculate the capillary rise onto a sphere instead of the numerical resolution of the complete Young-Laplace equation because it is much more straightforward. From Eq. (5) and (19), it is now easy to obtain σ (or $a = \sqrt{\frac{\sigma}{\rho g}}$) and θ independently if z_0 and p are measured. We have indeed from Eq. (19):

$$\sin\beta_0 = 1 - \frac{z_0^2}{2a^2} + \frac{4a}{3\sqrt{z_0(2b - z_0)}}\left[\left(1 - \frac{z_0^2}{4a^2}\right)^{\frac{3}{2}} - 1\right] \quad (21)$$

And from Eq. (5):

$$\cos\beta_0 = \frac{p - \rho g \pi z_0^2\left(b - \frac{2z_0}{3}\right)}{2\pi\rho g a^2\sqrt{z_0(2b - z_0)}} \quad (22)$$

Eliminating β_0 in Eqs. (21-22), we obtain an equation for the variable a alone that can be solved numerically (we used the Wolfram Mathematica package) and the surface tension σ can be deduced. Once a is known, β_0 can be obtained from either (21) or (22) and the contact angle θ is calculated using Eqs. (3-4). In the following section we experimentally test this new approach.

3 Experimental setup

Three common liquids were tested in order to validate the previous analysis: water ($\rho = 998\frac{kg}{m^3}$), castor oil ($\rho = 962\frac{kg}{m^3}$) and glycerin ($\rho = 1260\frac{kg}{m^3}$). We used steel spheres from ball bearings (100Cr6 steel alloy) with radii $b = 10.15\ mm$ and $b = 11.5\ mm$. According to the manufacturer (CIMAP), the accuracy on their radius is of the order of $2.5\ 10^{-6}m$. The sketch of the setup is presented in Fig. 6 below. The spheres are fastened to the precision balance (model Kern PLJ, $1\ mg$ read accuracy) by a rigid axis for the measurement of the force p . The height z_0 is measured by a cathetometer ($10^{-5}m$ accuracy) or by image processing (Miro 4 camera from Vision Research and ImageJ software). A LED backlight (OPT Machine Vision) is placed behind the sphere in order to obtain a contrasting image of the meniscus profile. The tank containing the liquid is the cup of a classical ring/plate tensiometer. Its radius is $R_c = 6\ cm$ and the liquid is filled to the brim so that the liquid interface slightly exceeds the top of the cup allowing one to see when the sphere touches the liquid.

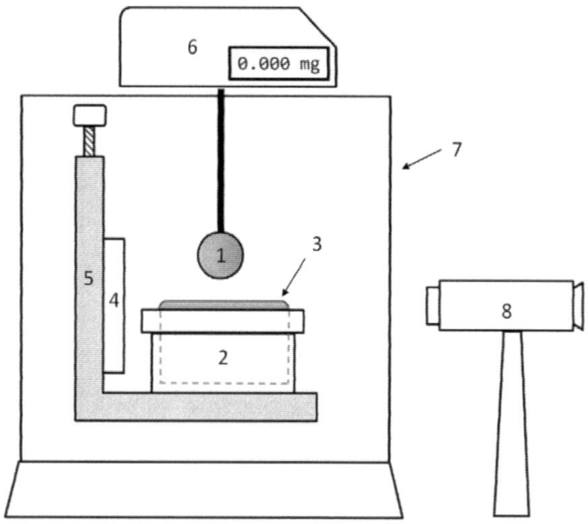

Fig 6. Experimental setup: (1) sphere, (2) tank, (3) liquid/air interface, (4) backlight, (5) micrometric table, (6) balance, (7) glass box, (8) optical device (cathetometer or camera)

The tank is mounted on a vertically moving micrometric table (OWIS, $10^{-5}\,\mathrm{m}$ accuracy) to accurately control the height of the liquid surface. The whole setup is placed under a glass box to reduce disturbance and evaporation. The liquid temperature is measured before and after each trial. In Table 1 below, the measured values of z_0 and P are presented for the 6 trials. The measured force P_{mes} has to be corrected to account for the slight decrease in the tank level when the meniscus forms. Using the conservation of the liquid volume, the corrected force is:

$$P_{cor} = P_{mes}\left(1 - \frac{r_0^2}{R_t^2}\right) \qquad (23)$$

In the present tests, this correction is in the range $0.936 < 1 - \frac{r_0^2}{R_t^2} < 0.970$. The measured meniscus height z_0 is also affected by the decrease in the liquid level in the tank but this correction is negligible (less than 0.8%). The last three lines of Table 1 give respectively the values of the surface tension σ, the capillary length a and the contact angle θ deduced from the present analysis using the Ferguson approximate solution. The radial extension of the meniscus being of the order of the capillary length a, we have for all our tests $23 < \frac{R_t}{a} < 32$.

Table 1. Experimental parameters and results.

	Water		Castor oil		Glycerin	
$b\,(mm)$	10.15	11.50	10.15	11.50	10.15	11.50
$T\,(°C)$	23.1	22.8	23.8	24.2	22.3	22.4
$z_0\,(mm)$	1.84	1.99	2.82	2.90	1.77	1.96
$\frac{P_{mes}}{g}\,(mg)$	285	347	344	409	305	385
$\frac{P_{cor}}{g}\,(mg)$	276	325	333	395	296	373
$\sigma\left(\frac{mN}{m}\right)$	64.66	64.27	33.60	35.11	63.59	63.56
$a\,(mm)$	2.57	2.60	1.89	1.93	2.27	2.27
$\theta\,(°)$	88.6	87.9	24.2	26.8	89.1	86.2

Consequently, the edge effects can be reasonably neglected (the free surface of the liquid is perfectly flat at the center of the cup before contact and far from the meniscus when the capillary bridge is formed; consequently the shape of the meniscus depends only on the contact with the sphere). Moreover, the validity of the Ferguson approximation is also respected ($3.9 < \frac{b}{a} < 6.1$) justifying the use of Eq. (19) to obtain z_0. Within the experimental uncertainties, the values of σ are independent of the sphere radius and are in agreement with the values found in the literature. For each liquid we also used a pendant drop tensiometer (KRÜSS G10) to compare these values.

Table 2. Comparison of σ obtained by the present method and the pendant drop method.

$\sigma\left(\frac{mN}{m}\right)$	*Water*	*Castor oil*	*Glycerin*
Present method	64.5	34.4	63.6
KRÜSS G10	65.8	35.2	64.9
Rel. difference (%)	1.98	2.33	2.04

The comparison is given in Table 2. The relative difference between both methods is around 2% which validates our approach (the average value of σ of Table 1 is considered in Table 2 for the present method). From the knowledge of θ and σ, it is now also possible to reconstruct the shape of the meniscus using the numerical method described in the previous section. Fig. 7 displays the superimposition of the real and numerically calculated menisci in the case of water and a sphere of radius $b = 11.5\,\mathrm{mm}$. The good agreement between both profiles gives confidence in the present technique. Experimentally we measure $z_0 = 1.99\,\mathrm{mm}$, the numerical calculation predicts $z_0 = 2.01\,\mathrm{mm}$ and the solution of the equation using the approximation of Ferguson is $z_0 = 2.03\,\mathrm{mm}$. The present profile always has a negative slope and the experimental determination of z_0 is easy

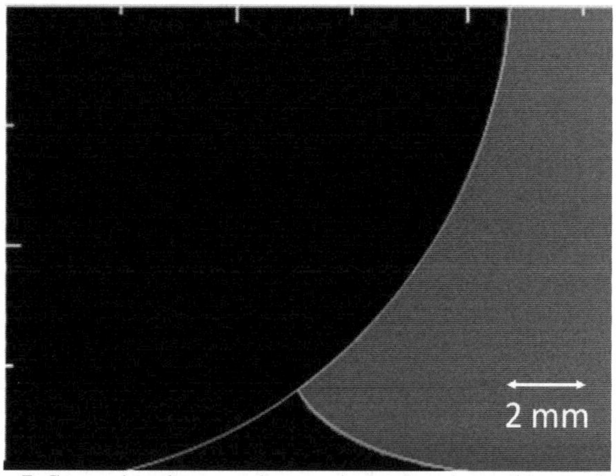

Fig. 7. Comparison between the experimental static meniscus and the theoretical shape (white line) derived from the numerical method for water and a steel sphere with radius $b = 11.5\,mm$.

As noted in the previous section (numerical section), it is also possible to observe menisci whose slope can change in sign when the liquid is non-wetting and/or the radius of the sphere is small compared to a. In those cases, the experimental measurement of z_0 requires special care. Moreover it is likely that the contact angle in the case of water is close to the advancing contact angle. Indeed as noted by Restagno [14] the capillary rise of the meniscus is very fast in the case of water and the final static contact angle may be close to an advancing contact angle. In fact following Clanet [20], we estimate the time of capillary rise for water to be of the order of $t \sim \sqrt{\frac{\rho a^3}{\sigma}} \sim 16\ ms$ (inertial regime) and for castor oil and glycerin of the order of $t \sim \frac{80 \mu a}{\sigma} \sim 3s$ (viscous regime). These dynamic effects are important when the viscosity of the liquid is low and the surface tension large. They are conveniently characterized by the Kapitsa number [20] (comparison of the capillary force to the gravity and viscosity forces):

$$\mathrm{Ka} = \left(\frac{\sigma^3}{\rho^3 g \nu^4}\right)^{\frac{1}{4}} \qquad (24)$$

This number is high in the case of water ($Ka \approx 400$) and low in the case of the castor oil and glycerin ($Ka \approx 0.3$) confirming that the contact angle is certainly close to an advancing contact angle in the case of water. For glycerin and castor oil the final contact angle is slightly different from the advancing contact angle. Finally the question of accuracy and sensitivity is of course of great significance in such a study. Due to the implicit and complex formulation, the uncertainty calculation for σ is difficult to perform using the Ferguson approximate solution for the capillary height z_0. It is however reasonable to suppose that it is of the same order of magnitude as the one obtained for the meniscus in the simpler 2D approximation. A numerical inspection of the two components of the force $\mathbf{P}$ in Eq. (5) reveals that they are of the same order of magnitude. Consequently, the order of magnitude of p is simply: $p \approx r_0 \sigma \cos\beta_0$. Using the expression of the meniscus height in the 2D approximation (11) and eliminating the contact angle β_0, we obtain for the surface tension:

$$\sigma \approx \rho g z_0^2 + \frac{p^2}{\rho g z_0^3 (2b - z_0)} \qquad (25)$$

A new inspection of both terms in (25) shows that the second term is prevailing. If the main uncertainties are those on p and z_0, the uncertainty calculation based on the second term of (25) gives:

$$\frac{\Delta\sigma}{\sigma} \approx \frac{2\Delta p}{p} + \frac{3\Delta z_0}{z_0} + \frac{\Delta z_0}{2b - z_0} \qquad (29)$$

Using $\Delta z_0 = 10\ \mu m$ and $\frac{\Delta p}{g} = 1\ mg$, we obtain a maximum relative uncertainty of the order of 2.5%. For the uncertainty concerning the contact angle, we can start again from the expression of z_0 in the 2D approximation (11). By differentiating this expression, we have: $z_0 dz_0 = a^2 \cos\beta_0 d\beta_0$. In our measurement, the angle α varies little ($\Delta\alpha \approx 10°$ compared to $\Delta\beta_0 \approx 56°$) and we can approximate $\Delta\beta_0 \approx \Delta\theta$. The sensitivity of the method is thus:

$$\frac{\Delta\theta}{\Delta z_0} \approx \frac{z_0}{a^2 \cos\beta_0} \qquad (30)$$

Taking again $\Delta z_0 = 10\ \mu m$, we obtain for the present measurements the uncertainties concerning the contact angle of the order of $\Delta\theta \approx 2°$ comparable to the other existing methods.

4 Conclusion

In this article we propose an original method allowing the simultaneous determination of the surface tension σ and of the contact angle θ contrary to all the other methods which require the knowledge of one of both parameters. This method is based on the combined measurements of the height of the meniscus on a sphere and of the weight of the meniscus. We adapt the Ferguson approximate solution (usually applied for the meniscus on cylindrical rods) to the spherical surface taking the sphere as the superimposition of cylindrical slices. This model allows one to calculate the static height z_0 of the meniscus on the sphere. Our numerical results clearly show that the Ferguson model is very accurate as soon as the sphere radius is greater than twice the capillary length, contrary to the largely used 2D approximation which necessitates a much greater sphere radius (introducing various experimental difficulties: tank edge effects, contamination…) to achieve the same precision. We use a very simple experimental setup composed of a balance and a camera. Using different liquids and spheres, the successful comparison of our results for σ with the pendant drop method confirms the validity of this technique.

References

1. P.G. de Gennes, Wetting: statics and dynamics, Rev. Mod. Phys. **57**, 827-863 (1985).
2. P.G. de Gennes, F. Brochard-Wiart and D. Quéré, *Capillarity and Wetting Phenomena: Drops, Bubbles, Pearls, Waves*, Springer (2004).
3. A. Marmur, Equilibrium contact angles: theory and measurement, Colloids and Surfaces A: Physicochemical and Engineering Aspects **116**, 55-61 (1996).
4. A.W. Adamson, A.P. Gast, *Dynamic Methods of Measuring Surface Tension, in Physical Chemistry of Surfaces*, 6th Ed.; John Wiley & Sons, Inc.: New York, 36-49 (1997).
5. T. Young, An Essay on the Cohesion of Fluids, Phil. Trans. Roy. Soc. London **95**, 65-87 (1805).
6. L. Gao and T. J. Mc Carthy, Contact Angle Hysteresis Explained, Langmuir **22**(14), 6234–6237 (2006).
7. L. Léger and J. F. Joanny, Liquid spreading, Reports on Progress in Physics **55**(4), 431-486 (1992).
8. S.Y. Lin, H.C. Chang, L.W. Lin, and P.Y. Huang, Measurement of dynamic/advancing/receding contact angle by video-enhanced sessile drop tensiometry, Rev. Sci. Instrum. **67**, 2852-2858 (1996).

9. Y. Yuan and T. R. Lee, Contact Angle and Wetting Properties" in "Surface Science Techniques, Springer Series in Surface Sciences **51**, 3-34 (2013).
10. A.I. Rusanov and V.A. Prokhorov, *Interfacial Tensiometry* in Studies of Interface Science 3, D. Möbius and R. Miller (Editors), Elsevier, Amsterdam (1996).
11. J. Drelich, C. Fang and C.L. White, *Measurement of interfacial tension in fluid-fluid systems* in "Encyclopedia of Surface and Colloid Science, Marcel Dekker, Inc., New York, 3152-3166 (2013).
12. K. J. Maloy, J. Feder and T. Jossang, An experimental technique for measurements of capillary waves, Rev. Sci. Instrum. **60**, 481-486 (1989).
13. F. Zhu, R. Miao, C. Xu and Z. Cao, Measurement of the dispersion relation of capillary waves by laser diffraction, Am. J. Phys. **75**, 896-898 (2007).
14. F. Restagno, C. Poulard, C. Cohen, L. Vagharchakian and L. Léger, Contact angle and contact angle hysteresis measurements using the capillary bridge technique, Langmuir **25**(18), 11188-11196 (2009).
15. C. Huh and L.E. Scriven, Shape of axisymmetric fluid interfaces of unbounded extent, J. of Colloid and Interface Science **30**(3), 323-337 (1969).
16. F. Bashforth and J.G. Adams, *An attempt to test the theories of capillary action by comparing the theoretical and measured forms of drops of fluid*, Cambridge Univ. Press (1883).
17. S. Hartland and R.W Hartley, *Axisymmetric Fluid-Liquid Interfaces*, Elsevier, Amsterdam (1976).
18. A. Ferguson, On the shape of the capillary surface formed by the external contact of a liquid with a cylinder of large radius, Phil. Mag. **24**(6), 837-844 (1912).
19. E.G. Shafrin, W.A. Zisman, Contact angle, wettability and adhesion, Adv. Chem. Ser. 43, 145-157 (1964).
20. C. Clanet and D. Quéré, Onset of menisci, J. of Fluid Mechanics **460**, 131-149 (2002).

Modeling of wind speed distribution for wind power analysis in the northwestern coast of Senegal

B. Ould Bilal[abde*], CMF Kebe[b], V. Sambou[b], A. Ndiaye[b], P.A. Ndiaye[c], A. Sava [d], K.H. Adjallah[d], D. Nourou[e], M. Ndongo[e],

[a]Ecole des Mines de Mauritanie (EMiM), BP 5259, Nouakchott, Mauritanie
[b]Centre International de Formation et de Recherche en Energie Solaire (C.I.F.R.E.S), ESP BP: 5085 Dakar Fann, Senegal
[c]Université Assane Seck de Ziguinchor, UFR – Sciences et Technologies, Département de Physique , BP : 523 Ziguinchor, Sénégal.
[d]Ecole Nationale D'ingénieurs de Metz, 1rte d'Ars Laquenexy, 57070 Metz, France,
[e]Laboratoire de Recherche Appliquée aux Energies Renouvelables de l'Eau et du Froid (LRAER)/FST/Université de Nouakchott, BP: 5026 Nouakchott, Mauritania

Abstract. Wind energy assessment plays a critical role on wind turbines exploitation in many countries worldwide. To evaluate the wind energy potential, probability density functions (pdf) are usually used to describe wind speed distributions. The selection of the appropriate pdf reduces the wind power estimation error. The most widely used pdf for wind energy applications is the Weibull probability density function. In this study, five distributions (Weibull, Gamma, Normal, Lognormal and Rayleigh distribution) were used to model the wind speed distribution. Used data were recorded at eight stations located in the northwestern coast of Senegal. A detailed comparison between the five approaches is carried out in the present work. The parameters of the distributions were calculated using the maximum likelihood method. The suitability of the theoretical distributions to real distribution was evaluated based on the performance criteria (coefficient of determination R^2, root mean square error and the maximum error between the real and the theoretical of the repartition function). Results indicate that, the used distributions show a good fit compared to the real distribution with a coefficient of determination between 88% and 99%. The Weibull distribution performs best for the sites of Sine Moussa Abdou, Botla and Sakhor with coefficient of determination of 99% for the three sites.

Keywords: Modeling, Wind potential, statistical analysis, wind speed distribution

1 Introduction

The statistical properties of the wind speed provide fundamental information to designers for predicting the output energy of a wind energy conversion system. Knowing the distribution of wind speeds is an important parameter for assessing the wind potential for a good estimate of the energy produced by a wind turbine. The output energy of wind turbines can be calculated by adding up the energy corresponding to the wind speeds distribution. Due to the high variability in measuring of wind data, it is essential to verify the method used for analysis.

The Weibull and Rayleigh distributions were used in many studies in the literature **[1-17]** to determine the average characteristics of wind (mean wind speed, power density, output energy from wind turbine, etc.). The reason is because of the easy estimation of the parameters to approximate the empirical distribution of wind observations for electricity generation.

Three other distributions **[10]**, were compared to the Weibull distribution in the region of Hungary. It was found that all three models give a good approximation. However, the Weibull distribution was recommended, due to the difficulty to identify the parameters for the other models. In another study **[9]**, ten probability distributions were compared using three goodness-of-fit tests at 95% confidence level and 5% significance. The Weibull distribution was identified to be the best distribution representing the wind data.

Recent studies **[18-26]** have concluded that the best area to use wind energy is on the northwest coast of Senegal. In these studies, the Wiebull distribution was used to model the wind speed distribution and analyze the wind potential for electricity generation.

The precedent works have shown that the model providing the best approximation depends, also, on the location.

In this study, we tried to categorize appropriate theoretical probability density distributions of wind speed at eight meteorological observatories located in the northwestern coast of Senegal. Five probability density distributions (Weibull, Rayleigh, log-normal, normal and the Gamma distribution) were tested and compared to determine the best fitting to real distribution of wind speed. The suitability of the theoretical distributions to real distribution was evaluated based on the performance criteria (coefficient of determination (R^2), mean square error (MSE) and the maximum error between the real and the theoretical of the repartition function). The appropriate model was determined for each site

2 Materiels and methods

2.1 Description of sites

The data used in this study, were collected at eight metrological stations in sites of Kayar, Potou, Gandon, Sakhor, Sine Moussa Abdou, Botla, Dara Andal and Nguebeul (Fig.1) located along the northwestern coast of Senegal. These stations were equipped with a data acquisition system that records every 10 min the average, the maximum and the minimum values for each sensor. Data are saved in a flash memory card. The evaluation of the collected data in the sites has showed that the coverage rate was between 82 % and 100 %. The minimum value (82 %) was observed for the site of Nguebeul. The coverage rate value is very high in generally and allows the use of these data in order to calculate the wind potential for the sites. Table 1 gives the locations of meteorological stations, period of collect and the coverage rate of data for each site.

Table 1. Characteristics of the eight meteorological stations

Site	Latitude north (°)	Longitude west (°)	Elevation (m)	Measures period	Coverage rate (%)
Kayar	14.92	17.12	06.00	August 2007 to July 2008	100
Potou	15.72	16.50	21.00	August 2007 to July 2008	100
Gondon	15.96	16.45	05.00	Jun 2004 to May 2005	99
Sine Moussa	15.18	16.74	54.00	November 2007 to October 2008	95
Botla	15.67	16.49	28.00	November 2007 to October 2008	94
Dara Andal	15.42	16.53	43.00	November 2007 to October 2008	86
Ngeubeul	15.35	16.59	51.00	November 2007 to October 2008	82
Sakhor	14.23	16.45	03.00	November 2007 to October 2008	96

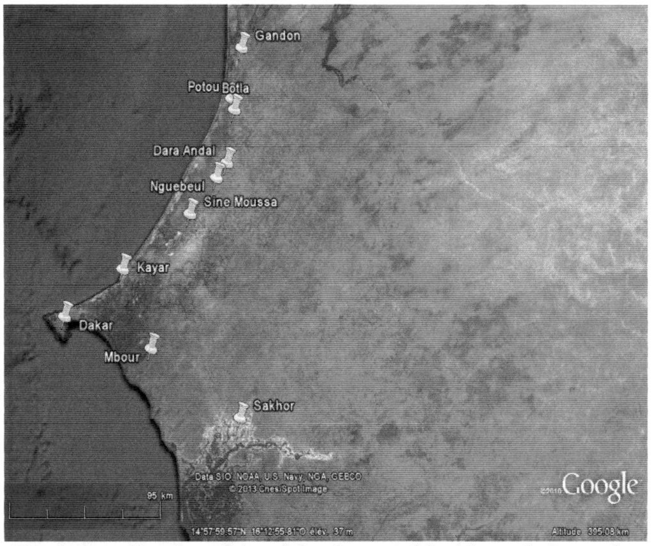

Fig.1. Localization of the eight sites used in this study located along the northwestern coast of Senegal

2.2 Theoretical models

The probability density distribution function models below were tested to approximate the frequency distribution of the wind speed data for the considered period of each site.

(a) Weibull distribution: Weibull distribution has been commonly used in the literature to express the wind speed frequency distribution and to estimate the wind power density. Weibull distribution provided good match with the experimental data. The Weibull probability density function is given by the equation (1) [27,28].

$$f(v)=\frac{k}{c}\cdot\left(\frac{v}{c}\right)^{k-1}\cdot\exp\left[-\left(\frac{v}{c}\right)^{k}\right] \quad \text{for v>0 k and c>0} \tag{1}$$

where v is the wind speed; k is the shape parameter and c is the scale parameter.

(b) Rayleigh distribution: For shape parameter k = 2, the Weibull distribution is called Rayleigh distribution [29,30]. The probability density is given by the equation (2) [31].

$$f(v)=f(v,c)=\frac{2\cdot v}{c^2}\cdot\exp\left[-\left(\frac{v}{c}\right)^2\right] \tag{2}$$

(c) Normal distribution: The random variable of the normal distribution in this case is the wind speed v. The probability density function is given by the equation:

$$f(v)=f(v;\ \mu;\lambda)=\frac{1}{\lambda\sqrt{2\cdot\pi}}\cdot\exp\left[-\frac{(v-\mu)^2}{2\cdot\lambda^2}\right] \tag{3}$$

μ, λ are mean and standard deviation of the variable [32,33].

(d) Log-normal distribution: The random variable of the log-normal distribution in this case is the wind speed v. The probability density function is given by the equation (4) [33].

$$f(v)=f(v;\ \mu;\lambda)=\frac{1}{\lambda\cdot v\cdot\sqrt{2\cdot\pi}}\cdot\exp\left[-\frac{(\ln(v)-\mu)^2}{2\cdot\lambda^2}\right] \tag{4}$$

μ expected value ; λ standard deviation of the ln(v) (v > 0)

(e) Gamma distribution: The Gamma distribution could be calculated using the equation (5). This distribution depend on two parameters which are the expected value μ and the standard deviation of the v probability variable [32,34].

$$f(v)=f(v\ ;\ \mu\ ;)=\frac{v^{\mu-1}}{\lambda^{\mu}\cdot\Gamma(\mu)}\exp\left(-\frac{v}{\lambda}\right) \tag{5}$$

2.3 Calculation of the models parameters

The parameters of the distributions were calculated using the maximum likelihood method. The detailed of this method can be found in the reference [24,25].

2.4 Fitting performance evaluation

The suitability of the theoretical distributions to real distribution was evaluated based on the performance criteria: coefficient of determination R^2, root mean square error and the maximum error between the real and the theoretical values of the repartition function [32,34,35]. These criteria can be expressed by the equation (6, 7 and 8) the best model to fit the real wind speed distribution must have the most high determination coefficient and the smallest root mean error and the maximum error between the theoretical and the real distribution.

$$RMSE = \left[\frac{1}{n}\cdot\sum_{i=1}^{n}(y_{ir}-y_{ic})^2\right]^{\frac{1}{2}} \quad (6)$$

$$R^2 = 1 - \frac{\sum_{i=1}^{n}(y_{ir}-y_{ic})^2}{\sum_{i=1}^{n}(y_{ir}-\overline{y}_{ir})^2} \quad (7)$$

$$EDC = \max\left|DCT(v) - DCO(v)\right| \quad (8)$$

Were y_{ir} and y_{ic} are real and theoretical value of the probability density ; n total number of samples ; $\overline{y}_{ir}$ is the mean of y_{ir} ; DCT and DCO are the theoretical and observed repartition function

3 Results and discussions

3.1 Comparison of the distribution on sites

Modeling of the wind speed distribution was performed using wind data measured at eight stations located in the northwestern coast of Senegal. So, the parameters of each site were determined and the performance of each model was computed for each site calculating the coefficient of determination R^2, the root mean square error and the maximum error between the real and the theoretical of the repartition function.

Fig.2 shows that, overall, the observed and theoretical distributions have the same paces.

Table 2 gives the values of these calculated parameters and table 3 shows the values of the statistical parameters for comparing distributions.

Table 2. Parameters of the distribution calculated on the sites

Site	Weibull		Rayleigh		Gamma		Normal		Log normal	
	c	k	c	K	μ	σ	μ	σ	μ	σ
Kayar	4,85	2,77	3,28	2,00	5,57	0,78	**4,32**	**1,68**	1,37	0,47
Potou	5,37	3,01	3,60	2,00	**7,26**	**0,66**	4,80	1,70	1,50	0,40
Gandon	4,85	3,02	3,26	2,00	6,54	0,66	**4,34**	**1,54**	1,39	0,44
Sine Moussa	**5,04**	**2,37**	3,46	2,00	4,19	1,07	4,47	1,99	1,37	0,56
Botla	**4,70**	**2,22**	3,26	2,00	3,81	1,09	4,16	1,98	1,29	0,57
Dara Andal	4,65	2,47	3,18	2,00	**4,96**	**0,83**	4,12	1,79	1,31	0,48
Nguebeul	4,91	2,77	3,31	2,00	6,35	0,69	4,36	1,69	**1,39**	**0,42**
Sakhor	**5,07**	**2,29**	3,50	2,00	4,04	1,11	4,49	2,08	1,37	0,55

3.2 Statistical analysis

For the eight sites, the most adapted distribution was the one having the smallest values of the root mean square error (RMSE) and highest values of coefficient of determination. The results given in table 3, show that the Weibull distribution was most suitable for sites of Sine Moussa Abdou (c = 5.0402 m / s and k = 2.3697), Botla (c = 4.7021 m/s and k = 2.2206) and Sakhor (c = 5.0662 m/s and k = 2.2928).

For the sites of Potou and Dara Andal, the Gamma distribution was most suitable. The obtained parameters of this model are (μ = 7.2581, σ = 0.66135) and (μ = 4.9638, σ = 0.82999) for the two sites respectively.

The normal distribution was the most suitable for the site of Kayar (μ = 4.3184 and σ =1.6798) and Gandon (μ = 4.3412 and σ = 1.5434à).

For the site of Nguebeul, the log-normal distribution was the most suitable with μ = 1.3923 and σ = 0.41678.

In general, the statistical analysis show a good fit compared to the real distribution. The coefficient of determination was between 88% and 99%. The Rayleigh distribution was the least suitable especially for the sites of Kayar, Potou, Gandon and Ngueubeul with coefficient of determination of 86%, 79%, 74% et 84%.

3.3 Theoretical and observed power density

Fig.3 shows that, for the low wind speed, the power density fallows the evolution of the wind speed distribution. However for high wind speeds, we can notice the decrease of the power density. These phenomena can be explained by the fact that the power density depends on the cub of the wind speed and on the distribution of the wind speed. Indeed, on high wind speeds, his frequency decreases (figure 2). So, the contribution of the wind speed frequency in the power density computing dominates the contribution of the cube of wind speed. Overall, a slight variation on the wind speed can result in a large variation on the distribution of power density.

Figure 4 gives a comparison between the theoretical and the observed power density. The theoretical power density was calculated using the most adapted model to the observed distribution. It could be noted (figure 4) a good fitting between the theoretical and the observed distribution with a maximum deviation of 11% observed for the site of Potou.

Figure 5 illustrates the evolution of the theoretical and the observed power density curves for the best model in each one of the eight sites. This figure shows a good correspondence between the theoretical and the observed power density curves. The maximum deviation is of 2% observed for the site of Kayar.

Table 3. Determination coefficient, root mean error and the maximum error between the theoretical and the real distribution

Site	Distribution	EQDM	R^2	EFD
Kayar	Weibull	0.350280	0.993080	0.013731
	Rayleigh	1.524400	0.868900	0.118450
	Gamma	0.979920	0.945830	0.054117
	Normal	**0.325800**	**0.994010**	**0.012611**
	Log normal	1.492700	0.874310	0.084736
Potou	Weibull	0.823090	0.966320	0.038280
	Raylegh	2.044800	0.792160	0.167510
	Gamma	**0.668170**	**0.977810**	**0.030724**
	Normal	0.785030	0.969370	0.043926
	Log normal	1.047800	0.945430	0.056981
Gandon	Weibull	0.471360	0.989440	0.0 38740
	Raylegh	2.302100	0.748070	0.153630
	Gamma	0.942130	0.957810	0.045888
	Normal	**0.418810**	**0.991660**	**0.021762**
	Log normal	1.598100	0.878590	0.076304
Sine Moussa	**Weibull**	**0.420080**	**0.986100**	**0.016509**
	Rayleigh	0.963700	0.926840	0.075230
	Gamma	0.664650	0.965200	0.037612
	Normal	0.813790	0.947830	0.040116
	Log normal	1.355700	0.855210	0.075095
Botla	**Weibull**	**0.327520**	**0.991440**	**0.010463**
	Raylegh	0.441330	0.984460	0.035642
	Gamma	0.483510	0.981340	0.028609
	Normal	1.022400	0.916580	0.046887
	Log normal	1.113400	0.901060	0.058229
Dara Andal	Weibull	0.908880	0.948190	0.035425
	Raylegh	1.051400	0.930670	0.074116
	Gamma	**0.736020**	**0.966030**	**0.027882**
	Normal	1.410500	0.875230	0.059179
	Log normal	0.914720	0.947530	0.047602
Nguebeul	Weibull	1.196000	0.920570	0.045067
	Raylegh	1.682500	0.842830	0.126300
	Gamma	0.902960	0.954730	0.030111
	Normal	1.535600	0.869070	0.063551
	Log normal	**0.894480**	**0.955580**	**0.029907**
Sakhor	**Weibull**	**0.214790**	**0.995870**	**0.006226**
	Rayleigh	0.594030	0.968400	0.049481
	Gamma	0.624830	0.965040	0.034987
	Normal	0.802690	0.942300	0.036083
	Log normal	1.262500	0.857250	0.070369

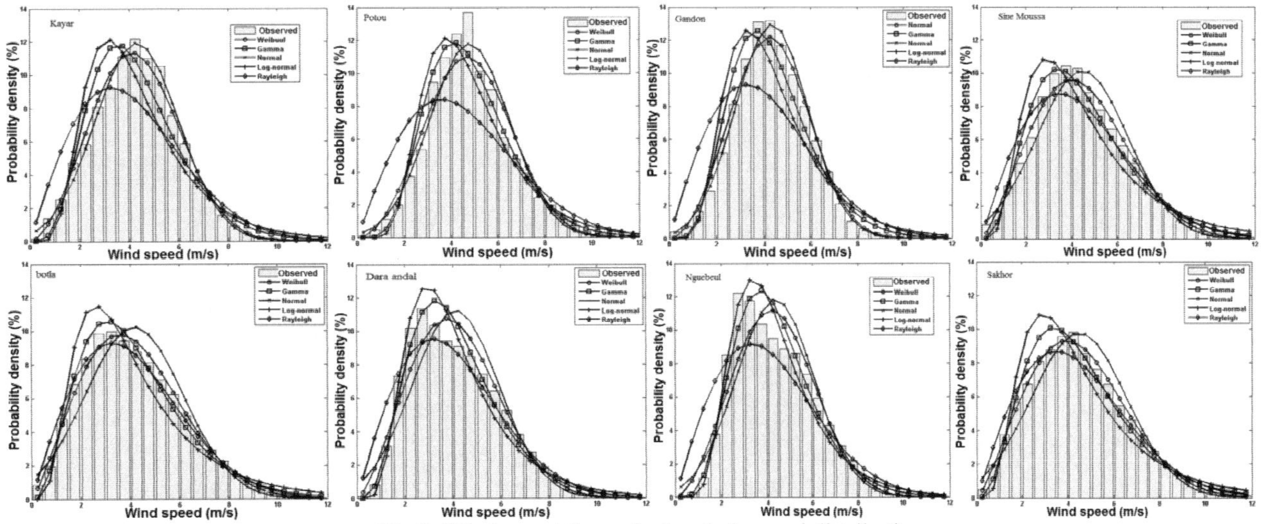

Fig.2. Wind speed theoretical and observed distribution

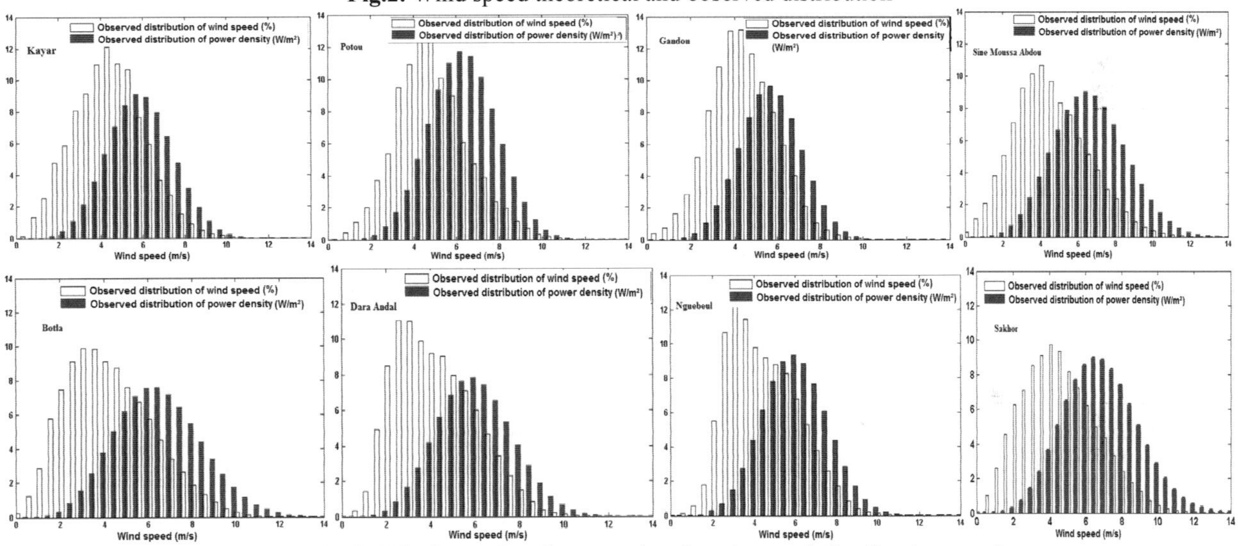

Fig.3. Wind speed and power density observed distribution on sites

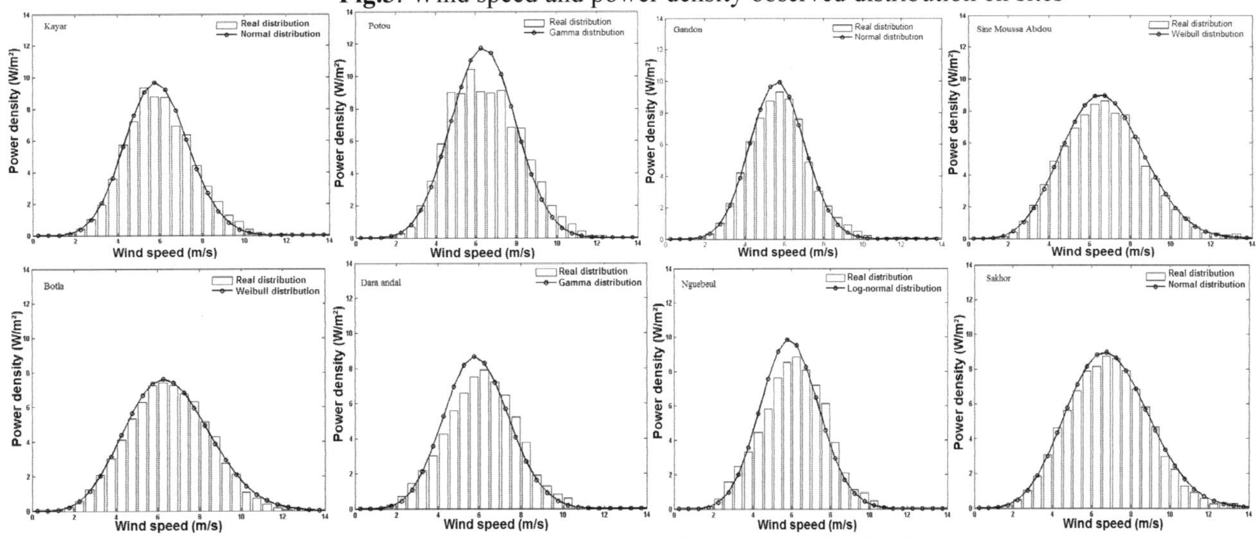

Fig.4. Theoretical and observed power density distribution on sites

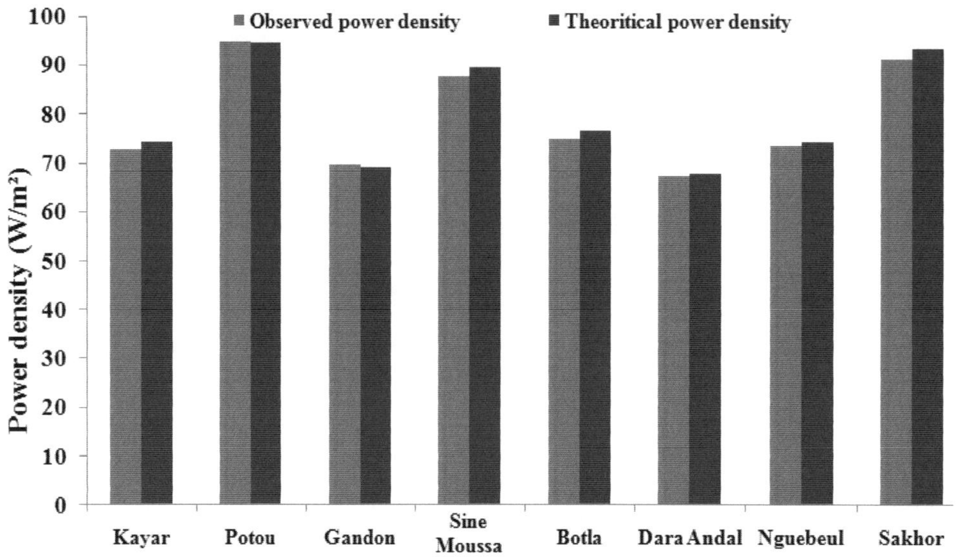

Fig.5. Comparison of theoretical and observed power density on sites

4 Conclusion

The object of this study was to propose an appropriate theoretical probability density distribution for wind speed at each one of eight meteorological data observatories located in the northwestern coast of Senegal.

Five probability density distributions (Weibull, Rayleigh, log-normal, normal and the Gamma distribution) were considered and compared to determine the best fitting to real distribution of wind speed.

The suitability of the theoretical distributions to real distribution was evaluated based on the performance criteria : coefficient of determination (R^2), mean square error (MSE) and the maximum error between the real and the theoretical of the repartition function.

The statistical analysis allowed determining the model parameters on each site; also the performance of each model was computed calculating the coefficient of determination R^2, the root mean square error and the maximum error between the real and the theoretical of the repartition function. The analysis enabled us to draw the following conclusions:

- The Weibull distribution was most suitable for the sites of Sine Moussa Abdou, Botla and Sakhor.
- For the sites of Potou and Dara Andal, the Gamma distribution was most suitable.
- The normal distribution is the most suitable for the site of Kayar and Gandon.
- For the site of Nguebeul, the log- normal distribution was the most suitable.

Power density estimations computed from the selected distributions for the eight sites exhibit potential wind energy for electricity generation (isolated or connected to grid), windmills and water pumping for rural areas.

References

1. O.S. Ohunakin. Wind resources in North-East geopolitical zone, Nigeria: An assessment of the monthly and seasonal characteristics. Renewable and Sustainable Energy Reviews. **15**, 1977–1987 (2011)
2. B. Ould Bilal , C.M.F. Kebe, V. Sambou, P.A. Ndiaye, and M. Ndongo. Economic analysis of wind electricity generation in the northern coast of Senegal. Int. J. Metrol. Qual. Eng. **5** , 302: 1-7 (2014)
3. S.M Boudia and O. Guerri. Investigation of wind power potential at Oran, northwest of Algeria. Energy Conversion and Management. 105, 81–92 (2015)
4. S.H. Pishgar-Komleh, A. Keyhani, P. Sefeedpari. Wind speed and power density analysis based on Weibull and Rayleigh distributions (a case study: Firouzkooh county of Iran). Renewable and Sustainable Energy Reviews. **42,** 313–322 (2015)
5. Z. Wei, H. Yang, Z. Fang. A novel model for photovoltaic array performance prediction. Applied Energy. **84**, 1187-98 (2007)
6. M. Gokcek, A. Bayulken, S. Bekdemir. Investigation of wind characteristics and wind energy potential in Kirklareli, Turkey. Renew Energy **32**, 1739-52 (2007)
7. M. Elamouri and F.B. Amar. Wind energy potential in Tunisia. Renew Energy. **33**, 758-68 (2008)
8. P. Ramırez and J.A. Carta. Influence of the data sampling interval in the estimation of the parameters of the Weibull wind speed probability density distribution: a case study. Energy Convers Manage. **46**, 2419-38 (2005)
9. V. Yilmaz and H.E. Celik. A statistical approach to estimate the wind speed distribution: the case of Gelibolu region. Dogus¸ Üniversitesi Dergisi. **9(1),** 122-32 (2008).

10. K. Tar. Some statistical characteristics of monthly average wind speed at various heights. Renewable Sustainable Energy Revews. **12**, 1712-24 (2008)
11. G. Justus, WR Hargraves, A. Mikhail, D. Graber. Methods for estimating wind speed frequency distributions. J Appl Meteorol. **17,** 350-3 (1978).
12. B. Safari and J. Gasore. A statistical investigation of wind characteristics and wind energy potential based on the Weibull and Rayleigh models in Rwanda. Renew Energy Renewable Energy. **35**, 2874-80 (2010)
13. Q. Pham, L. Thananchai. Assessment of wind energy potential for selecting wind turbines: An application to Thailand. Sustainable Energy Technologies and Assessments. **11**, 17–26 (2015)
14. D.A. Handri, S.A. Saad, I.A. Mohammad. Evaluation of wind energy potential and electricity generation at five locations in Jordan. Sustainable Cities and Society. **15**, 135–143 (2015)
15. B. Belabes, A. Youcefi, O. Guerri, M. Djamai, A. Kaabeche. Evaluation of wind energy potential and estimation of cost using wind energy turbines for electricity generation in north of Algeria. Renewable and Sustainable Energy Reviews. **51**, 1245–1255 (2015)
16. M. Ali, S. Ahmad, G. Morteza, D. Yagob, M. Mojtaba, S. Mohammad, Maryam. Evaluation of wind energy potential as a power generation source for electricity production in Binalood, Iran. Renewable Energy. **52**, 222-229 (2013)
17. S.S. Chandel, P. Ramasamy, K.S.R. Murthy. Wind power potential assessment of 12 locations in western Himalayan region of India. Renewable and Sustainable Energy Reviews. **39**, 530–545 (2014).
18. P. Ndiaye, C. Kraif, L. Protin, G. Fleury, Study and modelling of the wind power potential on the site in Dakar by a microcomputer, Electrical and power systems modeling and simulation. 95–98, (1989)
19. I. Youm, J. Sarr, M. Sall, A. Ndiaye, and M.M. Kane. Analysis of wind data and wind energy potential along the northern coast of Senegal, Rev. Energ. Ren. **8** , 95–108 (2005)
20. B. Ould Bilal, C.M.F. Kébé, V. Sambou, M. Ndongo, P.A. Ndiaye, Etude et modélisation du potentiel ´eolien du site de Nouakchott, Journal des Sciences Pour l'Ing´enieur. **9**, 28–34 (2008)
21. C.M.F. Kébé, V. Sambou, B. Ould Bilal, P.A. Ndiaye, S. Lo. Evaluation du potentiel ´eolien du site de Gandon dans la r´egion nord du S´en´egal, International Metrology Conference CAFMET. 1–6 (2008)
22. B. Ould Bilal, V. Sambou, C.M.F. Kébé, M. Ndongo, P.A. Ndiaye, Study and modelling of solar and wind power potential: Comparative Study of three sites in the West Coast of Africa, World Renewable Energy Congress X, Glasgow, Scotland (2008)
23. B. Ould Bilal, P.A. Ndiaye, C.M.F. Kébé, A. NDiay. Evaluation du potentiel éolien des sites de Kayar et de Potou Application au choix d'une ´eolienne adapt´ee au site, Journal Des Sciences pour l'Ing´enieur (JSPI). **12,** 33–41 (2010)
24. B. Ould Bilal, M. Ndongo, V. Sambou, P.A. Ndiaye, C.M.F. Kébé. Diurnal characteristics of the wind potential along the North-western coast of Senegal. *International Journal of the Physical Sciences*. **6**(35) 7950-60 (2011)
25. B. Ould Bilal, C.M.F. Kébé, P.A. Ndiaye, V. Sambou, M. Ndongo. Evaluation of wind energy potential and electricity generation in the northwestern coast of Senegal. *International Metrology Conference CAFMET*, 22-27 Avril. 1-9 (2012)
26. B. Ould Bilal, P.A. Ndiaye, C.M.F. Kebe, V. Sambou, M. Ndongo. Seasonal assement of wind energy chaeacteristics for electricity generation in the sites of Kayar and Potou Senegal. *Rev.CAMES-Série, A*. 13(1):9-13 (2012)
27. N.C. Ali . A statistical analysis of wind power density based on the Weibull and Rayleigh models at the southern region of Turkey. Renewable Energy. **29**, 593–604 (2003)
28. M. Gokcek, A. Bayulken, S. Bekdemir. Investigation of wind characteristics and wind energy potential in Kirklareli, Turkey. Renew Energy. **32**, 1739-52 (2007)
29. P.A. Ndiaye. Contribution à l'étude et à la réalisation d'un simulateur électrotechnique de turbine d'éolienne. Simulation des paramètres d'une éolienne adaptée sur le site du Havre. Thèse de Doctorat d'Université, le Havre. 119p (1998)
30. B. Ould Bilal. Méthodologie de dimensionnement d'un système hybride éolien-solaire-batterie optimisé : Analyse de l'influence du taux de non couverture de la charge, des potentiels éolien et solaire et des profils de charge sur la configuration optimale. Thése de troisième cycle, 145p (2010).
31. T. Karoly. Some statistical characteristics of monthly average wind speed at various heights. Renewable and Sustainable Energy Reviews. **12**, 1712-24 (2008)
32. S. Bonfils. Modeling wind speed and wind power distributions in Rwanda. Renewable and Sustainable Energy Reviews. **15**, 925-35 (2011).
33. P.C. Tian. Estimation of wind energy potential using different probability density functions. Applied Energy. **88**, 1848-56 (2011)
34. J. Zhou, E. Erdem, G. Li, J. Shi. Comprehensive evaluation of wind speed distribution models: a case study for North Dakota sites. Energy Convers Manage. **51**, 1449-58 (2010)
35. A.C.R. Paulo, C.S. Ricardo, F.A. Carla, E.V.S. Maria. Comparison of seven numerical methods for determining Weibull parameters for wind energy generation in the northeast region of Brazil. Applied Energy. **89,** 395-400 (2012)

How to monitor performance in proficiency testing

P. Briggs

Proficiency Testing Australia, Sydney, Australia

Abstract. Proficiency testing provides objective evidence of laboratories testing competence. laboratories quality control procedures can monitor the validity of tests and calibrations undertaken by measuring continuing performance in multiple rounds of a proficiency testing program. Such monitoring will allow laboratories to identify problems, check for testing bias and other trends and review the effectiveness of corrective actions where problems were highlighted by a proficiency test.

Keywords: Monitoring, Proficiency, Quality, Charts

1 Introduction

The competence of accredited laboratories is assessed by two complimentary techniques. One technique is the on-site evaluation by an assessment team, which examines the technical competence of the laboratories and their compliance with the requirements of ISO/IEC 17025 [1]. The other technique is by proficiency testing which involves the determination of laboratory testing performance by means of interlaboratory comparisons. The two techniques have their own advantages and when combined give a high degree of confidence in the overall competence of an accredited laboratory.

ISO/IEC 17025 recognises that participation in interlaboratory comparisons or proficiency testing programs as one way to assure the quality of test and calibration results. It is noted that the standard requires that if proficiency testing is used by the laboratory then this should be monitored:

ISO/IEC 17025 5.9.1 "The laboratory shall have quality control procedures for monitoring the validity of tests and calibrations undertaken. The resulting data shall be recorded in such a way that trends are detectable and, where practicable, statistical techniques shall be applied to the reviewing of the results. This monitoring shall be planned and reviewed and may include but not limited to: … (b) participation in interlaboratory comparison or proficiency-testing programmes"

Internal quality control for the laboratory involves a continuous, critical evaluation of the laboratory's own analytical methods and working routines. Internal quality control is conducted by the laboratory as a check that if the process is out of control then there is a need for an investigation and correction. The control encompasses the analytical process which can include the proficiency testing sample entering the laboratory and ending with the analytical report of results submitted to the proficiency testing provider.

Therefore this aspect of monitoring proficiency testing performance is a requirement of accreditation bodies using ISO/IEC 17025. The accreditation bodies assessing the technical competence of laboratories would require general satisfactory performance in proficiency testing over time as significant evidence of a laboratory's ability to produce reliable results.

2 Monitoring performance over time

For a single proficiency test ISO/IEC 17043 [2] clearly defines the criteria for performance evaluation by the statistical determination for z-scores as:
$|Z| \leq 2.0$ indicates "satisfactory" performance and generates no signal;
$2.0 < |Z| < 3.0$ indicates "questionable" performance and generates a warning signal;
$|Z| \geq 3.0$ indicates "unsatisfactory" performance and generates an action signal

However when laboratories monitor proficiency testing performance over time this single review of each performance may not be adequate as it may fail to identify a trend in testing that may lead to a future problem. There may be cases where single proficiency tests for a specific determination is satisfactory however when checked against past performance in a continuous program may indicate an action. Also a possible trend may be developing which could lead to a testing problem which could be confirmed with a review of the z-score for the next scheduled round of the program.

3 Control charts to monitor performance

Where a proficiency testing provider uses a standardised score such as a z-score to evaluate laboratory performance for a test over several rounds of a program then this information may be presented in a graph to monitor performance over time. The use of graphs in which the scores for several rounds are combined, may allow for the identification of trends and other inconsistencies and show performance which varies randomly. Such features of combining the results would not be apparent when each round is examined separately.

A laboratory's quality control procedures can monitor the analytical process for statistical control and alert users when corrective action is required. Control charts can be used as a simple graphical means of interpreting test data. Traditionally "Shewart" control charts are useful for graphical monitoring of combined standardised scores. The use of these control charts is detailed in ISO 13528 [3].

For proficiency testing Shewart control charts are the simplest and most convenient method to monitor results. A control chart can be maintained for any individual test with the z-score plotted sequentially (time ordered). Control charts are based on the distribution of the control values around a true or expected value (assigned value for proficiency testing) and assume that the distribution around the assigned value is normal. The Shewart control charts can easily identify the reporting bias by the laboratory.

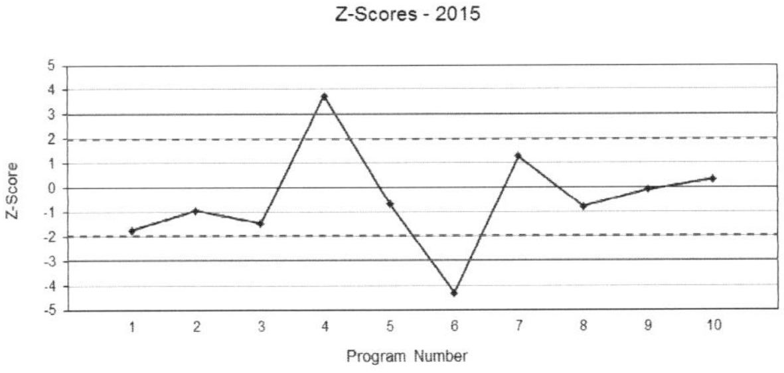

Fig. 1. Shewart Control Chart

The control limits can be based on the interpretation of z-scores. The z-scores may be plotted for each round where the warning limit may be based on the questionable performance $2.0 < | Z | < 3.0$ which equates to roughly 2 σ. This warning limit is set at a 95% confidence limit (1/20) and is expressed as: ± 2.0

The action limit based on unsatisfactory performance $| Z | \geq 3.0$ and equates to roughly 3 σ . This action limit is set at 99.7% confidence limit (1/1000) and is expressed as: ± 3.0

The acceptance range may be interpreted as per the satisfactory performance range for z-scores evaluation as: $| Z | \leq 2.0$ being satisfactory.

The probability of any sample point (z-score plot) falling above the centre line is equal to 0.5, provided that the laboratory quality control procedure is in statistical control. The probability that two consecutive sample points will fall above the centre line is equal to 0.5 times 0.5 = 0.25.

Accordingly, the probability that 9 consecutive points on one side of the centre line is 0.59 = 0.00195, which is approximately the probability that a sample point can be expected to fall outside the 3 σ limit. It is expected that approximately 5% of proficiency testing z-scores will fall between the warning limit and the action limit. When a sample point falls outside the control limits, the laboratory may no longer be in statistical control.

Additionally, laboratories should use the control charts to examine systematic trends, that is a series of sample points in the same direction or points in the same side of the centre line, even though they are all within the control limit. To use control charts for trend analysis they must be maintained and used on a real time basis. If laboratories prepare control charts after a considerable time delay they only provide a history of analytical performance with little opportunity for the laboratory to control the measurement process.

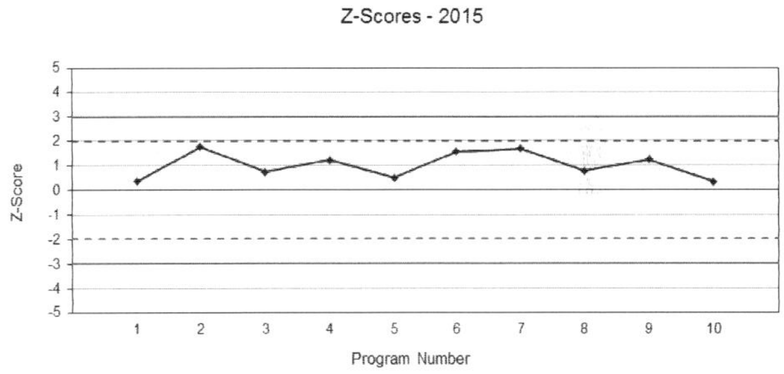

Fig. 2. Control chart with points above the centre line

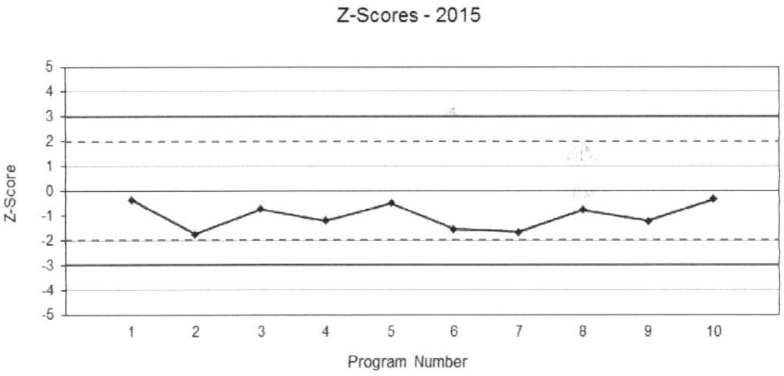

Fig. 3. Control chart with points below the centre line

The simplest interpretation of the control chart for z-scores is to identify any point greater than |3|. The probability of a point falling outside these warning limits is 0.3%. The probability of a point falling between the warning limit |2| and the control limit |3| is about 5%. Another simple check is to identify two consecutive points between the control and warning limits may need action.

Other simplified rules for action may be identification of seven consecutive points on the same side of the centre line. It can be considered that seven consecutive points increasing may need action. Similarly seven consecutive points decreasing may need action.

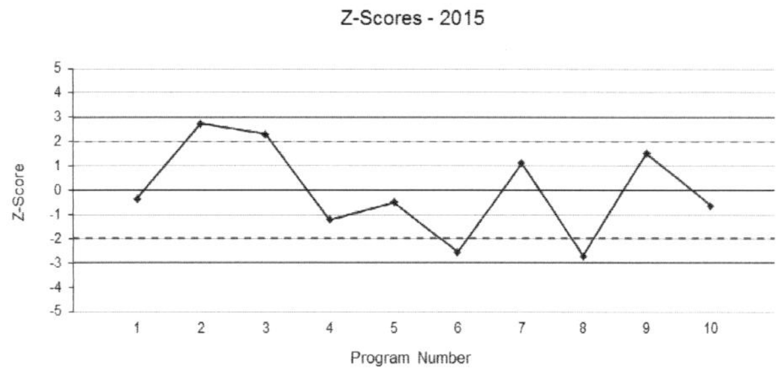

Fig. 4. Control chart indicating questionable performance

Whilst an investigation and corrective action should be implemented and monitored it is important that analysts then do not search for special causes that do not exist in order to adjust the process. The adjustments may distort a stable process as well as wasting time and energy.

Fig. 5. Control chart indicating increasing trend

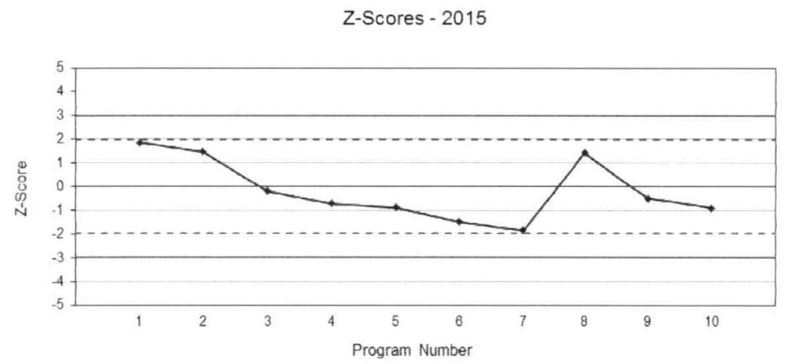

Fig. 6. Control chart indicating decreasing trend

Fig. 7. Control chart indicating performance in control

The best outcome for continuous monitoring in a proficiency testing program is where all points remain well within the warning limits and there is little evidence of a trend in the data. This would be where no results are identified as questionable, no results are outliers, there is no trend for increasing data or no trend for decreasing data and finally that there is data both above and below the centre line.

4 Benefits of control charts

Proficiency testing and other types of interlaboratory comparisons are highlighted in ISO/IEC 17025 as being an important means of monitoring quality. Regular participation in proficiency testing programs is one of the best ways for an analytical laboratory to monitor over a period of time its performance against both its own requirements and peer laboratories.

For the participating laboratory in a proficiency testing program the important part of the evaluation is that the use of control charts will easily identify systematic error or bias and other trends.

The control of the measurement process by proficiency testing is an important means to ensure valid results and should be considered as a continual monitoring process.

The control charts can be easily designed from proficiency test data as many programs reports generate z-score analysis. The z-scores are suitable to plot on a chart and can then identify the warning and action limits for the participating laboratory.

The control charts can be set up for to compare different analytical methods using separate control charts for each method or plotting different method results on the same chart. This may provide valuable method comparison information in particular when a laboratory is in the process of changing a method.

The control charts can be set up for an individual operator in the laboratory or for separate tests in a program as a means to monitor performance. This would be considered as a useful tool when training and qualifying new staff in the laboratory.

5 Conclusion

Important decisions are made based on the analytical data generated by laboratories. Therefore a laboratory's quality control procedures should be used considering fitness for purpose of the testing results.

The quality control procedures used should be well defined to assure the reporting of high quality data of a known accuracy and precision. Proficiency testing monitoring through the use of control charts is considered as an effective tool to include within a laboratory's documented procedures for quality control.

References

1. ISO/IEC 17025: 2005 General requirements for the competence of testing and calibration laboratories
2. ISO/IEC 17043: 2010 Conformity assessment – General requirements for proficiency testing
3. ISO 13528: 2005 Statistical methods for use in proficiency testing by interlaboratory comparisons

Trends of Mass measurement in Kenya

Ombati Wilson

Kenya Bureau of Standards
email: wombati@kebs.org

Abstract

Industrial mass measurements plays a critical role in supporting various industrial sectors such as healthcare, pharmaceutical/ drug manufacturing, food processing, research, construction, transport and trade etc. The significance of such measurements is presented in this paper on a case by case evaluation, and good measurement practices (including calibration of weighing instruments) is comparatively discussed as a premier alternative towards a sustainable industrial development. In line with this, various support frameworks offered by Kenya Bureau of Standards (KEBS) mass metrology services are also presented.

Key Terms: *Mass, weighing instrument, calibration*

1. Introduction

Mass is the measure of quantity of matter. It's a fundamental property of matter, independent of location. The SI unit of mass is kilogram (kg). A kilogram is equal to the mass of the International prototype kilogram (IPK). The IPK (cylindrical, and made alloy of platinum and iridium, 90% and 10 % respectively) is kept and maintained (since 1889) at the BIPM along with its six copies (BIPM, 2007). The IPK has however been observed to unstable over years due to environmental effects, wear & other material and surface properties, and currently it's undergoing redefinition (Davis, 2008).

Mass of a body is usually determined by weighing – using ***weighing instrument(s)***. These instruments are of various types and accuracy classes (OIML R76). Examples include analytical balances, platform balances, top-loading balances, spring scales, weighbridges, checkweighers etc. The choice of a weighing instrument(s) mainly depends on the intended purpose, desired accuracy/readability, repeatability/ reproducibility and capacity etc. Mass is one of the key measurands that drives various industrial processes.

2. Industrial applications of mass measurements

a) Mass measurements in healthcare sector

Determination of body mass index (BMI) (Table 1) is useful in supporting decisions and prescriptions in healthcare. Measurements of BMI have implications for epidemiologic research, obesity assessment, and nutritional status, as well as for screening and interventions for health problems/disorders such as osteoporosis,hypertension, high blood cholesterol, type 2 diabetes, heart disease, stroke, cardiovascular disease, gallbladder disease, sleep apnea, osteoarthritis etc (Macran,S., 2004;Tipton, *et al.*, 2012).The BMI values are also vital for **dosage calculation** of chemotherapeutic agents, anaesthetics, and other medications with a narrow therapeutic margin.Therefore, wrong determination of BMI subsequently leads to wrong diagnosis, prescription and monitoring of health status of patients and thus low productivity (WHO, 2013).

In spite of the considerable significance of mass measurements (BMI)in the provision of quality healthcare services, proper measurement practices have not been adequately embraced in Kenya. The essence of proper maintenance and calibration of weighing instruments in health care facilities can thus not be overemphasized.

Table 1: BMI values & weight status(WHO, 2013)

BMI value (kg/m^2)	Weight status
Below 18.50	Underweight
18.50 – 24.99	Normal
25.00 – 29.99	Overweight
30.00 & above	Obese

b) Mass measurements in Pharmaceutical industry

Pharmaceutical products/medicines or drugsdirectly impact the health and well-being of the population, making precision paramount throughout the manufacturing process.These products are expected to deliver consistent dose, form, texture and taste, producing the same symptomatic relief and health benefits pill-for-pill, tablet-to-tablet, or dose-after-dose. Accurate weighing instruments (automated or manual) thus play a critical and integral role in achieving such quality and consistency.For instance, by using calibrated balances at various stations on the processing line, operators have the ability to precisely measure each component prior to adding it to the mixture. Such balances (with defined inputtedtolerances) enable the operators to decipher immediately whether the product meets weight requirements. For example, if a given jug of powdered supplement is placed on the checkweigher, displaying Over/Under/Accept, fan graphs allows operators to determine if its weight corresponds to what is listed on its label (Alonzo, 2013).

c) Mass measurements in Food processing

Success in food preparation depends on the correct amount of ingredients in the recipe. The only way to get the correct amount is by weighing or measuring each ingredient. Scales are used to measure ingredients by weight. In food service, it is important to use scales that have been calibrated. Accuracy is very important when weighing ingredients and can be the difference in a product that is fabulous or one that is just okay.

d) Mass measurements in construction industry

Construction materials -such as sand, water, aggregate (rocks, gravel, etc.), fly ash, potash and cement- are measured by mass. For instance, cementitious materials are measured to within specified amounts/limits of mass; these materials permitted to be measured in bags of standard mass. Chemical admixture in liquid form is usually measured by mass or volume, whereas in powdered form it's measured by mass (ASTM C94; Fakere*et al.* 2012).

Batching plant, weighing equipment, serves the purpose of measuring and combining (mixing) various ingredients to form concrete. If proper ratios are not measured and mixed adequately, then the quality of concrete is compromised and may thus cause cracks and structural failure or collapse of the building leading to loss of life and economic impairment. These effects can be mitigated by ensuring that batching plant is well calibrated and maintained.

e) Mass measurements in transport industry

In **air transport**, aircraft performance and handling characteristics are affected by the gross weight and center of gravity limits. Exceeding these limits can be dangerous -the aircraft flight characteristics are adversely affected. Some of the aircraft performance characteristics adversely affected by overweight include increased takeoff speed, operational range, approach speed, increased take-off runway length, and manoeuvrability, landing distance, rate of climb, controllability, maximum altitude capability and stall speed. An overloaded or improperly balanced aircraft will require more power and greater fuel consumption to maintain flight, and the stability and controllability. The total weight of baggage, cargo, and fuel load should be adjusted accordingly to provide an adequate margin of safety.

3. Mass calibration services at KEBS

KEBS maintains the national standard for mass in the form of prototype kilogram BIPM/95, and reference mass standards, OIML Class E_1 (traceable to PTB (Germany) as shown in Figure 1). This has been established to enable the industry develop suitable measurement assurance program suitable for their processes. A normal mass calibration entails determination of true/conventional mass of weights and appropriate measurement uncertainty for that value and defined error limits.

Currently, the range of KEBS mass calibration services spans from 1 mg to 10 kg weight of Class E_2.

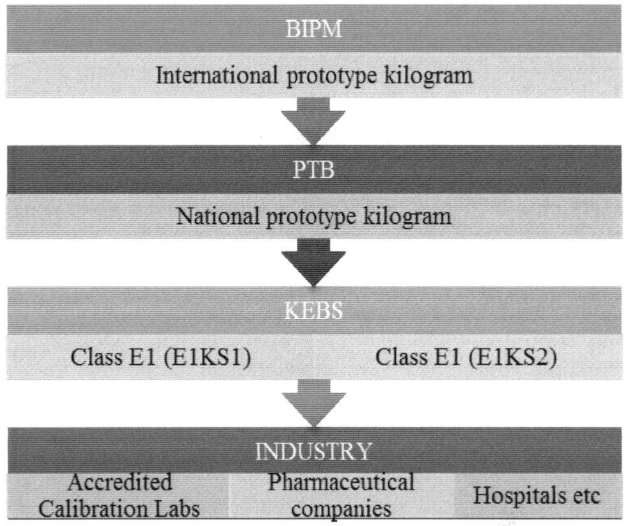

Figure 1: Traceability chain of mass

In a bid to support and enhance the aforementioned industrial processes, KEBS has recently upgraded its mass measurement and technical capabilities to calibration of mass standards (Class E_2, 1 mg to 10 kg). The laboratory is also currently undergoing audit for accreditation (by DAkkS) to density measurements (Class E_2, up to 1g to 20 kg) and balance calibration. The scope mass measurements and accreditation services as well as its participation in mass inter-comparison activities are respectively shown in Table 2 and 3 below.

Table 2: Mass measurement & accreditation

Measurand	Status	Year	Scope	Range
Convectional Mass Values	Accredited by DAkkS	2007	Class F_1 weights	1 mg - 1 kg
Convectional Mass Values	Accredited by DAkkS	2014	Class E_2 weights	1 mg - 10 kg
Density of standard weights	Equipment available & Measurements under establishment. *Accreditation in progress.*	2015	Class E_2 weights	1 g – 20 kg
Weighing instruments	Not accredited. *Accreditation in progress*	-	Balances	Up to 1000 kg
Moisture measuring instruments	Not accredited	-	Wood/ grain moisture meters	

Table 3: Mass inter-comparison measurements

Type	Participants	Period	Status
SADCMET.M.M.S1 [OIML F_1 1 kg] Kenya pilot	SADC states, Kenya, Tanzania & Ethiopia	2009	Completed
KEBS-ZMK [OIML E_2 200 g] ZMK pilot	Kenya & Germany	Oct–Nov 2014	Completed
KEBS-NIM (China) OIML 10 kg, 1 kg, 200 g, 50 g, 20 g, 2 g & 10 mg (Mass and density comparisons) KEBS Pilot	Kenya & China	2015/16	Planned

4. Conclusion

Mass is the quantity of matter, and most derived physical quantities (e.g. pressure, force, density etc) involve and revolve around mass. There is an increasing need for accuracy and traceability of mass measurements globally in support of health & safety, the environment, and trade, etc. Sustainable quality industrial products and services are hinged on quality mass measurements and calibration of weighing equipment. Calibration and related mass measurement services of KEBS provide means for manufacturers and users of such equipment to achieve levels of measurement accuracy that are necessary to attain quality, productivity and competitiveness.

5. References

Alonzo, L. (2013). *Weighing the benefits of scale equipment.* Retrieved from Pharmaceutical Manufacturing: http://www.pharmamanufacturing.com/articles/2013/1303-tech-at-work/

ASTM-94-c94 Batching, Mixing, and Transporting concrete

BIPM. (2007, April 27). *International Bureau of Weights and Measures*. Retrieved November 28, 2011, from Unit of mass (kilogram).

Chaikin (2014).Causes-of-Truck-Accidents/Overloaded-Trucks.http://www.chaikinandsherman.com/Personal-Injury/Truck-Accidents/Causes-of-Truck-Accidents/Overloaded-Trucks.aspx

EA10/18- Guidelines on the calibration of non-automatic weighing instruments.

FakereA., FadairoG., Fakere R. (2012). Assessment of Building Collapse in Nigeria: A Case of Naval Building, Abuja, Nigeria.*International Journal of Engineering and Technology2*(4), 581-591.

Macran, S. (2004).*The Relationship between Body Mass Index and Health-Related Quality of Life.*University of York, Outcomes Research Group.Heslington,: University of York.

OIML R76 Non-automatic Weighing Instruments Part 1: Metrological Requirements - Tests

Tipton, P. H., Aigner, J. M., Finto, D., Haislet, A. J., Pehl, L., Pamela, S., & Marjory, W. (2012). Patient Safety: Consider the accfuracy of height and weight measurements. *Nursing, 42*(5), 50-52.

WHO. (2013, 11 28). *BMI classification*. Retrieved 11 28, 2013, from World Health Organization (WHO): http://apps.who.int/bmi/index.jsp?introPage=intro_3.html

Modelization of SiPZ Photodiode Quantum Efficency

Z. Ben Achour[a], S. OUESLATI[a], O. Touayar[a]

a: National Institut of Applied Sciences and Technology, University of Carthage, INSAT BP 676 Centre Urbain Nord 1080 Tunis Cedex, Tunisia.

First Author/Corresponding Author : Zahra BEN ACHOUR, zbenachour@yahoo.fr, +21698317097, +21671703829, INSAT BP 676 Centre Urbain Nord 1080 Tunis Cedex, Tunisia.

Keywords :

Photodiode, quantum efficency, absorption model, photocurrent, front zone, depletion zone, base zone, sensitivity.

Abstarct :

The SiPZ photodiode is a radiometric detector realized at INSAT combining the silicon, porous silicon and doped ZnO layer. This photodiode serve as a transfer detector in the visible range for radiometric measurements. The present work consist in in studying and in modeling the SiPZ structure to determine its theoretical quantum efficiency and to compare it to the experimental one. The comparison has allowed us to conclude that the results of our elaborated model are in harmony with those obtained experimentally and allowed to have a precise idea of the contribution of the various layers constituting the photodiode.

Introduction:

Today, quantum detectors and thermal detectors enabled, first of measuring optical radiation, either in terms of the sensation produced on the eye but based on the energy transported by the radiation, and secondly to extend the spectral range below and beyond the visible spectrum. It is possible to measure the radiation power by using reference type of quantum detectors Detector Quantum Efficiency (QED) [1,3] whose quantum yield is 1 or electrical substitution radiometers operating at ambient or cryogenic temperature [4,5]. But this possibility is limited to low power lasers, typically a few milliwatts. Unfortunately quantum detectors QED type of reference have disappeared and cryogenic radiometers are heavy to implement. This unfortunately is a difficult problem for users and manufacturers looking to make in-situ measurements. Therefore, the realization of transfer standards for radiation measurements has become trivial and it is required [6].

Some Works already realized in the Materials, Measurements and Applications laboratory [7] have allowed the realization of a standard SiPZ photodiode with porous silicon to measure the energy flow, expressed in Watt. The SiPZ structure consists essentially of an n^+p homojonction, a porous silicon layer and an Al doped ZnO layer which serve at the same time as a passivation layer and a transparent electrode [7,8]. This original structure allowed to reduce considerably the front face reflection coefficient fluctuations of our photodiode. In addition to the achievement of the aforementioned photodiode, a research work was conducted in the laboratory. It consists in studying and in modeling this last structure and this to be able to determine its theoretical quantum efficiency and compare it afterward to that of this structure obtained experimentally. In this work we determined the equations governing the quantum efficiency of our photodiode. We simulated the quantum yield curves and we compared them with those measured experimentally.

1 - / The SiPZ photodiode Structure:

The originality of the SiPZ photodiode [7] lives in the use of the optical properties of the porous silicon structure and the electric properties of the ZnO layer in the same time. This was made to increase the light absorption in the created pores depths serving as traps to confine the incident radiation at the energetic point of view. In the figure 1 we represent the structure of the SiPZ photodiode.

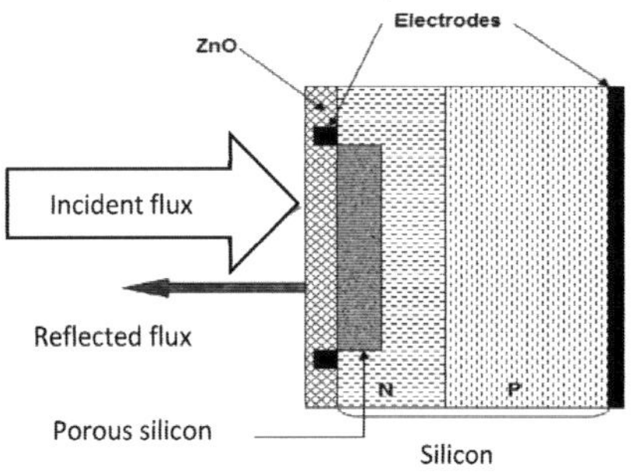

Figure 1: Schematic representation of the SiPZ photodiode [7].

This photodiode SiPZ presents many characteristics such as a reduced darkness current, because the surface of the n-p junction is small. The front recombination is also reduced because the active face of the photodiode is situated in an illuminated region.

Moreover, the SiPZ photodiode presents a high absorption coefficient of the incident light, and a low reflection coefficient equal to 7% for a wave length between 400 nm to 1100 nm.

2/ The proposed model for light absorption in the SiPZ photodiode

With the aim of modeling and determining the theoretical quantum efficiency on our structure, we studied the influence of the absorption of the light through the various passivation layers. Thus to model the quantum efficiency of our SiPZ photodiode, it is necessary to take into account various carriers diffusion mechanisms in various zone of the structure which are represented by the following figure:

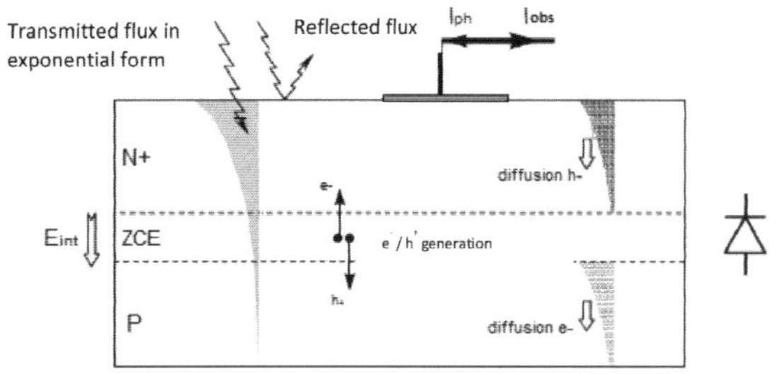

Figure 2 : Principle scheme illustrating the carriers diffusion mechanisms [9]

We have the case of a junction between an n type zone and a p type zone. This junction is constituted by three zones of different doping levels [7-10]: the n distribution is strongly doped (on 10^{19} atom / cm^3), the depletion zone devoid of free carriers, and the p substrate which is weakly doped (on 10^{16} atom / cm^3). The concentration of the free carriers determines the value of the absorption coefficient. We thus have a succession of three different absorption coefficients. Inside the depletion zone, we can consider that all the created free carriers are separated. We thus have a directly proportional quantum efficiency in the flux absorbed in this region.

The proposed model for light absorption in the SiPZ photodiode is the following one:

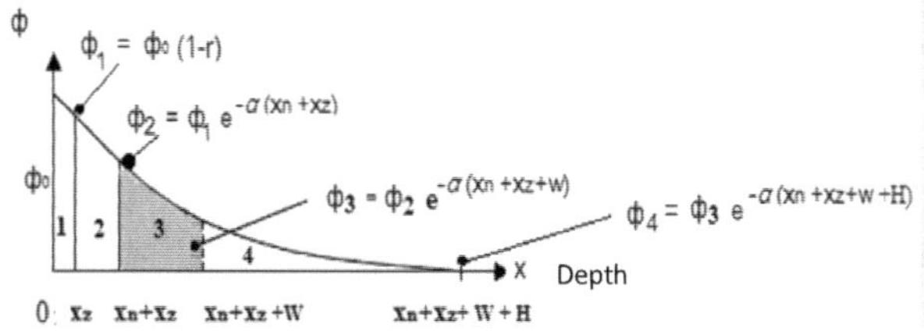

Figure 3 : Absoption proposed model in the various constituent regions of the SiPZ photodiode.

Each region of the photodiode absorbs a fraction of the incident energy, following the role which it plays: the front zone plays the transmitter role and it is composed of a ZnO layer with x_z=0,49µm as thickness (layer 1) and a porous silicon and n type silicon layer with a thickness of x_n=0,5µm (layer 2). Then the depletion region which is a highly disturbed buffer zone: (layer 3) (silicon with a thickness of W=0,28µm). The base is a p type silicon with thickness H=250µm, it absorbs the light and it is considrerd as the absorber (layer 4).

The light absorption in the photodiode follows a decreasing exponential law, because the part of the light which remains to be absorbed decreases as we penetrate into the photodiode. From this model, we are going to study the quantum efficiency on every region, by taking into account the absorption coefficient which varies according to the used material. For this purpose, we look for an absorption coefficient model optimized for our structure.

By simulation we obtained the result in the figure 4 below. The used values of the absorption coefficient $\alpha(\lambda)$ are published by K. Rajkanan [11].

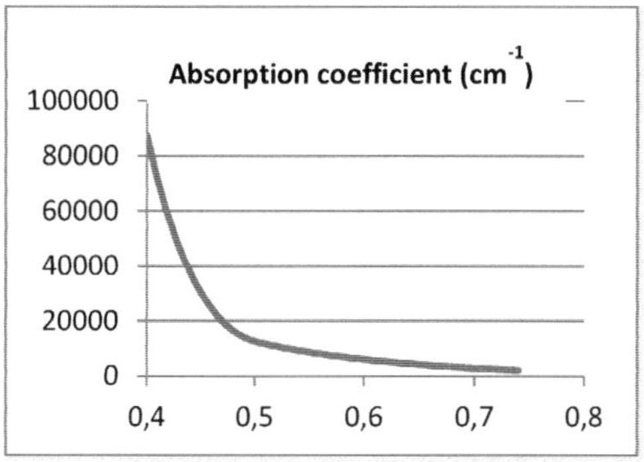

Figure 4 : Representative curve of Absorption Coefficient in cm-1 by RAJAKANA model

Where the mathematical model governing this evolution of the absorption is given by the following equation [12]:

$$\alpha(T) = \sum_{\substack{i=1,2\\ j=1,2}} C_i A_i \left[\frac{(hv-Eg+Eph)^2}{e^{Eph/KT}-1} + \frac{(hv-E_g+E_{ph})^2}{1-e^{-Eph/KT}}\right] + \sqrt{A_d(hv-E_{gd})^2} \quad (1)$$

Where hν is the energy of photons, E_{g1} = 1, 11 eV, E_{g2} = 2,45 eV and E_{gd} = 3,15 eV are the energies of both indirect gaps (1 and 2) and the direct gap in 300°K, respectively.
$E_{p1}=1,827\times10^{-2}$ eV and $E_{p2}=5,773\times10^{-2}$ eV are the phonon energy. C_1=5,5 ; C_2=4 ; $A_1=3,231\times10^{2}$ cm^{-1} eV^{-2} ; $C_2=7,237\times10^{3}$ cm^{-1} eV^{-2} and $A_d=1,052\times10^{6}$ cm^{-1} eV^{-2}.

3 -/ Modelization of the SiPZ quantum efficency:

3-1/ photocarriers distribution :

When the semiconductor is photoexcited, the surplus created and broadcast carriers recombine. The evolution of this non-equilibrium regime is governed by the equations of continuity, where G_n and G_p generation rates are the optical generation rate given by the following expression:

$$G_n(x,\lambda) = G_p(x,\lambda) = \phi\alpha(\lambda)e^{-\alpha x}$$

Où $\phi = (1-r)\phi_0$ is the absorbed flux of photons in the semiconductor and r is the reflection coefficient.

In the case of a one-dimensional approach along the propagation axis of the light beam (Ox), the illumination will be assumed uniform.

The rate of carrier generation in each layer depends only on the wavelength λ and the depth x, since the layers are not uniform, so the absorption coefficient is no longer the same at any point in the photodiode. The evolution of the photon flux ϕ (Wm^{-2}) is exponentially decreasing and depends on α.

The continuity equations for electrons and for holes are used to determine the density of minority carriers. These equations govern the condition of dynamic equilibrium of charge carriers in the semiconductor.

In one dimension, the continuity equations are thus written as follows:

$$\frac{\partial n}{\partial t} = n\mu_n\frac{\partial E}{\partial x} + \mu_n E\frac{\partial n}{\partial x} + D_n\frac{\partial^2 n}{\partial x^2} + \phi\alpha e^{-\alpha x} - \frac{(n-n_0)}{\tau_n} \qquad \text{(p zone : base)}$$

$$\frac{\partial p}{\partial t} = -p\mu_p\frac{\partial E}{\partial x} - \mu_p E\frac{\partial p}{\partial x} + D_p\frac{\partial^2 p}{\partial x^2} + \phi\alpha e^{-\alpha x} - \frac{(p-p_0)}{\tau_p} \qquad \text{(n zone : front)}$$

with p\n : the hole density\electron density ,

p_0 \ n_0 : equilibrium density,

D_p\ D_n : hole diffusion constant\electron diffusion constant,

μ_p\ μ_n : hole mobility\electron mobility,

τ_p\ τ_n : hole life time\electron life time.

The electric field component is the result of two contributions $E = E_a + E_i$.

With E_a: is the field applied to the sample by any bias voltage.

E_i: is an internal field, which results from the difference in mobility between electrons and holes. This field E_i accelerates the slowest carriers and slows the fastest ones.

The resolution of this system is relatively complex.

As a first approximation, and due to the significant relationship between the dielectric time constant τdiel $\approx 10^{-12}$ s [11] and the carriers life time $\tau \approx 10^{-3}$ à 10^{-3} s [11].

Electrical neutrality of the material recovered in a considerably shorter time than its return to equilibrium.

Therefore it can be assumed with a good approximation that the electrical neutrality of the semiconductor is kept under illumination, in other words $\Delta n(x,t) \approx \Delta p(x,t)$.

The electrons and excess holes created by photoexcitation, broadcast together it is the ambipolar diffusion.

We will try now to study the photocarriers distribution.

Consider that the photodiode is not subject to any external voltage (Ea = 0) and the internal electric field Ei is negligible in the front and in the basis of our structure.

As the regime is stationary $\frac{dn}{dt} = 0$, the ambipolar diffusion equation is therefore written

$$D\frac{\partial^2 \Delta n}{\partial x^2} - \frac{\Delta n}{\tau_n} + \phi\alpha e^{-\alpha x} = 0 \qquad (18)$$

Where according to the nature of the material, D is the ambipolar diffusion coefficient or minority carrier diffusion coefficient. By introducing the carriers diffusion length $L = \sqrt{D\tau}$, the equation (18) is written

$$\frac{\partial^2 \Delta n}{\partial x^2} - \frac{\Delta n}{L^2} = -\phi\alpha\frac{\tau_n}{L^2}e^{-\alpha x} \qquad (19)$$

The solution of this differential equation is the sum of the general solution of the equation without second member and a particular solution of the equation with the second member. The solution is of the form:

$$\Delta n = Ae^{\frac{-x}{L}} + Be^{\frac{x}{L}} + \frac{\phi\alpha\tau}{1-\alpha^2L^2}e^{-\alpha x} \qquad (20)$$

The determination of the constants A and B and the general solution requires the use of the limit conditions of each layer as it is thick or thin, type zone n or p ....

<u>3-2 / Determination of the photocurrent expression</u>

The mathematical resolution allowed us by taking in to account various photocarriers distributions in the various zones of the structure and using the continuities equations to determine the expression of the photocurrent in the various zones.

3-2-1/ photocurrent in the front zone

The front of this photodiode is composed of three different parts: a ZnO layer, a porous silicon layer and a n-type silicon layer.

- Study of the first front layer ZnO:

This layer has a thin size, therefore it is assumed that the surface recombination velocities (x=0) and ($x = x_z$) are negligible

The condition □$_Z$ <<1/α_Z implies that: □< □$_Z$ <<1/α_Z and thereafter □$_Z$□<<1 et $e^{-\alpha_z x} \approx 1$

the two boundary conditions are written as following:

In x=0 we have $0 = \frac{D_p}{\Delta p_0}\left(\frac{d\Delta p}{dx}\right)_{x_z}$ so A=B,

In x=x$_z$ we have $0 = \frac{D_p}{(\Delta p)_{x_z}}\left(\frac{d\Delta p}{dx}\right)_{x_z}$ so $A = Be^{\frac{2x_z}{Lp}}$,

Consequently A=B=0 hence $\Delta p = \alpha_z \phi_0 \tau_p$

Thus the change in concentration of minority carriers Δp is constant throughout the width of the ZnO electrode, on the other hand the corresponding photocurrent is written as: [13]

$$J_p = -qD_p \frac{\partial(p-p_0)}{\partial x} \text{ in } x=x_z$$

But $(p - p_0)$ is a constant, thereafter Jp = 0. So there's no photonic current creation in this layer. It is assumed that the current recovered in the external circuit is a current created in the active region (silicon) and which passes through the ZnO layer outwards. We adopted the assumption that the current flowing in the ZnO layer is no longer photonic but tunneling one. Which coincides with the above description of the ZnO layer as a transparent electrode.

- Study of the next layer of the front

This layer consists of porous silicon and n-type with xN thickness and which is illuminated by a uniform flow transmitted from the ZnO layer. The porous silicon layer is modeled as an homogeneous region with a short lifetime and a high recombination speed.

In $x = x_Z$ the flux is written $\phi_1 = \phi_0(1 - r)$,

where r is the reflection coefficient

The continuity equation of the minority carriers is as following :

$$\frac{d^2\Delta p}{dx^2} - \frac{\Delta p}{Lp^2} = -\frac{\alpha N \phi_1 \tau^p}{Lp^2} e^{-\alpha_N x} \quad \text{avec} \quad x_z \le x \le x_N + x_z$$

To solve this differential equation, we use the following boundary conditions :

$$D_p \frac{\partial \Delta p}{\partial x} = S_p \Delta p \quad \text{in} \quad x = x_Z$$

$$p - p_0 = 0 \quad \text{in} \quad x = x_N + x_Z$$

Therefore, the solution of the continuity equation is :

$$p - p_0 = \frac{\alpha\,\tau_p}{\alpha^2 {L_p}^2 - 1}\left[\frac{\phi_1\left(\alpha\,L_p + \frac{L_p S_p}{D_p}\right)e^{-\alpha x_z} sinh\left(\frac{x_1 - x}{L_p}\right) + \phi_2 e^{-\alpha x_1}\left(\cosh\left(\frac{x - x_z}{L_p}\right) + \frac{L_p S_p}{D_p}\sinh\left(\frac{x - x_z}{L_p}\right)\right)}{\frac{L_p S_p}{D_p}\sinh\left(\frac{x_1 - x_z}{L_p}\right) + \cosh\left(\frac{x_1 - x_z}{L_p}\right)} - \phi_1 \alpha e^{-\alpha x}\right]$$

The photocurrent expression in the front region (due to holes collected at the edge of the junction) is given by the following equation:

$$J_p = -\frac{\alpha\,\tau_p\,q\,D_p}{\alpha^2 {L_p}^2 - 1}\left[\frac{\phi_1\left(\alpha\,L_p + \frac{L_p S_p}{D_p}\right)e^{-\alpha x_z}\left(\frac{-1}{L_p}\right) + \phi_2 e^{-\alpha x_1}\left(\frac{1}{L_p}\right)\left(\sinh\left(\frac{x_1 - x_z}{L_p}\right) + \frac{L_p S_p}{D_p}\cosh\left(\frac{x_1 - x_z}{L_p}\right)\right)}{\frac{L_p S_p}{D_p}\sinh\left(\frac{x_1 - x_z}{L_p}\right) + \cosh\left(\frac{x_1 - x_z}{L_p}\right)} - \phi_1 \alpha e^{-\alpha x_1}\right]$$

3-2-2/ photocurrent in the depletion zone

Given the intense field prevailing in the depletion region, all the electron-hole pairs are separated and collected immediately.

The electrons and holes flux flowing in $x = x_N + x_Z$ et $x = x_N + x_Z + w$ respectively is equal to the number of electron-hole pairs created. It is assumed that no recombination occurs during the transit of a minority carrier across the junction.

Under these conditions the expression of the photocurrent in the depletion zone is written:

$$J_{ZCE} = -q = -q e^{-\alpha(x_N + x_Z)}\phi_2[1 - e^{-\alpha w}]$$

3-2-3/ photocurrent in the base zone

The current is mainly a minority electron current. The base is uniform in its electrical properties and we use the same reasoning as for the front. Hence, the boundary conditions used at the depth x_2 and x_3 are the following :

$$(n - n_0) = 0 \quad \text{in } x = x_2$$

$$-D_n \frac{\partial(n - n_0)}{\partial x} = S_n(n - n_0) \quad \text{in } x = x_3$$

with $x_2 = x_Z + x_N + w$

$x_3 = x_Z + x_N + w + H$

with w the depletion zone width and H is the hole photodide width

The electrons distribution in the uniform region forming the p-type base is given by the following equation :

$$n - n_0 = \frac{\alpha\tau_n}{\alpha^2 L_n^2 - 1}\left[\frac{\phi_3 e^{-\alpha x_2}\left(\frac{D_n}{L_n} cosh\left(\frac{x_3 - x}{L_n}\right) + S_n sinh\left(\frac{x_3 - x}{L_n}\right)\right) + \phi_4 e^{-\alpha x_3}(S_n - \alpha D_n) sinh\left(\frac{x - x_2}{L_n}\right)}{\frac{D_n}{L_n} cosh\left(\frac{x_3 - x_2}{L_n}\right) + S_n sinh\left(\frac{x_3 - x_2}{L_n}\right)} - \phi_3 e^{-\alpha x}\right]$$

The photocurrent expression in the region p:

$$J_n = \frac{q\,\alpha D_n \tau_n}{\alpha^2 {L_n}^2 - 1}\left[\frac{\phi_3 e^{-\alpha x_2}\left(\frac{-D_n}{L_n^2}\sinh\left(\frac{H}{L_n}\right) - \frac{S_n}{L_n}\cosh\left(\frac{H}{L_n}\right)\right) + \phi_4 e^{-\alpha x_3}(S_n - \alpha D_n)}{\frac{D_n}{L_n}\cosh\left(\frac{H}{L_n}\right) + S_n \sinh\left(\frac{H}{L_n}\right)} + \alpha \phi_3 e^{-\alpha x_2}\right]$$

Some photocurrent collections are held in the depletion area. The electric field in this region may be regarded as sufficiently high, and therefore the photogenerated carriers are accelerated out of the depletion region before they can recombine.

3-3 / Determination of the quantum efficency expression

The quantum efficency characterizes the photoelectric conversion of the photodiode. It essentially depends on the physical parameters of the silicon such as the absorption coefficient, the wavelength, the doping profile, the carriers diffusion constant, the depth of each zone and the generation/recombination rate of the electron-hole pairs. From the equations above, we determined the quantum efficency equations in the various zones of the SiPZ photodiode structure. We will also estimate the theoretical quantum efficiency in terms of the physical parameters : L_p, D_p, S_p, L_n, D_n, S_n, τ_n, τ_p and the experimental caracteristics : x_1, x_2, x_3, x_Z, x_N, w, H, ϕ_0, α and r.

The photocurrent of the region n essentially consists of a minority holes. The quantum efficiency on the front is written as :

$$Q_1 = \frac{\alpha L_p}{\alpha^2 {L_p}^2 - 1}(1-r)\left[\frac{\left(\alpha L_p + \frac{L_p S_p}{D_p}\right)e^{-\alpha x_z} + e^{-2\alpha x_1}\left(\sinh\left(\frac{x_1 - x_z}{L_p}\right) + \frac{L_p S_p}{D_p}\cosh\left(\frac{x_1 - x_z}{L_p}\right)\right)}{\frac{L_p S_p}{D_p}\sinh\left(\frac{x_1 - x_z}{L_p}\right) + \cosh\left(\frac{x_1 - x_z}{L_p}\right)} - \alpha L_p e^{-\alpha x_1}\right]$$

with: □$_p$ =1µm [13], □$_p$ =10^3 □□/□ [13], □$_p$ =1 □□^{2}/□ [13], r=0.07 [1-3-8], □$_z$ =0.39µ□ [1-3-8],

□$_1$ =0,89µ□ [1-3-8].

The equation of quantum efficiency for the depletion zone is the following :

$$Q_2 = e^{-\alpha(x_N + x_z)}\phi_2\left[1 - e^{-\alpha W}\right]$$

with: w= 0.28µ□ [1-3-8], □$_N$ =0.5µ□ [1-3-8].

The equation of the quantum efficiency for the p region is :

$$Q_3 = \frac{Ln\,\alpha}{\alpha^2 {L_n}^2 - 1}\left[\frac{e^{-2\alpha x_3}\left(\frac{L_n S_n}{D_n} - \alpha L_n\right) - e^{-\alpha x_2}\left(\frac{L_n S_n}{D_n}\cosh\left(\frac{H}{L_n}\right) + \sinh\left(\frac{H}{L_n}\right)\right)}{\cosh\left(\frac{H}{L_n}\right) + \frac{S_n L_n}{D_n}\sinh\left(\frac{H}{L_n}\right)} + \alpha L_n e^{-\alpha x_2}\right]$$

with: □$_n$ =140µ□ [13], □$_n$ =10^{2}c□/□ [13], □$_n$=20□□^{2}/□ [13], H=249.22µ□ [1-3-8],

□$_2$ =0.78µ□ [1-3-8], □$_3$ =250µ□ [1-3-8].

The pairs electrons-holes are generated in the base, in the load space zone and in the transmitter, thus the global quantum efficiency on the photodiode will be the sum of the partial quantum efficiencies on three regions for any wavelengths. We then deducted the quantum efficiency according to the wavelength for every region, then that global of the SiPZ photodiode. The quantum efficiency on the SiPZ photodiode possesses the appearance represented in the following figure:

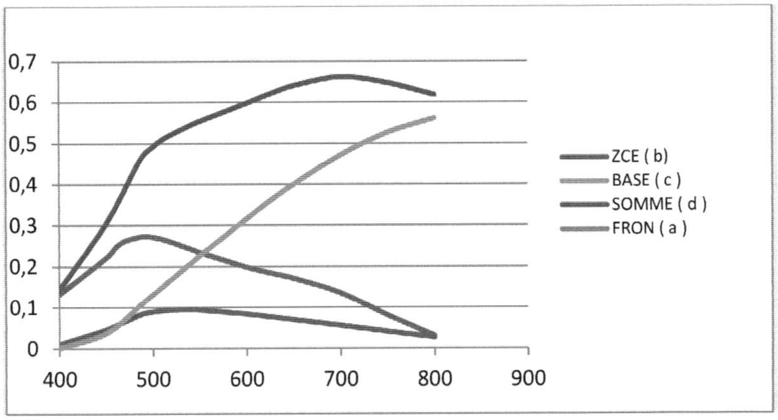

Figure 5 : Final simulation result of the SiPZ photodiode quantum efficiency, (a): front quantum efficiency, (b): depletion zone quantum efficiency, (c): base quantum efficiency, (d): the whole photodiode quantum efficiency.

The theoretical SiPZ photodiode quantum efficiency, represented in the figure 5 covers a range of wave lengths range from 400 nm to 800 nm (visible domain). This efficiency is lower than 10 % for wavelengths below 400 nm and increases until 50 % between 400 nm and 520 nm to reach its maximal value (62 %) at 700 nm. Beyond 700 nm, we note that the quantum efficiency decreases gradually. In fact, when the energy of the received photons becomes lower than the silicon gap energy, these cannot create any more free carriers and the efficiency becomes hopeless. We limit ourselves for description just on the visible spectral range.

4/ - comparison between theoretical and experimental sensitivities

We passed afterward in comparison with the theoretical spectral sensibility and in its comparison with that experimental.

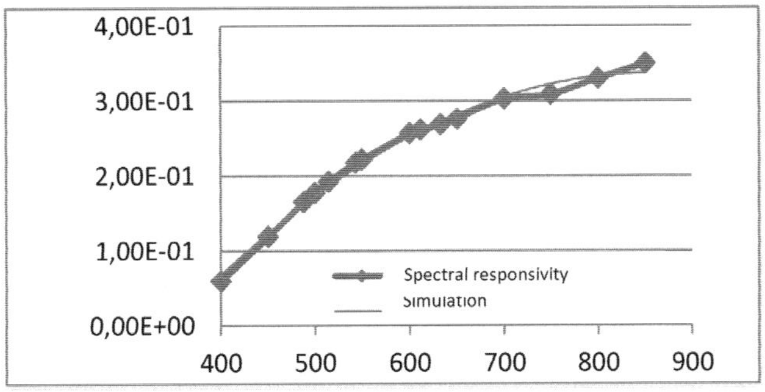

Figure 6 : Representative curve of the spectral responsivity of the SiPZ photodiode

According to the figure above, we observe that the spectral sensibility increases with the wavelengths, until a determined well wavelength equal to 900 nm approximately for which the spectral sensibility is maximal. Considering the equation (5), the quantum efficiency is proportional in the spectral sensibility thus it will have the same appearance as previously. This is compatible with the theoretical quantum efficiency curve. Once, we are going to compare the theoretical and experimental quantum efficiency. The figure 7 below gives the quantum efficiency obtained by both methods: simulation method and experimental method:

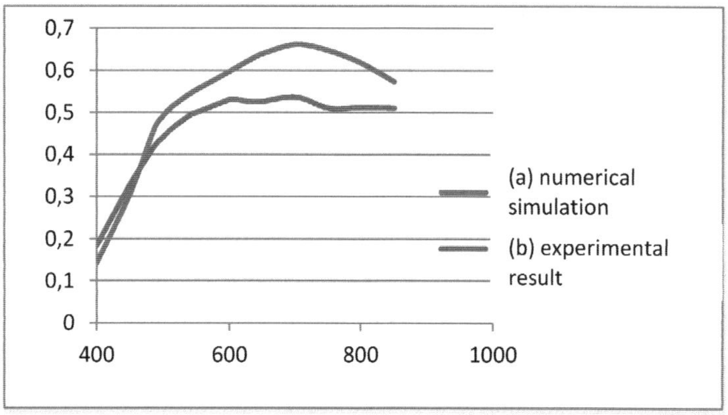

Figure 7 : The quantum efficiency on the SiPZphotodiode, (a): method of the digital simulation, (b): from the experimental values.

We notice that the behaviors of both curves are qualitatively identical to the low wave lengths and this for the front and depletion zone, but a light modification for the high wave lengths at the base zone.

It is difficult to realize a calculation model of the quantum efficiency which represent perfectly the reality, especially that a spectacular improvement of the photodiode exit tension was noted with the advent of the "back surface field" (BSF) of photodiode whom we did not take into account in the modeling and simulation of the photodiode quantum efficiency. This modification concerns essentially the parameter speed of recombination which quantifies the recombination on the back face.

In spite of the reflectivity decrease of our structure until 7% [7], the conversion rate of photons in pairs electrons-holes and the capacity of the structure to separate these pairs decreases. In fact from incident absorbed flow the maximal quantum efficiency value is in theory and experimentally more reduced. This implies that the recombination phenomenon has an important effect. This is mainly due to the fact that a part of the incident flow creates pairs electron-holes which we do not recover in the outside circuit.

The existence of a back field implies the existence of a back barrier. This barrier and the coexistence of two different semi-conductors with different gap energies involve the existence of discontinuities at the band energy. These discontinuities form probably wells and barriers of additional energies which increase the probability of recombination of the minority carriers created within our photodiode at every interface.

In the photodiode two phenomena of recombination have an important effect. It is on one hand, the recombinations which take place in front of the photodiode and which are due to carriers trapped in the interface Si-Si:O:H during the oxidation. These carriers create an electric field live as a parasite (causing interference) which modifies the concentration of the carrier loads. On the other hand, the second phenomenon of recombination takes place behind the photodiode. These recombinations are due to crystal defects of silicon and as we are relatively far from the zone of depletion, thus out of the intense electric field zone.

<u>Conclusion :</u>

In this work we studied and modeled the SiPZ photodiode quantum efficiency on, constituted essentially by a homojonction n+p, some porous silicon and an aluminum doped ZnO layer. For this purpose, we developed a theoretical study to determine a model connecting the quantum efficiency of our structure with the various parameters characterizing the photodiode. Then we feigned the equations of the quantum efficiency so determined according to the wavelength. The obtained results were confronted with those determined experimentally. Those last results were obtained by using the experimental sensibility values beforehand definite.

The results of our elaborate model are in perfect harmony with those obtained experimentally and allowed to have a precise idea of the contribution of our various layers constituting the photodiode.

One of the perspectives of this work would be to proceed to the improvement of the theoretical model of the quantum efficiency so developed by integrating into the place of the physical parameters extracted from the bibliography the same parameters which will be experimentally determined. Afterward, we shall proceed to the rectification of the model by trying to take into account all the characteristics of the base specially the "back surface field" (BSF). This will allow very probably a better approach of the experimental answer of the studied structure.

<u>Bibliography:</u>

. 1 Martin, J.E., Fox, N.P, and Key, P.J. (1985) 'A cryogenic radiometer for absolute radiometric measurement', Metrologia, Vol. 21, pp.147–155.

. 2 Zalewski, E.F. and Geist, J. (1990) 'Silicon photodiode absolute spectral response self-calibration', Appl. Opt., Vol. 19, pp.1214–1216.

. 3 Touayar, O., Reyn, H., Bastie, J. and Varpula, T. (1995–1996) 'Indirect comparison of cryogenic radiometers from the INM (France) and the VTT (Finland) with a QED-200 from the VSL (Netherlands)', Metrologia, Vol. 32, pp.561–564.

. 4 Mellouki, I., Touayar, O., Ktari, T., Saadallah, F., Bastie, J. and Yacoubi, N. (2004) 'Study and realization of a trap pyroelectric detector for absolute high radiant powers and energies', Measurem. Sci. Technol., Vol. 15, pp.384–388.

. 5 Touayar, O., Mellouki, I., Ben Achour, Z., Sifi, N., Yacoubi, N. and Bastie, J. (2006) 'Indirect comparison of the absolute LMR-Tunisia trap pyroelectric detector with the INM-France cryogenic absolute radiometer at 632.8 nm', Sens. Actuators, A, Vol. 132, pp.567–571.

. 6 Ben Achour, Z., Abbane, S., and Touayar, O., (2015) 'Study and realisation of an original silicon–germanium light trap detector for large band radiometric measurements', Int. J. Nanotechnol., Vol. 12, Nos. 8/9, pp.708-722.

. 7 Ben Achour, Z., Touayar, O., Akkari, E., Bastie, J., Bessais, B., Ben Brahim, J. (2007) 'Study and realization of a transfer detector based on porous silicon for radiometric measurements' Nuclear Instruments and Methods in Physics Research A, 579, pp.1117–1121.

. 8 Ben Achour, Z., Ktari, T., Ouertani, B., Touayar, O., Bessais, B., Ben Brahim, J. (2007) 'Effect of doping level and spray time on zinc oxide thin films produced by spray pyrolysis for transparent electrodes applications', Sensors and Actuators A, 134, pp.447–451.

. 9 Jérôme, G., (2009) 'Etude, conception, et réalisation d'un capteur d'image APS en technologie standard CMOS pour des applications faible flux de type viseur d'étoiles', Physique des semiconducteurs et des composants électroniques, Dunod.

. 10 Ben Achour, Z., (2009) 'Etude et élaboration d'une photodiode étalon à base de Silicium Poreux en vue d'une application en métrologie', Phd Report, FST, University of El Manar, Tunis, Tunisia.

. 11 Mathieu, H., Fanet, H., (2009), 'Physique des semiconducteurs et des composants électroniques', Dunod.

. 12 Rajkana, K., Singh, R., Shewcgun, J., (1979) 'Absorption coefficient of silicon for solar cell calculations Solid-State Electronics', vol. 22, Sept., pp.793-795.

. 13 Ricaud, A., (2009) 'De la physique de la conversion photovoltaique aux filiéres, matériaux et procédés électroniques', Photopile solaires, Ellipses.

Automatization of the primary level hydrometer calibration system of Volume, Density and Viscosity Laboratory in TUBITAK UME

U.Y. Akcadag*, G.S. Sariyerli, O. Sakarya

The Scientific and Technical Research Council of Turkey, National Metrology Institute (TUBITAK-UME), Gebze, Turkey

Received:

Abstract: In this project, the determination of weighing liquid by using automatic alignment system and the reference density standard to realize the calibration of scale division by hydrostatic weighing method introduced by Cuckow in computer controlled is planned. This system serves all projects of Volume, Density and Viscosity Laboratory for the calibration process of hydrometers and makes it fully automatic, fast, more precise and efficient in comparison with manuel calibration system. A new method refers automatically specific scale-marks for the calibration of hydrometers. A hydrometer calibration system adopting the new method consists of a vision system, positioning frame by servo motor and software to control the system. The vision system is composed of a camera to acquire images of meniscus level conflicted with scale level of hydrometer. The position of temperature controlled bath is provided by the positioning frame controlled with PLC. The stepping motor moves the camera, which is attached to the vessel containing a reference liquid, along the hydrometer. The aim of this study is to represent the automated hydrometer calibration system of TUBITAK UME.

Keywords: Cuckow's method, hydrostatic weighing, hydrometer, density, calibration, meniscus.

1 Introduction

Hydrometers, also known as gravimeters, areometers or densimeters, are the most ancient, simple and highly effective instruments, widely used at different levels of accuracy, to measure the density of liquids from 0,5 g/ cm^{-3} to 2,0 g/ cm^{-3}. Hydrometers can be used to measure any liquid property that is a function of density simply by putting an appropriate scale in the hydrometer stem.

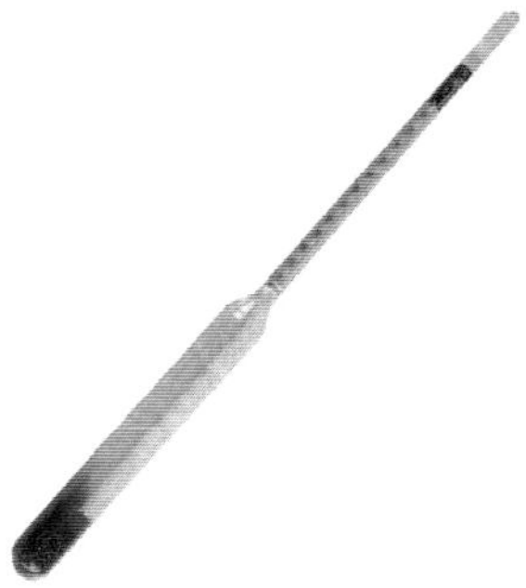

Fig.1. Density Hydrometer

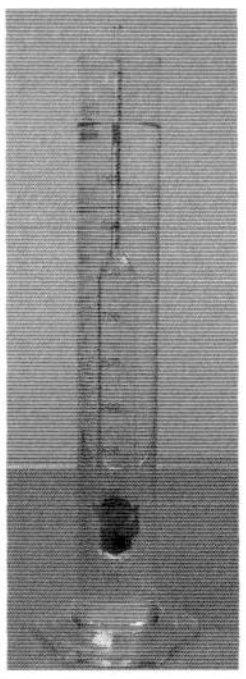

Fig.2. Hydrostatic reading in liquids

* Correspondence: umit.akcadag@tubitak.gov.tr

There are two primary methods for calibrating hydrometers. First one requires floating the hydrometer in several liquids of different densities, which are determined by applying Archimedes' principle to a sinker of known mass and volume. The second method (Cuckow's method) requires hydrostatic weighing, i.e. using a balance to measure the mass of the hydrometer while it is immersed to several levels in an unique liquid of known density.

Cuckow method has many advantages. It eliminates the inconvenience of storing a collection of liquids. It provides the calibration of a hydrometer at specified scale marks without the inconvenience of preparing liquid mixtures to specified densities. This method can be automated more easily.

Volume, density and viscosity laboratory of UME is willing to automate the calibration of hydrometers in order to reduce uncertainties and provide more accurate measurements. It was built an automated and primary standard system for the calibration of hydrometers using Cuckow's method .

The primary level hydrometer calibration system of volume, density and viscosity laboratory immerses the hydrometer chosen for test far enough into tridecane liquid so that the hydrometer mark to be calibrated is aligned with the free surface.

2 Method and theoritical equations

The method is based on weighing of the hydrometer when it has been floating at the scale mark, which is supposed to be calibrated. Density of the liquid must be previously measured. Hydrometer experiences an upthrust equal to its weight when it is immersed up to the scale mark and order of upthrust is proportional to the amount of immersion. If we weigh the body immersed to requested extent in two liquids of known density it would be possible to determine the density corresponding to requested extent which is supposed to be a scale mark. Application of this procedure requires special apparatus and special designs for sensitive immersion.
Theory of the method is based on the fact that, if we weigh a solid body at a point in between two media whose densities are known we may find the density of the medium in which the upthrust on the immersed portion would be equal to the weight of the body. Hydrometers are firstly weighed in air and then in a reference liquid of known density, which is used as reference. The weighing value is measured while the hydrometers were immersed up to different levels.
The density corresponds related scale line can be determined with the equation by using the measurement results according to the Cuckow method at reference temperature (20°C or 15°C).

$$\rho(t_B)=[\rho_F(t)-\rho_{LL}]\cdot\frac{W_L+(\pi/g)d.\gamma(t_B)}{W_L-W_F+(\pi/g)d.\gamma_F(t)}\cdot[1+\alpha_V.(t-t_B)]+\rho_{LL} \quad (1)$$

In equation 1;

$\rho(t_B)$: Density of calibrated scale line
W_L : Weighing value of hydrometer in air
W_F : Weighing value of hydrometer in liquid
t_B : Reference temperature
t : Temperature during measurement
d : Stem diameter of hydrometer at meniscus level
$\rho_F(t)$: Density of liquid during measurement
ρ_{LL} : Density of air during weighing in air
$\gamma(t_B)$: Surface tension of reference liquid
$\gamma_F(t)$: Surface tension of tridecane
α_V : Hydrometer's volumetric expansion coefficient
g : Local gravitational acceleration

The air density can be determined by equation 2;

$$\rho_a=\frac{0.34844\cdot P-h\cdot(0.00252\cdot t-0.020582)}{273.15+t} \quad (2)$$

The liquid density ($\rho_F(t)$) shall be determined by sinker (reference density standard) using substitute method with the same system in air and liquid media.

ρ_a : Air density (kg/m^3)
t : Environmental temperature (°C)
P : Atmospheric pressure (mbar / hPa)
h : Environmental humidity (% rh)

3 Automated hydrometer calibration system

A manual hydrometer calibration system had been used in Volume, Density and Viscosity Laboratory shown in Figure 3. The hydrometer shall be immersed into the calibration liquid up to the calibration scale mark by the hydrostatic weighing method for calibration process. The hydrometer is bounded up with balance by holder and hook assembly. The calibration liquid takes place in the glass tube positioned into the temperature controlled bath.

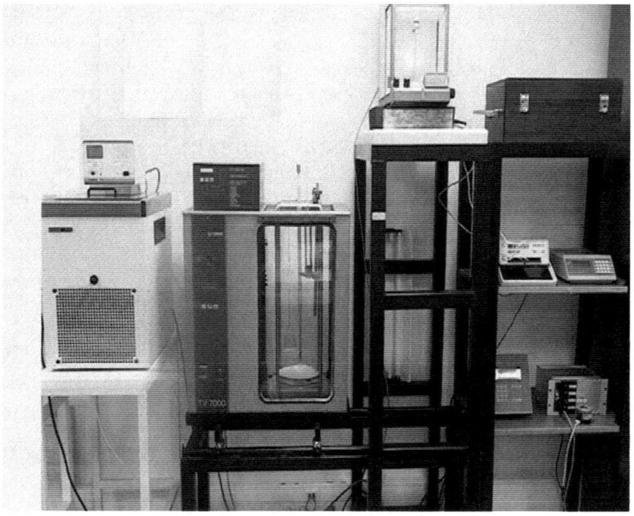

Fig.3. A manual hydrometer calibration system

The hydrometer calibration system described here consists of an electronic balance, a frame, a glass vessel containing a reference liquid, a thermometer, a hygrometer, a barometer and an automatic alignment system.

Fig.4. A cross section view of automated hydrometer system

Figure 6 shows the configuration of the automated hydrometer calibration system.The automatic alignment system consists of a camera, a frame grabber, a light, a stepping motor, and software to control the system. The distance between the hydrometer and the camera is 150 mm. The glass vessel is cylindirical with a height of 495 mm and diameter of 160 mm.

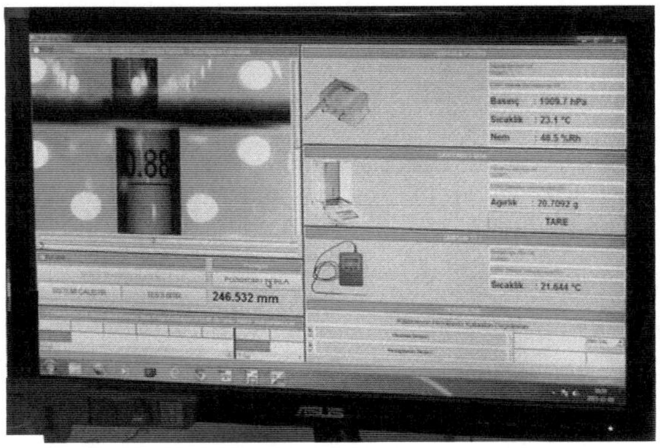

Fig.5. A camera image of immersed part of the hydrometer under test.

The software comprises a camera image to search for a meniscus and target scale-marks, and a program to control the stepping motor that aligns the temperature controlled bath on frame grabber (Fig.5).

Fig.6. Automated hydrometer calibration system

4 Experimental setup

Firstly measurements are carried out in air medium with a balance having 0.1 mg readability.

Calibrated weights are used in substitution method and air density is calculated by using ambient conditions so that air buoyancy correction would be concerned in weighing value. Right after weighing hydrometers in air, it is important to measure stem diameters at required scale marks of hydrometer, and reference surface tensions of the liquid, where the hydrometer is supposed to be used, are determined from related tables. Surface tension of the calibration liquid (tridecane) is already known. Second stage is to perform hydrostatic 'Cuckow' weighing. In this process; the balance is located at the top of the system and it has the ability to perform measurements inside the liquid via an apparatus, which connects the balance into the liquid. Temperature controlled bath is used for temperature stabilization. Actually, temperature is the major effect for the density of liquid in which the weighing takes place. Ambient conditions are monitored and recorded by PC during the weighing in liquid.

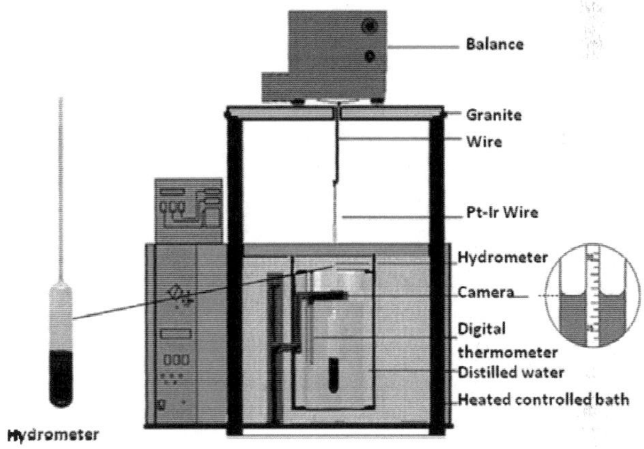

Fig. 5. The vertical movement section of hydrometer calibration system

The calibration process of hydrometer defined as follow. Heated controlled bath should be adjusted before the calibration process. A system should reach a thermal equilibrium with using heated controlled bath and cooler. After that an adjusted hydrometer holder hanging on balance in air ambient and is tared and environmental conditions (temperature, atmospheric pressure and humidity) are recorded. The hydrometer is tightened into the holder and then it is immersed in a liquid until a scale line overlaps with a liquid level. The liquid level can be displaced with the immersion of displacement object and the overlapping (reading can be realized with magnify) of scale line and liquid level are provided (If the calibration of scale line of lower density hydrometer is realized, known mass of stainless steel is used as an additional weight). After that weight value and temperature of liquid can be measured. The measurements are realized in 5 different scale lines (The scale lines can be adjusted by holder). The determination of density value of hydrometer scale lines are realized by using the measurement results as part of Cuckow method. The density values of calibrated hydrometer are given in calibration certificate at reference temperature (15 °C, 20 °C or a request of customer).

5 Conclusion

In this paper, it was described an automatic system for calibrating a hydrometer. The new system reduces errors caused by operator skills or attention when process is performed manually. The new calibration system automatically aligns specific hydrometer scale-marks with the horizontal plane of the reference liquid. A camera, a frame grabber, a step motor and a software program are used to realize this process. A linear-motion controller is added to the hydrometer calibration equipment, and approaches the desired position slowly in order not to disturb the horizontal plane of the reference liquid.

According to the ISO specification, when making a measurement, the centre of the scale-mark should be aligned with the horizontal plane of the reference liquid. In this study we match the meniscus with reference liquid line to focus on accurate calibration point.

A new procedure is realized to offer calibration services of reference standard hydrometers to their customers more accurate and with less uncertainty of measurement by Volume, Density and Viscosity Laboratory of TUBITAK UME.

Improvements are planned for future work to complete the characterization of automated hydrometer calibration system.

References

1. ISO 649-1: 1981, "Laboratory Glassware-Density Hydrometers for General Purposes, Part -1 Specification"

2. ISO 649- 2: 1981, "Laboratory Glassware-Density Hydrometers for General Purposes, Part -2 Test Methods and Use"

3. Cuckow F. W., " A new method of high accuracy for the calibration of reference standard hydrometers, Journal of the Society of Chemical Industry, 1949, 68, pp.44-49"

4. Salvatore Lorefice and Andrea Malengo, "Calibration of hydrometers, Meas. Sci. Technol. 17 (2006) 2560–2566"

5. NIST Special Publication 250-78, "NIST Calibration Services for Hydrometers, January 14, 2008"

6. Y J Lee, K H Chang, J C Chon and C Y Oh, "Automatic alignment method for calibration of hydrometers, Metrologia 41 (2004) S100–S104"

7. Luis M. Peña et al, "A new image processing system for hydrometer calibration developed at CENAM, IMEKO 20th TC3, 3rd TC16 and 1st TC22 International Conference Cultivating metrological knowledge 27th to 30th November, 2007. Merida, Mexico"

8. Luis Manuel Peña-Perez et al, "Alignment of the Measurement Scale Mark during Immersion Hydrometer Calibration Using an Image Processing System", Sensors 2013, 13, 14367-14397

9. Akcadag U.Y. and San S.E., "Newly Established Hydrometer Calibration Set Up at UME", Proceedings of the17th International Conference on Force, Mass, Torque and Pressure Measurements,IMEKO TC3, 17-21 Sept. 2001, Istanbul, Turkey.

Some important features of the proposed new definition of the International System of Units (SI) that the users should know about before 2018

F. Pavese*

Formerly at the National Research Council of Italy, IMGC-CNR, Torino, Italy.

Received:

Abstract. The paper is a digest of some problems to be timely considered should the proposed use of fundamental constants in the definition of measurement units of the SI be implemented in 2018: (a) more base units being multi-dimensional; (b) how the magnitude of the base units is established; (c) the use of CODATA adjusted values of the constants for this specific purpose; (d) limitations in new determinations that might arise from the stipulation of the values of several constants, for CODATA to continue performing meaningful least squares adjustments of the fundamental constants taking into account future measured data; (e) SI implementation at the NMI and Society level, namely introducing a hierarchy among Countries.

Keywords: International System of Units, SI; New SI; fundamental constants; Metre Convention; hierarchy between Countries

1 Introduction

The use of some "fundamental constants" (c_0, h, e, k_B, N_A) with stipulated numerical values has been proposed for the re-definition of the present International System of Units, the SI (Système International). This proposal was submitted to the Conférence Générale des Poids et Measures (CGPM) at its 2011 meeting, which decided in its Resolution 1 to "*take note of the intention of the CIPM*" for "*the possible future revision of the International System of Units*". This was confirmed in 2014 and a roadmap toward 2018 is now available.

Over the past decade problems can be found in the literature concerning the proposal on the floor related to four main questions: (i) how meaningful a progress can be achieved by using fundamental constants in defining the measurement units; (ii) how should use the selected constants; (iii) how should the definitions be formulated precisely; (iv) how to deal with future experimental data on these constants; (v) how well will the users' needs be fulfilled and, (vi) how much their present standards will still be valid and usable.

The following issues arising from the above problems will be addressed:

(1) how to deal with the indirect definition of the SI base units;
(2) how to take into account the multi-dimensionality in the new definitions;
(3) to what extent will the fundamental constants establish the magnitude of the SI base units;
(4) how to tackle formal issues in the stipulation of the definitions;
(5) how to take into account of future data on the constants;
(6) how is the resulting hierarchy by dealt with among Countries that are member states of the SI.

* Correspondence: frpavese@gmail.com

2 A short recall of the present and the new proposed SI

The definition of the present SI can be found on the website of the Bureau Internationale des Poids et Mesures (BIPM) under "Metre Convention" [1] and under "SI Brochure" [2]:

"*The Convention was signed in Paris in 1875 by representatives of seventeen nations. ... the Metre Convention established a permanent organizational structure for member governments to act in common accord on all matters relating to units of measurement. The Convention, ... remains the basis of international agreement on units of measurement. The BIPM now has fifty-seven Member States, including all the major industrialized countries.*" [1].

"*This SI consists of a set of base units, prefixes and derived units, as described in these pages. The SI base units are a choice of seven well-defined units which by convention are regarded as dimensionally independent: the metre, the kilogram, the second, the ampere, the kelvin, the mole, and the candela. Derived units are formed by combining the base units according to the algebraic relations linking the corresponding quantities.*" [2].

Each of the base unit is individually defined. The present definitions are of different types:

(a) Make use of an artefact: for mass "*The kilogram is the unit of mass; it is equal to the mass of the international prototype of the kilogram*";
(b) Make use of a physical state or condition: e.g., for temperature "*The kelvin, unit of thermodynamic temperature, is the fraction 1/273.16 of the thermodynamic temperature of the triple point of water*". Similarly for

time, amount of substance and luminous intensity;

(c) Define a realisation of the unit, e.g. for length: "*The metre is the length of the path travelled by light in vacuum during a time interval of* 1/299 792 45 8 *of a second*". Similar approach for the electrical current

"*Les unités choisies doivent être accessibles à tous, supposées constantes dans le temps et l'espace, et faciles à réaliser avec une exactitude élevée*" (from the official French text) [2]. Actually, indirectly also the base unit type (a) and (b) define a *realisation method* to be implemented with a procedure (not to be confused with the "mise en pratique" [3] that are approximations of the definition), according to clause 2.6 of VIM [9].

At present, four base units violate the above indication of the SI Brochure that "*Les grandeurs de base sont, par convention, considérées comme indépendantes.*" (Section 1.2 in [2]): the unit of length involves the second; the unit of amount of substance involves the kilogram; the unit of electric current involves the newton and the metre; the unit of luminous intensity involves the hertz, the watt and the steradian (notice that some of those are, in addition, derived units).

The definition of the proposed "New SI" can be found on the page "On the future revision of the SI" [4], where, under the title "What", one finds the following statement:

"... *In brief, the* [new] SI *will be the system of units in which:*

• *the unperturbed ground state hyperfine splitting frequency of the caesium 133 atom* $\Delta\nu(^{133}Cs)_{hfs}$ *is exactly 9 192 631 770 hertz,*

• *[and so forth for each of the seven base units: the [specific constant] is exactly [numerical value] [SI unit], using c, h, e, k and* N_A*], ...*

... *where the hertz, joule, coulomb, lumen, and watt, with unit symbols* Hz, J, C, lm, *and* W, *respectively, are related to the units second, metre, kilogram, ampere, kelvin, mole, and candela, with unit* symbols s, m, kg, A, K, mol, *and* cd, *respectively, ...*". Similar formulations are found in the draft of the SI Brochure, 9th Edition, prepared by the CCU [5]—where "will be" is simply replaced by "is".

This can be called the '*group-definition*' and considered the sufficient new SI definition. In fact, these constants should be considered and treated as a group.

However, in [4] the statement follows that "*The SI may alternatively be defined by statements that explicitly define seven individual base units: the second, metre, kilogram, ampere, kelvin, mole, and candela. These correspond to the seven base quantities time, length, mass, electric current, thermodynamic temperature, amount of substance, and luminous intensity. All other units are then obtained as products of powers of the seven base units, which involve no numerical factors; these are called coherent derived units*". This implies that also the 'single-unit' definitions of the base units should be provided, as, e.g., presently implemented in [5], e.g., for length: "... *its magnitude is set by fixing the numerical value of the [a constant] to be exactly [numerical value] when it is expressed in the SI unit for [kind-of-quantity] [new SI units]*", where the constant is the speed of light in vacuo, c_0, the numerical value is 299 792 458, the kind-of-quantity is length, and the new SI units are m s^{-1}.

Incidentally, this also implies that, in the "New SI" proposal, the base units remain the present ones. However, note that the definition would be totally differently based.

3 Basic differences between new and present definition

Until now the core of the formal definitions of the base units consisted in the specification of a definitional method of implementing a procedure for the realisation of each base unit: initially using more artefacts (mass, metre), then more invariant states of nature (temperature, ...), more recently by adopting the 'mise en pratique" for lower-rank realisation of some base units. As a consequence, the NMI wanting to realise a base unit in an independent way were restricted in the use of the definitional procedure. This, in some cases, was a strong limitation considering that new methods were developed in the mean time, often superior to the existing definitional method.

The new definition does *not* resort to any definitional method, but stands on declaring what is an important *consequence* of the use of the present definitions and their top realisations: the resulting numerical values of a group of fundamental constants—for five of the seven base units. This group uses six of the base units (excluding the candela, and including the second) for their measurement. Therefore, they are an indirect definition of the same base units. Conversely, each base unit contributes to the numerical value of each constant of the group:

$$\begin{aligned}
&[c_0/\Delta\nu(^{133}\mathrm{Cs})] = [\mathrm{metre}];\\
&[h\,\Delta\nu(^{133}\mathrm{Cs})/\,c_0^2] = [\mathrm{kilogram}];\\
&[h\,\Delta\nu(^{133}\mathrm{Cs})/k_\mathrm{B}] = [\mathrm{kelvin}];\\
&[e\,\Delta\nu(^{133}\mathrm{Cs})] = [\mathrm{ampere}];\\
&[1/N_\mathrm{A}] = [\mathrm{mole}].
\end{aligned} \tag{1}$$

(N_A depends only on the unit mol—but see [6]; $\Delta\nu(^{133}Cs)$ for the second, and K_{cd} for the candela are not "fundamental constants")

As said previously, the numerical value of these constants was obtained from measurements using the present SI definitions. The numerical value indicated in the New SI group definition was obtained by mean of a statistical and mathematical procedure applied to a critically reviewed set of experimental values, with associated uncertainties [7, 8]. Then, for the purpose of the definition, the uncertainty was dropped and the value of each constant set exact by convention (stipulated by the CGPM as a reference value. Thus, indirectly it sets the magnitude of the relevant unit involved in its dimensionality. However, the uncertainty does not disappear, but remains hidden and is still relevant to other aspects of the new definitions.

4 Advantages and disadvantages of the new definition

The new definition displays, in principle, some useful features, but also some unresolved difficulties.

4.1 Multiple methods satisfy the definition

The lack of a definitional method that each National Metrology Institute (NMI) must demonstrate to have implemented in a realisation procedure in order to comply with the top level of the metrological ladder, enables, in principle (see later), a wider flexibility in choosing the implementation best suited for each Country's needs. Multiple methods will be *allowed* next to the promulgation of the new definition.

However, a big question mark remains unexplained. In fact, the different implementation models, of the new definition can be subdivided in two categories:
(i) Those providing a *direct* use of the relevant constant(s) (e.g., the watt balance for the kilogram, acoustic gas thermometry for the kelvin), i.e., having the constant in their equation: they were the same methods used for determining the numerical values of the constants.
(ii) Providing indirect consistency with the relevant constant(s) (e.g., with the aid of a single crystal of highly enriched ^{28}Si for the kilogram, the ITS-90 Scale for the kelvin).

Are categories (i) and (ii) both realisation methods? Can all still be called "mise en pratique"? Probably not. In all instances they are to be promulgated by the CIPM, like the *mises en pratique*.

In addition, a disadvantage arises: are multiple methods all exactly providing the same magnitude of the new units? This is not possible, due to a feature called "non-uniqueness", a term of basic importance defined in the VIM [9] as "definitional uncertainty" (clause 2.27 "*component of measurement uncertainty resulting from the finite amount of detail in the definition of a measurand*"). Non-uniqueness, a term that must not be confused with the realisation uncertainty, means in this case that two methods do not provide exactly the same magnitude of the units, but only an approximation of the stipulated 'reference value'. If both are 'allowed', it means that the difference in magnitude provided by their different definition (and model) is within accepted limits. The acceptance criteria should be commensurate with the uncertainty associated with the original experimental 'best value' accepted for stipulation. Otherwise, the BIPM could not make a selection of '*allowed* methods'.
Presently, there is no illustration of these facts in the relevant official documents

4.2 Consistency of the base units proved

The new definition makes use of the same previous base units, but in a different way. The condition of their independent dimensionality, already broken, was definitely abandoned and replaced by the use of multidimensional quantities.
In fact, should the base units be dimensionally independent to a sufficient degree—as assumed by the historical promoters of the SI—the consistency requirement would be intrinsically respected, irrespective of the magnitude chosen for each of them. If not it must be proved, and cannot be obtained exactly but only to a certain degree.

The advantage of multidimensionality of the constants, directly or indirectly (in fact, often their numerical values are obtained from other constants—e.g., e through α—and by means of experiments critically involving other measurement units), is that, by setting an intricate network of relationships between the measurement units (Fig. 1), any significant discrepancy between the magnitudes of the units would become evident as a discrepancy in the results obtained with different methods. A presently sufficient consistency has been proved by the CODATA [7].

However, there is a disadvantage that is not yet taken into account in the draft of proposal [5]: all relevant constants should be included in the definition of each of the base units. They are listed in the above Eqs. (1). Instead, only one is presently included in the draft [5], as indicated by the definition for length reported above: also $\Delta\nu(^{133}\text{Cs})$ should appear instead for the second . It is true that the indicated constant for each of the base unit is the most important one, because its experimental uncertainty is the dominant one: for example, for the kelvin, the contributions to the uncertainty of $\Delta\nu(^{133}\text{Cs})$ and h are not significant ($u_{tot} = 4.16\cdot10^{-7}$ taking them into account, compared with $4.15\cdot10^{-7}$ for k_B only). Similarly for the kilogram ($u_{tot} = 3.01\cdot10^{-48}$ instead of $2.97\cdot10^{-48}$) and the ampere ($u_{tot} = 3.23\cdot10^{-12}$ instead of $3.22\cdot10^{-12}$), a bit less for the candela ($u_{tot} = 1.68\cdot10^{-18}$ instead of $1.58\cdot10^{-18}$) and for the metre ($u_{tot} = 9.64\cdot10^{-11}$ instead of $9.53\cdot10^{-11}$)—all referred to CODATA 2010 data. However, for the strict logic rules of a definition, this fact is *not* irrelevant. Consequently, the definitions for a single base unit become at least clumsy and, more substantially, showing in Fig. 1 an intricate relationship between the base units, so basically making these definitions useless [10]. Nevertheless, the group definition can stand alone.

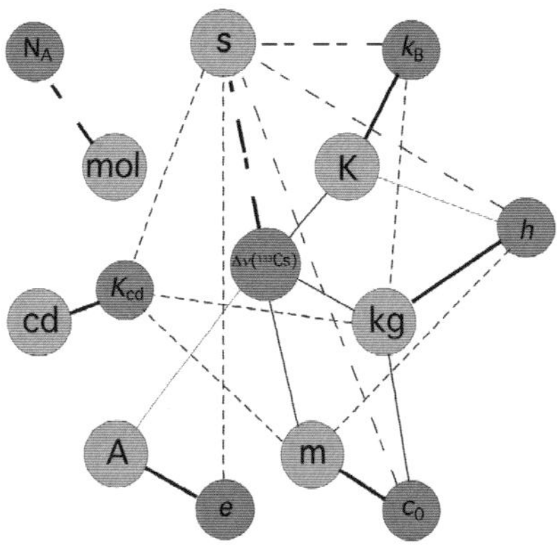

Fig. 1. Relationships between base units and proposed constants. Thick line for the 'dominant' constant (see text); dot-and-line when the inverse of the constant is used for the unit.

4.3 Magnitude continuity of the new and the previous base units: is it ensured ?

By retaining the values computed in [7] as the 'best' ones for the time being after the SI change of definition, one assumes that the continuity requirement for the magnitudes of the units is fulfilled to a sufficient degree.

When deciding to change the definition of a measurement unit, a universally recognised and most fundamental requirement in metrology is that the magnitude of the units defined in the old and new definitions does not change significantly: a discontinuity would cause a step change in the numerical values in the subsequent experimental results. See Fig. 2 for an illustration of the meaning of the *continuity condition*.

The literal meaning of the wording of the single-unit definitions derived from the group-definition, reported above, can thus be spelled out as follows: 'according to the new definition, the magnitude of each of the base units is *such that* the chosen stipulated numerical value of the relevant constant applies. This is the value measured with the previous units.

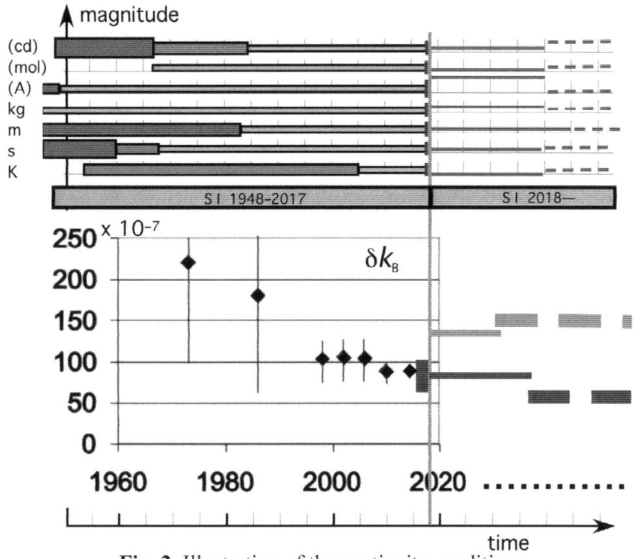

Fig. 2. Illustration of the continuity condition.
Upper part: changes in the base unit definitions since 1950; until 2018 the width of the box schematises the inaccuracy in a qualitative way; the vertical box at 2018 indicates the CODATA uncertainty level before SI change; the subsequent line indicates the magnitude continuity within that uncertainty; for electrical current is shows the present inconsistency (significant step change).
Lower part: as an example, the consequence for k_B (dimensionally depending on kg, m, s and K) is shown. The 1970-2014 changes of the CODATA recommended values [15] are shown on the left [7]. The vertical bar in 2015-18 is the foreseen experimental uncertainty interval (k = 1) [11]. If the base units will *not* show significant discontinuities in 2018 (surely not for the constants c_0 , $\Delta\nu(^{133}\text{Cs})$ and K_{cd}), the numerical value of k_B is expected to remain the same within that uncertainty, to possibly change in an unforeseeable future (broken thick line). Otherwise, the value will step-change since 2018 (light gray line).

In all instances, the continuity condition *cannot be said to be satisfied exactly*, for a reason that contradicts somewhat the definition of the numerical values of the constants as exact: it can be fulfilled only within the experimental uncertainty originally associated with those values [7]. For example, the kelvin is defined today by means of the value of the triple point of water defined as 273.16 K exactly. With the new definition, is defined instead by means of the Boltzmann constant "to be exactly 1.380 648 8 $\times 10^{-23}$ when it is expressed in the SI unit for energy per thermodynamic temperature J K^{-1} = kg m^2 s^{-2} K^{-1} " ([5], CODATA 2014 value is 1.380 648 5 $\times 10^{-23}$). It is not possible to tell that the two values are exactly consistent with each other, because the latter reflects on the former an original experimental uncertainty of $\approx$ 0.000 15 K.

However, that is the present state-of-the-art uncertainty in experimental science for k_B (note, not for the triple point of water, whose state-of-the-art uncertainty is 5 times better, 0.000 030 K), so the residual discontinuity can be considered non-significant.

If this may not the case for the electrical base unit [12], due to a significant inconsistency still unresolved in the "quantum metrological triangle", this would only mean that the new definition of the electrical base unit *should be delayed* until after 2018.

4.4 New measurements of the values of the constants: why should they be prevented in future?

The current intention in the SI is that the stipulated values of the constants should be established "once and for ever", i.e., that, once stipulated these value cannot be modified anymore by the current measurement unit system without incurring in a circular logical process. This has already happened after 1983 after the stipulation of the numerical value of c_0 for the length unit: as reported in the [8] digest, after that date no further determination was available, and even the CODATA analysis since then kept that value fixed until the 2014 adjustment [15].

However, "once and for ever" decisions are not permitted in the general interest of science and practice. In this case, "*tempore.* Any current numerical value obtained at a certain date can be found subsequently incorrect due to missed or misevaluated systematic effects, or advanced theoretical considerations.

In the case under examination, there is a specific situation that prevents circularity to happen: it is the "continuity condition" illustrated in the previous Section. Its possible imperfection does not impair its effect. The present values of the constants, adopted for the New SI, incorporate also the effects of possible present inconsistencies in the current units, and the uncertainty associated to the continuity condition is born from the uncertainty associated with those current values—the stipulation only hiding it.

All considered, the use of the 'best' current values for the numerical values entering the new definition, ensures a smooth transition from the current to the new units not only in a generic way, but in the sense that the new units have the same (nominal) magnitude as the old ones.

The consequence is that that the standards used so far can, in principle, still be used in future, at least in the "short period of time" that is allowed by the definition of "repeatability condition" in [9], term 2.20. Under this condition, *new* future determinations are possible under the same conditions they were performed so far—and should be performed [13].

4.5 Does the New SI induce a hierarchy between the Metre Treaty signatories?

This issue has been introduced in [14], where delete the different types of hierarchy concerning the SI in metrology are discussed, but it requires some further reflections. Table 1, taken from [14], summarises the different types. Here, hierarchy means that a country does depend on the standards of another country for their primary standards on a particular measurement unit, namely the base units (Type #2). It is only a matter of its *free* preference or convenience

Table 1. Hierarchy with respect to the SI in metrology.

Type #	Meaning
1	Between primary standards, including ranking between the very unit definition and the corresponding *mise en pratique*
2	Between countries for primary standards—BIPM not included
3	Between BIPM and all countries
4	National traceability pyramid, calibration hierarchy (VIM clause 2.40) [9]
5	Calibration services between countries

In this respect, there is a basic difference in the metrological ladder that establishes the hierarchy among the different realisation methods between the present SI and the New SI, summarised in Table 2.

In the *present* SI, according to the principle reported above, "*Les unités choisies doivent être accessibles à tous, supposées constantes dans le temps et l'espace, et faciles à réaliser avec une exactitude élevée*" [2], every country is, in principle, enabled to make its own standards, i.e., to realise "step 0" in Table 1, the realisation of the definition by using the definitional method.

This was true also after 1983, when the type (c) definition (see Section 1) was used for length. Actually, the definition does not explicitly say that it resorts to the fundamental constant c_0, and in fact does not resort to the quantity "velocity": the number 299 792 458 is not a speed but the reciprocal of a "time interval": thus, in principle, a different stipulation could follow later. These subtleties are important in a definition. However, the current practice has considered since then that c_0 was stipulated and that no more measurements of c_0 were *possible*. Actually none are available after that date. In addition, as illustrated in [14], step 0 and 1 were confounded when defining the *mise en pratique*.

In the *proposed New* SI, there is *not* a definitional method. As the top step of the hierarchical ladder, instead, one should demonstrate to comply with the *condition*: that one was able to obtain the stipulated value of each relevant constant.

Table 2. Metrological ladder for the SI (example: length).

Step	Today	New SI
0	Definitional method. Method using distance and time	No definitional method. Condition: to reproduce the stipulated value of the constant(s)
1	"Mise en pratique". Other method(s): frequency and period	"Primary" methods. c_0 and t explicitly in the model
2	Secondary methods. other method(s): stabilised laser	"Mise en pratique". Other method(s): frequency and period
3	Workshop methods. Gauge blocks	Secondary methods. Other method(s): stabilised laser
4 …	Lower ranks …	Workshop methods. Gauge blocks, …

Without definitional method, and without present official explanation about how this can happen, one can assume that he has to set up the procedure for a method that has shown, until the date of promulgation of the new definition, to have the capability to provide a value of the relevant constant(s) that is "metrologically compatible" [9] with the stipulated one(s), i.e. the uncertainty interval of which contains the stipulated value. The uncertainty interval does not need to have the narrowest width of the top experiments, but must be compatible with the uncertainty sufficient to that country.

Then, one has to understand that, in the lack of a definitional method, not all the methods—and consequently all procedures— comply with the new definitions. The methods and their procedures, to be compliant, need:

– to be traceable to the relevant constant(s);

– to "realise the stipulated value", i.e. the correct magnitude of the unit.

Hints for this issue cannot be found at present in official documents. Instead, it should be clarified that:

(i) This should mean that not all methods presently known are potentially able to realise a unit in a way that necessarily is fit for an intended use;

(ii) There should be a logical difference between those methods that explicitly contain, among the model quantities, the relevant constant(s) (the type reported in step 2 of Table 2), and the methods that do not, but that are traceable to the constant(s)' value(s) (the type reported in step 3 of Table 2);

(iii) The two types above should not be confounded in a

single set, because only the methods in step 2 can be considered equivalent to a definitional method, while only those in step 3 constitute a *mise en pratique* under the current meaning [3];

(iv) Methods in step 2 can only be those that are considered—or are presently used, for—obtaining a numerical value of the constant(s), but *used in the reverse way*.

To illustrate the last sentence, let us consider the case of the present definition of the kelvin, based on the value 273.16 K exactly of a physical state, the triple point of water. After the stipulation enters into effect, the *reversal* in the use of the method consists in that the same apparatus (e.g., a gas thermometer) used to determine the temperature value of this state, can then be used to measure thermodynamic temperature ratios T/T_{TPW}.

Everybody freezing a sample of water at its triple point should assign to it that numerical value on the SI unit kelvin as the resulting temperature (with the associated estimate of the realisation uncertainty). This does not mean that one is forbidden from assigning that same sample a different temperature numerical value, but this can be done only by:

a) comparing, in a distinct experiment called *inter-comparison*, that sample with another one;
b) taking note of the difference in the measured numerical values (if any) of temperature, and of the associated uncertainties;
c) assigning the other sample the function of *reference* standard, thus assigning it the SI value 273.16 K;
d) summing up the noted difference to the SI value, to obtain the SI value of the original sample; and, deciding if the latter numerical value is "metrologically compatible" with the reference one or not.

This is a simple experiment providing a different numerical value for the state to a specific sample, which can be done any time after the initial stipulation: however, it requires a reference standard to which the stipulated numerical value has been assigned.

For example, when k_B is used instead for the definition of the kelvin, the acoustic gas thermometer (AGT) used to determine k_B accurately, can then be used in the *reverse way*—by fixing in its model the k_B value to the stipulated one— and obtain the value of a generic T.

From the viewpoint of the hierarchy, this means that every country willing to be classified at the top of the hierarchical ladder for a specific base unit, should have implemented one of the methods at step 1 of the ladder (if not even step 0), e.g. for the mass, the watt balance.

If not specified in a suitable way in the official documents to be signed, there is the risk that only a very small number of countries in the world will have the scientific/technical competence and the resources needed to demonstrate the implementation of the *top three steps* (presently corresponding to the—affordable—upper two) of the metrological ladder.

5 Conclusion

A reflection similar to what has been started with the recent article [16] should extend from the Comité Consultatif des Unités (CCU) to the whole community of the users, to clear logical and formal issues and make the new definition sound and compatible with the Metre Treaty.

References

1. http://www.bipm.org/en/worldwide-metrology/metre-convention/
2. http://www.bipm.org/en/publications/si-brochure/
3. http://www.bipm.org/en/publications/mises-en-pratique/
4. http://www.bipm.org/en/measurement-units/new-si/
5. CCU, New SI, Draft Chapters1, 2 and 3 of the 9th SI Brochure, 2013 in Draft Documents on http://www.bipm.org/en/measurement-units/new_si/
6. Schwartz R, Richard Ph, Ehrlich C, Miki Y, OIML-Bulletin-New-SI-Draft-v4-20120831_Draft.doc, 2012, available online
7. CODATA http://physics.nist.gov/cuu/Constants/index.html, http://www.bipm.org/extra/codata/
8. F. Pavese, Metrologia 51 (2014) L1–L4, with online Supplementary Information
9. BIPM (2008). International Vocabulary of Metrology—Basic and General Concepts and Associated Terms (VIM) 3rd edn. http://www.bipm.org/en/publications/guides/
10. Knotts S, Mohr P J, Phillips W D, An introduction to the New SI, arXiv:1503.03496v2, 23 July 2015
11. J. Fischer, Low uncertainty Boltzmann constant determinations and the kelvin redefinition, Royal Society Meeting „Towards implementing the new kelvin“ Chicheley Hall, 18th May 2015, in press
12. Bronnikov K A, Ivashchuk V D, Kalinin M I, Khruschov V V, Kononogov S A, Melnikov V N, On new definitions of SI base units. Why is the "atomic" kilogram preferable, Measurement Techniques (english), May 2015, DOI 10.1007/s11018-015-0674-6; arXiv:1410.7906v1 29 October 2014
13. F. Pavese, Problems in implementing new measurement unit definitions of the SI by using fundamental constants, Proceedings IMEKO World Congress 2015, Praha; submitted to Measurement
14. F. Pavese, How much does the SI, namely the proposed 'new SI', conform the spirit of the Metre Treaty?, Accred. Qual. Assur. 19 (2014) 307–314
15. P.J. Mohr, D.B. Newell, B.N. Taylor (2015) CODATA recommended valuesof the fundamental constants 2014, arXiv:1507.07956v1
16. N. Fletcher, R.S. Davis, M. Stock and M.J.T. Milton, Modernizing the SI – implications of recent progress with the fundamental constants, arXiv 1510.08324 (October 15, 2015)

Realisation of the metre by using a femtosecond laser frequency comb: applications in length metrology

B. Samoudi

[1]National School of Applied Sciences of Safi, Cadi Ayyad University, Route Sidi Bouzid, BP 63, 46000 Safi, Morocco

Received:

Abstract. The appearance of the frequency comb technology; awarded the Nobel Prize in Physics 2005, has revolutionized enormously the metrology of optical frequencies. By allowing a direct link to stable microwave clocks, self-referencing systems eliminate the need for complicated frequency chains and thereby greatly facilitate the precise determination of absolute optical frequency measurements.
In this paper we present results obtained in the characterization of the Spanish Centre of Metrology frequency comb and the results of applying comb to the absolute measurement of the three Zeeman stabilized He-Ne lasers operating at 633 nm with a nominal frequency of 473.612 THz. A comparison of these results with those obtained by the current system based on iodine stabilized lasers is reported. A treatment for the estimating measurement uncertainty of laser frequency calibrations using a comb conform to GUM ISO/BIPM is also presented.

Keywords: Frequency combs; length standard; uncertainty; optical frequency metrology; mode-locked laser

1 Introduction

The definition of the unit of length and its practical realization are based on the adopted value for the speed of light, c = 299 792 458 m/s, and the frequency of an optical transition. Thus, length measurements are intrinsically related to the unit of time. It was adopted by the 17th Conference Générale des Poids et Mesures in 1983 [1]. At the same time, the Comité International des Poids et Mesures (CIPM) made recommendations for the practical realization of the metre, referred to as the *mise en pratique* (in later text referenced as MeP) of the definition. The metre should be realized by one of the following methods [2]:

(a) by means of the length l of the path travelled in vacuum by a plane electromagnetic wave in a time t ; this length is obtained from the measured time t , using the relation $l = c_0.t$ and the value of the speed of light in vacuum c_0 = 299 792 458 m/s,

(b) by means of the wavelength in vacuum λ of a plane electromagnetic wave of frequency f; this wavelength is obtained from the measured frequency f using the relation $\lambda = c_0/f$ and the value of the speed of light in vacuum c_0 = 299 792 458 m/s,

(c) by means of one of the radiations from a given list, whose stated wavelength in vacuum or whose stated frequency can be used with the uncertainty shown, provided that the given specifications and accepted good practice are followed;

Various sources of radiation have been recommended as standards of wavelength and have been updated by the CIPM over time [2-3]. One of the most important recommended radiations in the field of length metrology and worldwide precision measurements is that at 474 THz (633 nm) from a He-Ne laser, stabilized on an absorbing hyperfine component in $^{127}I_2$. This laser is used in many laboratories around the world as the practical means of realizing the SI metre and is commonly used for calibrating the frequency of lasers employed in length measurement and precision measurement in atomic physics. These lasers standards working according to method (c) of the CCL/CIPM Recommendation for realization of SI definition of the metre.

For checking values of the standards and possible improvement of uncertainty one needs to absolutely measure laser frequency (hundreds of terahertz) relative to caesium clocks (realizing SI definition of the second). This measurement (method b in MeP) was made easier by invention of optical frequency comb technique [4-6] awarded the Nobel Prize in Physics 2005.

With this system (frequency comb), the Spanish Centre of Metrology is establishing a new practical realization of the metre improved accuracy in two orders of magnitude with respect to the current system based on iodine stabilized lasers [7-8].

In this paper we briefly describe the state of art of femtosecond optical frequency comb including a theoretical background study. We measure absolutely the frequency of a Zeeman-stabilized He-Ne lasers operating at 633 nm against the frequency comb and compare the results with the one obtained by the current method of beating frequency against a standard iodine stabilized laser (CEM2). In both cases, we have studied the stability of the signal beat frequency. Finally, we estimate the measurement uncertainty for comb and laser frequency under calibrations using the GUM ISO/BIPM.

* Correspondence: b.samoudi@uca.ma

2 Theoretical backgrounds

Optical frequency combs are used routinely to generate optical radiation with a frequency uncertainty limited only by the uncertainty of the master clock that sets the repetition frequency of the combs. These frequency combs working in mode-lock regime have to be designed and so as the round trip time for all longitudinal modes is the same. To understand the mode structure of a femtosecond frequency comb and the techniques applied for its stabilization one can look at the idealized case of a pulse circulating in a laser cavity with length L with a carrier frequency f_c as shown in Figure 1. The output of this laser is a sequence of pulses that are essentially copies of the same pulse separated by the round trip time giving by:

$$T = 2L/v_g \quad (1)$$

Where v_g is the cavity's mean group velocity defined by the round trip time and the cavity length.

The pulses however are not quite identical. This is because the pulse envelope $A(t)$ propagates with v_g while the carrier wave travels with its phase velocity. As a result the carrier shifts with respect to the pulse envelope after each round trip by a phase angle $\Delta\varphi$ as shown in Figure 1. The shape of the pulse train in time domain is bound up with the amplitude and phase spectra by complex Fourier transform.

Let us describe the time evolution of the electric field at one point in space by carrier frequency f_c and periodic amplitude/envelope A. Unlike the envelope function, which provides us with a more rigorous definition of the pulse repetition time $f_r = 1/T$ by demanding $A(t) = A(t+T)$, the electric field is, in general, not expected to be periodic in time. If the periodicity of the envelope function is assumed the electric field at a given place outside the laser resonator can be written as

$$E(t) = Re[A(t)\exp(-i2\pi f_c)t] \quad (2)$$

Because the envelope is periodic

$$E(t) = Re[\sum_n A_n \exp(-i2\pi((f_c + nf_r)t)] \quad (3)$$

Where A_n are Fourier components of $A(t)$. This equation shows that, under the assumption of a periodic pulse envelope, the resulting spectrum consists of a comb of laser modes that are separated by the pulse repetition frequency. Since f_c is not necessarily an integer multiple of f_r the modes are shifted from being exact harmonics of the pulse repetition frequency by an

offset that can be chosen to obey $f_0 < f_r$ simply by renumbering the modes:

$$f_n = f_0 + nf_r \quad (4)$$

where n is a large integer of order 10^6 that indexes the comb line. This equation maps two radio frequencies f_r and f_0 onto the optical frequencies f_n. Although the detection of f_r is rather effortless and usually lies between a few 10 MHz and a few GHz depending on the length of the laser resonator, the determination of f_0 is far more challenging to access unless the frequency comb contains more than an optical octave. f_0 then is detected by the self-referencing technique with an f–$2f$ interferometer setup [9-10], by taking the difference of the frequencies of a comb mode at f_n and the second harmonic of the mode at f_{2n} (Figure 2).

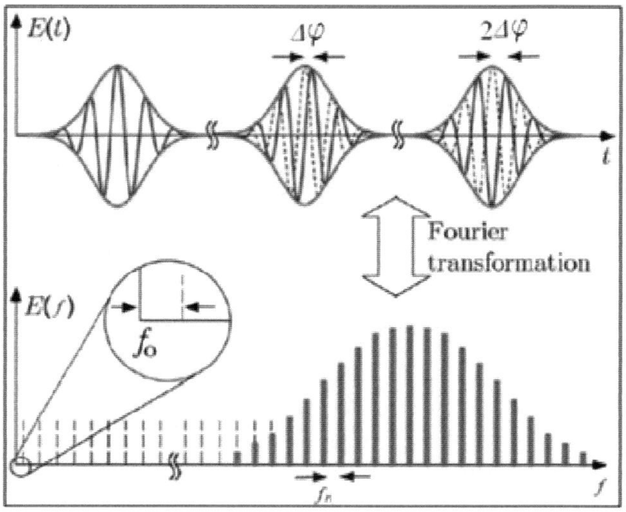

Fig. 1. Top: Consecutive pulses of the pulse train emitted by a laser mode locked and the corresponding spectrum. As the carrier wave at f_c moves with the phase velocity while the envelope moves with a different group velocity the carrier wave (blue) shifts by $\Delta\varphi$ after each round trip with respect to the pulse envelope (red). Bottom: This continuous shift results in a frequency offset $f_0 = \Delta\varphi/T$ of the comb from being exact harmonics of the pulse repetition frequency f_r .

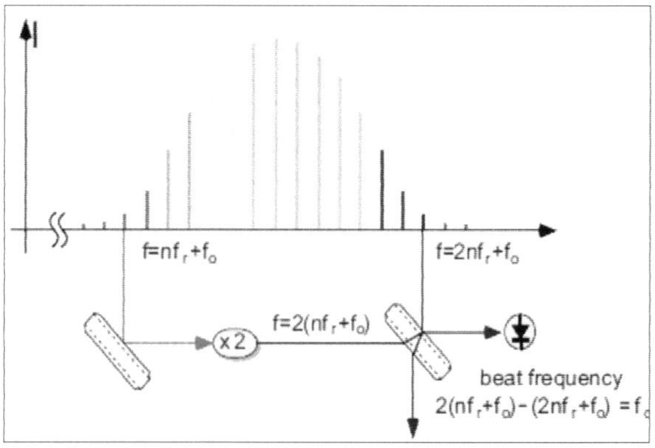

Fig. 2. The self-referencing technique of the optical frequency synthesizer: a mode with the mode number n at the red wing of the comb, whose frequency is given according to Equation (4), is

frequency doubled in a non-linear crystal. If the frequency comb covers a full optical octave a mode with the number 2n should oscillate simultaneously at $f_{2n} = f_0 + 2nf_r$. The beat note between the frequency doubled mode and the mode at 2n yields the offset frequency $2(f_0 + nf_r) - (f_0 + 2nf_r) = f_0$

The frequency of a laser under calibration (continuous wave), f_{cw}, is determined by observing a beat frequency, f_{beat}, with the nearest mode of the frequency comb system. Therefore, the f_{cw} is expressed as

$$f_{cw} = nf_r \pm f_0 \pm f_{beat} \quad (5)$$

The signs of the equation (5) depend on the measurement conditions and can be determined by changing f_0 and f_r while monitoring the resulting change in the beat signal.

If the visible cw lasers are measured after second harmonic generation (SHG), that is our case, equation (5) has to be modified to take the SHG process into consideration, the f_0 has to be multiplied by a factor of two:

$$f_{cw} = nf_r \pm 2f_0 \pm f_{beat} \quad (6)$$

The repetition rate remains unchanged due to the fact that the dominant process in the SHG is sum frequency generation.

3 Experimental setup

The details on experimental arrangements of the femtosecond laser frequency comb were published elsewhere [7-8], here a brief summary is presented in this paper. The experimental arrangement employed is sketched in Figure 3. Our version of the femtosecond laser frequency comb, the FC1500, developed by Menlo Systems GmbH, is based on a 250 MHz repetition rate mode-locked erbium fiber-ring laser and a nonlinear microstructured fiber.

The heart of the frequency comb generator is a fibre laser head with internal erbium doped fibre amplifier (EDFA) for generating high power IR light at 1500 nm with power up to 2 mW. The femtosecond laser output power is split into two branches and fed to the monitor port and the external parts of the system. One branch is amplified in an external EDFA and spectrally broadened in a highly nonlinear fibre (HNLF) to cover a spectrum of one octave in frequency space, for subsequent frequency doubling, the nonlinear interferometer for detection of the offset beat frequency f_0. The other branch for generating high power IR light at 1560 nm for subsequent frequency doubling at 780 nm radiation, and a photonic crystal fibre setup for subsequent broadening of the second harmonic generation (SHG) output to (530–1000) nm with power up to 60 mW.

We use a fast PIN diode to detect the offset frequency. The laser head features an internal fast PIN photo diode to detect the 4th harmonic of the repetition frequency which increases the phase sensitivity.

Two phase locked loops for locking the repetition rate and offset frequency to frequency standard allow to transfer the accuracy and stability between the radio frequency and optical domain and are part of the electronics. Frequency counters without dead time are used to measure beat signals with cw lasers and to control the phase locked loops for cycle slips. An oscilloscope and a spectrum analyzer are also included for monitoring purpose.

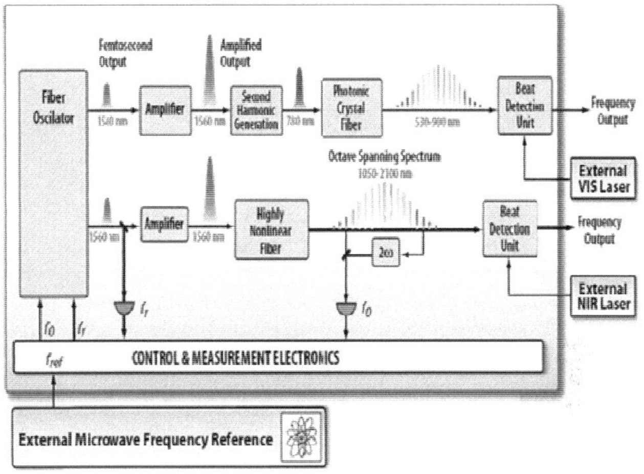

Fig. 3. Experimental setup used to measure the absolute frequency of different Zeeman-stabilized He-Ne lasers operating at 633 with a femtosecond comb generator.

The beat detection unit (Figure 4) consists of a series of mirrors coated with silver/gold, polarized beam splitters, λ/2 or λ/4 waveplates, which aim to place the beams from both the laser comb and calibration in the same polarisation plane, and lead them to a photodetector.

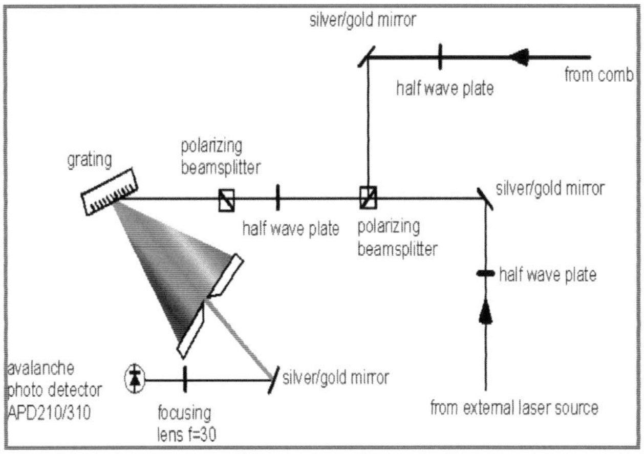

Fig. 4. Beat detection unit used for to measure the absolute frequency of different Zeeman-stabilized He-Ne lasers operating at 633 with a femtosecond comb generator.

The repetition rate frequency, f_r, and the carrier-envelope offset frequency (20 MHz), f_0, and f_{beat} were referenced to a primary frequency standard, a Cs atomic clock (Symmetricom, model 5071A), integrated into the network of atomic clocks of the Navy Observatory, ROA, in charge of maintaining the Spanish time and frequency standards.

For measuring the beat note between Zeeman-stabilized He-Ne lasers emitting in a nominal wavelength of 633 nm and the frequency comb mode, a grating (2100 lines/mm) for spectral filtering was used. The primary difficulties with measuring f_{beat} arises from the fact that only a very small fraction signal of the comb power is in the mode that gives rise to a beat signal. Several strategies are needed to maximize signal to noise and reduce detector saturation effects. Probably the most important single step is simply to take great care in aligning the beam from the test laser with the beam from the comb. To be more precise, what is ideally needed is perfect matching of the wave-fronts–two coaxial Gaussian beams with the same waist position and same size, travelling in the same direction. It's very important to assure that the beams overlap very well, travel accurately in the same direction, and have similar waist size to obtain a good beat signal. In this to get similar dimensions of beam diameters and output powers to obtain a good beat. Such beat note was detected by with an avalanche photodetector APD210. All relevant frequencies in the experiment have been analyzed and counted by a spectrum analyzer (Hameg, model HM5510) and frequency counters (Menlo Systems, model FXM50), respectively, which have been referenced to a primary frequency standard (Symmetricom, model 5071A) with a relative stability of 1×10^{-12} at short time, which is worse than real uncertainty of combs and reference RF signals but definitely sufficient for length measurements; therefore the stability of our system is predetermined by the reference source. Currently, to achieve long-term stability it is possible to use H-Masers and fountains based on cold atoms. In our case, we are using both a Cs clock and a Rb clock disciplined to the previous one, so ensuring long and short term stability.

During the process of measurement, the frequency comb system as well as remaining phase is very reliably locked. The frequency counters used for this measurements count continuously every second without dead time for more than 5 hours. In our case, the S/N ratio over 30 dB is sufficient for counting without cycle slips.

4 Results and discussions

At CEM we count with several Zeeman-stabilized He-Ne lasers operating at 633 nm. These lasers are traceable to the primary standard (CEM2) He-Ne laser stabilized to hyperfine spectral components of the transition 11-5 R(127) of $^{127}I_2$ vapour in internal cell with a nominal wavelength at 633 nm with third harmonic locking technique [8]. In this section we present results of absolute frequency measurement of three Zeeman stabilized He-Ne laser at 633 nm, using a frequency comb. A comparison of these results with those obtained with primary standard CEM2 laser has been treated.

The f_{beat} of Zeeman-stabilized He-Ne lasers deviation measurements from the mean value are shown in Figures 5a-5b. It can be seen that the standard deviations for these measurements are in agreement with the acceptance and rejection criteria established for obtaining reliable results.
The stability of the measured absolute frequency of our wavelength standard is limited by the stability of the reference Cs clock and a Rb clock disciplined to the previous one, for ensuring long and short term stability.

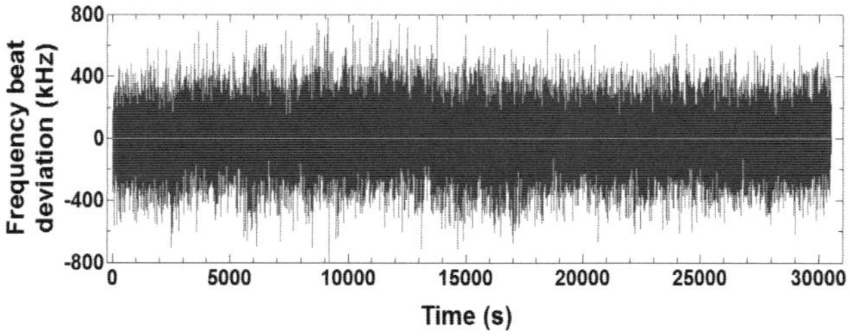

Fig. 5a. f_{beat} deviation of Tesa RSD/SR laser against frequency comb.

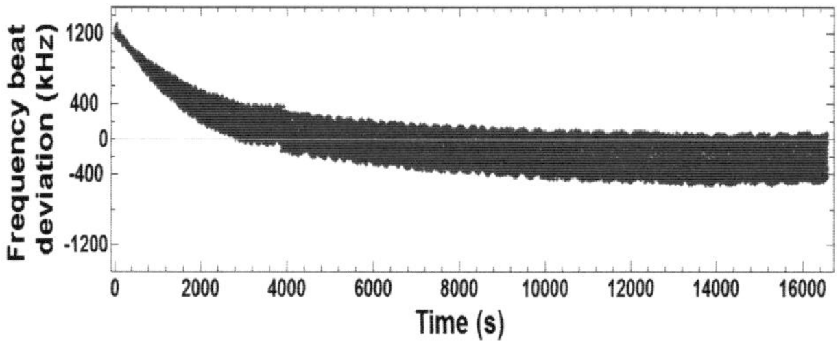

Fig. 5b. f_{beat} deviation of HP5517D laser against frequency comb.

In previous study we calculated the Allan deviation (square root of the Allan variance) the stability of the femtosecond comb reaches 8.38×10^{-11} at 1 s averaging and improves to 3.54×10^{-15} after 10 000 s [8]. Figures 6a–6b show the frequency beat obtained with our comb system.
The beat note and the Allan deviation of HP5519A laser look like the frequency beat and Allan deviation of HP5517D.

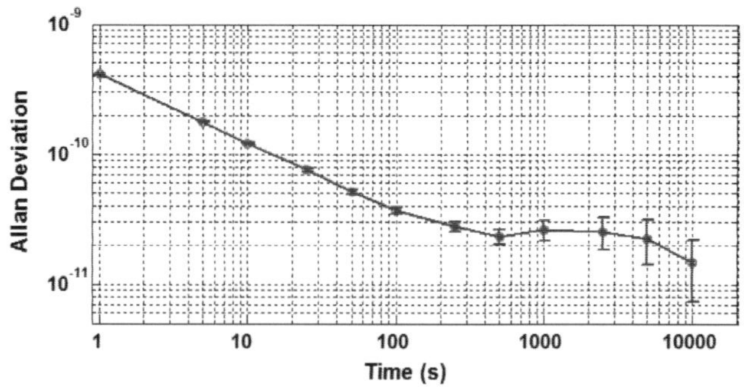

Fig. 6a. Allan deviation of f_{beat} between Tesa RSD/SR-L and femtosecond comb. Error bars corresponding to the standard

uncertainty are shown for longer averaging times, where the error is large enough to be significant.

It can be seen that Allan deviation of beat frequency obtained with the Tesa laser against the frequency comb describes the typical behaviour with white noise common in the caesium and rubidium time/frequency standards [11-12]. However the stability of HP5517D and HP5519A lasers (Figure 5b) at the longer averaging times is degraded. In particular, the stability plot has a τ^{+1} [11-12] slope (Time = τ) beyond 250 seconds that corresponds to the drift (i.e., about 5.6×10^{-9} at 5000 seconds)

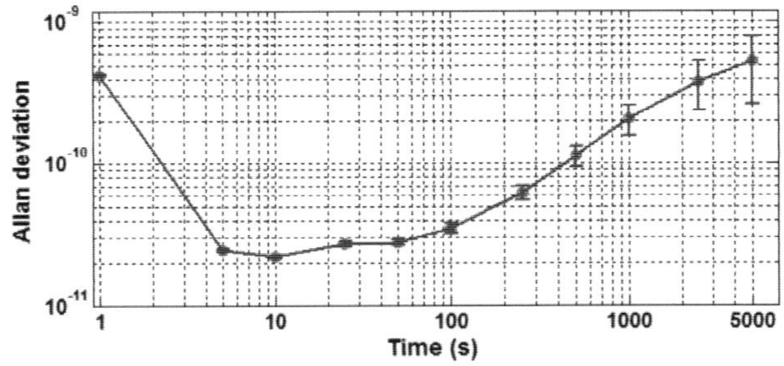

Fig. 6b. Allan deviation of f_{beat} note between HP5517D and femtosecond comb. Error bars corresponding to the standard uncertainty are shown for longer averaging times, where the error is large enough to be significant.

Evaluating the compatibility coefficient *C*, using the formula

$$C = |X_1 - X_2| \Big/ \sqrt{U_1^2 + U_2^2} \quad (7)$$

Where, X_1 and X_2 are the frequencies values of lasers under measurement obtained with CEM2 and frequency comb respectively. U_1 and U_2 are expanded uncertainties ($k = 2$) of lasers under measurement using a CEM2 and frequency comb respectively.
We obtained a *C* values less than 0.34, this result indicate the compatibility of these measurements using two different standards (CEM2 and frequency comb).

The table 1 shows a summary of these results measurements.

Type of lasers	Nominal frequency	Deviation from nominal frequency (with CEM2)	Deviation from nominal frequency (with Comb)
HP5517D	473 612 254	22,76 ± 1,2	22,79 ± 1.0
HP5519A	473 612 254	19,40 ± 9,5	19,10 ± 0.9
TESA-RSD/SR	473 612 750	9,99 ± 0,5	9,98 ± 0.3

Table 1. Frequencies of lasers under calibration measured by frequency comb and CEM2 printed as a difference from nominal frequency values. All values in MHz.

5 Evaluating measurement uncertainty

Estimating measurement uncertainty via studying the repeatability of the measurement is a well-established technique often used in dimensional metrology at many National Metrology Institutes. However, it often requires years of data to truly sample all sources of error in a typical dimensional measurement system.

Every GUM (Guide of Uncertainty Measurement) [13] compliant uncertainty calculation must start with the definition of the measurand and the formulation of the model equation for it. In frequency metrology special mathematical tools have been developed to deal with time series of correlated data. Also the use of relative uncertainties is common practice in this field. However we stay at a more traditional treatment [14], we start with the comb equation (6) which relates the laser frequency (the measurand) with the repetition, offset frequencies of the comb, and the beat frequency with the nth comb mode, respectively.

$$f_{cw} = nf_r \pm 2\bar{f}_0 \pm \bar{f}_{beat} \quad (8)$$

Where $\bar{f}_0$ and $\bar{f}_{beat}$ is calculated as the mean value of the offset and beat frequencies found in the measurement process, then

$$\bar{f}_0 = \left(\sum_i f_i\right) \Big/ m \quad ; \quad \bar{f}_{\text{beat}} = \left(\sum_j f_j\right) \Big/ m \quad (9)$$

Applying the law of propagation of uncertainty, the corresponding expression is obtained to the combined standard uncertainty $u_c(y)$ (assuming the absence of correlations).

$$u_c^2(y) = \sum_{i=1}^{N} \left[\frac{\partial f}{\partial x_i}\right]^2 u^2(x_i) = \sum_{i=1}^{N} [c_i u(x_i)]^2 = \sum_{i=1}^{N} u_i^2(y) \quad (10)$$

In our case

$$u^2(f_{cw}) = 2^2 u^2(\bar{f}_0) + n^2 u^2(f_r) + u^2(\bar{f}_{beat}) \quad (11)$$

By collecting everything and substituting, we end up with the model equation for a laser calibration using a comb

$$u^2(f_{cw}) = u^2(comb) + u^2(\bar{f}_{beat}) \quad (12)$$

Next we analyse each of the uncertainty contributions.

5.1. Uncertainty associated to the reference standard (frequency comb).

The uncertainty of the frequency comb depends on the uncertainty in determining the offset frequency, f_0 and the repetition frequency, f_r . But both frequencies depend in on two common contributions due to the stability of the synthesizer, due to the time reference that is given by the Cs atomic clock.

The uncertainty of the parameters that define the frequency comb is included within the stability of the frequency comb, characterized by the Allan variance, which is the internal counter of the comb synthesizer. Using the Allan variance as a contribution to the uncertainty avoids the correlations because the stability is considering the direct contribution of servos, PLLs (Phase Locked Loops) and system electronics. For an integration time of 1000 s, the Allan deviation $u_\sigma = 9.5 \times 10^{-14}$ [8]. In each calibration performed it has verified that the stability value is less than or equal u_σ. Furthermore the frequency comb is referenced to a primary frequency standard, a Cs atomic clock integrated into the network of atomic clocks of the Navy Observatory, ROA

$$u^2_{clock} = u^2_{Cs} \tag{13}$$

We take the certificate value emitted by ROA, which is for 24 hours, $u_{Cs} = 0.32 \times 10^{-13}$. Finally, the uncertainty of our reference standard frequency comb is, U(k=2) = 2 x 10^{-13}.

5.2. Uncertainty due to beat contribution

The uncertainty associated with the measured value of the beat signal is estimated using a type B evaluation of uncertainty. To do so is considered a type of rectangular distribution, amplitude, where the first is the maximum value and the second is the minimum one of the frequencies found.

$$u(f_{\text{beat}}) = \frac{\dfrac{f_{\text{máx}} - f_{\min}}{\sqrt{12}}}{f_{cw}} \tag{14}$$

Assigning a number of degrees of freedom $\nu_i = 100$, this is a conservative approach established in our Length Area by which the rectangular distributions are associated with an effective number of degrees of freedom equal to 100, to avoid an "infinite" number of degrees, which would suppose a total security as regard to the limits values of distribution. Therefore the (11) equation is written as

$$u^2(f_{\text{cw}}) = (u_\sigma)^2 + (u_{\text{Cs}}/2)^2 + \left(\frac{\dfrac{f_{\text{máx}} - f_{\min}}{\sqrt{12}}}{f_{cw}} \right)^2 \tag{15}$$

The expanded uncertainty, *U* is obtained by multiplying the combined standard uncertainty $u(f_{cw})$ by a coverage factor k

$$U = k.u(f_{cw}) \tag{16}$$

Where k is a function of the effective degrees of freedom obtained by Welch-Satterthwaite formula [13], from the values and the degrees of freedom of the partial uncertainties, for the desired confidence value, typically 95 %. If it can be assumed a normal distribution often the factor k = 2 is used. In table 2 we summarise the uncertainty budget.

Uncertainty Budget	*U* (k = 2)
u_σ (comb stability)	1.9 x 10^{-13}
u_{Cs} (24 hours)	0.3 x 10^{-13}
u_{comb}	2.0 x 10^{-13}
u_{beat} (Tesa RSD/SR)	6.1 x 10^{-10}
u_{beat} (HP5517D)	2.1 x 10^{-09}
u_{beat} (HP5519A)	2.2 x 10^{-09}

Table 2. The expanded uncertainty sources values involving in the measurement of frequency laser.

6 Conclusions

Optical frequency combs have received much attention in recent years due to their enormous potential in optical frequency metrology applications, taking advantage of the continuous breakthroughs in the field of time and frequency metrology. The absolute frequency measurements of Zeeman-stabilized He-Ne lasers with our femtosecond laser frequency comb are in good compatibility with previous studies using a CEM2 as primary standard. In addition the stability of beat frequency of Tesa RSD/SD is dominated by the typical white noise; while the stability of beat frequency of HP5517D and HP5519A at longer averaging times is degraded and corresponds to the drift.

By using Allan variance analysis we estimate a CMC of frequency comb in 2 x 10^{-13}. We evaluate the measurement uncertainty for comb based laser frequency calibrations conform to analysis GUM. Finally this realisation of metre based on femtosecond comb improves measurement precision more than 100 times compared with current method based on iodine stabilized lasers.

Acknowledgements: Author wish to thank the Spanish Centre of Metrology, CEM, and the Ministry of Industry, Energy and Tourism, MINETUR, for their support to this work in the period of 2009-2013.

References

1. Documents Concerning the New Definition of the Metre Metrologia **19**, 163-177 (1984)
2. T.J. Quinn International Report: Practical realization of the definition of the metre, including recommended radiations of other optical frequency standards (2001), Metrologia **40**, 103-133 (2003)
3. T.J. Quinn International Report: Practical realization of the definition of the metre (1997), Metrologia **36**, 211-244 (1999)
4. D.J. Jones, S.A. Diddams, J.K. Ranka, A. Stentz, R.S. Windeler, S.T. Cundiff, Carrier-envelope phase control of femtosecond mode-locked lasers and direct optical frequency synthesis, Science **288**, 635–639 (2000)

5. T. Udem, R. Holzwarth, T.W. Hänsch, Optical frequency metrology, Nature **416**, 233–237 (2002)
6. P. Balling, PhD, *Laser frequency stabilization and measurement of optical frequencies: Development of acetylene-stabilized DFB laser diode at 1542 nm and absolute frequency measurement by femtosecond comb*, Lambert Academic Publishing, 2009.
7. S. Ferreira-Barragáns, Ma.Mar Pérez-Hernández, B. Samoudi, E. Prieto, Realisation of the metre by optical frequency comb: applications in length metrology, Proc. SPIE **8001**, 1–8 (2011).
8. B. Samoudi, Mª Mar Pérez-Hernández; S. Ferreira-Barragáns, E. Prieto, Absolute optical frequency measurements on iodine-stabilized He-Ne at 633 nm by using a femtosecond laser frequency comb, International Journal of Metrology and Quality Engineering **3**, 101–106 (2012).
9. D.J. Jones, S.A. Diddams, J.K. Ranka, A. Stentz, R.S. Windeler, S.T. Cundiff, Carrier-envelope phase control of femtosecond mode-locked lasers and direct optical frequency synthesis, Science **288**, 635–639 (2000)
10. R. Holzwarth, T. Udem, T.W. Hänsch, J.C. Knight, W.J. Wadsworth, P.St.J. Russell, Optical frequency synthesizer for precision spectroscopy, Phys. Rev. Lett. **85**, 2264–2267 (2000)
11. W.J. Riley, *Handbook of Frequency Stability Analysis, NIST Special Publications* **1065** (2008).
12. D. W. Allan, Should the classical variance be used as a basic measure in standard metrology? IEEE Transactions on Instruments and Measurements, **IM-36, NO 2 (1987).**
13. BIPM, *Evaluation of measurement data-Guide to the expression of uncertainty in measurement*, **JCGM 100**:2008
14. M. Matus, P. Balling, W. Mache, A. Nieβner, P. Křen, Uncertainty estimation for comb based laser calibration by direct comparison of 3 different combs, MacroScale 2011 Proceedings Recent developments in traceable dimensional measurements.

Dynamic calibration of piezoelectric transducers for ballistic high-pressure measurement

L.Elkarous[1,2,3,*], C. Robbe[1], M. Pirlot[1], and J.C. Golinval[2]

[1]Royal Military Academy (RMA), Department of Weapons Systems and Ballistics, 30 avenue de la Renaissance, 1000 Brussels, Belgium
[2]University of Liège (ULg), Department of Aerospace & Mechanical Engineering, 1-Chemin des Chevreuils, 4000 Liège, Belgium
[3]Military Academy (AM), Fondouk-Jedid, Grombalia, 8012 Nabeul, Tunisia

Received:

Abstract. The development of a dynamic calibration standard for high-amplitude pressure piezoelectric transducers implies the implementation of a system which can provide reference pressure values with known characteristics and uncertainty. The reference pressure must be issued by a sensor, as a part of a measuring chain, with a guaranteed traceability to an international standard. However, this operation has not been completely addressed yet until today and is still calling further investigations. In this paper, we introduce an experimental study carried out in order to contribute to current efforts for the establishment of a reference dynamic calibration method. A suitable practical calibration method based on the calculation of the reference pressure by measurement of the displacement of the piston in contact with an oil-filled cylindrical chamber is presented. This measurement was achieved thanks to a high speed camera and an accelerometer. Both measurements are then compared. In the first way, pressure was generated by impacting the piston with a free falling weight and, in the second way, with strikers of known weights and accelerated to the impact velocities with an air gun. The aim of the experimental setup is to work out a system which may generate known hydraulic pressure pulses with high-accuracy and known uncertainty. Moreover, physical models were also introduced to consolidate the experimental study. The change of striker's velocities, diameters and lengths allows tuning the reference pressure pulses with different shapes and, therefore, permits to sweep a wide range of magnitudes and frequencies.

Keywords: pressure measurement, dynamic calibration, high speed camera, acceleration and displacement

1 Introduction

Ballistics is in general the study of a projectile's motion in three-dimensional space. When a solid gun powder burns inside fired ammunition, a ballistic time-dependant high-pressure is generated and leads therefore to a physical dynamic quantity. The measurement of this so-called ballistic pressure is paramount. Indeed, the evaluation of gun and ammunition performances is closely related to the knowledge of this parameter. However, fast changes of its amplitude in a short period of time complicate the measurement which involves specific measurement techniques.

Unfortunately, the measurement of this quantity depends on the used measurement technique. Crusher, strain gauges and piezoelectric transducers are the most known techniques and continue to be used depending on their importance. Until mid of the 1960, the crusher gauge method, invented in 1860 by Andrew Nobel was the commonly used method. Since the development of the charge amplifiers by W.P. Kistler in the 1950s, the piezoelectric transducers became the main technique and knew a great progress in ballistic high-pressure metrology [1]. Indeed, sensors with range over 1 kbar are called high-pressure sensors. Their main applications are in high-pressure hydraulics, in particular fuel injection pumps of diesel engines and ballistics.

* Correspondence: elkarouslamine@yahoo.fr

Depending on the weapon's caliber, the whole ballistic phenomenon takes only a few milliseconds when ammunition is fired. Regardless to this fact, the calibration techniques of the used piezoelectric transducers are still mainly static (dead-weight) or quasi-static (continuous). There is no adequate primary dynamic standard for ballistic transducers due to the absence of an absolute generator which can provide the reference dynamic pressure. An improper calibration certainly leads to incorrect measurement and increases the uncertainty. Hence, bad lots of ammunition can be accepted and good lots can be rejected. The safety of the use of a gun could also decrease if the maximum pressure is not known precisely.

Thereby, the need of a reliable dynamic calibration technique for such transducers has been increasing, particularly in the last twenty years. Many methods have been developed and employed to calibrate the variety of pressure sensors: shock tube, quick-opening device, explosive devices and the drop-weight devices [2-3]. But noone of them was able to satisfy entirely the need for ballistic high-pressure piezoelectric transducers. The reasons for this limitation is the range of amplitude (hundreds of MPa) and frequency (tens of kHz) of the gas pressure signal. They are all aperiodic generators which create step-like pressures or single pressure pulses similar to a half-sine wave. In most cases, the reference pressures are measured by reference transducers from the same categories and calibrated statically [3].

The present study falls within this topic with the aim of developing a dynamic calibration method. A suitable practical calibration method based on the calculation of the reference pressure by the measurement of the displacement of the piston in contact with an oil-filled cylindrical chamber is presented. This measurement was achieved thanks to a high speed camera or an accelerometer. Both measurement are then compared. In the first way, pressure was generated by impacting the piston with a free falling weight and, in the second way, with strikers of knows masses accelerated to the impact velocities with an air gun. The aim of the experimental setup is to work out a system which may generate known hydraulic pressure pulses with high-accuracy and controlled uncertainty. Moreover, a mathematical description based on different physical models is also introduced to consolidate the experimental method.

2 Dynamic pressure calibration

A Survey of the methods

The work of Schweppe et al. published in 1963 is considered the first reference document in the field of dynamic calibration of pressure sensors [4]. In 1972, ASME (American Society of Mechanical Engineers) published a guide for the dynamic calibration of pressure sensors [5]. A revised version of this guide by ISA (Instrumentation, Systems, and Automation Society) has been available since 2002 [6]. This second document consists of an elaborate version of the first one, where the pressure sensors properties and the dynamic calibration methods were presented more in detail. The diversity of periodic and aperiodic generators which have been developed was described. Each pressure generator has its range of operation. Periodic generators give pressures with low amplitudes and limited bandwidths, while aperiodic generators produce pressures with high amplitudes and large bandwidths. The choice of the required device is then determined by the conditions of use of the sensor to be calibrated. However, it should be noted that the transient and the harmonic tests are theoretically equivalents and allow both to characterize the dynamic behavior of the sensor [3].

The pressure standards under static conditions, as well as the associated uncertainties, are characterized precisely. The pressure balance is a primary standard that can provide highly accurate reference pressures with relative uncertainty of about 0.012 %. This method can only provide the sensitivity and linearity of a piezoelectric pressure sensor but does not provide any information on its dynamic behavior either in time and frequency domains [7].

A pressure primary standard for the dynamic calibration of high-pressure sensors does not exist yet. Indeed, the pressure signals provided by the existing aperiodic generators, especially shock tubes and quick-opening devices, are not perfectly known in amplitude and frequency except through a statically calibrated reference sensor. The shock tube may be an exception because the amplitude of the reference step signals can be calculated based on thermodynamic models. However, it requires precise knowledge of the gas properties and the shock wave speed in the tube. For this reason, a reference sensor is always used although the research aims to develop a shock tube primary standard. Few national institutes of metrology have developed series of shock tubes but they are still limited essentially for high-amplitude pressure. Indeed, the shock tube is very useful to study the dynamic behavior of the pressure sensors at high frequencies (usually up to 100 kHz), but the amplitude of the pressure remains limited to about 10 MPa which is still lower than most ballistic peak pressures [8]. Quick-opening devices generate positive or negative steps. A device generating amplitude pressure levels of about 1 GPa and a rise time less than 1 ms has been developed to calibrate high-pressure transducers [2]. In most cases, the frequency bandwidth of these devices is still limited.

Moreover, the concept of dynamic pressure generation by use of the close vessel has long been known. Mickevicz developed a bomb for generating pressures of about 300 MPa at the Naval Ordnance Laboratory [4]. This class of dynamic pressure generators which employs the burning of a gun powder has also been reviewed by Damion [3]. However, the lack of accuracy on the determination of the peak pressure, the high-rise time, the danger especially at high pressure and the time consuming handling of a single test were sufficient reasons to make this method rather unsuitable for dynamic pressure calibration. Nevertheless, some institutes continue to use it based on a so-called reference powder for dynamic tests on pressure transducers.

For ballistic high-pressure transducers, the only available method nowadays is static calibration. A dynamic verification or adjustement was also introduced to improve their behavior for dynamic measurements as in weapon barrels and closed vessels. First of all, only the working standard is calibrated statically by the use of a pressure balance as the primary standard (step-wise calibration). Then, a quasi-static calibration of the piezoelectric transducers is fulfilled by a high-continuous pressure generator as a routine calibration using that working standard. Finally, their dynamic behavior is checked against the same working standard [9]. For this purpose, the pressure pulse generators with free-falling weights are widely used due to the absence of a primary dynamic calibration system. When the drop weight hits a piston in contact with an oil-filled chamber, the generated pressure pulse is similar to a half-period sine; its amplitude depends on the compressibility of the fluid, the weight, the drop height and the piston section. The reference pressure is still unknown and also no-indications about the temperature and the pressure waves are given. This last is assumed to be perfect and both sensors, sensor under test (SUT) and reference sensor (RS), mounted in opposing ports are subject to the same wave.

However, differences between peak pressures and between ascending and descending phases, inherent to hysteresis phenomena, can be observed. Thus, based on the peak pressure given by the two sensors, a so called dynamic sensitivity is calculated. In the other way, a polynomial fitting is carried out to achieve an adjustment operation between the SUT and the RS. The polynomial degree has to be chosen carefully by comparing pressure-time signals. Hence, the pressure pulse generator is still used for a comparison calibration based on a reference sensor which provides the reference pressure measurements. In general, this generator has been adapted to get a pressure curve pattern quite similar to real gas pressure variation inside fired ammunition; both in its duration and in its shape. The aim of this method is to check that the dynamic behavior of the pressure transducer can mimic the real gas pressure which certainly improves the accuracy of the measurement. For almost all available systems such as those developed by HPI GmbH [7], Kistler AG [9], PTB [10] and PCB Piezotronics [11] sinusoidal pressure pulses are characterized with widths from 3 to 7 ms, rise times of about 2 ms and peak pressures up to 800 MPa.

The last researches in the field of dynamic high-pressure calibration were conducted in the works of Bartoli et al. [12], Bruns et al. [13] and Zhung et al. [14]. The goal of the studies was to establish traceable dynamic measurement of the mechanical pressure. In the first and the second work, which are made in the same EMRP framework, the reference pressure is deduced from laser interferometry and accelerometer measurements of the deceleration of drop-weight during impact or by laser interferometry measurements of the density change via the refractive index change in the pressurized media. However, in the third work, the Hopkinson bar principle was used to generate high-amplitude pressure pulses under highly-static conditions. The input excitation was measured using a strain gauge and the frequency response function of the pressure sensor was easily computed.

Calibration principle

Calibration is a procedure to find the relationship between a known input *e(t)* and a measured output *s(t)* in well-defined conditions, which means the determination of the transfer function [2-3-4-6]. The amplitude of this function represents the change in the sensitivity as a function of the frequency, so that its phase is used to find the phase shift between the output signal of the data sensor and a reference pressure ideally known. In static calibration, the ratio of output and input is constant and gives the sensitivity of the sensor. In dynamic calibration, the ratio leads to a complex function $H(\omega)$ which is defined as the ratio of the Fourier transforms of the output $S(\omega)$ and the input $E(\omega)$ [3-4-6]:

$$H(\omega) = \frac{S(\omega)}{E(\omega)} = \frac{\int_0^\infty s(t)e^{-j\omega t}dt}{\int_0^\infty e(t)e^{-j\omega t}dt} \qquad (1)$$

In practice, it's impossible to determine the characteristics of the pressure transducer analytically. Therefore, the transfer function is estimated from a knowledge of a pair of associated input and output signals *e(t)* and *s(t)* which are derived from the responses of the complete measuring chain (sensor, charge amplifier, data acquisition and processing system). The measured signals are sampled and non-periodic. Discrete Fourier Transform (DFT) is then used to compute the transfer function. The transfer function allows the full characterization of pressure sensors both in static and in dynamic. Besides the transfer function as amplitude response (AFR) and phase response (PRF), several properties of the pressure sensor such as resonance frequency, damping ratio, rise time and overshoot have to be assessed [6].

3 Dynamic description of ballistic pressure transducers

Piezoelectric ballistic pressure transducers are typically modeled by a single degree of freedom oscillating linear system. The model consists of at least a mass *m (kg)*, a spring with a spring constant *k (N/m)* and a damper with damping constant *c (N.s/m)* [6]. That is, the oscillatory movement would be limited to a direction (*x*) parallel to the line of action of the applied force *f(t)*. The characteristic differential equation which describes the motion of the system is obtained by application of d'Alembert's principle. When rearranged onto its canonical form, we get:

$$\frac{d^2x(t)}{dt^2} + 2\xi\omega_n\frac{dx(t)}{dt} + \omega_n^2x(t) = \frac{f(t)}{m} \qquad (2)$$

Where, $\omega_n = \sqrt{\frac{k}{m}}$ (rad/s) is the natural frequency of the system and $\xi = \frac{c}{2\sqrt{km}}$ is the damping ratio. Applying the Laplace transform to equation (2) yields to the transfer function of the pressure sensor:

$$H(s) = \frac{X(s)}{F(s)} = \frac{K\omega_n^2}{s^2 + 2\xi\omega_n s + \omega_n^2} \qquad (3)$$

Where, K *(pC/MPa)* is the steady-state sensitivity and $s = j\omega = j2\pi f$ is the complex variable (f is the frequency). Using the expression of the transfer function, the inverse Laplace transform is then applied to determine the time-domain response of the sensor to any input force (step, pulse or sine functions) can be obtained. Both the step and the impulse responses characterize the dynamic behavior of transducers as the impulse response is the derivate of the step response. If we apply a pressure step of amplitude A to the transducer, the time response is:

$$x(t) = A\left[1 - \frac{1}{\sqrt{1-\xi}}e^{\left(\frac{\xi\omega_d t}{\sqrt{1-\xi^2}}\right)}\sin\left(\omega_d t + \arctan\left(\frac{\sqrt{1-\xi^2}}{\xi}\right)\right)\right] \qquad (4)$$

Here, $\omega_d = \omega_n\sqrt{1-\xi^2}$ is the damping frequency.

4 Experimental study of the pressure pulses generator

The high pressure generator

A hydraulic pressure pulse generator Kistler type 6909 has been used for the assessment of the ballistic pressure transducers performance in a dynamic environment. The device consists of a piston/cylinder manifold and a drop tube containing a mass that can be dropped onto the piston from various heights [1]. When the mass is released from a certain height along the guiding tube, it transmits its Kinetics energy through the piston to the fluid inside the hard steel structure. The collision is perfectly inelastic. For that, the drop weight and the piston move downward with the same velocity. At the same time, the piston skins rapidly into the oil-filled chamber into which the pressure transducers are mounted. Its energy is then transformed to the fluid as compression energy which causes a pressure increase.

After releasing the total energy, the maximum pressure is reached and the reverse motion of the piston and drop weight starts. They are pushed upwards with the same velocity until the piston is stopped and the falling mass rebounds, and is generally caught. During this process, a pressure pulse is generated, which is similar to a single half cycle of a sine wave. Its amplitude depends on the fluid bulk modulus *K (MPa)*, the total mass (falling mass m_t and piston m_p), the height *h (m)* and the piston area *A* (m^2). The ultimate goal is to obtain a pressure-time signal that mimics the dynamics of weapon chamber pressures.

The principle of the calibration mode is depicted in Figure 1 below. The whole system was also modeled by a mass *m (kg)*, a spring with a spring constant *k (N/m)* and a damper with damping constant *c (N.s/m)*. The generated pressure *p(t)* is proportional to the displacement of the total mass *x(t)*.

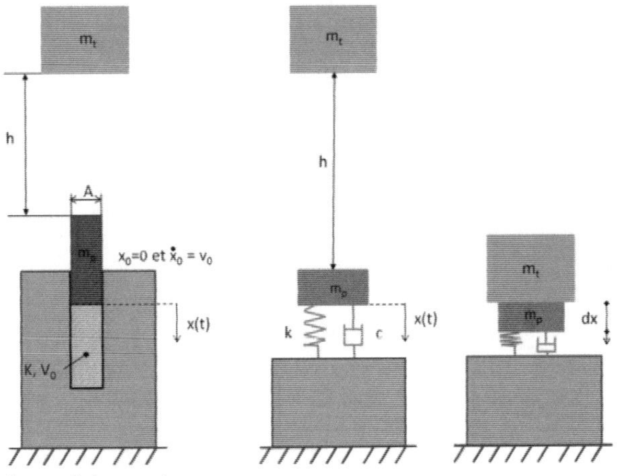

Fig. 1. The hydraulic pressure pulse generator

The velocity of the free falling mass just prior the impact was calculated considering only the acceleration due to the gravity *g* (m/s^2):

$$v_f = \sqrt{2gh} \tag{5}$$

During the impact, the collision was assumed perfectly inelastic i.e. the falling mass does not bounce but becomes permanently attached to the piston mass. In addition, the velocity v_0 of the total mass $m = m_t + m_p$ immediately after the impact was obtained using the conservation of momentum. Given that the mass of the piston (m_t = 0.006 kg) can be neglected comparing to the falling mass (m_p = 5.4 kg), we get:

$$v_0 = \frac{m_t}{m_t + m_p} v_f \approx v_f \tag{6}$$

Measurement and calculation of the reference pressure

In this study, the dynamic behavior of the pressure transducer will be assessed using the peak pressure values. However, the dynamics of the phenomenon will also be taken into account. The reference pressure calculation is based on the measurement of the deceleration and the displacement of the mass, during the compression and the expansion phases of the process. This measurement is performed thanks to a high speed camera and an accelerometer. Both measurements are performed in parallel, allowing a cross validation of both principles. High speed cameras have become widely used to measure dynamic phenomena such as in ballistics. This versatile technique has the advantage of the simplicity of handling, set-up and mainly no modification of the measuring system is required.

For the pressure pulses generator depicted in Figure 1, expression of the conservation of mechanical energy before and after the falling mass hits the piston yields to:

$$m_t g h = \frac{1}{2} m v^2 + \int_0^{x} pA\,dx \tag{7}$$

Where, v is the velocity of the total mass after the impact. Therewith, when all the potential energy is transmitted to the fluid as compression energy, we get:

$$m_t g h = p_{max} A x_{max}$$
$$\Leftrightarrow p_{max} = \frac{m_t g h}{A x_{max}} \tag{8}$$

Where, p_{max} is the maximum pressure and x_{max} is the maximum displacement of the piston.

In addition, the process is considered as isothermal. The isothermal bulk modulus **K** (MPa) given by equation (9) was thereby used as approximation to compute the pressure variation caused by the change in volume.

$$K = -dp\frac{V}{dV} = dp\frac{\rho}{d\rho} \tag{9}$$

Hence, a direct link can be made between the pressure and the displacement as follows:

$$dp = -K\frac{dV}{V} = K\frac{Adx}{V_0 - Ax}$$
$$\Rightarrow p = \int_0^x K\frac{A}{V_0 - Ax}dx \quad (10)$$

This method was also used at MIKES within the EMRP framework [12]. The obtained results of displacement and pressure were compared to the ones deduced from the equivalent mass-spring-damper model (EM) illustrated in Figure 1. The equation of motion of the total mass is described by the following second order differential equation.

$$m\frac{d^2x(t)}{dt^2} + c\frac{dx(t)}{dt} + kx(t) = mg \quad (11)$$

For the initial conditions $t = 0, x(0) = 0, \dot{x}(0) = v_0$, the solution of this equation is given by:

$$x(t) = ae^{-\delta t}\sin(\omega_d t + b) + \frac{mg}{k} \quad (12)$$

Where:

- $\delta = \xi\omega_n$
- $a = \dfrac{v_0}{\omega_d \cos(b) - \delta \sin(b)}$
- $b = arctg\left(\dfrac{\omega_d g}{\delta g - v_0(\omega_d^2 + \delta^2)}\right)$

Figure 2 gives an overview of the experimental set-up which was used to measure the deceleration and the displacement of the falling weight and the piston.

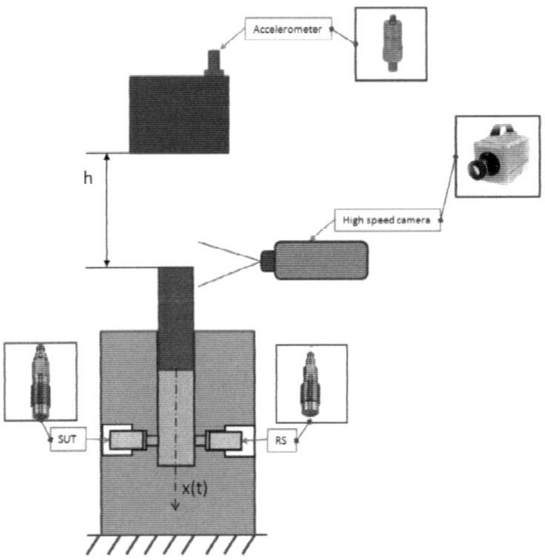

Fig. 2. The experimental set-up of the pressure pulse generator

An ICP shock accelerometer PCB type 305A03 with sensitivity equal to 0.477 mV/g was mounted adhesively onto the top of the drop weight. Moreover, the high speed camera was installed horizontally at a defined distance and level to get an optimal angle of view which permits to follow the whole collision process as shown in Figure 3.

The used camera is a Photron SA-5 high-speed camera (HSC). This HSC can achieve a frame rate up to one million frames per second (fps) [15]. For the calculation, the body formed by the piston and the drop weight is assumed to be rigid during the collision process and its movement is also supposed to be perfectly straight, always in the same plan of the camera axis.

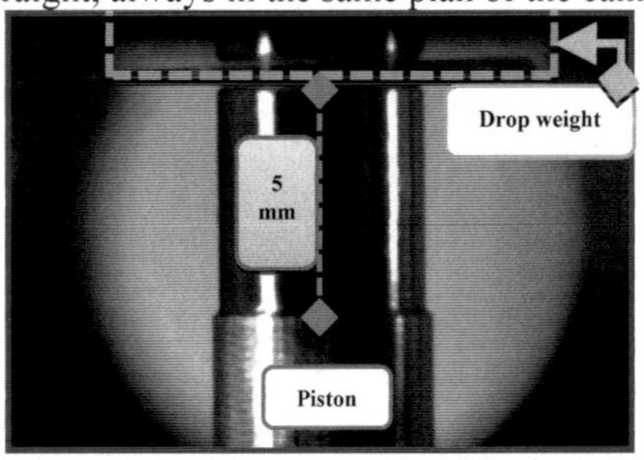

Fig. 3. A photograph of the process by HSC prior to the impact

The frame rate was set at 50000 fps. The calibration factor is 29.2 pixels/mm. In addition, taking into account the small dimensions of the piston and the lack of space in the measurement zone, a special lens with 12X magnification was used. Also, special attention was devoted to the problem of lighting to ensure a high quality measurement. A thorough explanation of the velocity computing based on the HSC measurement was performed by Robbe et al. [16].

The piezoelectric pressure transducers Kistler type 6215 (DUT) and type 6213BK (RS) delivers low amplitude and high impedance charge signal, generally expressed in pico-Coulomb (pC). Thus, a charge amplifier Kistler type 6907B with scale factor of 100 MPa/V was used. The data acquisition (DAQ) board consists in a multi-channel device of four high speed digitizers. Each digitizer has two channels of parallel with a resolution of 14 bits and a maximum sampling rate of 100 MHz. The major conversion occurring in the DAQ board is an analog to digital conversion.

In addition, signal processing was performed with programs developed with the LabVIEW software [17]. A Butterworth phaseless filter was used. For all signals, the frequency domain transform was computed by DFT for optimizing the filter cut off to the signal.

Results and discussions

Test series of 10 measurements for 10 chosen drop weight heights have been made with the experimental bench described in Figure 2. Figure 4 below shows typical pressure-time curves given by the hydraulic pulse generator for different selected heights.

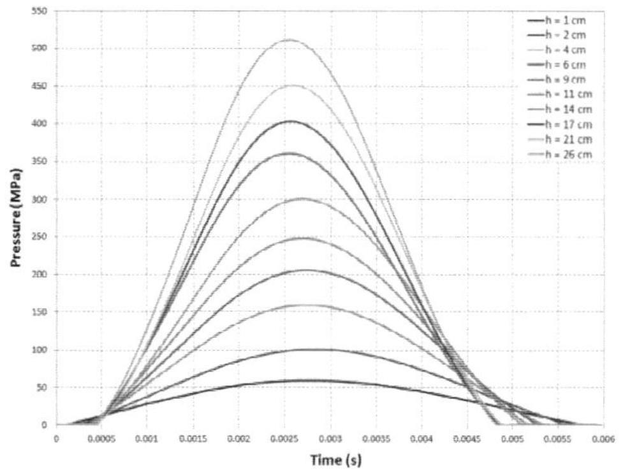

Fig. 4. Pressure-time curves for different heights

The pressure pulses are characterized by a width of about 5 ms and a rise time of about 2 ms. The maximum pressure varies from 60 to 510 MPa.

Similarly, Figure 5 illustrates a typical measured deceleration of the falling weight and piston during the collision process.

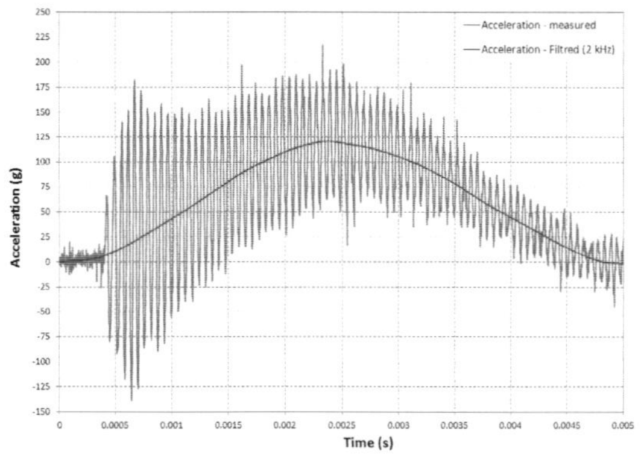

Fig. 5. Acceleration of the piston during the process

When the drop weight strikes the piston, an elastic wave is created directly and is transmitted into the piston. This wave is also reflected in the drop weight. As the falling weight and the piston remain attached during the whole compression and expansion process, the to-and-fro motion of the wave leads to the oscillations observed on the accelerometer signal in Figure 5. The amplitude of the reflected wave is also more important at the compression phase of the process but it decreases progressively at the expansion phase. The period of the oscillations is constant and is around 60 µs. This period corresponds to the duration (T_c) required for the wave to travel twice the drop weight length (L_{dw} = 0.15 m) which is given equation (13). The speed of the wave $c\left(\frac{m}{s}\right)$ is 5020 m/s.

$$T_c = \frac{2L_{dw}}{c} \qquad (13)$$

In addition, the Fast Fourier Transform (FFT) was used to investigate deeply the frequency content of the accelerometer signal.

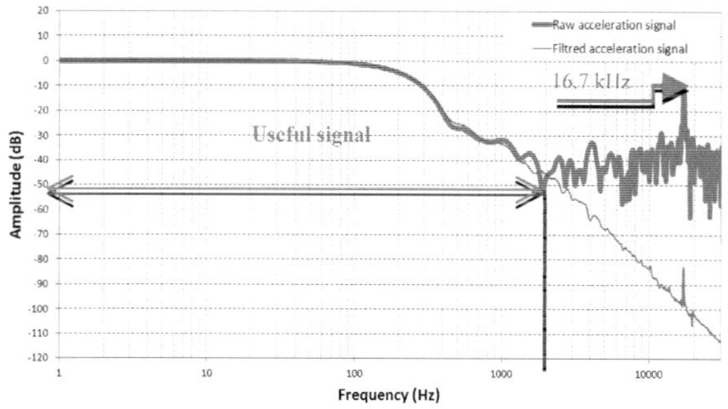

Fig. 6. FFT of the acceleration-time raw and filtered signals

First of all, as can be seen in Figure 6, there is peak around 16.7 kHz which matches the frequency of the oscillations as it was determined by equation (13). Secondly, it can also be noticed that the useful signal is mostly below the frequency of 2 kHz.

The velocity and the displacement of the piston and drop weight assembly, when it moves downward and upward after the collision, are obtained by the integration of the filtered acceleration-time signal. Figure 7 illustrate the three signals for a drop height of 14 cm.

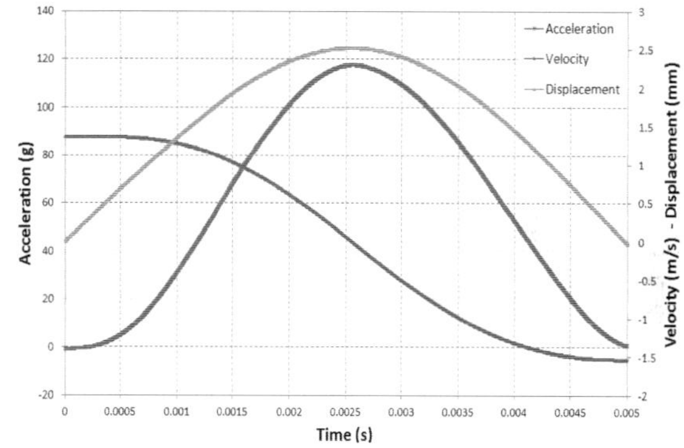

Fig. 7. Filtered acceleration, velocity and displacement

The shape of the displacement time-signal is in good accordance with the pressure curves presented in Figure 4. In Figure 8, the displacements given by the accelerometer, the HSC and the equivalent mechanical model (EM) are plotted together.

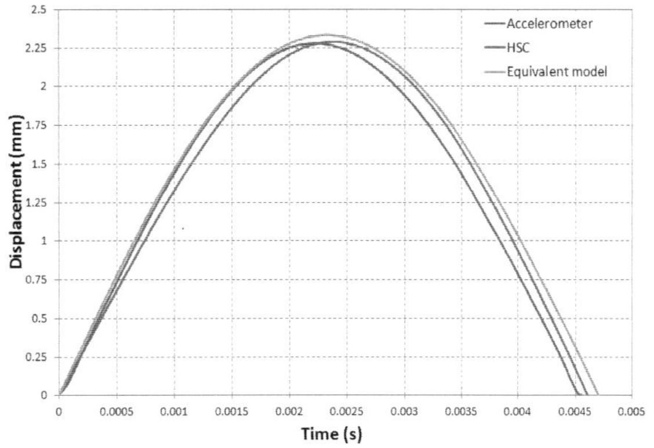

Fig. 8. Displacement: accelerometer, HSC and equivalent model

The partial conclusions are:

- The shapes of the time-displacement curves are similar.
- The peak values and duration are slightly different, which will be evaluated later.
- The proposed equivalent model fits the experimental results and can predict reliably the motion of the piston during the whole process.
- The displacements given by the HSC and the accelerometer are practically identical and always lower than the theoretical displacements.

Using the model described by equation (10), the pressure inside the oil-filled chamber was then computed as shown in Figure 9.

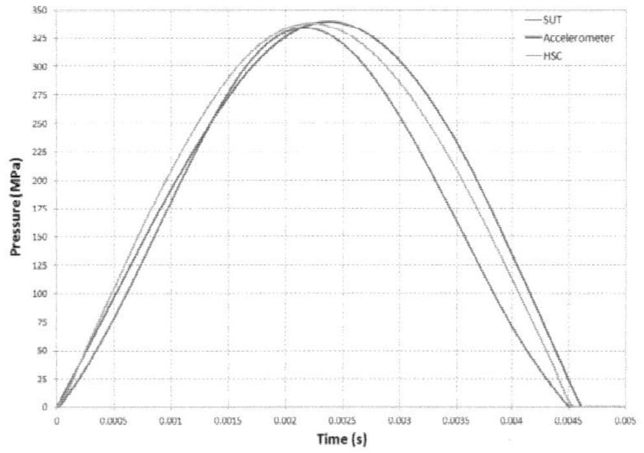

Fig. 9. Pressure inside the compression chamber

Comparing the pressure-time signals given by the accelerometer and the HSC to the one measured by the SUT, peak value and duration of the process can be determined. Figure 10 and 11 give the measured displacement for some selected heights of the drop weight.

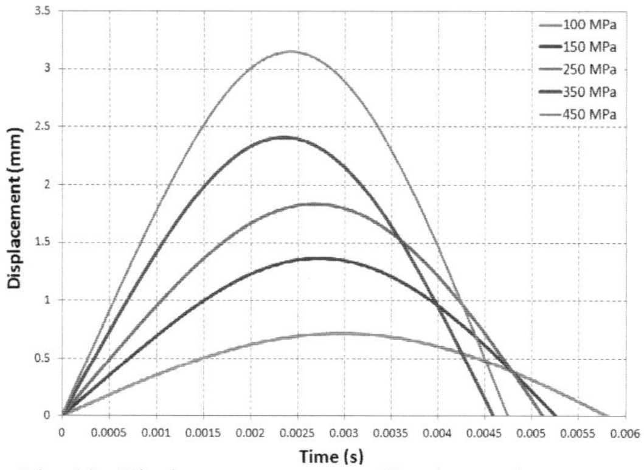

Fig. 10. Displacements measured by the accelerometer

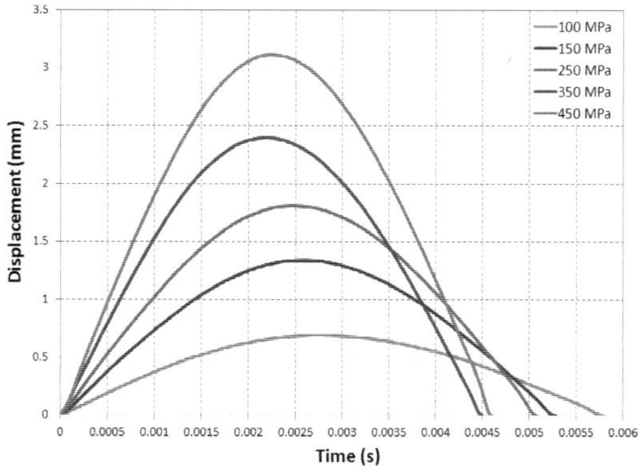

Fig. 11. Displacements measured by the HSC

The time-displacement curves of the drop weight/piston given by the accelerometer and the HSC for different falling heights are fairly similar.

In order to evaluate the two measuring methods, the peak values were taken as comparison criterion. Table 1 summarizes the measured maximum values of the displacement as well as for the pressure.

Table 1. Maximum values of displacement and pressure

h (cm)	x_{max} (mm)			P_{max} (MPa)			
	Accelerometer	HSC	Rel. error (%)	Accelerometer	HSC	Rel. error (%)	RS
1	0.511	0.503	1.57	65.75	64.71	1.59	60.83
2	0.821	0.810	1.34	106.78	105.31	1.38	101.60
4	1.257	1.241	1.27	166.03	163.82	1.33	160.01
6	1.593	1.572	1.32	213	210.01	1.39	207.90
9	2.035	2.013	1.08	276.56	273.35	1.16	270.50
11	2.270	2.250	0.88	311.26	308.28	0.96	303.17
14	2.608	2.597	0.42	362.30	360.61	0.46	357.75
17	2.929	2.918	0.38	412.07	410.34	0.42	407.20
21	3.186	3.176	0.31	452.90	451.27	0.35	450.24
26	3.466	3.461	0.14	498.36	497.54	0.16	495.05

The maximum values of displacement were therefore used to calculate the maximum pressure (P_{max}), i.e. the reference pressure (P_{ref}), using equation (14) which was derived from equation (10):

$$P_{max} = -K.\ln\left(1 - \frac{Ax_{max}}{V_0}\right) \quad (14)$$

Comparing the maximum pressure between each other, the obtained relative difference in (%) is presented in Figure 12.

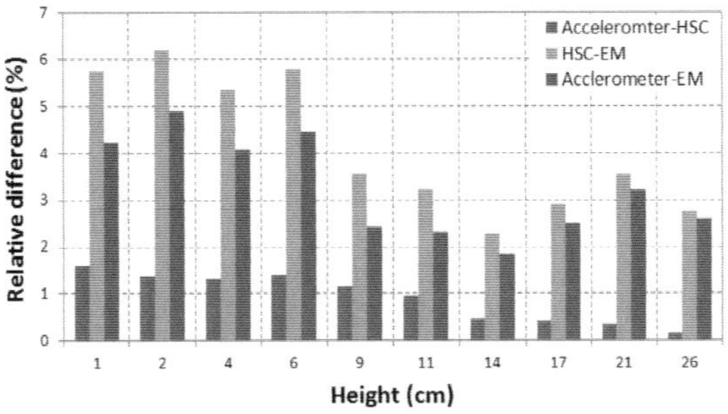

Fig. 12. Relative difference of maximum pressure

Despite the fact that the accelerometer always gives maximum pressure values slightly greater than the HSC, good agreement was observed between the two measuring techniques. The relative difference between the maximum pressures remains generally below 1 %. The equivalent model overestimates the maximum pressure with a relative difference almost exceeding the 3 % and could easily reach 6 % compared to the two measuring methods. Nevertheless, this estimation remains acceptable and leads to consider the physical model well enough to be used to predict the maximum displacement and pressure.

Fitting the maximum pressure to the height of falling weight with the power function, a relationship could be obtained as shown in Figure 13.

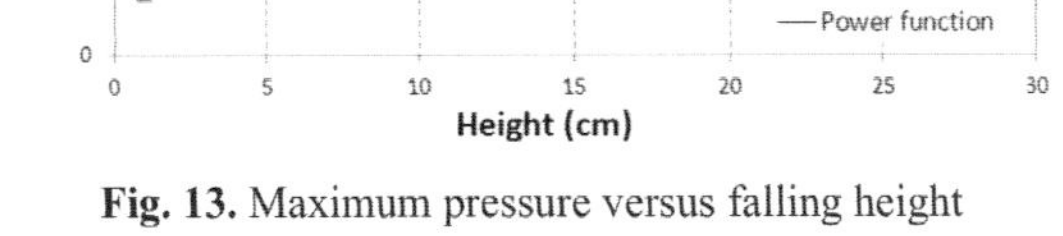

Fig. 13. Maximum pressure versus falling height

According to the described experiments, it follows that the measurement methods of the displacement, by an accelerometer or an HSC, are equivalent. The simultaneous measurement certainly improves the results. However, only the HSC was used to achieve the defined purpose especially as the HSC measurement uncertainties could be computed [16].

Dynamic sensitivity of the piezoelectric pressure transducer

As it was already mentioned, the measuring chain is constituted, in addition to the pressure transducer, of a charge amplifier, a data acquisition module and signal processing unit.

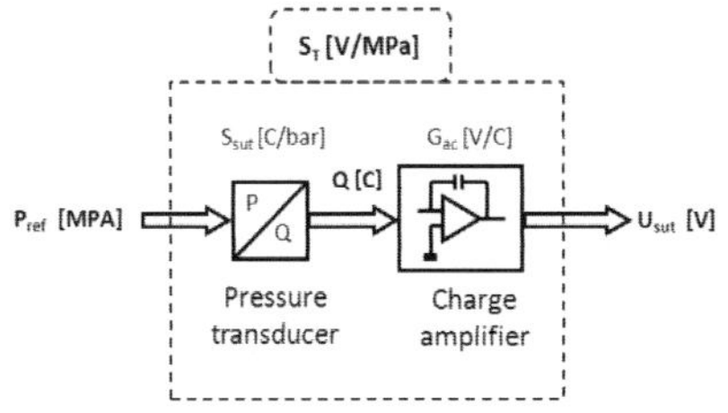

Fig. 14. The model of the measuring chain

Considering the sketch in Figure 14, the sensitivity of the sensor S_{sut} (pC/MPa) to be calibrated (SUT) could also be computed by the following relationship:

$$S_{sut} = \frac{Q}{P_{ref}} = \frac{U_{sut}}{P_{ref}.G_{ac}} \quad (15)$$

Where U_{sut} (V) denotes the maximum voltage delivered by the whole measuring chain of the SUT, P_{ref} (MPa) is the reference pressure which outcomes from the measurement of the HSC and $G_{ac} = \frac{U}{Q}$ (V/pC) is the gain of the charge amplifier. Practically, this gain was measured using a precision capacitor of 1000 pF. An AC voltage source was employed to provide voltage signals with different frequencies to the charge amplifier by way of the mentioned capacitor. Applying a voltage U across the 1000 pF capacitor is effectively applying U.1000 pC of charge into the charge amplifier ($Q = U.C$) . Figure 15 illustrate a typical amplitude frequency response of the charge amplifier. The dynamic measurements are carried out with a short time constant.

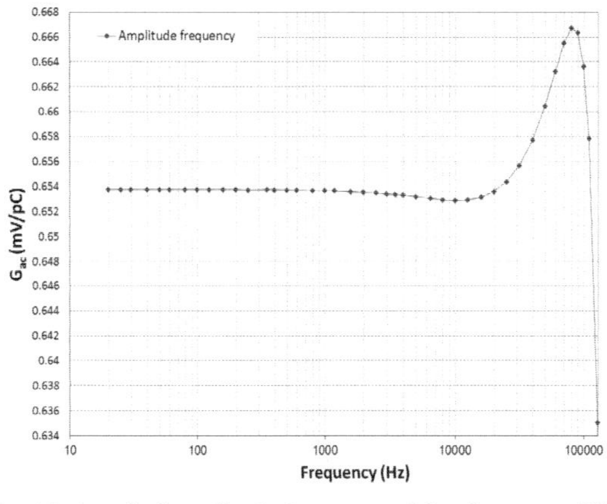

Fig. 15. A typical amplitude frequency of the charge amplifier

The gain of the charge amplifier in the frequency range up to 25 kHz showed no significant deviations. There is only a relatively small deviation of about 0.1 %. In the range up to 110 kHz, the relative deviation remains under 2 %.

Assessement of the calibration uncertainty

According to the Guide to the Expression of Uncertainty in Measurement (GUM) published by ISO in 1993 [18], the combined-standard uncertainty of measurements includes two general terms: one depends on the number of observations (u_A, type A uncertainty), and the other not (u_B, type B uncertainty), and can be expressed as follows:

$$u_c = \sqrt{u_A^2 + u_B^2} \tag{16}$$

Where $u_A = s(\bar{x}) = \frac{s}{\sqrt{n}}$ which is also defining the repeatability error and s is the experimental standard-deviation of a number of observations n. The estimators of the mean peak and standard deviation pressure value are given by:

$$\bar{x} = \frac{1}{n}\sum_{i=1}^{n} x_i \text{ and } s = \sqrt{\frac{1}{n-1}\sum_{i=1}^{n}[(x)_i - \bar{x}]^2} \tag{17}$$

In addition, u_B, the uncertainty of measurement due to different sources of independent uncertainty, is expressed by equation (18):

$$u_B = \sqrt{\sum_{i=1}^{n}\left(\frac{\partial f}{\partial x_i}\right)^2 u^2(x_i)} = \sqrt{\sum_{i=1}^{n} u_{Bi}^2} \tag{18}$$

Where f indicates the measurement which is also considered as a function of different parameters x_i and $u(x_i)$ is the equation of an individual uncertainty driven by the parameter x_i. Here, the elementary uncertainties $u(x_i)$ are supposed to be independent and approximately linear.

As mentioned above, the calculation of the displacement and its measurement uncertainty were performed by a dedicated program [16]. Individual uncertainties were computed and the global uncertainty was determined precisely. Figure 16 shows the displacement of the drop weight and piston during the collision as a function of time for a chosen falling height of 13 cm. By considering three sources of errors, the uncertainty computations allow to obtain a corridor around the nominal displacement curve in which the real measurement should exist.

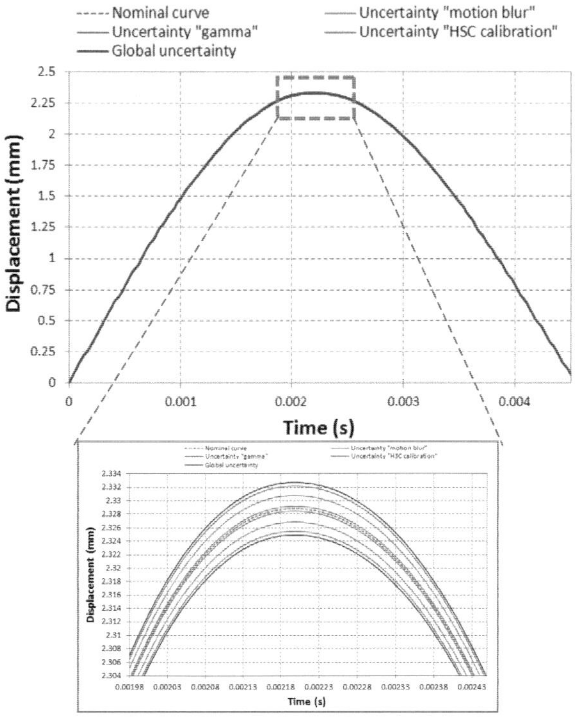

Fig. 16. Measurement uncertainty of displacement

The shape of the corridor changes along the curve due to the change of the individual contributions of all the uncertainties. Here, the global relative uncertainty on the maximum value is equal to 0.17 % which corresponds to a combined-standard uncertainty of 0.038 mm in displacement. Then, the expanded measurement uncertainty for a confidence level of approximately 95 % (k=2) is 0.076 mm.

According to equation (14), the uncertainty of measurement of the maximum pressure (P_{max}= 338.12 MPa) could be calculated as follow:

$$u_c^2(P_{max}) = \left(\frac{\partial P_{max}}{\partial x_{max}}\right)^2 u_{x_{max}}^2 + \left(\frac{\partial P_{max}}{\partial A}\right)^2 u_A^2 + \left(\frac{\partial P_{max}}{\partial V_0}\right)^2 u_{V_0}^2 \tag{19}$$

Table 2. Measurement uncertainty of the reference pressure by HSC

Sources	Contribution to uncertainty (MPa)
Displacement	2.3762
Piston section	0.79
Initial volume	0.8237
Combined-standard uncertainty	**2.63**
Expanded uncertainty (k=2)	**5.2**
Relative uncertainty	**1.55 %**

Moreover, the measurement uncertainty of the maximum pressure given by the SUT is estimated, based on the characteristics of the measuring chain components (technical documents and last calibration certificates of pressure transducers, charge amplifier and DAQ). Table 3 gives the contribution to uncertainty of each device and the resulting relative pressure uncertainty of the transducer under test.

Table 3. Measurement uncertainty of the pressure transducer

Sources	Type	Value	Distrib.	Contribution to Uncertainty (MPa)
Transducer				
Linearity	B1	0.14 %	$\sqrt{3}$	0.2705
Hysteresis	B2	1 %	$\sqrt{3}$	1.9318
Temperature sensitivity	B3	0.02 %/°C	$\sqrt{8}$	0.3691
Charge amplifier				
Linearity	B4	0.16 %	$\sqrt{3}$	0.3091
Resolution	B5	0.5	$\sqrt{3}$	0.0236
Precision	B6	0.5 %	$\sqrt{3}$	0.9659
Zero point deviation	B7	0.6 mV	$\sqrt{3}$	0.0116
Output Interference	B8	1.5 mV_{rms}	$\sqrt{3}$	0.0410
Gain accuracy	B9	0.1 %	$\sqrt{3}$	0.1932
Data Acquisition				
Resolution	B10	0.5	$\sqrt{3}$	0.0059
Offset accuracy	B11	0.4 %	$\sqrt{3}$	0.7727
DC accuracy	B12	0.65 %	$\sqrt{3}$	1.2557
AC amplitude accuracy	B13	0.7 %	$\sqrt{3}$	1.3523
RMS noise	B14	0.03 %	$\sqrt{3}$	0.0657
Repeatability error (10 measures, CL of 95 %)	A1	0.34 %	-	0.73
Combined-standard uncertainty	**3.1 MPa**			
Expanded uncertainty (k=2)	**6.2 MPa**			
Relative uncertainty	**1.85 %**			

According to Table 3, the measurement uncertainty of the SUT is arround 1.85 %. The combination of this uncertainty and the one of the reference pressure assessed in Table 2, gives the uncertainty of calibration which was evaluated to be around 2.40 %.

5 A practical method for high-pressure dynamic calibration

The peak value of the ballistic pressure inside a gun barrel, when an ammunition is fired, depends closely on the measurement method [19]. Given that the peak pressure and its uncertainty are the two most requested parameters, the fast changes of the ballistic pressure should be taken into account and performed with pressure transducers able to do it faithfully. Figure 17 permits to highlight the difference in pressure curve patterns depending on the caliber and the measurement method.

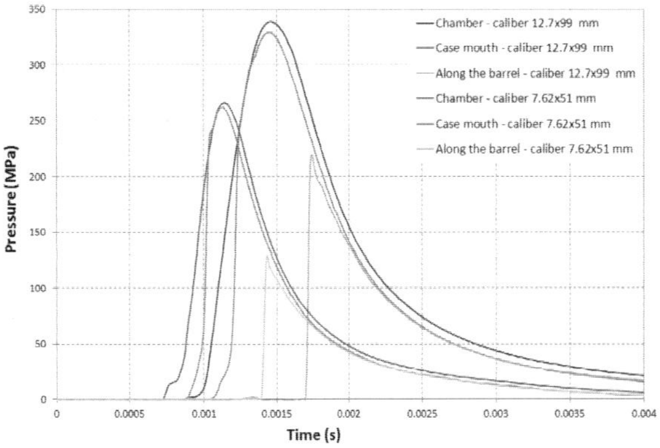

Fig. 17. Typical pressure curves of small calibers 12.7x99 mm and 7.62x51 mm with different measurement methods

The proposed calibration method falls within this optic. The reference dynamic pressure was generated by impacting the piston in contact with an oil-filled cylindrical chamber by strikers of known masses and accelerated to the impact velocities by an air gun. The aim of the experimental setup is to work out a system which may generate known hydraulic pressure pulses with high-accuracy and controlled uncertainty. It permits obtain a frequency bandwidth at the range of kHz in which the dynamic behavior of the transducer can be investigated. The calculation of the reference pressure was based on the measurement of the displacement of the piston by a HSC as it was explained for drop-weight pressure pulse generator.

A device based on the firing of a projectile which hits a piston in contact with a compression chamber was developed at the Combat Systems Testing Activity (CSTA) in Maryland in the United States of America [20]. The use of this method is restricted because a projectile is fired during the process which requires extensive safety provisions. Therefore, it cannot be available in most laboratories.

Figure 18 gives an overview on the experimental set-up which consists of four major components: a lunching device, an oil-filled compression chamber, a displacement measuring device (HSC) and a data acquisition and evaluation unit (DAQ). The strikers of different diameter, mass and velocity were launched by a sudden release of the compressed air in a gas gun and accelerated in a long barrel until impacting the piston.

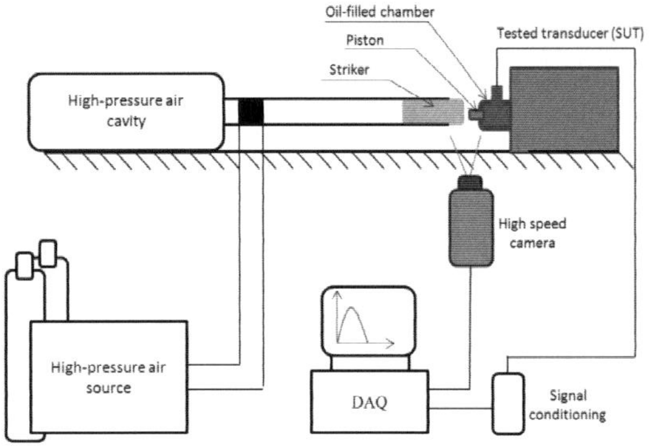

Fig. 18. The experimental set-up of dynamic pressure generator

As shown in Figure 19, the change of striker mass and velocity allows to obtain pressure pulses with different amplitudes and widths. A pressure pulse with peak value of 500 MPa and width of 0.4 ms can easily be generated.

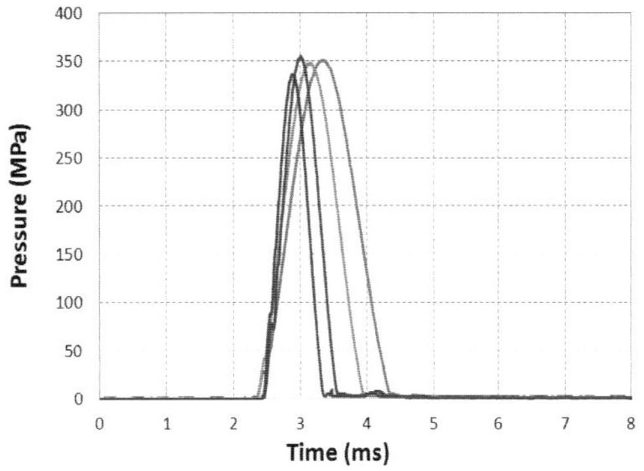

Fig. 19. The generated pressure pulses

Using the model described by equation (10), the reference pressure was computed from the displacement of the piston/striker given by HSC and compared to the measured one (SUT) as illustrated in Figure 20.

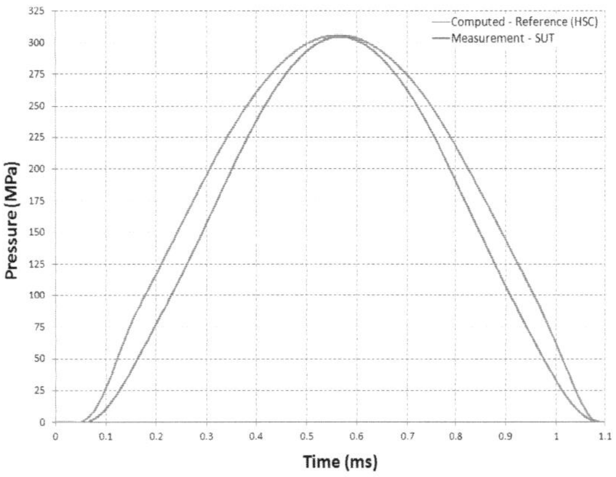

Fig. 20. Reference and SUT pressure pulses

5 Conclusion

The calibration of piezoelectric pressure transducers is paramount in ballistics. This operation should be achieved taking into account the characteristics of the mechanical quantity which must be measured. The presented study aimed at setting up a method for calibration under dynamic conditions of these transducers. The displacement measurement with a high speed camera is a promising approach for calculating the reference pressure. The measurement uncertainty was assessed to be around 2.40 %. Moreover, in order to perform calibration in a wide range of frequencies, an approach based on the launching of strikers from an air gun was presented. This method is simple and easy to use. The variation of the mass and velocity of the striker allows to produce pressure pulses of different amplitudes and frequencies.

References

1. KIAG, Technical documents, KISTLER Instrumente AG (KIAG). Available at http://www.kistler.com
2. V.E. Bean, Dynamic pressure metrology, Metrologia **30**, pp. 737-741, 1993.
3. J.P. Damion, Means of dynamic calibration for pressure transducers, Metrologia **30**, pp. 743-746, 1993.
4. J.L. Schweppe, L.C. Eichenberger, D.F. Muster, E.L. Michaels, G.F. Paskusz, Methods for the dynamic calibration of pressure transducers, NBS Monograph 67, 1963.
5. ASME, A Guide for the dynamic calibration of pressure transducers, ANSI B88.1-1972, USA, 1995.
6. ISA, A guide for the dynamic calibration of pressure transducers, ISA-37.1601-2002,USA, 2002.
7. J. Winkler, Quality improvement in piezoelectric pressure measurements by applying advanced calibration methods, 4e International Symposium on Ballistic Measurement, Switzerland, September 25-29, 1989.
8. J.P. Damion, Capteur de pression de référence pour l'étalonnage dynamique, 7e Congrès International de Métrologie, France, 1995.
9. C. Cater, Calibration of piezoelectric sensors for combustion pressure analysis, KIAG, 2006.
10. M. Kobusch, T. Bruns, E. Franke, Challenges in practical dynamic calibration, AMCTM, France, June 23-25, 2008.
11. J. Lally, D. Cummiskey, Dynamic pressure calibration, PRS-TN-15-0205, PCB Piezotronics, 2005.
12. C. Bartoli1, M. F. Beug, T. Bruns, C. Elster, T. Esward, L. Klaus, A. Knott, M. Kobusch, S. Saxholm and C. Schlegel, Traceable dynamic measurement of mechanical quantities: objectives and first results of this european project, Int. J. Metrol. Qual. Eng. **3**, pp. 127-135, 2012.
13. T. Bruns, E. Franke, M. Kobusch, Linking dynamic to static pressure by laser interferometry, Metrologia **50**, pp. 580–585, 2013.
14. Y. Zhang, J. Zu, H.Y. Zang, Dynamic calibration method of high-pressure transducer based on quasi-delta function excitation source, Measurement **45**, pp. 1981-1988, 2012.

15. Photron, FASTCAM SA-5 specifications. Available at http://www.photron.com
16. C. Robbe, N. Nsiampa, A. Oukara, A. Papy, Quantification of the uncertainties of high-speed camera measurements, Int. J. Metrol. Qual. Eng. **5**, n°201, 2014.
17. NI, Technical documents of LabVIEW, National Instruments (NI). Available at http://www.ni.com/labview
18. AFNOR, Norme AFNOR NF ENV 13005: Guide pour l'expression de l'incertitude de mesure, AFNOR, Août 1999.
19. L. Elkarous, F. Coghe, M Pirlot, J-C Golinval, Experimental techniques for ballistic pressure measurements and recent development in means of calibration, J. Phys.: Conf. Ser. **459** 012048, 2013.
20. A.A. Juhasz, C.D. Bullock, D.H. Newhall, Calibration of ballistic pressure transducers, Measurement and control, **146**, pp.123-127, April 1991.

Quantifying food quality: the case of alkyl-methoxypyrazines in wine

Gary J. Pickering [1,2,4,5*], Andreea Botezatu [1,5], Yorgos Kotseridis [3], and Debbie Inglis [1,2]

[1] Department of Biological Sciences, [2] Cool Climate Oenology and Viticulture Institute, [3] Agricultural University of Athens, Greece, [4] Department of Psychology, [5] Environmental Sustainability Research Centre, Brock University, St. Catharines, Ontario L2S 3A1, Canada
* Correspondence: gpickering@brocku.ca.

Abstract. Wine is the oldest alcoholic beverage, and the most commonly consumed in many countries, including France, Sweden, Italy and Argentina. Its sensory quality is dependent on the relative prevalence of the 200+ odorants known to influence wine flavor. Many of these odor-active compounds exist at trace concentrations, yet still exhibit potent effects due to their low detection thresholds in humans. An important example is 3-alkyl-2-methoxypyrazines (MPs), which are capable of tainting both grape juice and wine, yet possess sensory thresholds well below the sensitivity of established analytical methods. Here we describe the development of a method based on multi dimensional gas chromatography coupled with mass spectrometry and headspace solid phase microextraction (SPME-MDGCMS) that allows for the measurement of MPs in wine down to the low ng/L range. We then apply this method to a range of commercial wines (n=187) from 14 countries to elucidate for the first time the relative concentrations of all four MPs implicated in wine quality - 2,5-dimethyl-3-methoxypyrazine (DMMP), *iso*propyl methoxypyrazine (IPMP), secbutyl methoxypyrazine (SBMP) and *iso*butyl methoxypyrazine (IBMP). IPMP and SBMP concentrations were consistently lower than IBMP. DMMP was detected in approximately half of the samples, and was above the limit of quantitation in 87% of those wines, suggesting it contributes to the aroma of many wines, especially reds. These results illustrate the capacity of modern chromatography techniques to determine the prevalence and importance of trace compounds in food contamination and quality.

Keywords: methoxypyrazines, wine, survey, wine quality, wine composition, ladybug taint, wine flavour, odorants, Coccinellidae, multi dimensional gas chromatography.

1 Introduction

Alkyl-methoxypyrazines (MPs) are trace yet potent odorants found in a variety of vegetables, nuts, and spices as well as several grape and wine varietals [1-4]. For some grape varietals and at low concentrations they play an important role in their characteristic aroma profiles, while at higher concentrations they can lead to unpleasant green characters. MPs can also be introduced into grape juice and wine through accidental incorporation of Coccinellidae beetles during harvest and subsequent processing, producing an off-flavour known as 'ladybug taint' [5]. Cocccinellidae secrete haemolymph, which contain several MPs: isobutyl methoxypyrazine (IBMP), isopropyl methoxypyrazine (IPMP), secbutyl methoxypyrazine (SBMP) and dimethyl methoxypyrazine (DMMP) [6-7], all of which have also been tentatively identified in grape products.

MPs have very low human detection thresholds ranging from 0.3 ng/L to 31 ng/L [8-10]. Given their potency and that elevated MP levels are associated with both under-ripe grapes and ladybug taint [11-12], it is necessary to be able to reliably quantify these compounds in juice and wine. However, this is challenging due to their very low concentrations and the inherent complexity of the wine matrix, making them difficult to separate and quantify. To address some of the challenges and limitations of previous analytical methods [reviewed in 13], the use of multi dimensional gas chromatography coupled with mass spectrometry, headspace solid phase microextraction (SPME-MDGCMS) and deuterated MPs as internal standards has been proposed as a promising approach to meet these measurement challenges.

The main objectives of this study are to describe the development of a SPME-MDGCMS method, and report on its application in a large survey of MP composition in wines from around the world in order to more fully understand the impact and importance of this class of odorant compounds to wine quality.

2 Experimental setup

Part I. Method development.

Initially, we designed a trial to determine the optimum column for MP separation and subsequent quantification on a single column GC–MS system. The general method of [14] was used, and the performance of three columns compared separately for model wine, model juice, grape juice and wine spiked with 50 ng/L of all the four internal MP standards (IBMP, IPMP, SBMP, DMMP). Pure DMMP and the isotopically labeled internal standards [$^2H_3$] DMMP, [$^2H_3$] IPMP, [$^2H_3$] SBMP and [$^2H_3$] IBMP were synthesized at Brock University based on the methods of [14] and [15]. The columns were a HP5MS non-polar column, a DB-WAX highly polar column and a DB17 mid-polar column (all Agilent Technologies, DATU, Geneva, NY, USA).

After determining the two best performing columns from the trial described above, we then sought to adapt the approach in [14] to develop a reliable and sensitive multi-dimensional method for quantifying MPs in white and red wine. Analyses were performed using an Agilent 7890A Gas-Chromatographer coupled with an Agilent MS 5975 Mass Spectrometer.

The Gas-Chromatographer was equipped with a Dean Switch (Agilent Inc., USA) that permitted switching the effluent flow between the first (HP5MS) and second (DB-WAX) columns. Quantifying and qualifying ions, gases, temperature regimes, performance measures and other method details are given in [16].

Part II. Application to commercial wines.

187 wines were analyzed for IBMP, IPMP, SBMP, and DMMP using the optimized SPME-MDGCMS method. Wines were collected from seven different grape cultivars and 14 countries with varying climatological conditions. Samples were represented by nine vintages and were donated by the Liquor Control Board of Ontario.

The column temperature was held at 70° C then ramped to 100° C at a rate of 6° C/min , further ramped to 130° C at a rate of 2° C/min and to 240° C at a rate of 35° C/min where it was held for 8 min. The front inlet was set to splitless mode and held at 250° C under 23.2 psi pressure. The purge flow was turned on after 3 min with a flow to the split vent of 50 mL/min. The dean-switch was programmed for two heart-cuts, the first one between min 10.1 and min 13.5, the second one between min 14.1 and min 14.88. The MSD interface was held at 240° C and the temperature of the ion source was 200° C. The carrier gas was helium, with an initial flow of 0.8 L/min . Identification was performed using Selected Ion Monitoring Mode (SIM). For IPMP, ions 137 and 152 were monitored as quantifying and qualifying ions, respectively. For [$^2H_3$] – IPMP, ions 140 and 127 were monitored as the quantifying and qualifying ion, respectively.

The selected mass channels for IBMP were m/z 124 and 81, and for [$^2H_3$] – IBMP they were 127 and 154. Ions 124 and 127 were used as quantifying ions while 81 and 154 were qualifying ions.

For SBMP the selected mass channels were 138 and 124 (quantifying and qualifying, respectively) while for the [$^2H_3$] – SBMP they were 141 and 127. For DMMP the mass channels were 109, 123 and 138. DMMP was quantitated using the [$^2H_3$] – IBMP internal standard. The MS was operated in SIM, with a gain factor of 7. The methods are fully described in [13].

3 Results and discussions

Method development.

As a measure of individual column performance, the proportions of the qualifier to quantifier ions as expressed in chromatographic area were calculated for samples and compared. When proper separation of the analytes from other matrix components occurs, the proportions should stay constant throughout evaluations.

There were inconsistencies with the ion ratios for all columns as well as problems in detecting some peaks of interest, indicating likely interference from co-eluting compounds (data not shown). The data suggest that improved separation of the target compounds across the range of matrices of interest might be possible by combining columns, with HP5MS and DB-WAX showing the most potential.

The SPME-MDGCMS system that used both HP5MS and DB-WAX columns in series provided much better separation, resolution and quantification of MPs. Figure 1 shows a typical chromatogram. There was good standard curve linearity for all four MPs, with r^2 >0.99. Repeatability was satisfactory, with relative standard deviations for replicate (n=4) wine samples of <15% for MP concentrations at 5 ng/L, and <10% for MP concentrations at 50 ng/L. The recoveries varied between 98% and 105%, with RSDs between 1% and 6%. The limits of detection were 1 - 2 ng/L for IPMP, SBMP and IBMP, and 5 ng/L for DMMP.

Application – survey results.

113 red wines and 74 white wines were assessed for MP composition. IPMP and SBMP concentrations are consistently lower than for IBMP, and are within previously reported ranges (1, 11, 27, 28, 32) with SBMP levels ranging between <2 -12.5 ng/L and IBMP ranging between <2 - 54.3 ng/L . Average values for each varietal wine style for the four MPs are presented in Figure 2. Most IPMP values fall within the <2 - 17.4 ng/L range previously reported (11, 16, 33), although concentrations as high as 27 ng/L were observed in some cool climate Merlot and Cabernet franc wines, consistent with the more intense vegetative aroma and flavor often described in this varietal in wines from cool climates.

DMMP, which has not previously been determined in a large sampling of commercial wine, was detected in 48% of the samples, and was above the limit of quantitation in 87% of those wines (75 red, 4 white).

For the red wines, DMMP levels ranged between 18.8 - 166 ng/L, with an average of 66 ng/L. Thirty five percent of the wines examined had DMMP levels higher than the human detection threshold of 31 ng L (23) suggesting that DMMP contributes significantly to the aroma of many wines, especially red.

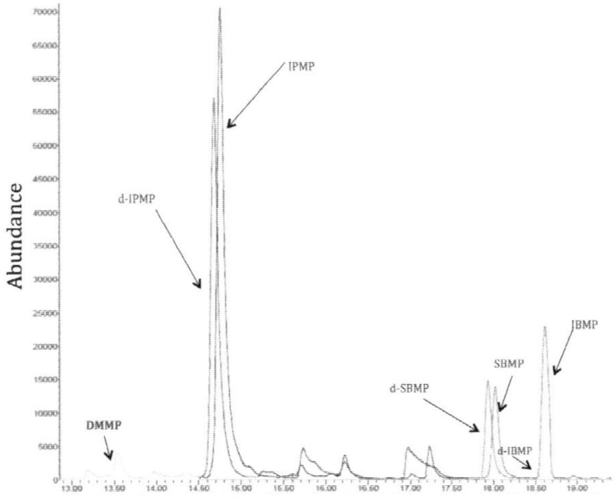

Fig. 1. Chromatogram of a red wine spiked with 40 ng/L dimethyl methoxypyrazine (DMMP), *iso*propyl methoxypyrazine (IBMP), *sec*butyl methoxypyrazine (SBMP) and *iso*butyl methoxypyrazine (IBMP) and their deuterated (d-) analogs. The optimized SPME-MDGCMS method offers good separation of methoxypyrazines, no interferences, and good sensitivity (LOQ = 1-5 ng/L).

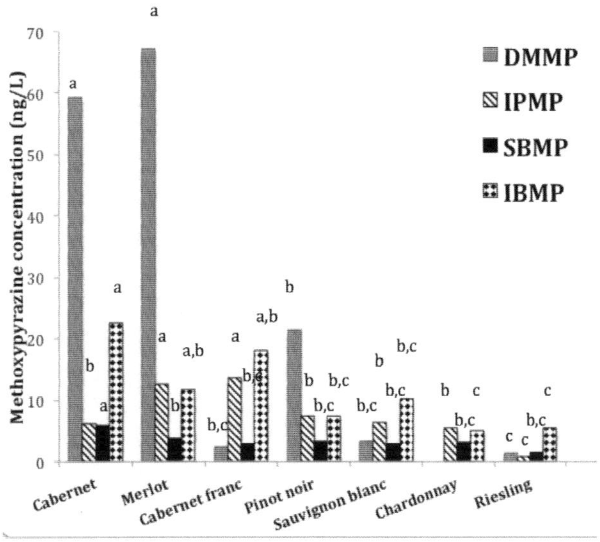

Fig. 2. Average concentrations ± SD of dimethyl methoxypyrazine (DMMP), *iso*propyl methoxypyrazine (IBMP), *sec*butyl methoxypyrazine (SBMP) and *iso*butyl methoxypyrazine (IBMP) for each varietal wine style. Styles with the same letter are not significantly different (Tukey's HSD, p=0.05). Adapted from [13].

4 Conclusion

The analytical method described here based on multi dimensional gas chromatography coupled with mass spectrometry and headspace solid phase microextraction allows for rapid, sensitive and reliable measurement of alkyl-methoxypyrazines associated with wine quality. The application of this method to a large sample of commercial wines from around the world reveals the relative prevalence of *iso*propyl methoxypyrazine, *sec*butyl methoxypyrazine, *iso*butyl methoxypyrazine and dimethyl methoxypyrazine, and suggests that dimethyl methoxypyrazine may be a more important odor-active constituent of wine quality than previously thought.

5 Acknowledgements

We would like to thank Linda Tremblay, Nigel Cocks, Hannah Pickering, Jamie-Lee Robb and Drs Ian Brindle, Thomas Hudlicky, David Adams, Susanne Kögel and Cristoph Hoffmann for technical support and advice. We would also like to gratefully acknowledge the financial support of the Ontario Research Fund, the Ontario Grape and Wine Research Inc, and the Faculty of Mathematics and Science, Brock University. This paper is based on two studies previously reported [13, 16].

References

1. D.R. Boubee, C.V. Leeuwen, D. Dubourdieu, Organoleptic impact of 2-methoxypyrazine on red Bordeaux and Loire wines. Effect of environmental conditions on concentrations in grapes during ripening, J. Agric. Food Chem. **48**, 4830–4834 (2000)

2. G. Buchbauer, C.T. Klein, B. Wailzer, P. Wolschann, Threshold-based structure activity relationships of pyrazines with bell-pepper flavor, J. Agric. Food Chem. **48**, 4273–4278 (2000)

3. C. Sala, M. Mestres, M.P. Marti, O. Busto, J. Guasch, Headspace solid-phase microextraction analysis of 3-alkyl-2-methoxypyrazines in wines, J. Chromatogr. **A 953**, 1-6 (2002)

4. T. Jagella, W. Grosch, Flavour and off-flavour compounds of black and white pepper (Piper nigrum L.), Eur. Food Res. Technol. **209**, 16-21 (1999)

5. G.J. Pickering, J.Y. Lin, R. Riesen, A. Reynolds, I. Brindle, G. Soleas, Influence of Harmonia axyridis on the sensory

properties of white and red wine, Am. J. Enol. Vitic. **55**, 153-159 (2004)
6. L. Cai, J. Koziel, M. O'Neal, Determination of characteristic odorants from Harmonia axyridis beetles using in vivo solid-phase microextraction and multidimensional gas chromatography-mass spectrometry-olfactometry, J. Chromatogr. **A 1147**, 66-78 (2007)
7. E. Cudjoe, T.B. Wiederkehr, I.D. Brindle, Headspace gas chromatography-mass spectrometry: a fast approach to the identification and determination of 2-alkyl-3-methoxypyrazine pheromone in ladybugs, Analyst **130**, 52–155 (2005)
8. A. Botezatu, G.J. Pickering, Determination of ortho- and retronasal detection thresholds and odor impact of 2, 5-dimethyl-3-methoxypyrazine in wine, J. Food Sci. **77**, S394-S398 (2012b)
9. G.J. Pickering, A. Karthik, D. Inglis, N. Sears, K. Ker, Determination of ortho- and retro-nasal detection thresholds for 2-isopropyl-3-methoxypyrazine in wine, J. Food Sci. **72**, S468-S472 (2007)
10. C. Sala, O. Busto, J. Guasch, F. Zamora, Factors affecting the presence of 3-alkyl-2-methoxypyrazines in grapes and wine, A review as found on, http://tdx.cat/bitstream/handle/10803/8653/15-PaperC2.pdf?sequence=15, (2004)
11. G.J. Pickering, L. Yong, A. Reynolds, G. Soleas, R. Riesen, I. Brindle, The influence of Harmonia axyridis on wine composition and aging, J. Food Sci. **70**, 128 (2005)
12. C.F. Ross, K. Weller, Sensory evaluation of suspected Harmonia axyridis - tainted red wine using untrained panelists, J. Wine Res. **18**, 187-193 (2007).
13. A. Botezatu, Y.S. Kotseridis, D. Inglis, G.J. Pickering, A survey of methoxypyrazines in wine, J. Food Agric. Environ. **14**, in press, (2016)
14. Y.S. Kotseridis, M. Spink, I.D. Brindle, A.J. Blake, M. Sears, X. Chen, G. Soleas, D. Inglis, G.J. Pickering, Quantitative analysis of 3-alkyl-2-methoxypyrazines in juice and wine using stable isotope labeled internal standard assay, J. Chromatogr. **A 1190**, 294-301 (2008)
15. M. Czerny, W. Grosch, Potent odorants of raw Arabica coffee. Their changes during roasting, J. Agric. Food Chem. **48**, 868-872 (2000)
16. A. Botezatu, G.J. Pickering, Y. S. Kotseridis, Development of a rapid method for the quantitative analysis of four 3-alkyl-2-methoxypyrazines in white and red wine using multi-dimensional Gas Chromatography – Mass Spectrometry, Food Chem. **160**, 141-147 (2014)

Preventive actions for fraud and questionable research practices by EERM (Ethical and Efficient Research Management)

Reine Bareille*, Bordeaux, Béatrice Baudouin- Massot**, Paris, Marie Paule Carreno, Sandra Fournier***, Nelly Lebret****, Isabelle Remy-Jouet*****, and Eva Giesen

Institut National de la Santé et Recherche Médicale (Inserm), Inserm U 1026*, UMRS 702**, *** Desp Inserm, **** Institut Mondor de Recherche Biomédicale, Paris, ***** Inserm U 1096, Rouen, Directorate General, Paris, France

Received:

Abstract. Preventive actions for scientific misconduct and Questionable research practice must be taken at an institutional level but also by scientist themselves at the lab bench as part of their role of science managers. Here we propose a concept "Ethical and efficient research management" (EERM) and a panoply of easy to use tools which are designed to favour ethical behaviour, sound data and robust methods.

Keywords: Ethical and efficient research management, quality management, questionable research practice, scientific misconduct

1 Introduction

Scientific misconduct (SM) and questionable research practices (QRP) occur on occasion in private and in public research institutions. When competition for limited resources and publication-orientated evaluation practice in research increase, pressure on scientists to produce and to publish results increases too: "Publish or Perish". The societal request for accountability of science is stronger than before. Moreover, the availability of specific computer programs and other tools make the detection of plagiarism easier. All these have probably contributed to an increase of the number of reported cases. Some scientists underline the fact that a researcher is a professional like any other and that todays' culture being more materialistic and less concerned with moral and ethos, we will less automatically do "the right thing even when no one is watching"[1]. These deviations were initially reported in biomedical research, but are now occurring in all fields of science. When SM or QRP are detected in a published paper, the latter has to be amended or, if necessary, retracted by the scientific journal.

Van Noorden [2] has reported that between 2005 and 2011 the retraction of scientific articles in biomedical journals had increased more than 10 fold in 10 years. He also showed that 44% of retractions occurred because of scientific misconduct (e.g. fabrication, falsification, or plagiarism of data or information) and 28% because of scientific errors.

Cases of fraud, poor quality of data but also unethical and inefficient research management will ruin the trust of citizens in science and the trust of scientists in their managers and head of laboratory or unit. Therefore the scientific community is concerned with this phenomenon and adopted Codes of conduct and structures for investigations for misconduct in most fields and places.

Preventive actions would be helpful, but are more difficult to design and to use because in many cases managerial tools are missing or unknown by scientists.

The Inserm-Quality-Network (Riq) uses currently management tools from different sources such as quality management, quality control, knowledge management, project management and so forth. Certain tools have been adapted or developed for purpose of good research practice [3]

Here we describe the concept of Ethical and efficient research management and its use for preventive measures against bad research practice. The concept is based on the belief that sustainable management of a research team, project or collaboration is not possible without ethical conduct of management. Ethical research management and efficient research management are thus intrinsically connected.

2 Scientific misconduct and Questionable research practice exist in all fields of science

Initially pinned down in biomedical research, there is evidence that SM and QRP occur in all fields of science and since a long time.

As early as 1830, the British mathematician Charles Babbage wrote about fraud and defined different types of misconduct: trimming (eliminate data points that do not "fit" with the mean), cooking (selecting of data which are not representative of the measurements but taken out of the context, provide a spectacular finding) and forgery ("pulling numbers out of the thin air")[4].

In archaeology, cases of fraud have been reported as early as in the 19th century. The "Piltdown case" (1912) is a commonly quoted example of a fake and a rather sophisticated scientific fraud, since the authors Charles Dawson and Arthur Smith Woodward had modified their finds artificially and deliberately by adding artifacts and trimming down pieces of skull and teeth to more adequate size in order a match a 500 000 year old human skull[5]. It clearly appears here that findings were not used to establish an interpretation or hypothesis, but that they were fabricated to prove a desired and "stunning" discovery.
Grieneisen and Zhang [6] surveyed 42 of the largest bibliographic databases for mayor academic fields using journals with Web of science category assignments. They found that "the PubMed retractions per year outnumbered the non –PubMed retractions until 2002, indicating the dominance of the medical literature among retractions in the past; however roughly equal numbers have appeared each year thereafter, with 1,402 PubMed and 1,442 non-PubMed retractions from the beginning of 2003 to 22 Sep 2011" (end of the study).

3 Who reports suspicions of Scientific misconduct and Questionable research practice?

In most cases, allegations of misconduct are made by coworkers and other members of the institution; reviewers of scientific publications, too, question reported data, note inconsistencies, redundancies or question the names of authors on a manuscript. Senior scientists are alerted either by their own observations or those of their coworkers or, at a late state, by a scientific journal or the scientific community. Whistle blowers often hesitate to report an allegation because relationships and dependencies are strong in science. Students and young researchers do sometimes not dare report what seems SM or QPR to them, because they depend on the head of a team or institution for their research and their career. Senior researchers and reviewers may not report items of concern, because they realize that they may be in a situation in the future where they depend themselves on the favorable outcome of an evaluation. Only when rules are strict, measurable, transparent and ubiquitous, objective evaluation is possible. In the opposite case plenty of room is left for playing games.

4 Prevention of misconduct and Questionable research practice at the institutional level

Scientific institutions are partly or fully responsible for evaluation practices. Today, evaluation of a scientist or of a team is strongly based on "productivity" e. g. the number and the visibility of a publication. Although heavily debated in the scientific community, "Quality" is almost always appraised by using the impact factor of the scientific journal in which the paper was published. Career, tenure-ship and financing of projects and personnel strongly depend on the publication record of the investigator. Therefore a large number publications and high profile journals are aimed for by researchers. Improvement of the very methods of evaluation may offer a possible preventive action of SM and QRP. Evaluation committees should reflect on possible overestimation of the value of scientific publications and of publication in high profile journals for the quality as a good researcher and team leader. Creativity as such, accuracy and critical questioning are also part of good research. Team leaders and coordinators of large or complicated collaborative networks need to develop particular skills which cannot be boiled down to publication index. For a preventive measure, more differentiated criteria have to be identified and put into practice.
Scientific institutions should question the value and possible negative side effects of career incentives, including fast track promotion, and cash rewards.
Scientific institutions and evaluation bodies also have social responsibility when selecting evaluation criteria. With resources for research becoming rare and increasingly contract related, the question of efficient and good allocation of resources for science is posed by the citizens. Competition is clearly a motor for people, but it also holds a number of dangers such as possible incentive for SM and QRP. Therefore, increasing competition should go hand in hand with increasing awareness of codes and rules of conduct. Moreover, in tomorrow's economy, additional skills are requested from scientists such as enforced skills in management, communication, knowledge management and risk assessment. These must also be taken into account when scientists are evaluated.

Scientific editors have recently adopted editing rules in a White paper, which have to be used by all scientific journals. Negative data, validation of a methodology or scientific approach are difficult to publish today. Those should also be valued by the scientific community and research organizations.
Codes of conduct such as the Singapore Statement of research integrity [7], the Montreal Statement [8], the European charter of researchers [9], the standard NF X 50-553[10], and several guides and publications [11] are available. These have laid the groundwork for teaching at different levels (master, doctorate and live-long-learning). These can be part of classes or through an e-learning program.

5 Preventive actions by research management

Most researchers care about responsible conduct of research, publication and reviewing of scientific publications; also, best practices and codes of conduct exist for scientific integrity in general and different codes of conduct for various areas of science have been identified and made public. The question remains, how to translate them into daily life at the lab bench, in the office and so on.
Ethical and Efficient Research Management (EERM) is a concept of good research management and at the same time a toolbox. It contains managerial tools which are appropriate in science and used to implement good research practice.
The concept, like the standards ISO 9001, "Quality management systems" and NF 50-553 "Management of research activities" are based on the PDCA (Plan-Do-Check-Act) principle. This principle suggests that good planning (P), operation and traceability (D), control in order to detect errors early(C), and correction of errors and nonconforming outputs plus improvement of recurrent activities offers the structure, or the spine, for good research management.
In order to implement this principle, different tools are helpful. Here we present several examples.
1/ The definition of tasks and responsibilities, of roles and codes in the lab (e. g. publication policy, authorship and publication acknowledgement), helps assure fair treatment of co-workers and transparency of management. Managers have designed "task-charts", "Identity cards" for each process and other tools so that the characteristics of a process can easily be viewed. Figure 1a and 1b give examples of ID cards of the process "Arrival of a new co-worker" and "Departure of a co-worker" respectively. Co-workers are treated

like customers in the sense that their needs and expectations are taken into account and that the "give-and-take" principle in the unit is documented in the ID card as well as indicators which reflect to what degree mutual expectations have been met.

Fig. 1°) ID card of process "Arrival of a new co-worker" and Fig. 1b) ID card of process "Departure of a co-worker"

PROCESS « Arrival of new co-worker »		
Value : « Professional courtesy and fairness »	Pilot of process : Peter, senior scientist	
Customers	**Conformity of products (Customer satisfaction)**	**Indicators**
New co-worker	- Easy integration into the team - Appropriate information on his/her rights and responsibilities	- Ratio of persons leaving the team before end of contract over total of new co-workers - Reported defaults and dysfunctions
Laboratory which hires new co-worker	- Easy integration into the team - Quick leaning - New competences - Integration as planned	- Ratio of persons leaving the team before end of contract over total of new co-workers - Reported defaults and dysfunctions
University	- Hiring process compliant with legal requirements - Good image	- No complaints of administration - Number of candidates for a position - Customer loyalty
Sponsors and funding agencies	- Good communication	- Number of contracts

Identity Card		
PROCESS « Departure of a co-worker »		
Value : « « Professional courtesy and fairness »	Pilot of process : Peter, senior scientist	
Customers/Interested Parties	**Conformity of products (Customer satisfaction)**	**Indicators**
New co-worker	- Professional experience, diploma - Evolution of CV and competences - Satisfaction	- Ratio of co-workers who increased professional experience and obtained diploma over total - Satisfaction (inquiry)
Laboratory which hires new co-worker	- Seamless continuation of project - Transmission of knowledge - Data reproducible to previous investigations - Project progression as planned	- Professional objectives attained - Sustainability - Nonconformities
University	- Respect of legal requirements - Increase of favorable image	- Alerts from administration - New candidates coming from the environment of previous co-workers
Sponsors and funding agencies	- information on the satisfactory outcome of the funded project	- Number of satisfying projects to total

2/ When quality management is used in a research lab, actions will not be performed as such and individually, but connected to an "objective", that is the goal that the action should achieve and to an "indicator" which permits objective measurement of the outcome of the action. This approach of managing actions (including scientific actions) is scientific in nature, because it enables the science manager to make fact-based decisions and to step-wise improve the efficiency of the actions.

3/ Moreover, fact based decisions and rules are likely to improve adherence to regulations. Specific efforts are made to make research methods appropriate, robust and comparable to other methods and to ensure fiability and availability of research data (Giesen et al).

4/ Research records and other records which are important in a publication, or, more globally, for a project or a research unit, should not only be clear, complete and accurate, but also allow easy verification and replication of work. Young researchers have to be trained and supervised in order that log-books and other records meet these requirements. Records need to remain in the research unit when a co-worker leaves the unit and knowledge, materials and record have to be transferred to his/her supervisor or an appropriate senior researcher.

5/ The steps of an activity or a project can be materialized on a flow chart to make it easy for everybody to gain information on how a process is set up (Figure 2 and Figure 5). As an illustration we use in all the following figures the previous example "Arrival" and "Departure of a co-worker" and give flow-charts which show the actions of different stake-holders (supervisor or senior researcher, head of the unit, new co-worker etc.), responsibilities, and records related to the different steps (orange boxes in the figures).

Figure 2 Arrival of a new co-worker

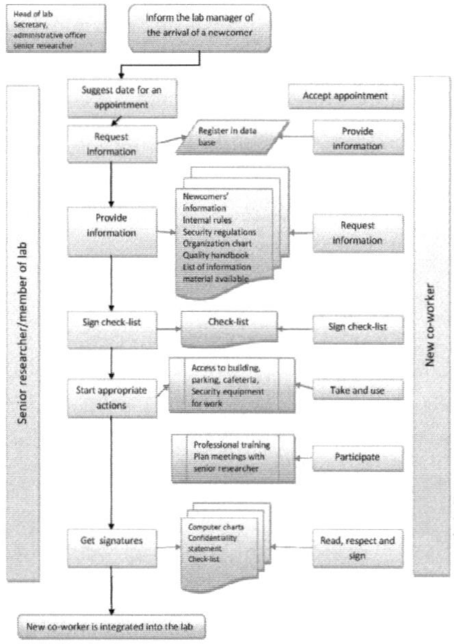

Figure 5 Departure of a co-worker

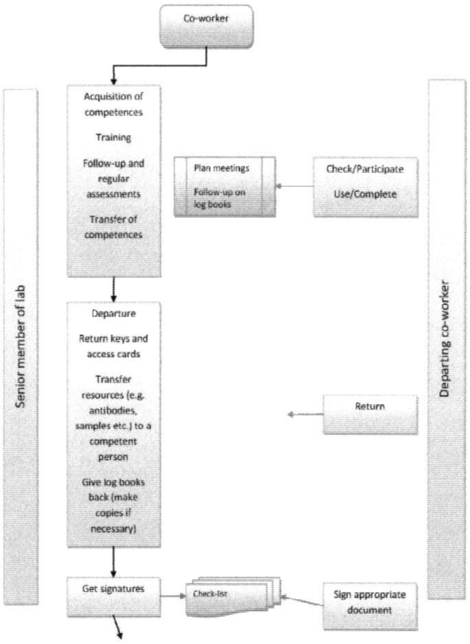

Figure 3 Arrival of a new co-worker

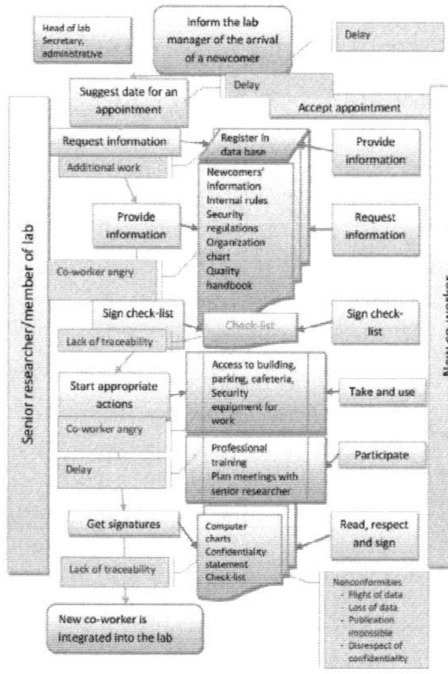

Figure 3 and figure 6 show at which steps critical situations may occur and what risk or threat may be encountered .

Figure 6 Departure of a co-worker

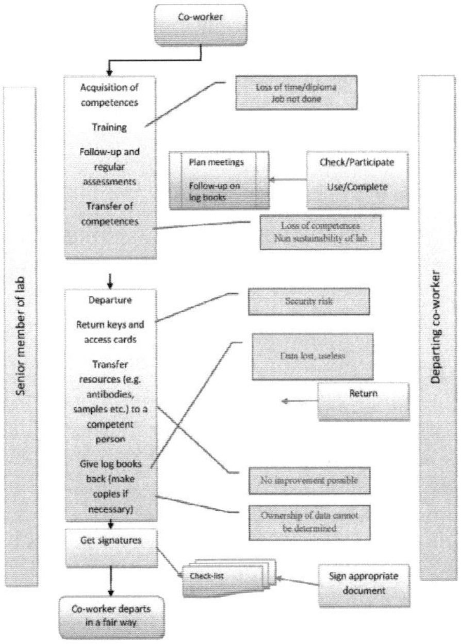

Figure 4 Arrival of a new co-worker

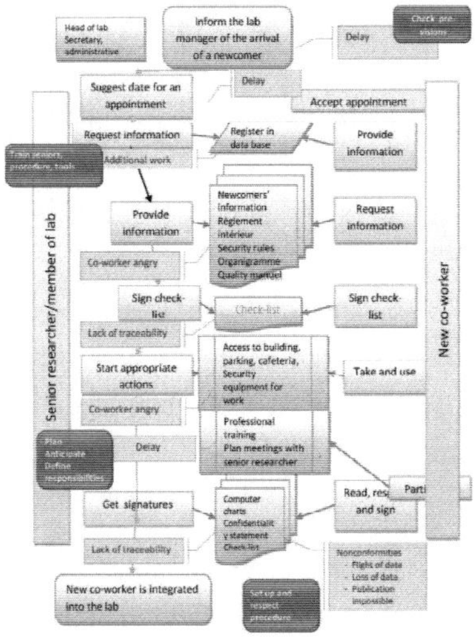

On Figure 4 and Figure 7 is indicated what is planned to do in order to manage the risk.

Figure 7 Departure of a co-worker

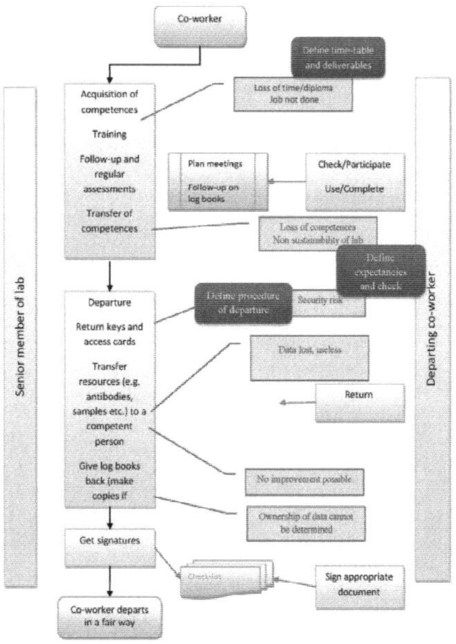

Risks and threats related to the different steps are listed by the team in a most complete fashion. In a second step, a hierarchy of risks is established either by simple appreciation by the team or by using one of the available risk-assessment tools, such as the SWOT-analysis. Then, possible ways of management of the risk are devised (red boxes).

These flow-charts do of course not replace appropriate actions (objectives, indicators) to be taken, but document and accompany the actions as a reminder and an alert. Their usefulness depends on their appropriateness and acceptance by the stakeholders. For this reason, an EERM management system has to be designed by the team in order to have maximum usefulness. Like in a Quality management system, the documentation of the system has to be in conformity with the actions; the records document the way actions are really performed and not what should be done.

5 Conclusion

Honesty, Accountability, Professional courtesy and fairness, and Good stewardship, the four principles of Research integrity, according to the Singapore Statement, are the gold standard in public and private research. In order to diminish possible deviations, such as Scientific misconduct or Questionable research practices, corrective and preventive actions at the institutional and at the operational level are necessary. Here we showed what has been done and what can be done to help sustain, as much as possible, decent research practice. Supervisors, heads of a laboratory or unit and senior researchers have become research managers too. For this reason, research management and its tools must be made available, useful and acceptable to these research managers. The use of the process orientated approach which offers quality management, the PDCA cycle of the new ISO management standards and some simple tools for risk management we declined here to show that Ethical and efficient research management (EERM) is easy to perform and can be used when Codes of conduct for good research management have to be put into practice.

References

1. Scientific Integrity and solid research practices, TU Delft, 28th of March/2014 http://www.tudelft.nl/fileadmin/UD/MenC/Support/Internet/TU_Website/TU_Delft_portal/Over_TU_Delft/Strategie/Integriteit/Schuyt_Scientific_Integrity_and_Solid_Research_Practices___TU_Delft__28th_of_March_2013.pdf
2. Van Noorden R. The trouble with retractions. Nature **478** (2011)
3. http://extranet.inserm.fr/demarche-qualite/reseau-inserm-qualite
4. Cited in: Royal Netherlands Academy of Arts and Sciences. Responsible research data management and the prevention of scientific misconduct. Advisory report by the committee on scientific research data (2013).
5. Piltdown man www.nhm.ac.uk/our-science
6. Grieneisen ML and Zhang M A comprehensive Survey on retracted articles from the scholarly literature PLoS ONE 7(10) e44118.doi: 10.1371/journal.pone.0044118 (2012)
7. www.singaporestatement.org
8. www.researchintegrity.org/Statements/Montreal%20Statement%20English.pdf
9. http://ec.europa.eu/euraxess/index.cfm/rights/europeanCharter
10. Afnor NF X50-553 Management des activités de recherche (2014)
11.Giesen E et al Ethical and efficient research management: a new challenge for an old problem. Int.J. Qual. Eng. 2015, **6**, 460-471
12. NF EN ISO 9001, Quality management systems-Requirements (2015)

Design of an optimization algorithm using PSO method for the determination of the dynamic properties of a pyroelectric sensor

M.H Raouadi, N. Sifi and O. Touayar

University of Carthage, National Institute of Applied Sciences and Technology, INSAT, Research Laboratory « Materials, Measurements and Applications » Dépt. de Génie Physique et Instrumentation, BP676, 1080 Tunis Cedex, Tunisia.

Abstract:

We modeled a pyroelectric sensor by a current source connected in parallel with an output impedance. The dynamic behavior of the sensor is described using a transfer function designed using the MATLAB Simulink environment. The transfer function parameters are optimized using the optimization algorithm Particle Swarm Optimization PSO implemented in the MATLAB environment. This optimization is performed from a comparison with the measured signal. The transfer function thus determined is used to determine the dynamic properties of a pyroelectric sensor. To justify the validity of the proposed approach, we used pyroelectric sensor based on PVDF.

Keywords: Pyroelectric Sensor; transfer function; dynamic properties MATLAB/Simulink; PSO method.

1- Introduction:

Recently, uncooled infrared (IR) sensors are being increasingly demanded for many applications such as automobile, biomedical, plant monitoring, gas detection, fire monitoring, and security system [1-3]. IR sensors can be classified into two major types including photon sensors and thermal sensors. Compared with photon sensors, thermal type IR sensors, such as bolometer, thermopile, and pyroelectric sensors, can be operated at room temperature with little wavelength dependence of the response over a wide IR range. IR sensors using pyroelectric material have the highest sensitivity in thermal-type IR sensors. To realize uncooled pyroelectric IR sensors, an integration of pyroelectric material and circuitry using silicon devices is required [4].

The dynamic properties of the pyroelectric sensor have been identified theoretically [5-8] (mathematical model, electronic model and transfer function model) and experimentally by using different facilities and experiences [9]. However, it was noticed that after the conceptual design of the sensor, the use (in situ) of the sensor affects those already predefined parameters. The best way then is to redefine the parameters from the recorded actual signal [10].

The objective of this research is headed in that direction. It involves using the actual measurements recorded after the sensor design and develop the PSO algorithm to optimize the parameters of the transfer function of the pyroelectric sensor. This algorithm is based on virtual instrumentation and is developed in MATLAB environment. The number of model parameters is determined as an approximation of the solution of an optimization problem.

2- Transfer function of the pyroelectric sensor:

The equivalent circuit includes three blocks of signal conversion for the pyroelectric sensor (Fig. 1) - thermal conversion, thermal to electrical conversion, and current to voltage conversion described by equations (1), (2) and (3) respectively.

$$C_{th}\frac{dT(t)}{dt}+G_{th}T(t)=\eta\Phi(t), \quad (1)$$

$$I_p = pA\frac{dT(t)}{dt}, \quad (2)$$

$$C\frac{dV(t)}{dt}+\frac{V(t)}{R}=I_p(t), \quad (3)$$

where: T- Temperature of the sensor,
I_p- pyroelectric current,
V – pyroelectrec voltage,
ϕ- heat flux,
Cth – thermal capacity of pyroelectric sensor,
Gth - thermal conductance of pyroelectric sensor,
η – absorption coefficient of radiation,
p – pyroelectric coefficient,
C – equivalent capacitance for parallel connected pyroelectric capacitance C_p and input amplifier capacitance: $C=C_p$,
R - equivalent resistance for parallel connected leakage resistance of pyroelectric sensor and input amplifier resistance R_f: $R = R_f$.

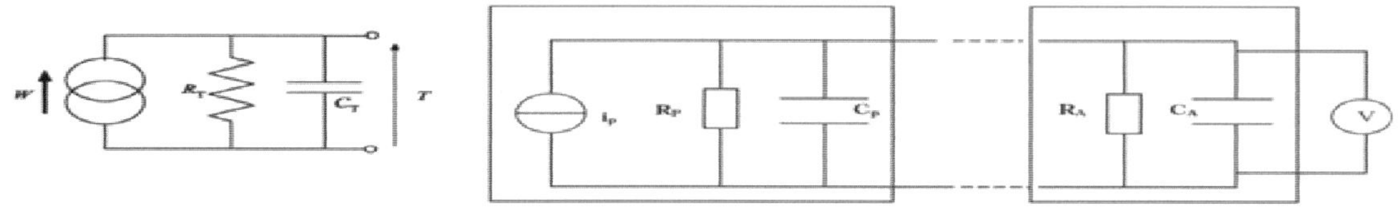

Fig. 1. Equivalent thermo-electrical model with system amplifier.

Each of the conversion stages shown in Fig.1 are described by differential equations (1-3) can be modelled by a Laplace transfer function G(s) defined as the ratio of the Laplace transform of the output signal to the Laplace transform of the input signal under the assumption that all initial conditions are zero.

Circuit amplification are used to amplify the signal of the pyroelectric sensor and then added to equivalent thermo-electrical model (fig 1).

3- The software program:

In this section we present our measurement system and the software that we developed with MTALAB platform.
We have tow part in our software program. The first is the implementation of the transfer function on the SIMULINK tool of MATLAB. The second part is the algorithm developed in MATLAB edit file. So the two parts of the software communicate easily because we have the same platform of the programming simulation.

The mechanism of the identification system of the parameters of the pyroelectric sensor, which includes the measurement records and software developed with MATLAB platform is described in Fig. 2.

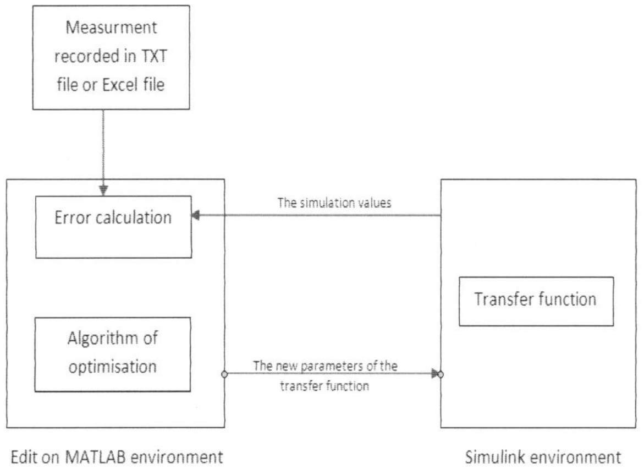

Fig. 2. Mechanism of the system identification parameters.

3.1- Measurement system:

We use in this case the experimental setup described in Fig 4: an incoming radiation chopped at increasing frequencies (up to 300 Hz) is focused on the sensor while the sensor output and the chopper driver signal are acquired by the oscilloscope connected to the PC with the usb port for real time acquisition Fig 5 and all the data of the signal is saved in Excel files.

We add a capacity C_f to the current-voltage amplifier Fig 3 to avoid the problem of the parasite signals and we have the low pass amplifier filter.

$$Vs = \frac{Rf}{1 + jRfCf\omega} Ip$$

The detection card is characterized by an integration time constant $\tau e = R_f C_f$, where R_f is the gate resistance value of the field effect transistor and C_f the capacity.

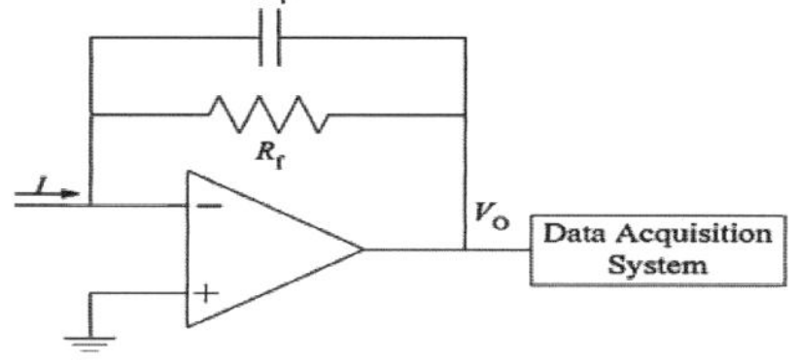

Fig.3. The amplifier used to amplify the generated currant. C_f is the equivalent capacity of the system amplification.

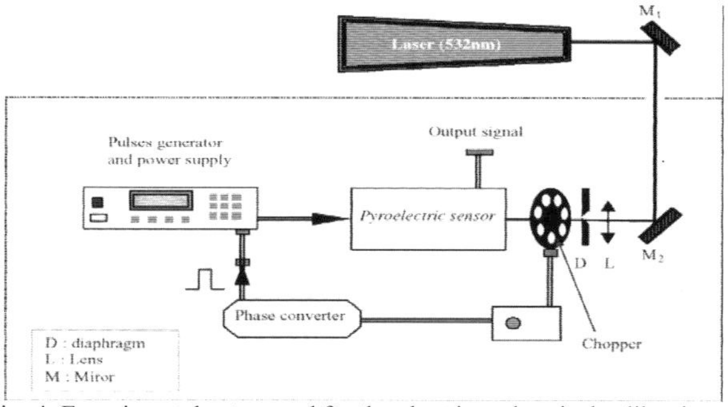

Fig. 4. Experimental setup used for the electric and optical calibration of the pyroelectric sensor.

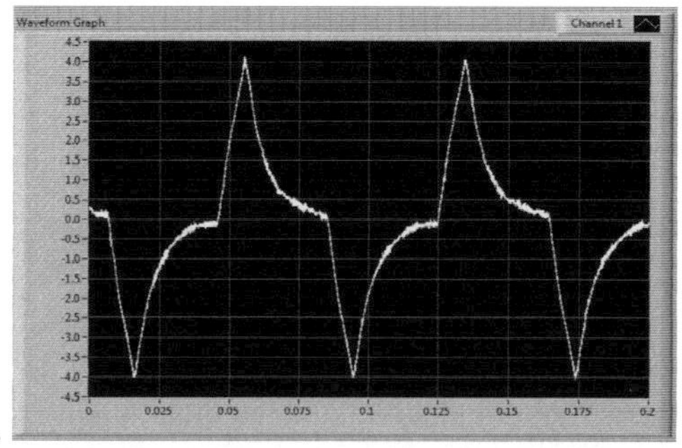

Fig 5. Real time acquisition signal for the pyroelectric sensor

3.2- Implementation of the transfer function in SIMULINK tool:

The Laplace transfer function model $G(s)$ of the pyroelectric sensor described by eq. (4) can be easily implemented in Simulink. For simulation study it is convenient to express the transfer function model $G(s)$ in the form of a product of three blocks connected in series

and characterised by transmittances of Gs=(□□s)/C'dA(C_{th}s

+ G_{th}), G_{Ip}=pAs and G_A= $R_f/(1+\tau_f s)$. It is not a necessary operation but it permits minimization of errors on modification of the detector parameters and easier prediction of consequences of these changes. Fig. 6 shows the simulation diagram which is equivalent to the abovementioned mathematical model of the pyroelectric sensor. The amplitude of the radiation power Φ = 0.1 W

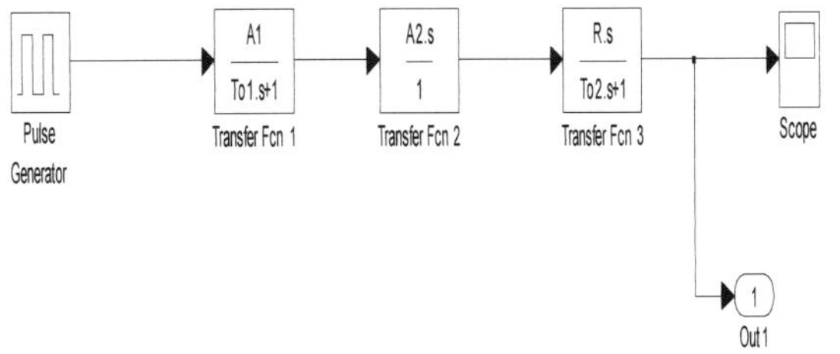

Fig.6. Simulink block diagram for simulation of voltage response of the pyroelectric sensor

3.3- Software algorithm and its validation:

The computer program of PSO algorithm for the identification and prediction of the dynamic properties of the pyroelectric sensor was developed in the MATLAB programming edit file. A block diagram of the software algorithm is presented in Fig. 7. The transfer function is estimated by employing the SIMULINK tool environment developed above in section 2.1.

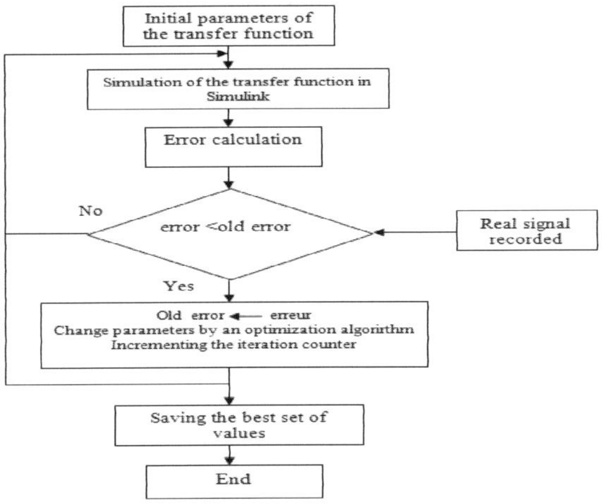

The virtual instrument contains a multi-stage algorithm for the identification of the transfer function. In the first step, the parameters of the model (developed in SIMULINK) are estimated consecutively by employing the random method to have the start of the simulation. The second step was to compare the real signal with the estimated one using the standard error of estimate. The corresponding approximation responses to the measured excitation signal are then calculated. The quality of each approximation response is evaluated using the standard error of estimate [11]:

$$SEE(\Theta_a, \Theta_s) = \sqrt{\frac{1}{N_s - M}\sum_{i=1}^{N_s}[\Theta_a(t_i) - \Theta_s(t_i)]^2}, \quad (5)$$

where Θs(ti) is the sensor's response at the discrete time ti and Θa(ti) is its approximation, Ns is the number of samples in the signal and M = m + n is the number of parameters in the approximation model.

The solution is rearranged into the OE model (output error model) and the parameters of the transfer function were optimized using the Newton-Raphson method. The transfer function with the corresponding approximation response that exhibits the minimum value of SEE after several iterations is selected as the most suitable transfer function for the pyroelectric sensor under test.

The real signal can also be taken from recorded measures in Excel or TXT file. So we can build a model of pyroelectric sensor only from measures recorded without the test facilities.

4- Results and discussions: parameters determination of a PVDF sensor:

The measurement system presented in Fig. 4 was employed to carry out a case study. The area of the pyroelectric sensor is 2 mm^2. The tested sensor was connected to the measurement electronics. This measurement system was calibrated in the laboratory temperature at 25 °C with the reference temperature having an expanded measurement uncertainty of 2 °C.

The static calibration was conducted in the Laboratory of Materials Measurements and Applications (MMA) at the National Institute of Applied Sciences and Technology (INSAT, Tunisia).

The sensor under test was therefore experimentally validated to be suitable for predicting its dynamic properties Fig. 8.

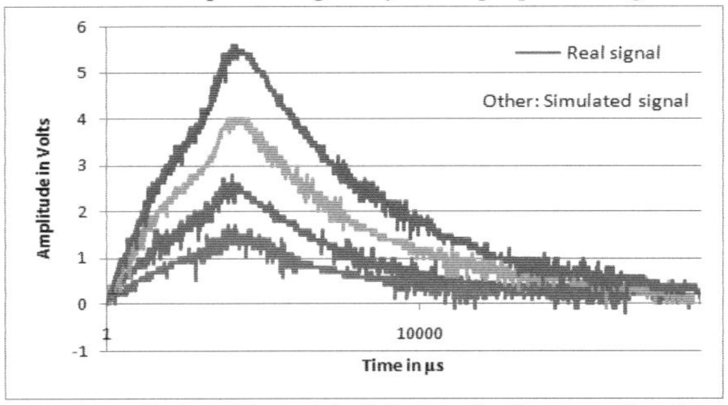

Fig. 8. Evolution of the result of the transfer function using the optimization algorithm

The prediction error after iterations done with the software is equal to 7.4% and, as a result, it lies within the specified acceptance interval of ±10%.

The accuracy of the estimated transfer function depends on a variety of parameters, such as the signal length, the sampling frequency and the signal noise. A careful visual examination of the resulting approximation response is recommended. In the case of inappropriate results the identification procedure should be repeated, using, e.g., signals with a modified length or down sampled. It is also reasonable to minimize the noise of each signal, e.g., by employing a moving average or an ensemble average of a few measured signals. Another possibility is to change the convergence criteria of the PSO algorithms within the system identification process.

Further testing with different settings and by employing both the simulation and the experimental signals should be performed in order to analyze and improve the capabilities of the developed software.

For the purposes of the system identification, the lengths of the signals in SIMULINK tool were set to 0.01 s (equivalent to radiation after chopper modulation). The minimum values of the SEE are equal to 1.27×10^{-2}. The following transfer functions were identified as the most suitable for the sensor under test:

$$G(s) = 0.064s \,/\, [(0.002s + 1) \times (0.0008s + 1)]$$

And the best signal of the optimized transfer function of the pyroelectric sensor by our developed software is presented in Fig. 9.

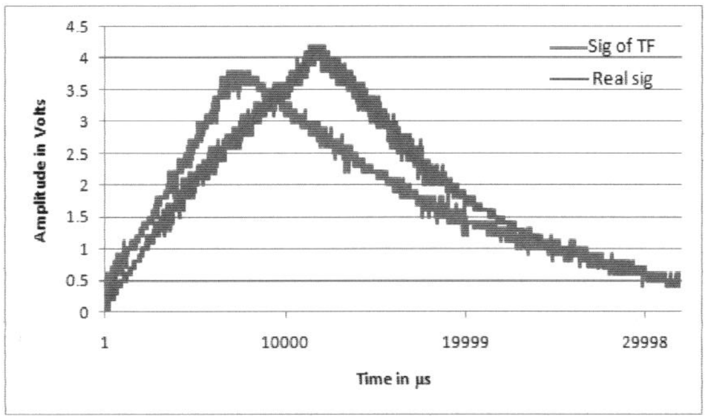

Fig. 9. The signal of the transfer function with the real signal

We have as result the thermal constant of the pyroelectric sensor wish is τ_{th}=**0.002s**. It describes the propagation thermal wave in the sensor after its design and conception. We can therefore compare the theoretical result and the experience result to see the difference and the impact of conception process on the pyroelectric sensor. Also we can have the value of the C_p=**0,23 pF** of the pyroelectric sensor after the identification of the $\tau e = R_pC_p$=**0.0008**s because we have the value of the R_p=34MΩ (in our circuit measurement). It's simple and fast way to identify the experimental C_p of a pyroelectric sensor without use a developed instrumentation.

We apply this easy method to identify the C_p of any pyroelectric sensor from measuring its signal output or from recorded measuring of the sensor and apply our developed software to identify the characteristic C_p.

4- conclusion:

In the literature, the determination of the dynamic properties of the pyroelectric sensor is usually performed either from theoretical models or appropriate experimental techniques. We have developed a method for the identification of these parameters by combining these two approaches. The measuring device can record the output signal from the sensor. We designed an appropriate transfer function and developed an optimization algorithm implemented in the MATLAB environment to determine the parameters of the transfer function of the pyroelectric sensor and its dynamic properties. The advantage of this method, in addition to its instrumentation at very low cost (we used the standard electrical components: resistances, capacitors, TLO71 amplifier, oscilloscope and usb interface with a PC), is the determination of the parameters of the pyroelectric sensor just after conception to study the effects of the fabrication process on the sensor specially on its thermal parameters by comparing the theoretical parameters and the experimental parameters we get with our measurement system for a better integration in automated system (intrusion detection, high temperature control, thermal vision system…).

REFERENCES

1. M. Henini, M. Razeghi, Handbook of Infrared Detection Technologies, Elsevier Science, Oxford, 2002.
2. A.D. Stuart, Some applications of infrared optical sensing, Sens. Actuators B 11 (1–3) (1993) 185–193.
3. H. Schneider, H.C. Liu, Quantum Well Infrared Photodetectors: Physics and Applications, Springer-Verlag, Berlin, Heidelberg, 2007, pp. 175–199.
4. L. Capineri, L. Masotti, V. Ferrari, D. Marioli, A. Taroni, M. Mazzoni, Comparisons between PZT and PVDF thick films technologies in the design of low cost pyroelectric sensors, Review of Scientific Instruments 75 (2004) 4906–4910.
5. A. Odon, Modelling and Simulation of the Pyroelectric Detector Using MATLAB/Simulink. MEASUREMENT SCIENCE REVIEW, Volume 10, No. 6, 2010
6. Ramos, P., Meca, F.J., Mendiola, J., Martin, E. (2002). A
7. Wheless, W.P., Wurtz, L.T., Wells, J.A. (1994). An equivalent-circuit radiation sensor model. In *Southeastcon '94: Creative Technology Transfer – A Global Affair,* April 10-13, 1994. IEEE, 7-11.
8. E. Fatuzzo, H. Kiess, R. Nitsche, Theoretical efficiency of pyroelectric power converters, Journal of Applied Physics 37 (1966) 510–514.
9. V. Ferrari, A. Ghisla, D. Marioli, A. Taroni, Array of PZT pyroelectric thick-film sensors for contactless measurement of XY position, IEEE Sensor Journal 3 (2003) 212–217.
10. W. Minkina, S. Grys, Dynamics of contact thermometric sensors with electric output and methods of its improvement, Metrology and Measurement Systems 12 (2005) 371–392.
11. H.M. Hashemian, Sensor Performance and Reliability, ISA – The Instrumentation, Systems, and Automation Society, Durham, 2005.

Bayes, ou une façon si enthousiasmante de (re)considérer les mesures…

Jean-Michel POU

Delta Mu

Résumé
L'incertitude de mesure est au centre (ou devrait être au centre) des préoccupations des métrologues. Néanmoins, et pour ceux qui se sont investis dans leur évaluation, force est de constater qu'elles sont rarement prises en considération, même dans la déclaration de conformité. Dans cet article, nous voyons comment les incertitudes de mesure peuvent permettre - paradoxalement - d'améliorer la fiabilité d'un résultat de mesure dans le cas où l'entité mesurée fait l'objet d'une connaissance a priori.

Mots clefs : Conformité, inférence baysienne, risque, probabilité, loi a priori, loi a posteriori, incertitude de mesure

1. Préambule

Le métrologue sait aujourd'hui qu'il se doit d'évaluer les incertitudes de mesure. Même si cette mission est encore loin de son quotidien, la pression se fait de plus en plus ressentir, souvent par l'intermédiaire des auditeurs, quelques fois par les clients. Mais, une fois l'incertitude calculée, que faut-il en faire ? Il nous faut bien constater que dans la plupart des cas, elle ne sert à rien, elle n'est pas considérée et on peut comprendre pourquoi : on a toujours fait sans et ça va bien ainsi !

2. Incertitude et statistique

À force de GUM, de GUM S1, d'études R&R et d'ISO 5725, le métrologue a également compris que la statistique était au cœur des mesures. Pour la part de l'erreur qui est systématique, elle peut être corrigée mais pour la part aléatoire, il faut la considérer avec cette propriété troublante : on ne sait pas quelle valeur elle va prendre au moment de la mesure. De ce fait, on ne sait pas, et on ne saura jamais, qu'elle est la valeur vraie de l'entité mesurée. Et pourtant, comme dit un ami qui travaille dans le nucléaire, ce sont bien les champignons que nous mangeons, pas les msures qu'on en fait. Ainsi, seules les valeurs vraies nous intéressent (les champignons sont-ils contaminés ?) mais nous devons nous y résoudre, nous ne la connaitrons jamais…

Une chance dans notre (presque) malheur, les statisticiens nous aident largement pour comprendre et évaluer les phénomènes, qu'ils soient systématique ou aléatoires. Ils ont démontré que lorsque plusieurs facteurs aléatoires élémentaires contribuent à un phénomène global, la somme des **réalisations**[1] de chaque facteur élémentaire se distribue suivant une **loi de probabilité** dite **normale**. Ce cas est tellement fréquent que les propriétés de cette loi normale ont été étudiées, décortiquées, analysées, publiées à de maintes reprises. Nous savons tout ou presque sur elle, mais dans la joie et l'allégresse d'avoir enfin trouvé une réponse à sa question existentielle (le GUM), il semblerait que le métrologue se soit un peu emballé…

3. Réalité d'une mesure

[1] On appelle **réalisation** d'une variable aléatoire une valeur que prend le phénomène lorsqu'on l'observe à un moment donné. Par exemple, si je lance un dé, la réalisation de la variable aléatoire « Lancé de 1 dé » peut-être 2, 1 ou 5 suivant la valeur sur laquelle le dé voudra bien s'arrêter. Une nouvelle réalisation pourra être la valeur 5, 6 ou 1, suivant là encore le hasard des choses…

La mesure est un processus comme un autre, qui met en jeu, pour résumer, les désormais fameux 5 M. Il est donc logique que l'incertitude de mesure, c'est-à-dire l'ensemble des erreurs de mesure possibles, puisse être considérée comme une variable aléatoire de loi de probabilité gaussienne, de moyenne 0 (ou de moyenne « biais », somme algébrique de tous les biais de tous les facteurs élémentaires participants à la réalisation de la mesure si les effets systématiques ne sont pas corrigés) et d'écart type u_c (incertitude-type composée). Notons $\mathcal{N}(0; uc)$ la loi de cette variable aléatoire.

Chaque mesure voit donc se produire une réalisation de la variable aléatoire $\mathcal{N}(0; uc)$ autour de la valeur « vraie » de la grandeur d'intérêt. En effet, une valeur mesurée peut s'écrire sous la forme :

$$V_{mesurée} = V_{Vraie} + e_{mesure} \quad (1)$$

Où e_{mesure} est une réalisation de $\mathcal{N}(0; uc)$.

La représentation « graphique » que le métrologue se fait de l'incertitude de mesure, associée à la valeur numérique produite par son processus de mesure, et parfois corrigée (cas des erreurs systématiques prises en compte), est la suivante :

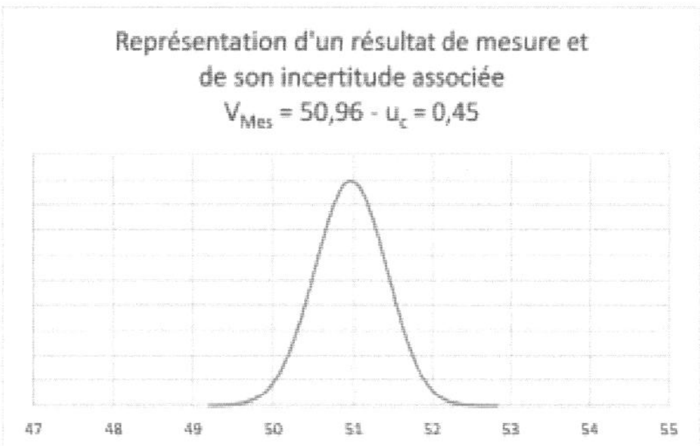

Si cette représentation ne choque pas de prime abord (puisqu'elle est « traditionnelle »), il suffit de se poser une seule question pour la remettre en cause : la valeur mesurée est-elle vraiment, **systématiquement**, la valeur la plus probable ? Évidemment non, et il suffit pour s'en convaincre de répéter la mesure, ou de la faire faire à une autre personne, pour constater que **la valeur mesurée varie**... De ce fait, la valeur mesurée n'est pas la plus probable et la représentation graphique ci-dessus n'est donc pas correcte. Notre raisonnement, souvent appuyé sur la représentation graphique classique, est souvent erroné...

Une fois ce constat fait, le métrologue se trouve face à une autre question : comment faire autrement ?

4. Mesure, résultat de mesure et inférence bayésienne

Bayes a, en quelque sorte, donné la réponse, et il y a déjà longtemps. Dans la relation (1) ci-dessus, on a bien considéré l'erreur de mesure comme une réalisation d'une variable aléatoire, mais quid de la valeur vraie ? Dans bien des cas, l'entité d'intérêt (**LE** champignon choisi pour être mesuré ou **LE** patient qui demande à connaître sa glycémie) est également la réalisation d'une variable aléatoire ! **Ce** champignon est **un champignon parmi les champignons disponibles**, **ce** patient est **l'un des patients possibles**. Ainsi, la valeur « vraie » est **elle aussi** une réalisation d'une variable aléatoire du phénomène d'intérêt (la contamination des champignons ou la glycémie d'un patient). Notons donc $Ph_{Intérêt}(\mu; \sigma)$ la loi du phénomène d'intérêt duquel *l'échantillon mesuré* a été extrait.

Ce simple constat permet d'aborder la question de la mesure sous un angle différent. **Une mesure est donc la conjonction de deux phénomènes aléatoires indépendants : une réalisation du phénomène d'intérêt $Ph_{Intérêt}(\mu; \sigma)$ + la réalisation de la variable aléatoire « Incertitude de mesure » $\mathcal{N}(0; uc)$.** Fort de cette nouvelle vision, et sous réserves de connaître les propriétés respectives de $Ph_{Intérêt}(\mu; \sigma)$ et de $\mathcal{N}(0; uc)$, il est possible de calculer la probabilité d'obtenir le résultat trouvé suivant différentes configurations pour la valeur vraie et, par conséquent, pour l'erreur de mesure qu'il a fallu que le processus produise pour obtenir une valeur mesurée donnée. En effet, et suivant les propriétés statistiques bien connues, la probabilité de voir la conjonction de phénomènes indépendants se réaliser est égale au produit des probabilités de ces termes. Ainsi, la probabilité de trouver une mesure donnée est égale à la probabilité d'une valeur vraie donnée et d'une erreur de mesure associée égale à :

$$e_{mesure} = V_{mesurée} - V_{vraie}$$

pour que la relation (1) soit respectée.

5. Application

Considérons la situation suivante[2] :

A priori	Moyenne	50
	Ecart-type	1
Loi mesure	Biais	0
	Ecart-type	0,5

Dans le cas où nous mesurons, dans un tel contexte, une valeur de 52, on peut estimer la probabilité d'un tel résultat pour différentes valeurs possibles de la valeur vraie :

[illegible]	Loi "Process"	Erreur de mesure	Loi mesure	P1xP2
[illegible]	[illegible]	[illegible]	[illegible]	[illegible]
[illegible]	[illegible]	[illegible]	[illegible]	[illegible]
[illegible]	[illegible]	[illegible]	[illegible]	[illegible]
[illegible]	[illegible]	[illegible]	[illegible]	[illegible]
[illegible]	[illegible]	[illegible]	[illegible]	[illegible]
[illegible]	[illegible]	[illegible]	[illegible]	[illegible]
[illegible]	[illegible]	[illegible]	[illegible]	[illegible]
[illegible]	[illegible]	[illegible]	[illegible]	[illegible]
[illegible]	[illegible]	[illegible]	[illegible]	[illegible]
[illegible]	[illegible]	[illegible]	[illegible]	[illegible]
[illegible]	[illegible]	[illegible]	[illegible]	[illegible]
[illegible]	[illegible]	[illegible]	[illegible]	[illegible]
[illegible]	[illegible]	[illegible]	[illegible]	[illegible]
[illegible]	[illegible]	[illegible]	[illegible]	[illegible]
[illegible]	[illegible]	[illegible]	[illegible]	[illegible]
[illegible]	[illegible]	[illegible]	[illegible]	[illegible]
[illegible]	[illegible]	[illegible]	[illegible]	[illegible]
[illegible]	[illegible]	[illegible]	[illegible]	[illegible]
[illegible]	[illegible]	[illegible]	[illegible]	[illegible]
52	[illegible]	[illegible]	[illegible]	[illegible]
[illegible]	[illegible]	[illegible]	[illegible]	[illegible]
[illegible]	[illegible]	[illegible]	[illegible]	[illegible]
[illegible]	[illegible]	[illegible]	[illegible]	[illegible]
[illegible]	[illegible]	[illegible]	[illegible]	[illegible]
[illegible]	[illegible]	[illegible]	[illegible]	[illegible]
[illegible]	[illegible]	[illegible]	[illegible]	[illegible]
[illegible]	[illegible]	[illegible]	[illegible]	[illegible]
[illegible]	[illegible]	[illegible]	[illegible]	[illegible]
[illegible]	[illegible]	[illegible]	[illegible]	[illegible]
[illegible]	[illegible]	[illegible]	[illegible]	[illegible]
[illegible]	[illegible]	[illegible]	[illegible]	[illegible]

L'observation des lois en présence (A priori, Mesure et A posteriori) conduit au graphique suivant :

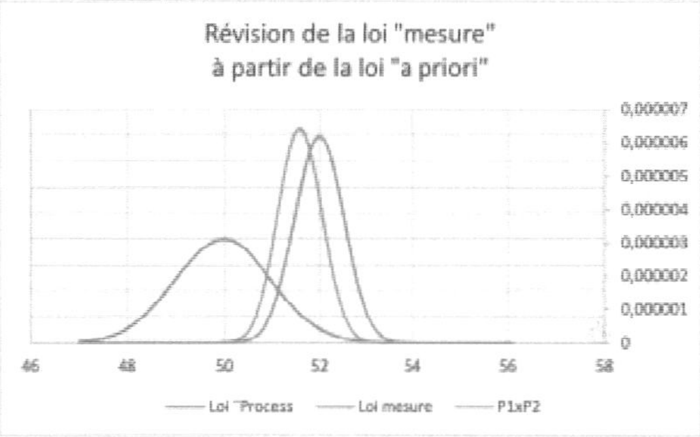

En ne disposant que de la valeur mesurée (52 ± 0,5 à 1 écart-type), on ne peut rien dire de plus… En revanche, et en disposant d'une information « a priori » sur les valeurs vraies possibles (ce qui est souvent le cas finalement…), la valeur mesurée (52), l'incertitude associée (0,5) et les propriétés de la loi « a priori » ($Ph_{Intérêt}$ gaussien, de paramètres $\mu = 50$, $\sigma=1$), il est possible de réviser la valeur mesurée pour obtenir :

- La valeur la plus probable sous-jacente : 51,6 (en lieu et place de 52)
- L'écart type de la loi « a posteriori », gaussienne elle aussi dans ce cas : 0,45 (en lieu et place de 0,5)

[2] Dans le monde bayésien, on appelle la loi du procédé, qui « produit » la valeur vraie, la loi « a priori ». La loi résultant du produit des probabilités de la réalité et de la mesure s'appelle loi « a posteriori ».

Avec cette nouvelle connaissance de la grandeur d'intérêt, établie sur la valeur la plus probable (et pas uniquement sur une valeur mesurée non fiable) et l'écart type associé, il est possible de quantifier la probabilité que valeur vraie soit ou pas au-delà de certaines limites (les champignons sont-ils contaminés ou le patient est-il malade ?). Ces évaluations de probabilité, puisqu'il s'agit bien de cela, deviennent des évaluations de risques, dès lors que la décision est prise de manger, ou de soigner, qui les champignons, qui le patient…

6. Conclusion

Voilà donc que se dessine un bel avenir pour la métrologie. Calculer une incertitude pour calculer une incertitude ne sert finalement pas à grand-chose (la preuve : nos pratiques actuelles). En revanche, connaître l'incertitude associée à un résultat et connaître suffisamment le phénomène d'intérêt duquel provient l'entité à mesurer (ce qui me parait finalement un minimum, les mesures doivent servir à cela !) permet d'améliorer la connaissance de chaque entité considérée, donc de mieux évaluer les risques liés à une décision la concernant !

ORRASA©: a modern audit approach Application to the metrological process

V. Lemarquis, F. Nimanbeg

CRB Management
Bandol, France

Received:

Abstract. The traditional approach of the évaluation which consists in comparing the prescriptions of the laboratory with accreditation requirements and to demonstrate their application through the examination of proofs present limits in term of effectiveness.
With the version 2012 of the standard ISO15189 [2] and even more with the revision of the future standard ISO9001 [5] diffusion which is planned in September, 2015, the accent is clearly placed on the notion of effectiveness of the internal évaluation.
With the imperatives of profitability to which are subject the laboratories of medical biology, beyond the effectiveness, it is to the efficiency of the évaluation that it is necessary to become attached. This article presents the notion of efficiency of the évaluation and an original approach in 4 phases names ORRASA© to put it into practice during the internal évaluations of the laboratories of biology. The évaluation based on the efficiency is besides compatible with the process approach and the risk analysis required by the version 2012 of the standard ISO15189 [2]. An example of application to the metrological process [6] is presented in this paper.

Keywords: audit, efficiency, metrology, effectiveness, performance.

1 Introduction

L'évaluation reste l'un des outils de la Qualité les plus puissants pour faire progresser les pratiques d'un laboratoire. Dans son acception pure, l'évaluation consiste à examiner les prescriptions du Laboratoire formalisées dans sa documentation interne et dans les documents externes (fournisseurs, partenaires...) et à en vérifier l'appropriation et l'application sur des cas concrets.
Pour autant, l'efficacité [4] de l'évaluation reste trop souvent bridée par la recherche de la conformité des pratiques aux standards de fonctionnement du Laboratoire et de la conformité de ces standards aux exigences d'accréditation.
Si on fait l'analogie d'une évaluation avec un moteur - le moteur du progrès - cette approche centrée sur la conformité [4] ne permet pas d'exploiter le plein potentiel du moteur. Le rendement d'une évaluation centrée sur la conformité reste donc largement insuffisant en regard de l'investissement consenti.
Pour rentabiliser cet investissement, il devient incontournable de rentabiliser le temps d'exécution de l'évaluation qui représente généralement les 2/3 du temps total consacré à l'évaluation.
Il importe donc d'orienter l'évaluation vers une autre voie : celle de la recherche d'efficience [4].

2. Méthodologie d'un audit basé sur l'efficience

Les évaluateurs expérimentés le savent bien. En évaluation le temps passe très vite et chaque instant d'évaluation compte pour permettre de mettre en lumière les gisements de progrès du laboratoire [3].
L'approche ORRASA© permet de centrer l'évaluation sur la recherche de l'efficience et d'optimiser le temps d'évaluation afin d'en tirer un maximum de rendement.
Cette méthode est structurée selon 4 phases successives.
Le principe de base d'une évaluation basée sur l'efficience est de la structurer par processus du Laboratoire et de la centrer sur la démonstration de l'efficacité du processus en plus de la démonstration de sa conformité.

Etape OBJECTIFS – RISQUES – RESULTATS (ORRASA©)
Qui dit efficacité d'un SMQ dit atteinte des objectifs associés à un processus et maîtrise des risques de ce processus: la première phase d'une évaluation basée sur l'approche ORRASA© consiste donc à procéder à l'examen approfondi des résultats Qualité en regard des cibles Qualité du processus et des risques identifiés du processus.
Cet examen permet d'apprécier le niveau d'efficacité du processus du Laboratoire. Ce premier constat permet de vérifier si les cibles Qualité sont atteintes et si les risques vis-à-vis de la satisfaction des clients sont maîtrisés.

Etape ACTION (ORRASA©)
Cette phase permet d'une part de vérifier que le Laboratoire engage les actions nécessaires pour améliorer ses pratiques dans le cas où les objectifs Qualité du processus évalué ne sont pas atteints. L'évaluateur vérifie ainsi la pertinence et la mise

en place des actions correctives engagées pour redresser la trajectoire Qualité des indicateurs Qualité du processus.
D'autre part, cette phase d'évaluation va se consacrer à l'examen approfondi de la maîtrise des risques du processus : les documents d'analyse de risques sont- ils exhaustifs ? Tous les risques sont-ils bien pris en compte avec des actions préventives ? Ces actions préventives sont-elles pertinentes et en place ? Quels en sont les critères de vérification d'efficacité ? Quels sont les résultats de l'évaluation de leur efficacité selon ces critères ?
L'évaluation basée sur l'efficience explore, dans cette phase, le cœur du dispositif d'amélioration continue du Laboratoire en permettant de fournir un jugement sans appel sur la maturité du SMQ du Laboratoire. S'engage alors la phase 3 de l'évaluation baséee sur l'efficience.

Etape STANDARDISATION (ORRASA©)
Cette phase permet de vérifier que les progrès accomplis par le Laboratoire à l'issue de la phase précédente à travers la mise en oeuvre et la vérification de l'efficacité des actions correctives et des actions préventives sont consolidés dans les standards (procédures, instructions, modes opératoires, fiches techniques, formulaires..) et dans les documents d'analyses de risques du Laboratoire afin de pérenniser les progrès accomplis et de les généraliser à d'autres sites notamment dans le cas des laboratoires multi-sites.
L'évaluation basée sur l'efficience s'attache donc à vérifier l'ancrage des améliorations réalisées et jugées efficaces dans les pratiques opérationnelles du Laboratoire. Il reste à en vérifier l'appropriation par les opérationnels, les acteurs du processus. C'est l'objet de la dernière phase de l'évaluation basée sur la recherche d'efficience.

Etape APPLICATION (ORRASA ©)
Cette dernière phase de l'évaluation basée sur l'efficience permet de s'assurer que l'ancrage des améliorations réalisées et standardisées lors de la phase précédente est effectif au sein du Laboratoire ou au sein des différents sites du Laboratoire dans le cas d'une configuration multisites. L'évaluation basée sur l'efficience rejoint ici l'évaluation classique de recherche de conformité. Il s'agit de vérifier l'appropriation des standards ((procédures, instructions, modes opératoires, fiches techniques, formulaires..) par le personnel du Laboratoire. Il 'agit aussi de vérifier leur connaissance des objectifs Qualité relatifs au processus dont ils sont acteurs et leur contribution aux résultats Qualité de ce processus.

3. Discussion

L'évaluation basée sur l'efficience apparaît adaptée à l'évaluation des processus dans le cadre de l'approche processus et de la maîtrise des risques prônées par la norme ISO15189 :2012.
En effet, les 2 premières étapes pourront être menées avec le pilote du processus afin d'apprécier le mode de management du processus évalué. Alors que les 2 dernières étapes trouveront toute leur valeur ajoutée par un questionnement ciblé auprès des acteurs du processus.
L'évaluation basée sur l'efficience selon l'approche ORRASA© constitue donc une suite logique de l'approche processus et de la maîtrise des risques. Cette approche incite également à explorer l'ensemble de la ligne hiérarchique : du bureau au terrain. Ce qui contribue à sa crédibilité auprès des évalués en focalisant sur les pistes d'évaluation identifiées pendant les 2 premières étapes.
L'approche ORRASA© permet également de s'assurer que le rebouclage entre les retours d'expérience du terrain avec les objectifs (ce que le Laboratoire souhaite) et les risques (ce que le Laboratoire redoute) est bien effectué : gage d'amélioration.

4. Exemple d'application dans un Laboratoire de Biologie Médicale

Prenons l'exemple du processus Métrologie [6].

Etape ORR
Dans le cadre de l'évaluation basée sur l'efficience, l'évaluateur questionne le Responsable Métrologie – Pilote du Processus Métrologie - sur l'atteinte des objectifs attribués à ce processus. Il examine les résultats mensuels de l'indicateur Qualité *Nombre d'équipements en retard d'étalonnage* et constate une augmentation significative de cet indicateur sur les 3 derniers mois. L'analyse des causes montre que la charge croissante du laboratoire sur les 3 derniers mois impose une activité continue qui amène une indisponibilité des moyens de mesure pour étalonnage. Il constate que l'analyse de risques menée pour ce processus n'inclut pas le risque «Non disponibité des équipements pour étalonnage». Il demande alors le plan d'actions correctives engagé par le Laboratoire.

Etape A
L'examen du plan d'actions avec le Pilote de Processus montre que des actions correctives sont engagées: notamment une action visant à louer ponctuellement des équipements de mesure en substitution des équipements qui pourront alors être envoyés en étalonnage dans les délais sans pénaliser l'exploitation.

Etape S
L'évaluation basée sur l'efficience conduit notre évaluateur à examiner la liste des équipements critiques du Laboratoire. L'évaluateur vérifie que cette liste intègre désormais les équipements de substitution et que la procédure de maîtrise métrologique encadre désormais cette pratique de substitution.

Etape A
Notre évaluateur vérifie sur le terrain auprès du personnel opérationnel l'application du programme d'étalonnage et la disponibilité des enregistrements d'étalonnage des équipements de substitution afin de s'assurer que la pratique de substitution

des équipements de mesure est désormais appliquée et que les conditions sont à présent réunies pour redresser la tendance de l'indicateur Qualité *Nombre d'équipements en retard d'étalonnage*.

En cas de défaillance constatée par l'évaluateur lors de ces diverses vérifications, une non-conformité est ouverte afin d'améliorer le management de la performance du processus Métrologie.

5. Conclusions

L'évaluation [3] basée sur l'efficience [4] présente les avantages suivants :

Compatibilité avec l'approche processus déjà perceptible dans la norme ISO17025:2005 [2] et la maîtrise des risques largement renforcées avec la nouvelle norme ISO15189:2012 [1]. Les 4 étapes de l'évaluation basée sur l'efficience sont applicables à tout type de processus du Laboratoire : managérial, opérationnel et support.

Mise en valeur du mode de management par objectif et par la maîtrise des risques qui se centre sur l'efficacité [4]

L'évaluateur passe d'un rôle de vérificateur centré sur le respect des normes et des standards à celui d'un agent du changement afin de stimuler le Laboratoire à résoudre ses problèmes de performance [4]

Repositionnement des standards du Laboratoire à leur juste place : le standard est un outil de pérennisation et de transversalisation d'une bonne pratique du Laboratoire destinée à maîtriser un risque [4] et/ou à atteindre un niveau de performance

Rééquilibrage des investigations d'évaluation [4] entre le niveau managérial et le niveau opérationnel en disposant d'une filière d'évaluation [3]

Pertinence de l'échantillonnage d'évaluation en identifiant d'emblée avec le Pilote de Processus les domaines de contre-performance et de risques à explorer pendant l'évaluation [3]

Centrage sur l'efficacité [4] du SMQ afin de porter un jugement sur la maturité de cet outil de management du Laboratoire qu'est le SMQ. A ce titre, l'approche ORRASA© est applicable plus largement à tout type d'audit (interne, seconde partie, tierce partie) et pour tout système de management (Qualité [5], Environnement, Sécurité…).

Références

[1] ISO/IEC 17025:2005, Exigences générales concernant la compétence des laboratoires d'étalonnage et d'essais

[2] ISO 15189:2012, Laboratoires de biologie médicale. Exigences concernant la qualité et la compétence.

[3] ISO 19011:2011, Lignes directrices pour l'audit des systèmes de management
[4] ISO 9000:2015, Systèmes de management de la qualité - Principes essentiels et vocabulaire

[5] ISO 9001:2015, Systèmes de management de la qualité - Exigences

[6] ISO 10012:2003, Systèmes de management de la mesure - Exigences pour les processus et les équipements de mesure.

Main gaps in metrology during evaluation of accreditation in Laboratory of Medical Biology

Les principaux écarts en métrologie lors d'évaluation d'accréditation en Laboratoire de Biologie Médicale

MME LEMARQUIS V- F NIMANBEG

* *Véronique Lemarquis- veroniquelemarquis@orange.fr*
www.crb-management.fr

Abstract

The management of metrology in a laboratory of Medical biology accredited, requires the definition of our needs, the identification of the critical equipment. A quality policy is defined for each size and each equipment. Metrology becomes a key function in the laboratory, is managed by a person in metrologist, who animates and ensures the coherence of the whole of measurements of the laboratory.
This process is the object of internal audit in laboratories and is systematically estimated during accreditation visits.
We looked for the weak points of the metrology in the laboratories based on the main gaps encountered during the audits.
Keywords: Accreditation, audit gaps, metrological traceability, metrological policy; CAFMET2016; papers.

Résumé

La gestion de la métrologie dans un laboratoire de biologie Médicale accrédité , passe par la définition de nos besoins, l'identification des équipements critiques. Une politique qualité est définie pour chaque grandeur ; La métrologie devenue une fonction clé dans le laboratoire, est gérée par un responsable métrologue, qui anime et assure la cohérence de l'ensemble des mesures du laboratoire. Ce processus est l'objet d'audit interne dans les laboratoires et est évalué systématiquement dans les évaluations d'accréditation.
Nous avons cherché les points faibles de la mise en conformité de la métrologie dans les laboratoires de biologie médicale au travers des principaux écarts rencontrés.

Mots clés: Accréditation; écarts ; raccordement ; politique métrologique; CAFMET2016; article.

1. Introduction

Le suivi métrologique du matériel prend une place de plus en plus importante dans les laboratoires de biologie médicale (LBM) ; Il intervient dans la maîtrise des conditions ambiantes, la conservation et préparation des échantillons, des réactifs, la réalisation de la phase analytique et participe à l'exactitude des résultats d'examens de biologie médicale.

Ce processus métrologique fait l'objet d'audit périodique en interne pour vérifier sa conformité aux dispositions prévues et son efficience au sein du LBM [7]; il est systématiquement audité pendant les évaluations COFRAC des LBM dans les processus d'accréditation selon les Normes EN ISO 15189[2], ISO CEI 17025[1], ISO EN ISO 22870. [6],

2. Les Grandeurs concernées au LBM

Nous ne parlerons pas dans cet article de la métrologie des automates d'analyse.

Matériel	Grandeurs susceptibles d'avoir un impact
Enceintes thermiques	Température, PCO2
Pipettes en verre, micropipettes	Volume
Centrifugeuse	Température, Vitesse angulaire, Temps
Balance de précision	Masse
Spectrophotomètre	Longueur d'onde
PH mètre	PH
Environnement	
Locaux	Température, Pression, Hygrométrie,

Figure 1 Matériels et grandeurs concernées

3/ Définition des écarts d'audit

Lors de l'audit, l'évaluateur va vérifier que les dispositions techniques et organisationnelles établies et mises en œuvre pour assurer la qualité des prestations sont conformes aux exigences d'accréditation et réglementaires et qu'elles sont appliquées; le rapport d'audit comprend des points forts, des points sensibles, des écarts d'audits; les points sensibles correspondent à une situation qui est conforme aux exigences mais qui paraît fragile et pourrait, et peut en cas de dérive, conduire à un écart.

Un écart est défini comme la différence entre une situation attendue et une situation observée, dans le cadre de l'examen de la prise en compte des exigences d'accréditation.

Un écart peut mettre en évidence :

- le non-respect d'une exigence.
Exemple : la balance n°2 utilisée pour la pesée des réactifs n'a pas été étalonnée ou vérifiée avant mise en service et ne fait l'objet d'opérations de suivi.

- un traitement incomplet ou inefficace du risque justifiant l'exigence.
Exemple : Le programme d'étalonnage du laboratoire ne prend pas en compte tous les instruments jugés critiques.

- une description insuffisante des pratiques pour répondre à une exigence donnée, qui ne permet pas de donner l'assurance que les actions mises en place sont uniformément appliquées, pérennes et/ou traçables.
Exemple : Les critères d'habilitation du responsable métrologie ne sont pas définis.

Les écarts peuvent être critiques ou pas ; les écarts critiques mettent en cause la fiabilité des résultats ou l'aptitude du système de management à maintenir le niveau de qualité des examens.

L'écart peut avoir un effet avéré et quantifiable par l'évaluateur, ou peut présenter un risque théorique fort que le laboratoire doit évaluer en pratique et prendre en compte pour confirmer la qualité de ses résultats. Un écart critique peut être d'ordre technique ou organisationnel.

4/Organisation de la métrologie ; définition des besoins

Lors de l'audit, l'évaluateur va vérifier la maitrise des données métrologiques sur les phases pré-per-post analytiques. La métrologie mise en oeuvre est définie en fonction des besoins du laboratoire et des données de la veille réglementaire et scientifique.

Le laboratoire doit définir en fonction de ses besoins :
- les limites acceptables en se référant aux exigences réglementaires,
- les plages de température utilisées en se référant aux exigences fournisseurs fiches techniques réactifs, guide automate.
- les équipements et les grandeurs à surveiller et à quelle fréquence: une analyse de risque est possible en fonction des pratiques et des équipements utilisés. Différentes publications, recommandations, guides techniques peuvent être utilisés.

Norme EN ISO 15189 -[2], Norme ISO CEI 17025-[1] Norme EN ISO 22870-[6],
Référentiel d'accréditation COFRAC SH REF 02-[5], LAB REF 02-[3].
Recommandations des fournisseurs (fiches techniques réactifs, guides automates...)
Publications des instances (OMS, HAS…)
Recommandations des sociétés professionnelles (GEHT, SFBC...)
Guide Technique COFRAC SH GTA01-[4],
Guide du Collège Français de Métrologie

Figure 2. Les documents de référence

5/ Organisation de la métrologie; les différentes phases

Lors de l'audit, l'évaluateur va vérifier également les différentes phases de mise en place de la métrologie au sein du laboratoire.

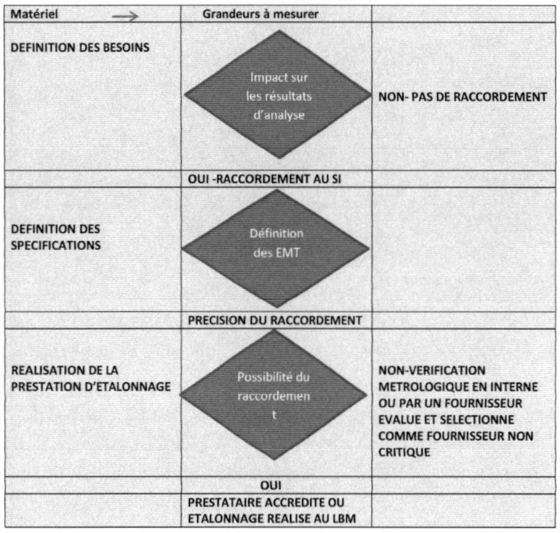

Figure 3 Les différentes phases d'organisation de la métrologie dans un LBM

5/ Les principaux écarts enregistrés

Le recensement des écarts enregistrés concernant les processus de mesure pendant les différents audits internes et visites d'évaluation d'accréditation est réalisé avec la méthode 5M qui sert à rechercher et à représenter de manière synthétique les différentes causes d'un problème.

Egalement appelée méthode Ishikawa, elle permet de rechercher l'ensemble des « causes possibles » en les classant dans les 5 familles suivantes.

1/ Matière : les différents consommables utilisés, matières premières…
2/ Milieu : le lieu de travail, son aspect, son organisation physique…
3/Méthodes : les procédures, le flux d'information…
4/ Matériel : les équipements, machines, outillages, pièces de rechange…
5/Main d'œuvre : les ressources humaines, les qualifications du personnel

1/ MATIERE	Mesurande mal défini
	Matériaux de référence non suivis (pas de périodicité d'étalonnage des poids étalon définie)
	Absence de politique concernant les déclarations de conformité ; absence de comparaison des valeurs d'étalonnage obtenues aux EMT ou aux spécifications définies
2/ MILIEU	Défaut de stockage du matériel dans des locaux appropriés (température, hygrométrie, poussières)
	Les relevés de températures effectués dans les enceintes thermiques ont dépassé les spécifications du laboratoire sans qu'aucune étude d'impact ne soit réalisée ni fiche d'anomalie enregistrée.
	Absence de prise en compte des grandeurs d'influence lié à l'environnement lors des étalonnages et calcul d'incertitude.
	Protection inadéquate du matériel lors des déplacements et défaut de traçabilité.
	Absence de dispositions prises par le laboratoire pour s'assurer que le transport du matériel (micropipettes) est sécurisé et absence de contrôle effectué à la réception de celui-ci.

3/ METHODE	Mode opératoire incomplet, Absence de dispositions concernant la réalisation des mesures, l'étalonnage, le passage des CIQ (exemple d'un PH mètre)
	Absence de planning de contrôle métrologique des équipements de mesure Périodicité de contrôle non définie.
	Conditions d'étalonnage et ou de vérification insuffisamment définies : Les opérations préliminaires (nettoyage, mise en température, zéro) ne sont pas précisées ; Appareil étalonné sur une gamme de mesure pas utilisée en pratique Absence de certificats d'étalonnage Absence d'étalonnage du matériel défini comme critique par le LBM.
	Vérification : pas de comparaison des résultats d'un étalonnage aux EMT Points de vérification non représentatifs de l'étendue de mesure
	Défaut de qualification et de suivi métrologique des enceintes thermiques Les cartographies n'enregistrent pas un cycle complet de fonctionnement de l'enceinte thermique.

3/ METHODE	Traçabilité du raccordement métrologique incomplète. Le calcul d'incertitude d'étalonnage ne tient pas compte des facteurs liés à la chaine de mesure et à la variabilité du milieu (homogénéité, stabilité).
	Défaut de traçabilité documentaire prouvant le raccordement.
	Absence de veille réglementaire et scientifique
	Absence de cahier des charges concernant les prestations métrologiques externalisées Evaluation des sous- traitants incomplète La prestation de sous traitance ne correspond pas aux besoins définis par le laboratoire. Le prestataire d'étalonnage n'est pas accrédité pour la prestation réalisée. Pas d'enregistrement de non-conforrmité ou de dérogation alors que la validité de l'étalonnage a expiré.

4/MATERIEL	Logiciel de suivi des températures: absence de maîtrise du paramétrage Le paramétrage des limites de contrôle ne tient pas compte des incertitudes des sondes.
	Performances de l'appareil utilisé (PH mètre) non documentées
	Utilisation d'un appareil comme référence non documentée
	Réception d'un appareil : éléments manquants : fiche de vie, identification, introduction dans l'inventaire, confirmation métrologique avant mise en service, marquage de confirmation métrologique
	Appareil remis en service sans contrôle métrologique
	Appareil interchangé : appareil de prêt mis en service, sans contrôle métrologique de ce dernier.
5/ MAIN D OEUVRE	Habilitation du personnel et maintien d'habilitation non démontrés
	Responsabilités concernant la gestion de la métrologie indéfinies
	Absence de prérequis pour assurer le poste de métrologue
	Les suppléances au poste de métrologue ne sont pas définies. Habilitation du suppléant non enregistrée.

6/ Interpréter un résultat d'audit

Vous venez de recevoir le rapport d'audit interne ou d'évaluation d'accréditation dont une partie concerne la métrologie. Il contient des points forts, des points faibles, des écarts critiques ou non critiques. Il est important de traiter en priorité les fiches d'écarts critiques:

1/Analyse de l'étendue de l'écart (antériorités - prestations et clients) ; le laboratoire doit analyser systématiquement l'impact de la non-conformité:
- le risque, c'est-à-dire évaluer le risque éventuel sur le résultat de la mesure métrologique et son impact sur les résultats d'examens antérieurs et ceux à venir
- l'étendue de la NC : est-ce que cela concerne un ou plusieurs instruments de même nature ou de natures différentes, un site ou plusieurs sites, d'autres domaines de mesure .
-les causes à analyser selon les règles des 5 pourquoi
-la récurrence de la non-conformité, la fréquence d'apparition de la NC dans les mois précédents.

2/Mise en place d'un plan d'actions adapté.

Le plan d'action réunit l'ensemble actions curatives et des actions correctives planifiées pour traiter un écart. Ces actions sont définies dans des délais convenus, les responsables des actions sont nommés et informés, les ressources nécessaires débloquées. Les moyens sont mis en place au laboratoire pour vérifier en interne l'efficacité de ces actions et pour éviter la reproduction de la non-conformité.
L'évaluateur se prononce alors sur la pertinence des actions et les délais annoncés pour maîtriser la situation.

3/ Apport de preuves aux évaluateurs

Les preuves doivent permettre de montrer la correction de l'écart et la capacité du laboratoire à éviter sa reproduction. L'évaluateur examinera les preuves d'actions jointes et appréciera si elles sont suffisantes pour conclure à la maîtrise de la situation d'écart. L'évaluateur tient notamment compte de la criticité (risque) liée à l'écart mais aussi en la confiance acquise lors de l'audit. Ces preuves sont obligatoires dans le cas d'un écart critique dans des délais définis.

7/ Conclusion

La fonction métrologie et le processus métrologie ont un rôle et un positionnement important au sein des LBM[7]; l'audit du processus métrologie doit être basé sur les risques et la performance sans oublier la conformité aux référentiels externes et aux dispositions interne du laboratoire.
La méthode d'audit ORRASA© basée sur l'efficience paraît tout à fait appropriée pour réaliser les audits internes et se préparer ainsi aux évaluations d'accréditation.

8/Références

[1] EN ISO/CEI 17025, Exigences générales concernant la compétence des laboratoires d'étalonnage et d'essais, septembre 2005.

[2] EN ISO 15189, Laboratoires de biologie médicale. Exigences particulières concernant la qualité et la compétence, Décembre 2012

[3] Cofrac - LAB REF 02- rév10-12/2015- Exigences pour l'accréditation des laboratoires selon la norme EN ISO 17025.

[4] Cofrac - SH GTA 01-rév 01-04/15 - Guide technique d'accréditation en biologie médicale-

[5] Cofrac - SH REF 02- rév 04-10/2013- Recueil d'exigences spécifiques pour l'accréditation des

laboratoires de biologie médicale selon la norme EN ISO 15189 :2012

[6].Norme ISO 22870 :2006-Analyses de biologie délocalisées (ADBD)-Exigences concernant la qualité et la compétence.

[7] ISO 10012:2003, Systèmes de management de la mesure - Exigences pour les processus et les équipements de mesure.

La comparaison inter-instruments

Pascal COQUET[1], Jean-Michel POU[2]

1 LA Métrologie, 271 bd de la Paix, 64000 Pau, France
2 Delta Mu, 48 rue de Sarliève, 63800 Cournon d'Auvergne, France

Received:

Résumé: Inspirée des comparaisons inter-laboratoires, la comparaison inter-instruments (C2I) permet, en faisant mesurer le même objet à un ensemble d'instruments de même type, de déterminer si l'un d'eux (ou plusieurs) est statistiquement différent. La méthode repose sur des tests d'égalité de populations et de détection de valeurs aberrantes. Idéalement, les instruments comparés constituent le seul facteur variable, la méthode, les conditions ambiantes et l'opérateur demeurant, si possible, identiques.

Keywords: Raccordement, traçabilité, étalonnage

1. Présentation

Son application la plus évidente est la surveillance de dérive d'instruments entre deux confirmations métrologiques ; mais son potentiel est nettement plus élevé : selon la manière dont elle est mise en œuvre, elle peut répondre à certains cas de raccordements difficiles, lever un doute sur un instrument ou encore optimiser les périodicités d'étalonnage.

1.1. Détection de dérive

Comparer un lot d'instruments permet de détecter celui ou ceux qui sont statistiquement différents. Si ces instruments n'ont pas été détectés lors de la précédente confirmation (étalonnage, C2I...), c'est qu'ils ont probablement dérivé.

1.2. Levée de doute

Si un instrument est mis en doute lors d'un mesurage, la C2I peut, en l'absence d'étalon, confirmer ou infirmer ce doute.

Note : Dans ce cadre, la C2I est déjà souvent pratiquée, au moins en « bilatéral » (Un instrument « contre » un autre) sans porter ce nom ...

1.3. Optimisation de la périodicité

Le fait de réaliser des C2I sur une famille d'instruments permet d'optimiser leur périodicité d'étalonnage d'une manière inédite : tant que les instruments, puisqu'ils ont tous été étalonnés au moins une fois (au minimum à la mise en service), ne sont pas statistiquement différents entre eux, on peut légitimement penser que leur raccordement n'est pas remis en question. La C2I peut alors devenir un outil d'optimisation d'une périodicité devenue conditionnelle : on peut ne recourir à l'étalonnage qu'en cas de détection lors d'une C2I, c'est-à-dire seulement lorsqu'il y a un doute, plutôt que de le faire comme aujourd'hui, arbitrairement.

Note : Il faut évidemment, dans ce cas, être en mesure de prouver que tous les instruments ne risquent pas de dériver de la même quantité, dans le même sens. Ce cas est peu probable mais doit être considéré.

1.4. Etalonnage dans les cas difficiles

Lorsque l'étalonnage « sur site » classique présente des difficultés de mise en œuvre, la C2I peut apporter une réponse adaptée au raccordement de chaînes de mesure difficilement démontables ou intégrées au process.

Il est par exemple possible de comparer des thermomètres montés sur des lignes différentes à des températures proches. Dans ce cas précis, l'objet à mesurer (milieu de comparaison) n'étant pas commun, un thermomètre supplémentaire est nécessaire ; la comparaison porte alors sur les écarts mesurés entre celui-ci et chacun des thermomètres en ligne.

2. La sélection des participants

Il est évident que cette méthode ne s'appliquera pas à tous les types d'instruments. Il conviendra en cas de doute, d'intégrer un étalon dans la première comparaison. De plus, la méthode repose sur une hypothèse forte : un lot d'instruments n'a statistiquement aucune raison de dériver dans le même sens et dans la même proportion durant le même intervalle de temps.

La sélection des instruments participant à la comparaison doit être réalisée avec le plus grand soin de manière à respecter cette hypothèse : on évitera par exemple de ne choisir que des instruments issus du même lot de fabrication car ils auraient précisément des chances de porter en eux les mêmes défauts, voire de dériver de manière quelque peu synchronisée. Cette étape est primordiale ; le non respect de l'hypothèse de départ peut mener à des décisions préjudiciables sur le plan du management de qualité.

3. Les mesures

Une fois la sélection réalisée, les mesures doivent être faites. Dans le cadre d'une C2I, on teste la fidélité de chaque instrument (sa capacité intrinsèque à reproduire la même mesure) et sa « justesse » (sa capacité à donner des valeurs proches de la réalité). De ce fait, il convient de réaliser plusieurs mesures de la même entité (la répétabilité du processus de mesure se mélange alors à la fidélité intrinsèque de l'instrument), avec tous les instruments.

A titre d'exemple, les tableaux et figures ci-dessous présentent les résultats d'une C2I menée sur un lot de balances de laboratoire d'échelon 0,1mg et de portée inférieure ou égale à 220g. Les objets de comparaison sont deux masses 50 et 100g (non raccordées).

Tableau 1 Mesure d'une masse de 50g

BAL001	BAL002	BAL003	BAL004	BAL005
49,9999	49,9994	50,0000	50,0000	50,0000
49,9999	49,9995	50,0001	50,0001	50,0001
49,9999	49,9995	50,0003	50,0001	50,0001
50,0000	49,9994	50,0002	50,0000	50,0001
49,9999	49,9995	50,0002	50,0000	50,0002

BAL006	BAL007	BAL008	BAL009
50,0004	49,9999	50,0002	50,0004
50,0003	50,0000	50,0002	50,0003
49,9999	50,0000	50,0000	50,0003
49,9997	49,9999	50,0002	50,0002
50,0004	49,9999	50,0002	50,0003

Tableau 2 Mesure d'une masse de 100g

BAL001	BAL002	BAL003	BAL004	BAL005
99,9999	99,9991	100,0002	100,0001	99,9999
99,9999	99,9990	100,0001	100,0000	99,9998
99,9999	99,9993	100,0002	100,0001	99,9999
99,9999	99,9992	100,0002	100,0001	99,9999
99,9998	99,9990	100,0002	100,0001	100,0000

BAL006	BAL007	BAL008	BAL009
100,0012	100,0000	100,0004	100,0003
100,0009	100,0000	100,0003	100,0002
100,0008	100,0001	100,0004	100,0002
100,0011	100,0000	100,0003	100,0003
100,0008	100,0000	100,0004	100,0001

4. Les tests

Si le nombre d'instruments est suffisant, il convient de commencer par un test de normalité. Qu'il soit graphique ou numérique, le test du caractère aléatoire gaussien de la distribution constitue un indicateur de la pertinence de la sélection.

Dans notre exemple, l'hypothèse de distribution gaussienne n'est pas évidente :

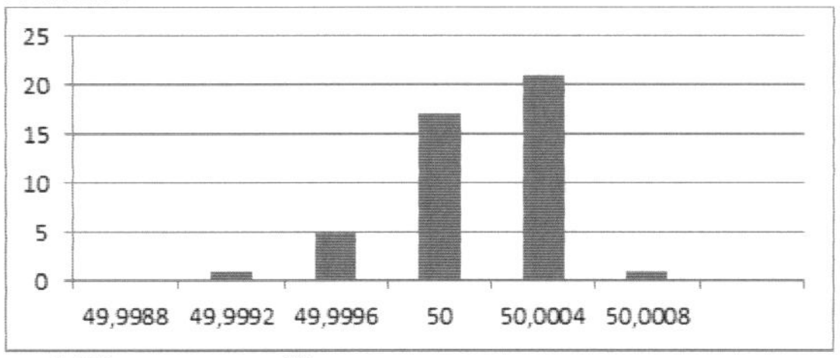

Figure 1 Histogramme 50g

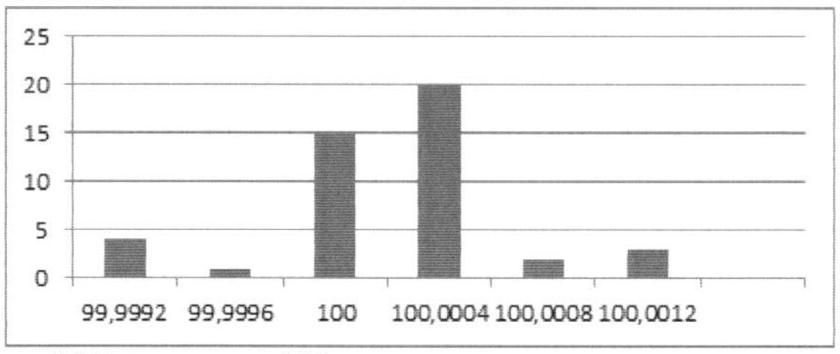

Figure 2 Histogramme 100g

Il est aussi possible de considérer la répartition des écarts moyens de chaque instrument par rapport à la moyenne générale pour évaluer la distribution aléatoire du lot :

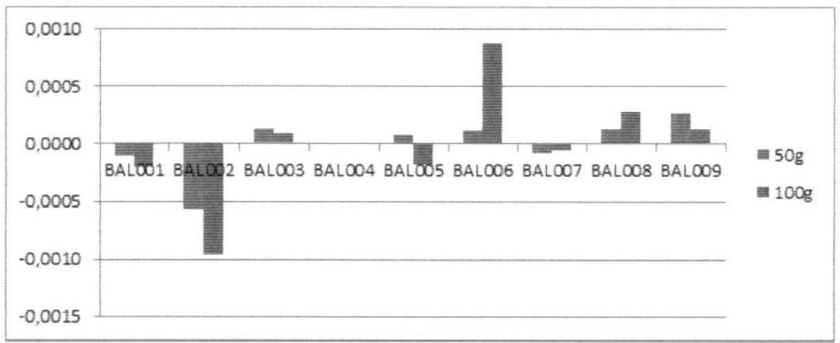

Figure 3 Répartition des écarts

La figure 3 met en évidence un déséquilibre parmi les barres négatives : la balance 002 représente à elle seule la quasi-totalité de l'écart négatif, tirant la moyenne générale vers le bas.

Au plus simple, un test aux écarts normalisés permet de détecter une valeur aberrante, c'est-à-dire ici un instrument statistiquement différent.

Note : le caractère gaussien de la population permet de donner un niveau de performance à ce test.

Tableau 3 Test aux écarts normalisés (50g)

	BAL001	BAL002	BAL003	BAL004
Moyenne	49,9999	49,9995	50,0002	50,0000
SCE	8,00E-09	1,20E-08	5,20E-08	1,20E-08
Ecart N	-0,43	-2,33	0,56	0,06

BAL005	BAL006	BAL007	BAL008	BAL009
50,0001	50,0001	49,9999	50,0002	50,0003
2,00E-08	4,12E-07	1,20E-08	3,20E-08	2,00E-08
0,31	0,48	-0,35	0,56	1,14

Tableau 4 Test aux écarts normalisés (100g)

	BAL001	BAL002	BAL003	BAL004
Moyenne	99,9999	99,9991	100,0002	100,0001
SCE	8,00E-09	6,80E-08	8,00E-09	8,00E-09
Ecart norm	-0,41	-1,98	0,21	0,00

BAL005	BAL006	BAL007	BAL008	BAL009
99,9999	100,0010	100,0000	100,0004	100,0002
2,00E-08	1,32E-07	8,00E-09	1,20E-08	2,80E-08
-0,37	1,82	-0,12	0,58	0,29

Note : La ligne « SCE » (Somme des Carrés des Ecarts) des tableaux 3 et 4 sera utilisée lors du test de Cochran afin de déterminer la variance la plus élevée.

La normalité de la distribution n'ayant pas été démontrée précédemment, il convient de considérer le résultat de ce test avec précaution. Cependant, il confirme l'interprétation de la figure 3 en détectant la balance 002. Il semble donc raisonnable d'écarter cet instrument.

Lorsqu'un instrument est écarté, il convient de refaire les calculs des tests avec les instruments restants :

Tableau 5 Second test aux écarts normalisés (50g)

	BAL001	BAL003	BAL004	BAL005
Moyenne	49,9999	50,0002	50,0000	50,0001
SCE	8,00E-09	5,20E-08	1,20E-08	2,00E-08
Ecart N	-1,39	0,52	-0,44	0,04

	BAL006	BAL007	BAL008	BAL009
Moyenne	50,0001	49,9999	50,0002	50,0003
SCE	4,12E-07	1,20E-08	3,20E-08	2,00E-08
Ecart N	0,36	-1,24	0,52	1,63

Tableau 6 Second test aux écarts normalisés (100g)

	BAL001	BAL003	BAL004	BAL005
Moyenne	99,9999	100,0002	100,0001	99,9999
SCE	8,00E-09	8,00E-09	8,00E-09	2,00E-08
Ecart N	-0,92	-0,06	-0,35	-0,86

	BAL006	BAL007	BAL008	BAL009
Moyenne	100,0010	100,0000	100,0004	100,0002
SCE	1,32E-07	8,00E-09	1,20E-08	2,80E-08
Ecart N	2,19	-0,52	0,46	0,06

Le second test aux écarts normalisés de notre exemple détecte la balance 006 sur un point seulement ; l'instrument est conservé pour les tests suivants.

Afin d'évaluer l'égalité des variances, il est possible d'utiliser un test de Cochran dont le principe est de tester la variance la plus élevée du lot. Le fait de ne pas tester la plus faible (même si elle est la plus éloignée de la moyenne) est logique : il serait injuste d'incriminer un instrument pour cause d'excellente répétabilité. En revanche, il faut souligner qu'un instrument présentant une variance trop élevée relativement au groupe ne constitue pas forcément une anomalie. En effet, un tel instrument est à écarter mais il peut y avoir deux raisons à cela : soit il s'est effectivement dégradé en terme de fidélité, soit il est différent de par sa technologie, sa gamme (au sens de la qualité) et n'a pas sa place dans cette comparaison. Ce test est donc l'occasion de réévaluer la pertinence de la sélection.

Dans notre exemple, c'est la variance de la balance 006 qui est testée :

Tableau 7 Premier test de Cochran

50g	100g	Ccrit5%
0,725	0,589	0,391

La valeur critique à 5% est dépassée sur les deux points, confirmant la détection du test précédent. La balance est écartée et le test renouvelé :

Tableau 8 Second test de Cochran

50g	100g	Ccrit5%
0,333	0,304	0,431

Le test est concluant avec les 7 balances restantes.

Note : le test de Cochran suppose que toutes les variances ont le même nombre de degrés de liberté ce qui signifie qu'il y a le même nombre de répétitions de mesure par instrument.

Le test de Fisher constitue une alternative possible au test de Cochran ; n'imposant pas de conditions quant au nombre de degrés de liberté, il nécessite en revanche de comparer les variances deux à deux.

Un test de Grubbs peut être utilisé pour comparer les moyennes. Cette comparaison de moyenne permet de vérifier qu'un instrument ne s'éloigne pas des autres instruments participant. Dans ce cas en effet, cela signifierait que ledit instrument a dérivé. Le principe étant de tester la valeur la plus éloignée de la moyenne générale en tenant compte de toutes les variances, il convient de réaliser ce test après celui de Cochran pour identifier préalablement les instruments ayant une dispersion trop importante.

Appliqué à notre exemple, le test de Grubbs donne les résultats suivants :

Tableau 9 Test de Grubbs

50g	100g	Gcrit
1,577	1,537	2,020

Les 7 balances passent ce dernier test, nous permettant de conclure que ces instruments ne sont pas statistiquement différents.

Evidemment, la C2I peut porter sur des entités de valeurs nominales différentes, de façon à explorer une étendue de mesure, et pas uniquement un point de ladite étendue.

5. L'interprétation

A ce stade, il est convenu que si la sélection a été correctement réalisée, les instruments écartés devraient en principe faire l'objet d'un étalonnage, voire d'une maintenance.

Les instruments restant à l'issue des tests n'ayant eu, d'une part, aucune raison de dériver de la même manière (hypothèse de départ) et ayant été, d'autre part, étalonnés dans le passé, ne se sont pas « éparpillés » dans le temps du fait qu'ils ne sont pas statistiquement différents (résultat des tests). Leur raccordement est donc encore assuré au moment de la C2I.

En outre, si nous pouvons admettre que les instruments ayant passé les tests sont toujours raccordés, il devient possible de déterminer la variance liée à ce type d'instruments, variance qui peut alors être utilisée dans un calcul d'incertitude d'un processus qui met en œuvre un tel type de moyen. Cette variance, déterminée expérimentalement, semble plus pertinente qu'une évaluation de type B souvent calculée à partir des résultats d'étalonnage (Erreur maximale constatée) ou de vérification (Erreur Maximale Tolérée). Par ailleurs, il semblerait qu'on puisse régler en partie la question récurrente des « limites d'acceptation (E.M.T) ». En effet, une C2I permet de finalement de conclure quant à l'homogénéité d'une famille d'instruments, ce qui revient à dire que tous les instruments sont statistiquement identiques entre eux, donc « conformes ».Il serait évidemment curieux que l'entreprise ne se soit pas rendu compte que les moyens de mesure qu'elle utilise au quotidien ne sont pas adaptés à son besoin.

Ionizing radiation metrology applied to the medical monitoring of persons exposed to a risk of internal contamination.

Métrologie des rayonnements ionisants appliquée à la surveillance médicale des personnes exposées au risque de contamination interne

P. Gerasimo*, J. Y. Arriat**.

*Centre d'Expertise et d'inspection dans les domaines de la réalisation et de l'exploitation France 2 rue Ampère 93206 Saint Denis Cedex01France/
**Ascent Consulting 25 re de paris 92101 Clichy France

Abstract. When considering internal exposure, especially as for the occupational health care many possible causes of uncertainties are involved into the measurements. Those are different from any methodological ones. Our article aims at refining uncertainties estimation when performing dose calculation for internal dosimetry by1) Examining causes of uncertainties using mainly the diagram of Ichikawa, 2) Demonstrating they can be apprehended. We are looking at two main examples of measurement in the assessment of intake, of the workers of nuclear power plant to EDF :
- Whole body gamma counting, which is direct measurement of radionuclides of body content of radionuclides;
- The radiochemical analysis, which is the measurement of radionuclides excreted.

Résumé. Dans le cas d'une exposition interne, particulièrement en médecine du travail, les mesures de contamination interne sont pénalisées par de nombreuses causes d'incertitudes de mesure autres que méthodologiques. Notre communication a pour objet d'approfondir l'estimation des incertitudes lors du calcul de dose en dosimétrie interne : 1) en inventoriant les causes d'incertitudes au moyen de diagramme d'Ichikawa, 2) en montrant comment il est possible de les appréhender.Nous prendrons pour exemple les deux principales méthodes de mesure de la contamination interne, utilisées pour le suivi des travailleurs du nucléaire à EDF :
- l'anthroporadiamétrie, qui est la mesure directe des radionucléides présents dans le corps humain ;
- l'analyse radiochimique, qui est la mesure des radionucléides dans les excrétions.

Keywords: ionizing radiation, health, radionuclides, intakes, doses, measurements, uncertainties.
Mots clefs : rayonnements ionisants, santé, radionucléides, incorporation, dose, mesure, incertitudes.

1 Introduction

La radiotoxicologie se situe au carrefour de deux sciences la physique nucléaire et la toxicologie. La toxicologie est celle des radionucléides : ces derniers manifestent leurs effets toxiques par l'intermédiaire des rayonnements ionisants qu'ils émettent ; comme leurs homologues chimiques ils ont un devenir biologique particulier dans l'organisme qui explique pour quelle raison tel ou tel organe ou tissu est atteint préférentiellement ; enfin pour les éléments les plus lourds qui sont émetteurs alpha, il faut utiliser de la même façon que pour les toxiques chimiques, des méthodes de purification et d'isolement souvent délicates. Quant à la physique nucléaire, ses principes sont appliqués à la détection et à la mesure des rayonnements qui permettent d'identifier et de quantifier ces radionucléides, le phénomène physique fondamental étant constitué par l'interaction d'un rayonnement avec la matière sensible d'un détecteur, qu'il s'agisse d'un rayonnement particulaire, comme le rayonnement alpha (ou bêta) ou d'un rayonnement électromagnétique, comme le rayonnement gamma.

L'application pratique de la radiotoxicologie consiste en la surveillance des travailleurs exposés au risque de contamination. En milieu professionnel le risque de contaminations radioactives survient

* Correspondence: patrick.gerasimo@edf.fr

lors de l'emploi de substances contenant des radionucléides, ou bien à la suite d'un accident au cours d'un processus industriel nucléaire par exemple. On parle de contamination radioactive interne si les substances radioactives sont incorporées à l'organisme, après y avoir pénétré par différentes voies possibles : inhalation, ingestion, blessure, voie transcutanée. La prévention de la contamination interne ressemble à celle qui s'applique dans les industries de chimie classique, à la différence près que les masses de matière en jeu sont souvent infimes (de l'ordre ou inférieures au nanogramme ou picogramme) et que la sensibilité des méthodes de détection radioactive est de ce fait beaucoup plus performante. Le but final est de fournir une dose efficace équivalente qui exprime l'impact sur l'organisme humain des personnes exposées au risque de contamination radioactive interne dans l'exercice de leurs professions, cet impact étant la conséquence de l'action des rayonnements ionisants sur la matière vivante.

De l'une et l'autre science, la radiotoxicologie a hérité des méthodes de travail et notamment de la façon d'établir les incertitudes de mesure, de façon à avoir une indication quantitative sur la variabilité de ces résultats. Cette information est essentielle pour que ceux qui utilisent ces résultast puissent en estimer sa fiabilité, c'est à dire la probabilité de représenter la valeur vraie. Elle s'exprime sous la forme d'une étendue de valeurs dans laquelle se situe la valeur vraie de la grandeur mesurée Sans incertitude les résultats de mesure ne peuvent plus être comparés entre eux, ou à des valeurs de référence..

Il est important de faire la distinction entre erreur et incertitude. L'incertitude se rapporte au concept de doute, elle caractérise la dispersion des valeurs et à la forme d'un intervalle qui est établi avec un niveau de confiance défini (en général 95 %). L'erreur, quant à elle, est définie comme la différence entre les valeurs obtenues et la valeur vraie. Souvent les erreurs ne sont pas connues exactement et de ce fait ne peuvent pas servir à corriger le résultat final. Il en résulte que l'on a toujours intérêt à ce qu'elles restent négligeables. Il existe deux types d'erreur, les erreurs aléatoires et les erreurs systématiques.

Au travers de cet article, notre objectif est de présenter comment se fait l'évaluation des incertitudes en radiotoxicologie, au travers des deux principales techniques utilisées pour la surveillance des travailleurs exposés au risque de contamination interne.

- l'anthroporadiométrie qui consiste à mesurer les rayonnements gamma émis par une personne placée dans une enceinte comportant un système de détection corps entier de radioactivité gamma,
- L'analyse radiotoxicologique des excréta qui permet de mesurer les radionucléides émetteurs alpha notament dans les fèces

Pour estimer cette incertitude, notre approche consiste à estimer les différentes sources de variabilité en prenant chacune des étapes de la méthodologie utilisée, puis à appliquer la loi de propagation des incertitudes. C'est la démarche recommandée par le GUM (1995), nous la compléterons en évaluant la répétabilité et la reproductibilité. Le processus de radiotoxicologie ne se réduit pas à l'obtention d'un résultat de mesure, il se poursuit par le calcul de dose que nous présenterons de façon simplifiée pour indiquer les incertitudes qui pèsent sur cette détermination et montrer quel est son intérêt.

2 Matériels et méthodes

Anthroporadiométrie

L'anthroporadiométrie consiste à évaluer les radionucléides incorporés dans un organisme humain en détectant à l'extérieur du corps les rayonnements gamma (ou X) émis lors de leurs désintégrations. Le rayonnement gamma est facile à détecter, car il s'agit d'ondes électromagnétiques de même nature que la lumière. Il est capable de traverser les milieux matériels et en particulier le corps humain, d'où la possibilité de le détecter à l'extérieur du corps humain. Sa grande portée dans l'air (plusieurs centaines de mètres) lui permet d'atteindre sans difficulté un détecteur. Le terme, *portée,* correspond à la distance que ce rayonnement peut parcourir avant de perdre toute son énergie. L'anthroporadiométrie est également appelée mesure « in vivo », elle permet de quantifier directement l'activité contenue dans l'organisme (ou dans un organe en particulier).

L'utilisation en anthroporadiométrie de détecteur à scintillation constitué d'un cristal d'iodure de sodium activé par le thallium repose sur les travaux de Miller et Marinelli (1956, 1957).

Pour minimiser les interférences du bruit de fond, un blindage est placé de telle sorte qu'il fasse écran sur la surface sensible du détecteur. Dans ces conditions, l'appareil de type *Fastscan Canberra*® directement hérité de ces travaux, est spécifique des mesures de haute énergie (jusqu'à 3 MeV) et permet d'évaluer la dose interne des individus sur une partie ou sur l'ensemble du corps. De ce fait, il est classé dans la catégorie type 2) de la norme NF EN 61582.

L'appareil utilisé de type *Fastscan* est composé de 2 détecteurs NaI (TI) de grande dimension 7.6 x 12.7 x 40.6 cm (3 x 5 x 16 in.) NaI(Tl) detectors (iodure de sodium (NaI). La résolution est d'environ 8,5%. La limite de détection est de l'ordre de 150 Bq pour le cobalt 60. La figure 1 montre l'installation ATP : le sujet se positionne sur la ligne centrale. La chaîne de mesure comporte une alimentation haute tension, Les signaux émis par chacun des détecteurs passent par un amplificateur et sont mis en forme par un préamplificateur. Un codeur analogique numérique transforme l'amplitude du signal en un nombre proportionnel à l'énergie du rayonnement, puis les différents signaux sont classés par un analyseur multicanaux. Un logiciel d'exploitation démarre et arrête les mesures, visualise les spectres, réalise les analyses (identification des radionucléides et calcul d'activités).

Le résultat de l'analyse est un spectre de raies avec un numéro de canal en abscisse et un nombre d'impulsions (présentes dans chaque canal) en ordonnée. Ce spectre correspond à un histogramme représentant le nombre de photons mesurés, pendant un temps donné, en fonction de leur énergie. L'émission gamma apparaît sous la forme d'un pic. L'énergie du maximum du pic permet l'identification du radionucléide. Quant à la surface du pic (c'est-à-dire l'intégrale des impulsions trouvées dans le pic), elle permet de calculer l'activité du radionucléide.

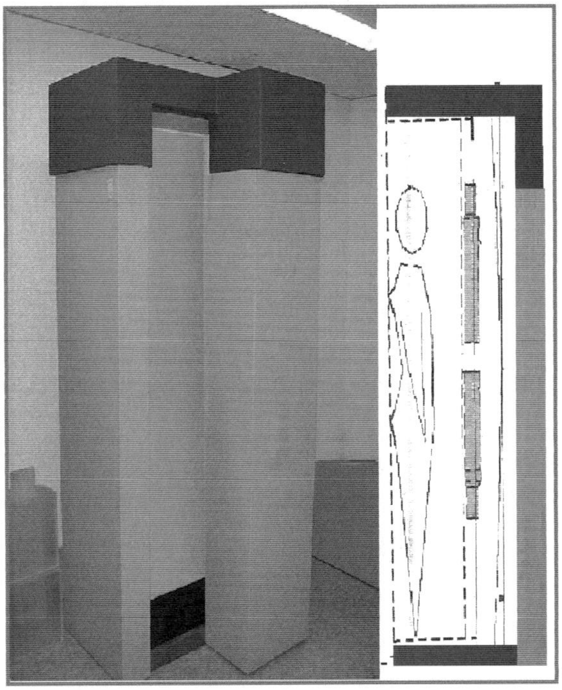

Fig. 1. Installation d'anthroporadiométrie montrant de façon schématique le positionnement du patient et l'emplacement des deux détecteurs.

Spectrométrie alpha

Le rayonnement alpha est un rayonnement particulaire, il a une faible portée. La distance que peut parcourir une particule alpha est faible : elle est de l'ordre du centimètre dans l'air. C'est la raison pour laquelle, les radionucléides émetteurs alpha, lorsqu'ils ont été incorporés ne peuvent pas être mesurés directement par anthroporadiométrie, mais indirectement dans les excréta. L'incorporation est calculée grâce à des modèles qui décrivent le devenir biologique et l'excrétion des radionucléides. Autre conséquence de cette faible portée : les prélèvements doivent subir un traitement chimique avant d'être mesuré en spectrométrie alpha, pour les débarrasser de tous les composants organiques susceptibles d'absorber le rayonnement. Ce traitement est long (environ une semaine) et nécessite un savoir-faire important. Dans le cas, par exemple, d'un prélèvement de fèces. L'analyse comporte trois temps principaux : l'ajout de traceur, la séparation chimique et l'analyse spectrométrique.

1) Ajout de traceur

Les traitements de purification n'ont pas un rendement de 100 %. Il varie habituellement entre 25 et 95 % en fonction de la charge minérale et organique de l'échantillon. Il en résulte qu'une partie plus ou moins grande du radionucléide recherché se trouve perdue. Pour déterminer le rendement, une quantité connue d'un traceur est ajoutée à l'échantillon lors de la mise en solution du prélèvement après obtention de cendres par passage au four à 700°C. Le traceur est un isotope du radionucléide recherché. Du fait qu'il a les mêmes propriétés, il se comporte chimiquement de la même manière. C'est ainsi que le pourcentage de traceur perdu est égal au pourcentage d'échantillon perdue.

2) Séparation chimique

Il s'agit d'une étape essentielle qui détermine la bonne qualité d'une mesure de spectrométrie alpha.. Il faut séparer chimiquement le radionucléide recherché si l'on veut pouvoir le mesurer de façon satisfaisante. Les techniques de séparation impliquent des chromatographies par échange d'ions ou par extraction, avec bien souvent une combinaison des deux. Cette purification a deux objectifs : 1) éliminer les composants organiques qui atténuent l'énergie des rayonnements alpha, rendant impossible toute identification, 2) éliminer également les radionucléides émetteurs alpha naturels qui vont interférer avec le rayonnement du radionucléide recherché.

Le dépôt sur support intervient à la fin du traitement. Il doit être le plus fin, le plus uniforme et le plus stable possible, afin de se laisser traverser par le rayonnement alpha. Il existe deux méthodes de dépôt par électrodéposition et par précipitation. Bien que la première fournit des dépôts d'excellente qualité, elle dure une à deux heures. Cet inconvénient fait qu'il lui est souvent préféré la méthode par précipitation lorsque la production en analyses est élevée.

3) Spectrométrie alpha

Les émissions alpha des radionucléides étant formées de particules alpha lentes et lourdes, facilement arrêtées par l'air lui même. Il faut les mesurer dans le vide. Ainsi elles ont plus de chance d'atteindre la surface sensible du détecteur. Un type de détecteur très utilisé en spectrométrie alpha est représenté par des semi conducteur au silicium de type PIPS.

Les détecteur *silicium plans implantés passivés* (Passivated Implanted Planar Silicon PIPS Canberra) sont parmi les plus modernes: ils sont fabriquées par le ***procédé planaire*** une jonction P N type P est réalisée par diffusion d`atomes d`impuretés dans le cristal. Une particule ionisante à l'origine des signaux permettant de construire un spectre en amplitude.

Si nous prenons l'exemple du plutonium 238, l'énergie avec laquelle est émise la particule alpha est de 5499 keV, elle est très proche de celle de l'américium 241 (5486 keV). L'identification du radionucléide, ainsi que sa quantification, sont effectuées par la reconnaissance de son énergie d'émission.

Comme en anthroporadiométrie, le signal en spectrométrie alpha apparaît sous la forme d'un pic dont le maximum est représenté par l'énergie d'émission. Si la résolution d'un pic (c'est à dire sa largeur à mi hauteur) est de l'ordre de 100 keV en anthroporadiométrie NaI(Tl), elle n'est plus que de 20 keV en spectrométrie alpha. à la condition qu'il n'y ait pas d'impuretés dans la préparation à mesurer. En spectrométrie alpha, le plutonium et l'américium ne sont séparés que par 13 keV les meilleurs détecteurs ne peuvent pas distinguer des pics séparer de plus de 17 keV. S'il n'y avait pas de séparation chimique, il serait impossible de les distinguer.

3 Résultats et discussion

L'incertitude de mesure permet de quantifier la confiance que l'on peut accorder à un résultat. Nos estimations concernent deux examens important en radiotoxicologie : l'anthroporadiométrie et l'analyse par spectrométrie alpha.

3.1. Anthroporadiométrie

Comme le montre le diagramme d'Ichikawa, Les facteurs influençant la mesure sont divers (figure 2).

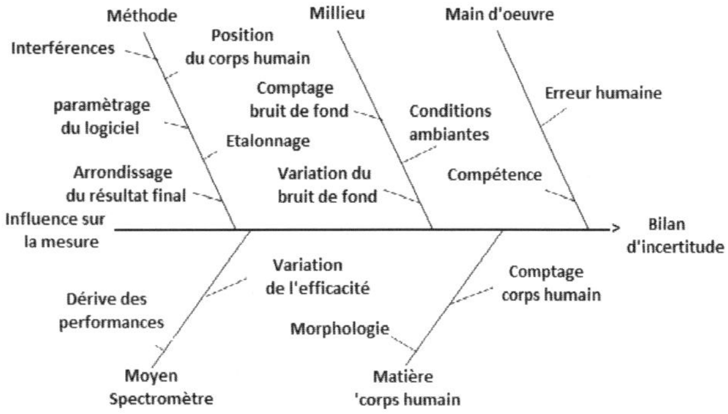

Fig. 2. Diagramme d'Ichikawa

Inventaires des facteurs de variabilité

Cet inventaire est déduit du diagramme d'Ichikawa en figure 2.

a) Facteurs relatifs au corps humain

Statistique de comptage du corps humains

Les désintégrations radioactives du radionucléide recherché sont transformées en impulsions après détection. La probabilité de mesurer x désintégrations pendant un temps t est donnée en pratique par une loi de Gauss où m est la valeur moyenne et σ l'écart-type qui est égal à √m. L'activité se calcule de la façon suivante:

$$A = \frac{S}{\rho_e . i_e . t} . f_{ie}(k_1.k_2...)$$

A : activité en becquerels du radionucléide recherché mesuré à l'énergie e,

S : surface nette du pic (en nombre d'impulsions), : $S = S_T - S_o$ avec S_T, surface totale du pic et S_o surface du fond continu sous le pic

i : probabilité d'émission photonique du radionucléide recherché à l'énergie e,

t : temps de mesure en secondes,

$f_{ie}(k_1.k_2...)$: représente l'ensemble des paramètres correctifs lies aux différences de matrice et de géométrie entre le corps entier à mesurer et l'étalon

L'incertitude type u découle de la formule de calcul d'activité, elle est de la forme :

$$u_A/A = \sqrt{\left[\frac{u_S}{S}\right]^2 + \left[\frac{u_\rho}{\rho}\right]^2 + \left[\frac{u_{ie}}{i_e}\right]^2 + \left[\frac{u_{fe}(k1.k2...)}{u_{fe}(k1.k2...)}\right]^2}$$

avec : $$u_S/S = \frac{\sqrt{S_T + S_o}}{(S_T - S_o)}$$

En principe, plus le temps de mesure est long, plus le nombre de désintégration est grand et plus le rapport u_s/S diminue, avec comme conséquence une amélioration de la précisions. En principe, sauf en cas d'incident, on utilise peu cette possibilité et tous les examens sont standardisés pour un temps de 60 secondes.

Morphologie

Chaque patient possède une morphologie particulière qui se traduit par un volume géométrique et un poids différent. La norme S92501 nous indique qu'il faut tenir compte du fait que les patients sont différents des caractéristiques de l'étalon anthropomorphe IGOR de 70 kg qui dans nos conditions opératoires repésente l'homme standard (ICRP 23 1975). Nous avons estimé cette incertitude à 25%.

Ce pourcentage est légèrement supérieur à celui donné par la Norme S92501 (2013). Il a été établi à partir des mesures de potassium effectuées entre 1956 et 1961à Los Alamos sur 2960 sujets âgés de 20 et 79 ans (Anderson 1963) en prenant le rapport de la variation maximale du potassium par rapport au potassium de l'homme standard de 70kg, soit 140 g (ICRP 1975), ce rapport étant exprimé en pourcentage. Les quantités de potassium étant corrélées au poids et à la stature de l'individu, cette variation par rapport à l'homme standard représente l'incertitude sur la morphologie.

b) Facteurs relatifs au milieu

Statistique de comptage du bruit de fond

Même en l'absence de corps humain, le spectromètre d'anthroporadiométrie fournit un signal. Ce dernier possède deux composantes une partie électronique et une partie environnementale que nous étudions dans ce paragraphe.

Lorsque le bruit de fond varie au-delà de certaines limites, les résultats peuvent être modifiés : si le bruit de fond est trop bas, comme il est retranché de la mesure, on commet une erreur par excès. S'il est trop élevé, on risque de ne plus pouvoir détecter les activités les plus faibles. Cette variabilité peut être exprimée par le seuil de décision (SD), il représente la limite maximale au-delà de laquelle on considère que l'activité détectée est vraie et significativement différente du bruit de fond :
Les seuils de décision mesurés sur une personne non exposé sont légèrement plus élevé que ceux mesurés sur le bruit de fond (installation vide), cela est du à la présence d'un fond Compton plus élevé dans le cas d'une personne non exposé, conséquence de la présence d'ans l'organisme de radionucléides naturels (potassium 40, radium 226 et descendants), d'où la pratique des examens d'anthroporadiométrie sans déduction du bruit de fond, le calcul d'activité s'effectuant à partir du pic net Tableau I.

Mesure cellule vide		
SD	*Co-60*	*Cs-137*
1	*213*	*261*
2	*219*	*240*
3	198	264
Moyenne	**210**	**255**
Ecart-type	**11**	**13**
Mesure d'une personne non exposée		
SD	**Co-60**	**Cs-137**
1	**237**	**270**
2	**240**	**267**
3	**240**	**282**
Moyenne	**240**	**273**
Ecart-type	**11**	**8**

Tableau I. Seuil de décision en impulsions pour un examen d'anthroporadiométrie de 1 minute, lors d'une mesure cellule vide et lors d'une mesure d'une personne non exposée.

Soit S la surface nette du pic d'un radionucléide à rechercher, Lorsque S est très petit devant So, surface du fond continu (cas du radionucléide absent ou en très petite activité), le seuil de décision a pour expression :

$$SD = 4{,}4.\sqrt{\frac{R_{ie}.B_c}{t}}.\frac{1}{i_e.\rho}.f(k1.k2...)$$

Avec SD : seuil de décision,
R_{ie} : résolution à mi hauteur du pic étudié exprimé en keV,
B_c : valeur moyenne du fond continu sur l'intervalle I = 2,52 R_{ie} (centré sur l'énergie d'émission du radionucléide recherché) en impulsions keV^{-1}.

Cette formule montre que la résolution des pics majore le seuil de décision. Plus la résolution est élevée, plus il sera difficile d'avoir un résultat d'activité qui dépasse le seuil de décision et l'on risque de conclure à tard qu'il n'y a pas d'activité pour le radionucléide recherché.

Avec une aire sous le pic de l'ordre de 70 impulsions, un rendement variant entre 0,70 et 1,15 %, le seuil de décision exprimé en activité varie entre 200 et 250 Bq, pour des énergies comprises entre 500 et 1000 Bq. Ces valeurs rapportées à l'énergie représentent les performances optimales de l'installation en matière de détection. .

Conditions ambiantes
Les variations de température peuvent occasionner un décalage en énergie du spectre. Pour éviter ce phénomène, un intervalle de température de 15 °C à 28 °C est préconisé. En cas de dépassement de ces bornes, il faut effectuer un recalage ponctuel en énergie par modification du gain de l'électronique des détecteurs.
Le radon et ses descendants peuvent être à l'origine d'interférence, leur impact est réduit, si les conditions ambiantes soient bien maîtrisées. Par exemple, L'humidité peut jouer un rôle, en effet le radon après son émanation du sol et des murs se dilue d'autant plus facilement dans l'air que celui-ci est humide. Le contrôle de l'humidité permet de réguler le bruit de fond.

c) Facteurs relatifs à la méthode

Temps de comptage
La plupart des mesures avec des détecteurs de type scintillateur NaI(Tl)) font intervenir des résolutions faibles (comparés à celle des détecteurs germanium) qui nécessite seulement 10 et 12 bits (1024 canaux) avec des fréquences d'échantillonnage de l'ordre de la dizaine de MHz. En pratique un numériseur VENUS® d'ITECH instrument associé à un détecteur NaI(Tl) possède une période d'échantillonnage d'au minimum 20 MHz, ce qui nous donne une précision de 0,05 µs pour la mesure du temps actif. La mesure durant 60 secondes, l'incertitude est négligeable.

Activité de la source d'étalonnage
Elle est égale à 2,5 % (certificat d'étalonnage n° 415/2000 établi par la Mendelev Institute for Metrology Russia, St. Petersburg, 190005 Moskovsky pr., 19).

Incertitude sur la décroissance de l'activité de la source d'étalonnage
L'incertitude sur la décroissance radioactive est de l'ordre de 0,01 % pour le cobalt 60, de l'ordre de 0,003 % pour le césium 137. Le logiciel calcule automatiquement l'activité actualisée à la date d'utilisation. L'incertitude sur le calcul de cette décroissance peut-être considéré comme négligeable.

Arrondissage
L'erreur d'arrondissage est inférieure au 1/10ème de l'incertitude (LNHB 2004). Elle s'évalue de la façon suivante : si le premier

chiffre significatif de l'incertitude est compris entre 5 et 9, le résultat sera arrondi à cette décimale (l'incertitude comportera un seul chiffre significatif ; si le premier chiffre significatif est inférieur à 5, le résultat est arrondi à la décimale suivante (incertitude à 2 chiffres).

Autres variables

Les variations sur la méthode peuvent souvent être assimilées à des erreurs humaines, c'est le cas par exemple de défaut de paramétrage du logiciel, erreur limitée étant donné que le paramétrage n'est effectué que par des personnes dument habilités et que les principaux paramètres sont répertoriés sur les feuillets d'analyse édités lors de la sortie de résultats. D'autres facteurs, comme la position du corps humain sont plus difficiles à appréhender, on peut en avoir une idée par la répétabilité ou la reproductibilité (dont l'étude fait l'objet d'un paragraphe particulier).

d) Facteurs relatifs au spectromètre

Efficacité & maintien des performances

L'incertitude-type sur l'efficacité de détection, ρ_e, à l'énergie e, est déduite du lissage des points expérimentaux obtenus lors de l'étalonnage. Elle est estimée à moins de 5 % : ce pourcentage correspond à l'EMT des points lissés par rapport aux points expérimentaux.

Le maintien des performances peut ne pas influer directement sur le résultat de mesure, il rend simplement plus difficile la réalisation de la mesure par l'opérateur et peut être à l'origine d'erreurs humaines concernant l'interprétation des spectres. C'est la raison pour laquelle un suivi est effectué au moyen de cartes de contrôle des différents paramètres de performances (résolution, calage en énergie, centroïde, bruit de fond pour sa composante électronique) pour mettre en évidence toute dérive au-delà des limites de contrôle, ainsi on est assuré d'effectuer une mesure dans de bonnes conditions.

e) Erreurs humaines

Les erreurs par défaut de vigilance conduisent le plus souvent à l'impossibilité d'obtenir un résultat, elles sont néanmoins réduites en anthroporadiométrie, car d'une part les spectres sont peu complexes et ne comportent qu'un petit nombre de pics et d'autre part les manipulations humaines sont réduites, le logiciel sortant par voie automatique un résultat que l'opérateur doit vérifier.

La seule erreur possible réside dans l'encadrement du pic, elle est limitée du fait que dans les laboratoires les opérateurs font l'objet d'un apprentissage, de plus un maintien de leurs compétences est vérifié périodiquement. Avec du personnel bien entrainé, la variabilité ne dépasse pas 1 %.

f) Incertitude globale

Les incertitudes types et les incertitudes composées uc_c, ainsi que l'incertitude élargie U, toutes exprimées en pourcentage sont présentées dans le tableau II. Il s'agit de la mesure du cobalt présent dans un corps humain, suite à un incident.

Cobalt 60 : 515 Bq		**Incertitude type %**
Comptage brut	466 impulsions	10,25
Comptage surface sous le pic	212 impulsions	
Comptage net	254 impulsions	
Temps de mesure	60 secondes	0,00
Efficacité		0,56
Activité de la source radioactive d'étalonnage	Certificat d'étalonnage	5
Variabilité de la lecture du pic dans le spectre		1
$u_{c\ Mesure}$		11,5
Morphologie		25
$u_{c\ Mesure+Morphologie}$		28
Erreur d'arrondissage	2 chiffres significatifs	0,1
U (2.k)		**56**

Tableau II. Calcul des incertitudes composées u_c etargies U (les calculs sont effectués sur les valeurs exactes, l'incertityde type (Mesure et morphologie), ainsi que l'incertitude élargie sont des valeurs arrondies.

g) Répétabilité & reproductibilité

Qu'il s'agisse de la répétabilité ou de la reproductibilité, l'objectif est d'exprimer la variabilité des résultats sous la forme d'un coefficient de variation d'une série de mesure, CV. Ce dernier consiste à faire le rapport entre la moyenne et l'écart-type d'une série de mesure :

$$CV = \frac{\sigma}{m}.100$$

Les facteurs pouvant expliquer cette variabilité des résultats sont indiqués dans le diagramme d'Ichikawa (figure 1)

Des séries de 5 mesures d'europium 152 ont été effectués pendant un temps de comptage de 60 secondes, pour trois niveaux d'activité 300, 3000 et 30 000 Bq. Les mesures sont réalisés à 778 keV pour éviter les phénomènes d'interférence entre pics. Les résultats sont présentés dans le tableau III.

Cobalt 60	Niveau I (500 Bq)	Niveau II (3000 Bq)	Niveau III (30 000 Bq)
Mesures	535	2823	31910
	541	2836	35260
	385	3173	32640
	409	2779	33460
	520	2774	34570
Moyenne	478	2877	33570
Ecart-type	35	368	1368121
Répétabilité CV %	16	5	4
Reproductibilité CV %	21	7	5
Incertitude radioactive %	13	4	1

Tableau III. Répétabilité et reproductibilité estimés à partir d'une série de résultats de mesure.

Il est possible de corréler la répétabilité et la reproductibilité. La reproductibilité est égale à environ 1,33 fois la répétabilité (Vassault 1999). L'incertitude obtenue en reproductibilité est inférieure celle obtenue par la méthode GUM. Les données présentées montrent qu'il y a d'autres facteurs à prendre en compte que l'incertitude radioactive (qui ne participe à l'incertitude qu'à hauteur de 13%). Elles montrent également que les répétabilités et les reproductibilités sous estiment l'incertitude sur le résultat.

3.2. ANALYSE DES FECES PAR SPECTROMETRIE ALPHA

Diagramme cause-effet

Comme le montre le diagramme d'Ichikawa, Les paramètres influençant la mesure sont aussi divers que pour l'anthroporadiométrie, mais en plus, de nouveaux facteurs interviennent liés à la chimie nécessaire à la séparation du radionucléide recherché (figure 3).

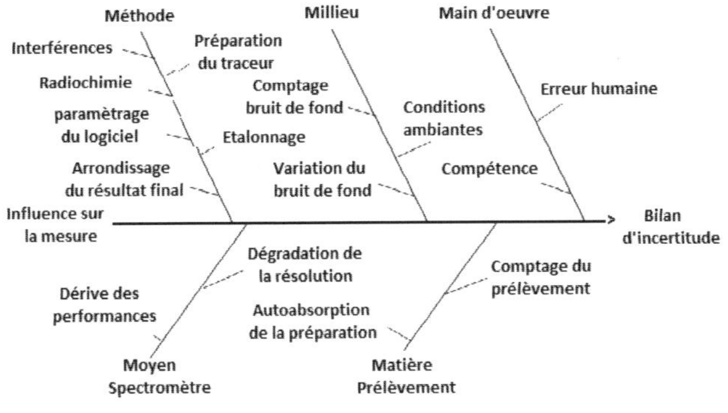

Fig. 3.. Diagramme d'Ichikawa

Inventaires des facteurs de variabilité

Dans les paragraphes qui suivent, nous ne détaillerons que les facteurs qui sont différents de ceux déjà décrits à propos de l'anthroporadiométrie.

a) Statistique de comptage : radionucléide recherché & traceur.

L'activité se calcule de la façon suivante :

$$A_e = \frac{S}{R.i_e.t.q}$$

A : activité en becquerels du radionucléide recherché mesuré à l'énergie e.

S : surface nette du pic, : $S = N_T - N_o$.

avec S_T, surface totale du pic ; N_T, nombre d'impulsions dans le pic ; N_o nombre d'impulsions dans le bruit de fond correspondant au pic. En spectrométrie alpha, N_o est proche de zéro, c'est la raison pour laquelle se terme est négligé.

i_e : probabilité d'émission alpha du radionucléide recherché à l'énergie ; en spectrométrie alpha est de l'ordre de 100 %, étant donné que les émission sont incluses dans le pic (seule exception l'uranium 235, pour lequel, il faut tenir compte de l'émission détectée)

t : temps de mesure en secondes.

q : quantité de prélèvement, elle est égale à 1 car la totalité du prélèvement est analysé.;

La formule peut alors se simplifier

$$A_e = \frac{N_T}{R.t}$$

R es le rendement de recouvrement du radionucléide recherché : il est composé du rendement physique (efficacité) ρ_{phys} de l'appareil de mesure et du rendement chimique ρ_{chem} de séparation.

$R = \rho_{phys} \cdot \rho_{chem}$

Le rendement chimique correspond à l'activité du traceur retrouvé après séparation $a_{traceur}$ rapporté à l'activité du traceur introduite dans le prélèvement en début de manipulation, soit a_o.

$$\rho_{chem} = \frac{a_{traceur}}{a_{0traceur}}$$

L'activité en traceur retrouvée après séparation est donné par l'équation, q correspond à la quantité de traceur introduite (masse ou volume) :

$$A_{traceur} = \frac{S_{traceur}}{\rho_{traceur}.t.q}$$

Le rendement chimique s'exprime alors :

$$\rho_{chem} = \frac{S_{traceur} / (\rho_{phys}.t.q_{traceur})}{a_{0traceur}}$$

L'activité du radionucléide recherché devient.

$$A_e = \frac{N_T}{\left(S_{Ttraceur} / a_{Otraceur}\right)} R$$

L'expression de l'incertitude est :

$$u_{Ae} / A_e = \sqrt{\left[\frac{u_S}{N_T}\right]^2 + \left[\frac{u_R}{R}\right]^2} + Incert_{syt}$$

avec, $u_S / N_T = \frac{\sqrt{N_T}}{N_T}$

Dans le cas du traceur, l'incertitude est donnée par l'expression suivante :

$$u_R / R = \sqrt{\left[\frac{u_{Straceur}}{S_{Ttraceur}}\right] + \left[\frac{u_{aotraceur}}{a_{Otraceur}}\right]^2 + \left[\frac{u_{qtraceur}}{q_{traceur}}\right]^2}$$

Rapporté dans l'expression de l'incertitude de l'activité du prélèvement, on obtiens :

$$u_A / A_e = \sqrt{\left[\frac{u_S}{S}\right]^2 + \left[\frac{u_{Straceur}}{S_{Ttraceur}}\right] + \left[\frac{u_{aotraceur}}{a_{Otraceur}}\right]^2 + \left[\frac{u_{qtraceur}}{q_{traceur}}\right]^2}$$

avec pour le prélèvement, $u_S / S_T = \frac{\sqrt{N_T}}{N_T}$ et pour le traceur

$$u_{Straceur} / S_{Ttraceur} = \frac{\sqrt{N_{Ttraceur}}}{N_{Ttraceur}}$$

b)Temps de comptage

Les convertisseurs analogiques numériques étant plus performant que ceux d'anthroporadiométrie NaI, on obtiens une incertitude de l'ordre de ou inférieure à 0,01 µs, pour un comptage d'une durée de 54 000 secondes, donc négligeable.

c) Probabilité d'émission

Elle négligeable car de l'ordre de 100 %, car pour un radionucléide donné, les émissions sont proches et en deçà de la résolution des spectromètres.

d) Activité du traceur

Il est donné par le certificat d'étalonnage : exemple pour le plutonium 242 : u = 1,12 à k=3

e) Facteur de forme

En spectrométrie alpha, le pic est accompagné par une traîne plus ou moins importante, selon la qualité de la préparation. On doit tenir compte de cette variabilité dans le calcul du seuil de décision (GTN 5 1990). La forme du pic a donc une importance et intervient dans le calcul de la MDA, elle se traduit par l'introduction d'un coefficient, le **facteur de forme F.** Ce dernier est déterminé à partir du pic le plus important, en général celui du traceur :

$$F = X_{(T)} / X_{(L)}$$

$X_{(T)}$: surface totale du pic (traine comprise)
$X_{(L)}$: la demi surface droite du correspondant au sommet du pic, jusqu'au canal correspondant à la base droite du pic.
Le facteur de forme est de l'ordre de 2, lorsque les pics sont bien résolus. Il peut s'élever jusqu'à 4 et parfois au delà. Son évaluation se fait en prenant la forme du pic du traceur comme modèle qui est appliqué aux isotopes recherchés. En fonction de la composition de l'échantillon et de sa préparation, la forme des pics est différentes et par voie de conséquence le facteur de forme.
En prenant en compte le facteur de forme, le seuil de décision et la *limite de détection* sont multipliée d'autant. Si le pic est parfaitement gaussien le résultat est à multiplier par 2, car dans ce cas F = 2. En réalité ce facteur est souvent plus élevé.

f) Statistique de comptage du bruit de fond

Le bruit de fond en spectrométrie alpha est estimé à 0
Nous avons déterminé dans un premier temps les seuils de décision puis ensuite les limites de détection (formules modifiées du GTN5 Groupe Technique n°5 du calculé.
Calcul du seuil de détection :

$$SD_{[impulsions]} = 2.(1+\sqrt{2(B+1)})$$

Si B est égal à 0, le seuil de décision arrondi au chiffre supérieur donne une valeur de 3

Traduit en activité (avec un temps de comptage de 172800 secondes, un rendement de détection de 0, 25 et un rendement chimique de 0,75) on obtiens un seuil d'environ 0,15 mBq.

g) Erreurs humaines

Les erreurs humaines ont pour origine des défauts de vigilance. Elles concernent principalement la radiochimie et conduisent en général à des résultats inexploitables. Avec du personnel bien entraîné, elles ne doivent pas dépasser 5 % des analyses

h) Incertitude globale

Les incertitudes types et les incertitudes composées uc_c, ainsi que l'incertitude élargie U, toutes exprimées en pourcentage sont présentées dans le tableau IV. Elle sont déterminées pour une activité 1 milli becquerel en plutonium 239.

i) Répétabilité & reproductibilité

Les essais de répétabilité et la reproductibilité été menés sur des « blancs de selles » constitués de phosphate de calcium (2 g) et de chlorure ferrique (1 g), principaux composants des selles. On dispose ainsi d'échantillons parfaitement connus, présentant les mêmes difficultés de traitement que les échantillons biologiques. Ces blancs ont fait l'objet d'une charge en plutonium 239.

On constate que la reproductibilité est du même ordre de grandeur que l'incertitude élargie ournie par la méthode GUM (respectivement 28 et 34 %). A la différence de ce quel'on a observé en anthroporadiométrie, l'incertitude radioactive participe peu à la variabilité (4%).

Plutonium 239 : 1mBq	**Incertitude type %**
Comptage du prélèvement : 36 impulsions	17
Comptage du traceur : 548 impulsions	4,2
Temps de mesure : 172800 secondes	0,00
Activité du traceur Pu 242 (certificat d'étalonnage) *Activité marqueur :* 14,74 mBq ; $U_{Pu242} = 1,12\ \%\ (k=3)$	0,37
Pipette préparation du traceur : 250 µl $EMT_{justesse + fidélité} = 11 \mu l$	2,5
Dilution (mesurée en masse) Balance : $EMT_{justesse + fidélité} = 0{,}010\ g$ 243 g HNO_3 + 83 g $H20_{distillée}$	0,01
Pipette addition du traceur à échantillon :1000 µl $EMT_{justesse + fidélité} = 11 \mu l$	0,63
Incertitude type composée u_c	16,9
Incertitude élargie U (k=2)	**34**

Tableau IV. Calcul des incertitudes composées u_c et élargies U (les calculs sont effectués sur les valeurs exactes, l'incertityde type, ainsi que l'incertitude élargie sont des valeurs arrondies).

Plutonium 239	Activité mBq	Ecart par rapport à la valeur vraie %
Mesures	1,3	8
	1,1	-8
	1,0	-17
	1,6	33
	1,8	50
	1,2	0
	0,9	-25
	1,2	0
	1,5	25
	1,1	-8
	1,2	0
moyenne	1,3	5
Ecart-type	0,26	
Répétabilité CV %	21	
Reproductibilité CV %	28	
Incertitude radioactive	4	

Tableau V. Répétabilité et reproductibilité estimés à partir d'une série de résultats de mesure.

3.3. Dosimétrie

Les résultats en activité obtenus par anthroporadiométrie directement ou par analyse radiotoxicologique indirectement à partir des excréta permettent de remonter à la quantité incorporée (à la condition que la date d'incorporation soit connue) grâce à des modèles métaboliques biocinétiques. La quantité incorporée multipliée par un coefficient de dose permet alors d'obtenir la dose interne. Ces coefficients sont issus de modèle biophysique d'interaction entre le rayonnement ionisant et les tissus vivants. La dose interne désigne l'énergie transférée à l'organisme (ou à l'organe) par le rayonnement ionisant émis par le radionucléide incorporé.

Plusieurs facteurs contribuent à l'incertitude lors du calcul de dose.

- le manque de connaissances concernant le moment et la façon dont se fait l'incorporation,
- la variabilité de l'excrétion (cas des analyses radiotoxicologiques),
- les différences du métabolisme d'une personne à l'autre,
- les caractéristiques incertaines ou variables des matières radioactives auxquelles le travailleur peut avoir été exposé (en particulier la taille des particules de poussière),

Cetaines de ces incertitudes peuvent être évaluée : par exemple l'erreur sur moment exact où se fait l'incorporation est de l'ordre de 70 % (ICRP 78 1997), en multipliant les prélèvements, on peut abaisser raisonnablement la variabilité sur l'excrétion à environ 10 %.

D'autres incertitudes sont difficiles à évaluer en pratique,. C'est la raison pour laquelle la dose calculée doit être comprise comme une dose nominale, qui représente d'une façon théorique le risque induit par les rayonnements ionisants de cancerogénése, suite à l'incorporation de radionucléide.

4 Conclusion

Pour établir l'incertitude de mesure, deux approches ont été mises en œuvre. Dans une première approche analytique, nous avons dégagé à partir du processus opératoire les facteurs d'influence. La seconde approche dite de performance consiste à estimer l'incertitude à partir des caractéristiques que sont la répétabilité et la reproductibilité.

Les valeurs d'incertitude sont similaires que dans le cas des analyses de spectrométrie alpha. L'approche de performance ayant tendance à sous estimer les incertitudes, car elle comporte un certain nombre de biais, car les différents examens ou analyses sont réalisés dans un temps limité.

A la différence du résultat de mesure, par anthroporadiométrie ou par analyses radiotoxicologiques, dont les incertitudes peuvent être quantifiées de façon exhaustive, la dose interne est pénalisé par des facteurs d'incertitudes très difficile à apprécier en pratique, car liées aux variabilité individuelles. C'est la raison pour laquelle, La dose interne correspond à une donnée nominale en relation avec le risque à long terme d'effets pathologiques aléatoires

References

Anderson E. C . (1963) Three component body composition analysis based on potassium and water détermination. Ann NY Acad. Sci.110 189-212.
GUM (1995) NF ISO/CEI Guide 98-3 de Juillet 2014 3 Incertitude de mesure partie 3 : guide pour l'expression de l'incertitude mesure.
GTN5 (1990) Groupe de Travail n° 11 de la Commission d'Etablissement des Méthodes d'Analyses de la CETAMA. Limite de détection en spectrométrie alpha.
ICRP (1975) International Commission on Radiological Protection. Publication 23. report of the task group on reference Man.
ICRP (1997) International Commission on Radiological Protection. Publication 78. Individual monitoring for internal exposure of workers.
LNHB (2004). Arrondissage des résultats de mesure, Nombre de chiffres significatifs. Note technique LNHB/04-13, 2004.
Marinelli E (1957). The Use of NaI-Tl Crystal Spectrometers in the Study of Gamma-Ray Activity in Vivo: A Summary of Developments at the Argonne National Laboratory. Brit. J. Radiol. Suppl., 7.
Miller C Marinelli E (1956). Gamma-ray activity of contemporary man. Science, 124 (3212), 122-123.
Norme NF EN 61582 (2006) Instrumentation pour la radioprotection – Systèmes de mesure in vivo – Classification, exigences générales et procédures d'essai pour les appareils portables, mobiles et à poste fixe.
Norme S92501 (2013) Mesures anthroporadiométriques - Coprs entier – Mesures des émissions gamma d'énergie supérieure à 100 keV).
Vassault A., Graftmeyer D., De Graeve J. et al (1999). Quality specifications and available limits for validation of methods used in clinical biochemistry. Annales de Biologie Clinique, 57, 685-695).

Viscosimètre absolu à chute de bille adapté aux faibles viscosités des liquides

P. Ballereau, D. Truong

Laboratoire Commun de Métrologie LNE-CNAM, 1 rue Gaston Boissier 75724 Paris Cedex 15

Résumé. Le Laboratoire Commun de Métrologie LNE-CNAM disposait d'un viscosimètre absolu à chute de bille fonctionnant uniquement à la température du laboratoire. Son développement arrêté en 2005, a été repris en 2010 pour le rendre opérationnel en régulant, dans un premier temps, sa température entre 15° C et 50 °C, et pour l'adapter aux faibles viscosités des liquides jusqu'à une valeur de 15 mPa.s. L'objectif de cette étude est de se rapprocher des viscosités des carburants ou des biocarburants. Leur faible viscosité nécessite l'utilisation d'une bille de faible diamètre. Une bille en silicium d'un diamètre de 0,48 mm a été choisie. Le faible diamètre de la bille a rendu obligatoire la conception et la réalisation d'un préhenseur. Celui-ci utilise une technique propre aux microsystèmes : l'adhésion par des forces de Van der Walls. Le fonctionnement de ce préhenseur est décrit dans cet article. Il a été conçu pour réaliser deux fonctions : libérer la bille dans le liquide en partie haute, puis la récupérer au fond du viscosimètre, pour la repositionner prête à être lâchée à nouveau.

Mots clefs: viscosimètre absolu à chute de bille, biocarburant, microsystème, rhéologie, contrainte seuil

1 Introduction

Dans le contexte d'une nécessaire réduction mondiale des émissions de gaz à effet de serre et d'une économie forcée des énergies d'origine fossile, l'utilisation des biocarburants [1] s'avère nécessaire. Les législateurs européens ont pris des mesures dans ce sens [2].

La viscosité des biocarburants et de leurs mélanges avec des carburants fossiles est assez mal connue et elle est une caractéristique essentielle pour leur transport dans les pipelines. Ces biocarburants ainsi que les carburants fossiles ont de faibles viscosités (quelques mPa.s) et sont utilisés d'après TRAPIL société des transports pétroliers par pipeline, dans des conditions de température pouvant varier de –10 °C à + 50 °C et de pression variable de 0,1 MPa à 10 MPa.

La viscosité qui varie en fonction de la température et de la pression est donc un paramètre important dans le transport des carburants et des biocarburants.

L'objectif du projet est de rendre opérationnel un viscosimètre à chute de bille pour pouvoir mesurer la viscosité de mélanges de biocarburants et de carburants sur une plage de température de – 10 °C à + 50 °C et également avec une pression pouvant atteindre 10 MPa. Dans un premier temps, ce projet se limite à une plage de température de + 15 °C à + 50 °C et uniquement à la pression atmosphérique.

L'objectif ultime de ces recherches est de rendre opérationnel le viscosimètre à chute de bille afin qu'il devienne **une référence absolue,** en reliant la viscosité dynamique aux différentes grandeurs : masse, longueur et temps.

2 Etat de l'art

D'assez nombreuses études sur les viscosimètres à chute de bille ont été menées avec des fluides newtoniens [3], et également avec des fluides possédant des particules en suspension [4].

Dans le domaine de la métrologie, des travaux menés au National Metrology Institute of Japon NMIJ ont abouti à construire un viscosimètre absolu pour réaliser des mesures à des pressions élevées (500 MPa) [5]. Le NMIJ a également décidé en 1998 [6] de construire un viscosimètre absolu à chute de bille, pour déterminer une nouvelle valeur de la viscosité de l'eau avec une nouvelle incertitude. L'état d'avancement du viscosimètre du NMIJ et celui du LCM/LNE-CNAM ont été présentés au CCM Working Group on Viscosity au BIPM en mai 2011 [7] [8].

3 Objectif scientifique et technique

Le LCM/LNE-CNAM disposait en 2005 d'un viscosimètre à chute de bille développé et étudié par Matthieu Brizard [9] au cours de sa thèse.

* correspondance : patrick.ballereau@cnam.fr

La photographie de la figure 1 montre la cellule de mesure qui fonctionnait uniquement à la température du laboratoire.

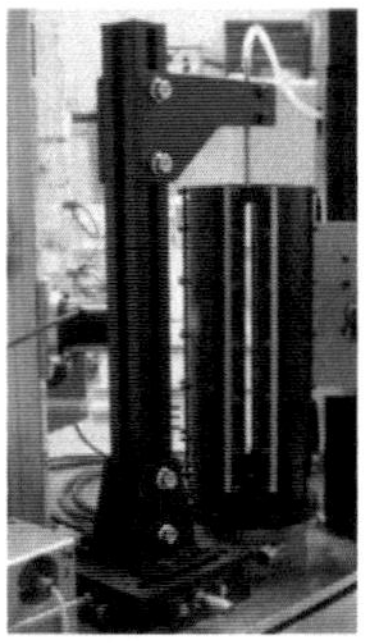

Fig.1. Cellule de mesure du viscosimètre à chute de bille

L'étude métrologique réalisée au cours de cette thèse a montré la possibilité d'obtenir des incertitudes relatives de 10^{-3} pour des viscosités égales ou supérieures à 10 Pa.s. D'autre part les incertitudes relatives du viscosimètre à chute de bille deviennent meilleures que celles des viscosimètres capillaires pour des viscosités supérieures à 1 Pa.s.

Le développement de ce viscosimètre arrêté en 2005 a repris en 2010, pour l'adapter aux faibles viscosités des biocarburants, le réguler à des températures comprises entre – 10 °C et + 50 °C, et construire une cellule de petit volume pour participer à des inter-comparaisons.

Les modifications du viscosimètre ont été réalisées en trois étapes principales :

Etape 1 - adaptation aux faibles viscosités (des biocarburants) par l'utilisation de billes spécifiques.

Etape 2 - adaptation aux températures contrôlées par le développement d'une enceinte thermostatée.

Etape 3 - construction d'une cellule pour inter-comparaisons.

3.1 Projet d'adaptation du viscosimètre aux faibles viscosités

3.1.1. Ordre de grandeur de la viscosité d'un biofuel

Les premiers résultats réalisés par le LCM/LNE-CNAM sur les biocarburants: en viscosité cinématique et en masse volumique ont été présentés au cours de la réunion annuelle de l'ENG09–Biofuel (programme européen financé par EURAMET) à Helsinki [10] en janvier 2011. Les mesures de viscosité cinématique ont été réalisées avec des viscosimètres capillaires. Quant aux mesures de masse volumique, elles ont été réalisées avec des pycnomètres.

Remarque: la viscosité cinématique ν est définie comme le rapport de la viscosité dynamique η sur la masse volumique ρ.

$$\nu = \frac{\eta}{\rho} \quad (1)$$

Les évolutions de la viscosité cinématique et de la masse volumique, de deux biofuels purs fabriqués à partir de colza et de soja, en fonction de la température sont présentées sur les figures 2 et 3.

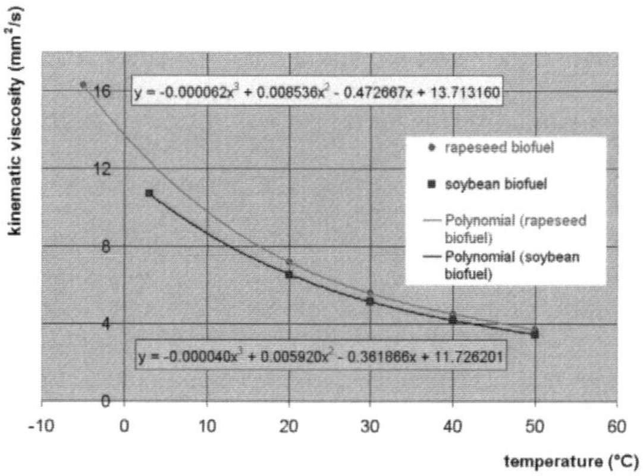

Fig. 2. Evolution de la viscosité cinématique en fonction de la température [10] (à la pression atmosphérique)

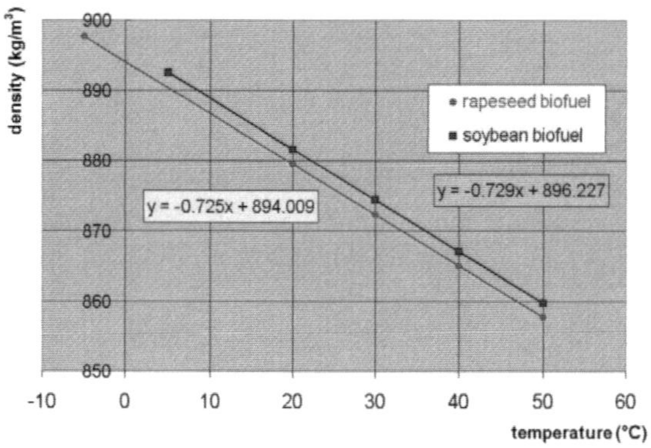

Fig. 3. Evolution de la masse volumique en fonction de la température [10] (à la pression atmosphérique)

A la température de 20 °C, la viscosité dynamique de ces biocarburants est de l'ordre de 6 mPa.s soit 6 fois supérieure à celle de l'eau.

3.1.2 Rappel du principe du viscosimètre à chute de bille

La viscosité dynamique η d'un liquide est obtenue à partir de la mesure de la vitesse de chute U_∞ d'une bille de diamètre d et de masse volumique ρ_b dans ce liquide de masse volumique ρ_l

L'équation d'équilibre dynamique de la bille donne la relation suivante:

$$\eta = \frac{d^2}{18U_\infty}(\rho_b - \rho_l)g \quad (2)$$

avec g : accélération de la pesanteur

* correspondance : patrick.ballereau@cnam.fr

Cette relation a été obtenue en utilisant la formule de Stokes (issue de l'équation de Stokes) pour la traînée aérodynamique F_{Stokes} (quelques explications sur la détermination de cette loi sont données dans le paragraphe "correction de l'effet de Reynolds") :

$$F_{Stokes} = 6\pi\eta U_{\infty} d \qquad (3)$$

Sachant que la formule implique deux hypothèses :

Première hypothèse (effet de paroi):

La bille tombe dans un milieu de dimension infinie. Ce qui revient à dire que la bille se déplace dans un cylindre de diamètre D infini. Soit :

$$\frac{d}{D} \rightarrow 0 \qquad (4)$$

Dans la pratique, D est de dimension finie (pour cette cellule, D = 99,61 mm).

Mais, il est possible d'introduire un coefficient de correction k_1 fonction de $\frac{d}{D}$ dans la formule de Stokes.

Deuxième hypothèse (effet de Reynolds):

Le nombre de Reynolds R_e doit tendre vers 0.

$$R_e \rightarrow 0 \qquad (5)$$

avec
$$R_e = \frac{\rho_l U_{\infty} d}{\eta} \qquad (6)$$

Pour les nombres de Reynolds non nuls mais de valeurs faibles, il est possible d'introduire un second facteur de correction k_2 fonction de R_e dans la formule de Stokes.

L'analyse dimensionnelle montre que la force de traînée F_x peut prendre la forme suivante :

$$F_x = F_{Stokes} \times f(\frac{d}{D}) \times f(R_e) \qquad (7)$$

D'où l'équation d'équilibre de la bille:

$$\eta = \frac{d^2}{18U_{\infty}}(\rho_b - \rho_l) g \times k_1(\frac{d}{D}) \times k_2(R_e) \qquad (8)$$

Correction de l'effet de paroi

L'équation de Stokes a été résolue pour une sphère en mouvement avec des conditions limites cylindriques par Bohlin [11] en 1960. C'est le cas d'une bille qui tombe le long de l'axe de symétrie d'un cylindre de révolution de diamètre D avec un nombre de Reynolds qui tend vers zéro.

La fonction de correction $k_1(\frac{d}{D})$ est la suivante :

$$k_1 = 1/[1 - 2.10443(\frac{d}{D}) + 2.08877(\frac{d}{D})^3 - 0.94813(\frac{d}{D})^5 - 1.372(\frac{d}{D})^6 + 3.87(\frac{d}{D})^8 - 4.19(\frac{d}{D})^{10} + ...] \qquad (9)$$

Son domaine de validité est limité à:

$$\frac{d}{D} \prec 0.6 \qquad (10)$$

Correction de l'effet de Reynolds

La formule de Stokes exprime la force exercée sur la bille en mouvement dans un milieu infini avec $R_e \rightarrow 0$.

De manière générale la force aérodynamique exercée sur un corps par un écoulement est égale à la somme de l'intégrale des forces de pression et de l'intégrale des forces de frottement autour de ce corps. Ces forces de pression et de frottement sont connues à partir de la connaissance de l'écoulement autour du corps qui est régi par la loi de Navier-Stokes [12] [13] [14]:

$$\rho\frac{\partial\vec{U}}{\partial t} + \rho(\vec{U}.\vec{grad}).\vec{U} = \rho\vec{g} - \vec{grad}.p + \eta\nabla^2\vec{U}$$

(a) (b) (c) (d) (e) (11)

Cette équation possède les 5 termes suivants:

(a): représente la quantité d'accélération instationnaire par unité de volume

(b): représente la quantité d'accélération advective par unité de volume (les forces d'inertie)

(c): représente la force de gravité par unité de volume

(d): représente la force de pression par unité de volume

(e) : représente les forces visqueuses par unité de volume

L'équation de Navier-Stokes n'a une solution analytique exacte que pour des cas simples, principalement pour des fluides isovolumes et des conditions limites particulières [15].

L'adimensionnement de cette équation [16] [17] fait apparaître un nombre sans dimension, le nombre de Reynolds. Ce nombre caractérise l'importance des forces d'inertie sur les forces de viscosité. Lorsque $R_e \rightarrow 0$, le terme advectif disparaît.

Cette équation linéaire est l'équation de Stokes [18].

$$\rho\frac{\partial\vec{U}}{\partial t} = \rho\vec{g} - \vec{grad}.p + \eta\nabla^2\vec{U} \qquad (12)$$

Dans le cas d'un écoulement stationnaire, le membre de gauche de l'équation est nul.

La solution de Stokes (1851) fournit le champ de vitesse et de pression autour de la sphère. Ces deux champs de vitesses et de pressions autour de la sphère permettent de calculer l'effort exercé sur celle-ci pour aboutir à la formule de Stokes présentée précédemment.

La démonstration est présentée dans d'assez nombreux livres scientifiques [19] [20] [21].

Différents auteurs, par approximation (par exemple par linéarisation) du terme advectif de l'équation de Navier Stokes ont calculé analytiquement la traînée de la sphère. Le graphique de la figure 4 donné par Shi-Jun Liao [22] compare son propre résultat à différents autres résultats analytiques et à des résultats expérimentaux (la force de traînée est ici présentée sous sa forme adimensionnelle, le coefficient de traînée aérodynamique [23]).

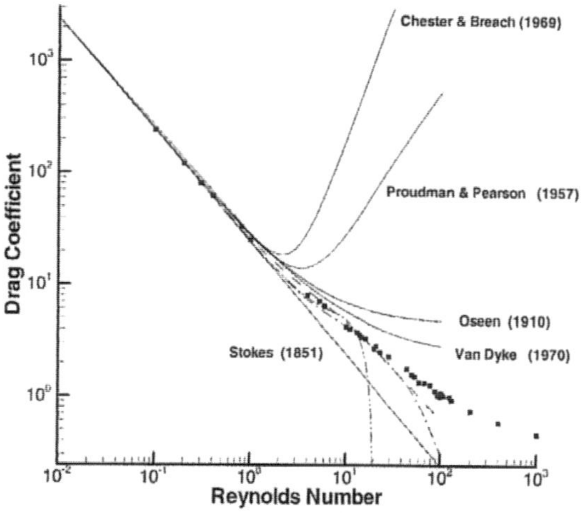

Fig.4. Résultats analytiques comparés à des résultats expérimentaux d'après Shi-Jun Liao (2002) [22]

3.1.3. Choix de la bille

Un faible diamètre de bille favorise l'obtention d'un faible nombre de Reynolds.

Une bille en silicium de 0,48 mm de diamètre a été choisie à cause de sa relativement faible masse volumique (2329 kg/m^3) pour diminuer la vitesse de chute. Cette bille a été sélectionnée aussi pour ces caractéristiques : dimensionnelles (Grade 10 norme ISO 3290-1998), thermiques, mécaniques, et chimiques. D'autres billes d'un diamètre plus important ont été sélectionnées, des billes de 1,73 mm et 2 mm.

Pour la viscosité d'un biodiesel ayant une viscosité de 6 mPa.s, la vitesse de chute à l'équilibre dynamique est de l'ordre de 30,3 mm/s et le nombre de Reynolds est d'environ 2,1. Dans cette configuration, il paraît difficile d'utiliser directement le viscosimètre à chute de bille pour mesurer la viscosité des biocarburants.

Mais, si on choisit une huile référencée possédant à la température de 20 °C une viscosité de 14,9 mPa.s et une masse volumique ρ= 835 kg/m^3, les valeurs approchées de la vitesse de chute et du nombre de Reynolds sont les suivantes:

$$U_{\infty} = 12{,}6 \text{ mm/s} \qquad R_e = 0{,}34$$

Comme on peut le voir sur la courbe précédente (figure 4), ce nombre de Reynolds semble acceptable.

Cela nous ouvre donc une autre possibilité de raccordement en permettant d'étalonner en absolu une huile de référence avec le viscosimètre à chute de bille. Cette huile servira ensuite à raccorder les viscosimètres utilisés pour les biocarburants.

Mais, le faible diamètre de la bille oblige à construire un préhenseur adapté au lâcher et à la récupération de la bille.

3.1.4 Conception et réalisation d'un préhenseur

Un dispositif de préhension pour la bille a été conçu pour avoir deux fonctions:
- maintenir la bille sous la surface libre du liquide et la lâcher à un instant donné (phase « lâcher de bille » figure 5a).
- récupérer la bille au fond du cylindre, pour la replacer sous le niveau de la surface libre et la relâcher de nouveau (phase «récupération de la bille» figure 5b).

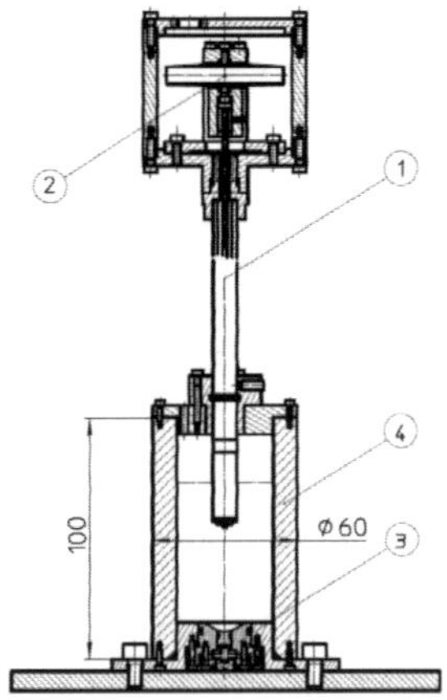

a) Position "lâcher de la bille"

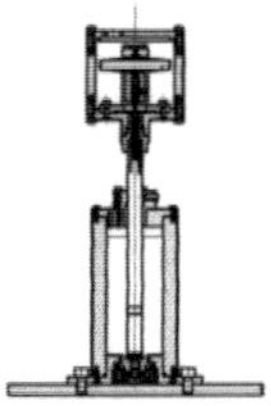

b) position "récupération de la bille"

c) Photographie du préhenseur

Fig. 5. Préhenseur monté dans la cellule de mise au point

Le croquis de la figure 5a montre le préhenseur (1), avec son actionneur (2) et la partie réception (3). Le préhenseur, ici en position « lâcher de bille » est installé sur une cellule de mise au point (4) dont le cylindre a des dimensions réduites par rapport au cylindre du viscosimètre.

La photographie de la figure 5c montre cet ensemble avec le générateur de tension alimentant l'actionneur.

Compte tenu du faible diamètre des billes, de l'ordre du millimètre, on utilise pour la réalisation du système de préhension des techniques propres aux microsystèmes, l'adhésion par des forces de type Van der Walls [24].

En effet à cette échelle (de l'ordre de 1 mm), les forces de surface (force d'adhésion) peuvent devenir prépondérantes devant les forces de volume (force de gravité). Ces types de forces sont des forces inter-atomiques qui dépendent de la nature des matériaux et du liquide situé à l'interface.

Des explications sur le déroulement des deux phases « lâcher de bille » et « récupération de la bille» sont présentées dans les deux paragraphes qui suivent.

Lâcher de la bille

La figure 6 montre l'extrémité inférieure du préhenseur pour une bille de 2 mm.

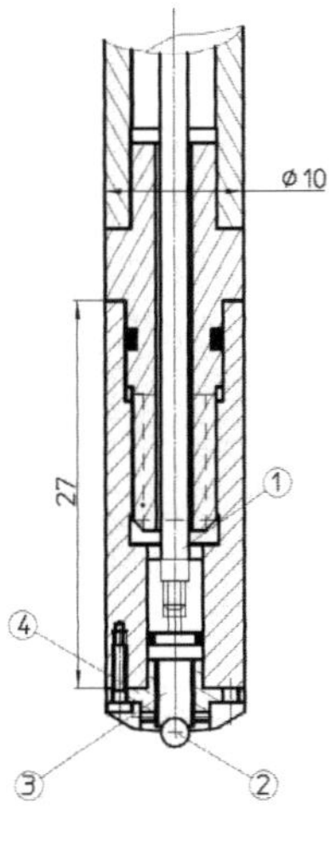

Fig. 6. Extrémité du préhenseur pour la bille de 2 mm

- dans un premier temps, la tige (1) est descendue pour que la bille (2) puisse être saisie par contact avec le noyau (3) fixé sur la tige.

- dans un deuxième temps, lorsqu'est actionnée la commande pour soulever la tige, les deux surfaces en contact bille-noyau se séparent. Alors les forces d'adhésion entre la bille et le séparateur (4) sont insuffisantes pour maintenir l'équilibre de la bille, et la bille tombe.

Le déplacement vers le haut de la tige est provoqué par la contraction de l'actionneur piézo-amplifié. L'amplitude de déplacement de l'actionneur est proportionnelle à la tension appliquée. Un déplacement maximum de 0,4 mm est produit par une tension de + 150 V. Cette tension est fournie par un générateur (voir figure 5c).

La figure 7 montre les photographies de l'extrémité du préhenseur respectivement en position « adhérence » et en position « lâcher» de la bille pour une bille de 2 mm de diamètre.

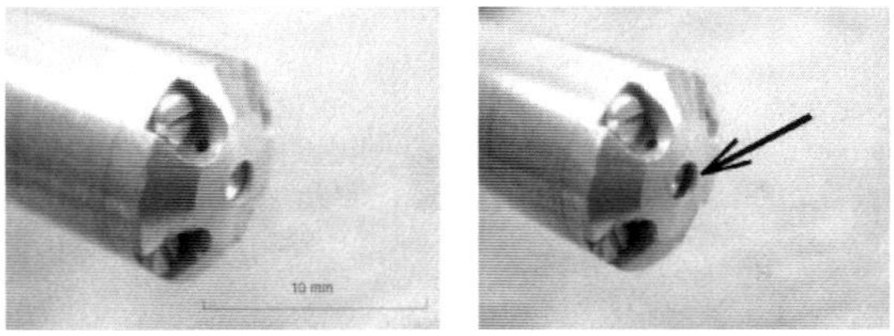

Fig. 7 - Position «adhérence » pour une bille de 2 mm

Le préhenseur fonctionne pour des billes d'un diamètre de 2 mm, de 1,73 mm ou de 0,48 mm, en changeant le noyau et le séparateur. L'ensemble des éléments constituant le préhenseur est réalisé avec un acier inoxydable.

L'adhésion des billes sur leur noyau est satisfaisante grâce à des polissages réalisés après l'usinage. Cette opération de mise au point du préhenseur a permis de rendre les surfaces de contact très proches l'une de l'autre, de diminuer la rugosité de celles-ci et d'augmenter ainsi l'intensité des forces de Van der Walls.

Une autre forme de séparateur possédant des encoches, pour limiter les forces de contact bille-séparateur, a été testée. Une photographie, prise à l'aide d'un microscope optique, montre un séparateur pour une bille d'un diamètre de 2 mm. Ce séparateur est présenté sur la figure 8.

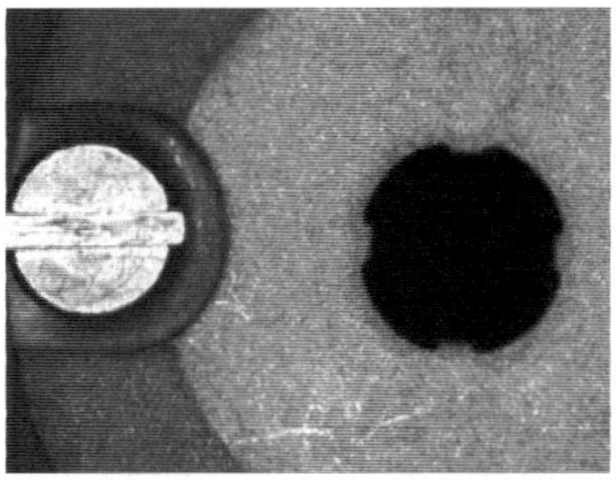

Fig. 8. Séparateur avec encoches (microscope optique)

La photographie 9 montre la bille de 0,48 mm adhérant sur son noyau retiré du préhenseur.

Fig. 9 - Adhésion de la bille de 0,48 mm sur son noyau (microscope optique)

Une autre alternative à ce type de solution a été étudiée en faisant adhérer la bille sur la partie «séparateur» et en poussant celle-ci avec un noyau modifié comme le montre la figure 10.

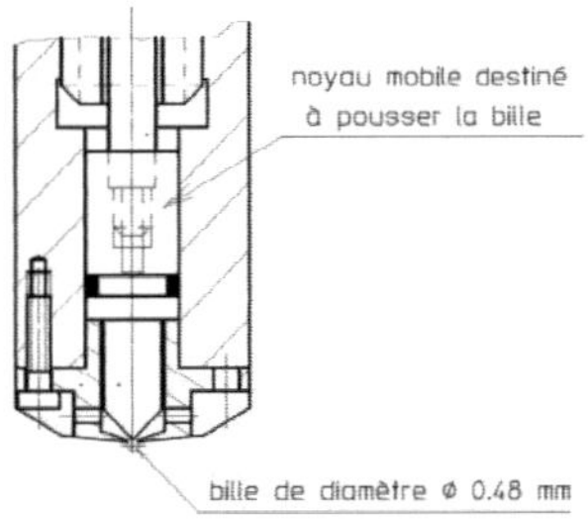

Fig. 10. Solution alternative en poussant la bille pour déclencher sa chute

Récupération de la bille

Pour récupérer la bille, il faut descendre le préhenseur jusqu'au système de récupération présenté sur la figure 11.

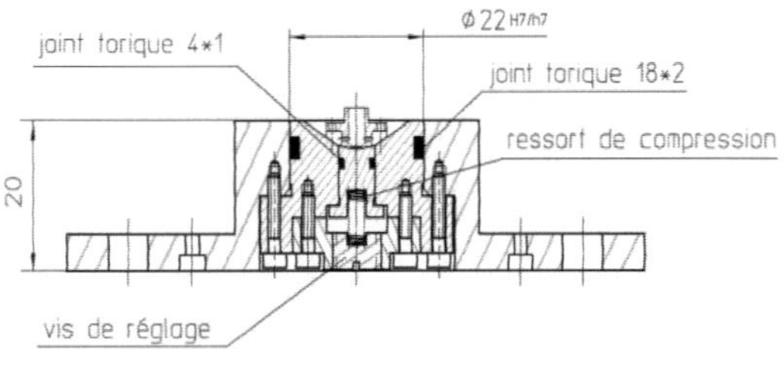

Fig. 11. Croquis du récupérateur de la bille

La photographie de la figure 12 montre le récupérateur. Une bille de 2 mm adhérant sur son noyau a été placée juste au-dessus, pour donner une indication de l'échelle.

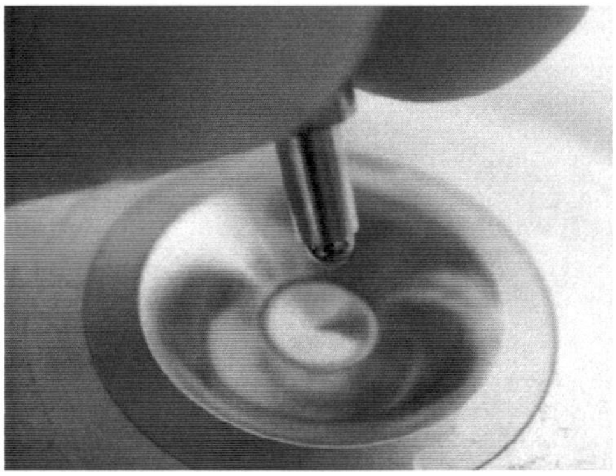

Fig. 12. Photographie du récupérateur de la bille (avec la bille de diamètre 2 mm pour donner une indication de l'échelle)

La partie conique de réception a été polie à la main de manière à ce que la bille puisse rouler jusqu'à l'axe de symétrie du récepteur, si pour une cause accidentelle, elle ne tombait pas sur l'axe. La mise au point du récupérateur a été rendue assez difficile par le fait que les forces de Van der Walls augmentent considérablement le moment de résistance au roulement.

En fonctionnement normal, la bille tombe sur l'axe et elle est maintenue dans cette position grâce à la partie conique du récepteur pendant la phase d'adhésion sur le noyau.

Ensuite, lorsque l'on remonte le préhenseur, on récupère la bille, pour la repositionner prêt à être relâchée de nouveau.

Remarque : la partie conique centrale du récupérateur possède un ressort de rappel et peut translater. Ce système en imposant une force de contact faible entre la bille et le récupérateur peut éviter d'éventuelles déformations, de celle-ci ou du séparateur.

Un film montrant le lâché et la récupération de la bille dans une huile de lin possédant une viscosité de l'ordre de 50 mPa.s, pour des billes de 0,48 mm et 2 mm, a été réalisé.

3.2 Adaptation aux températures contrôlées (- 10 °C à + 50 °C)

Un bain thermostaté possédant des parois optiques a été conçu et réalisé pour y plonger le viscosimètre. Il est présenté sur la figure 13. Ce bain est réalisé à partir d'un produit semi-fini, en alliage d'aluminium.

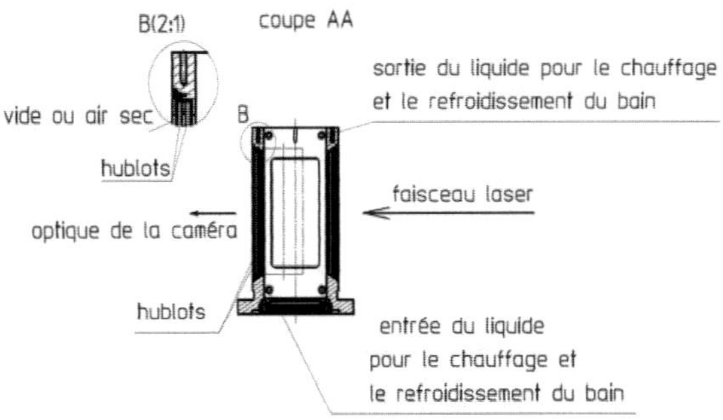

Fig. 13. Bain thermostaté

Ce bain thermostaté possède deux configurations. La figure 14 montre les hublots du bain en version « hautes températures » (une seule optique en verre borosilicaté) et en version « basses températures » (deux optiques en verre borosilicaté).

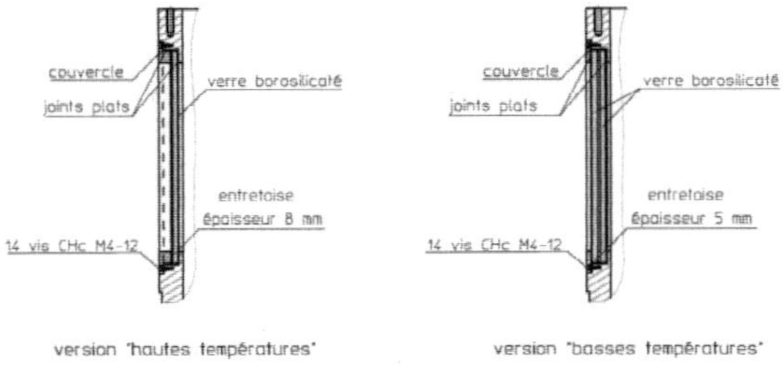

Fig. 14. Hublots du bain thermostaté

Les deux configurations ont été testées. Tout d'abord en configuration «hautes températures», voir figure 15a.

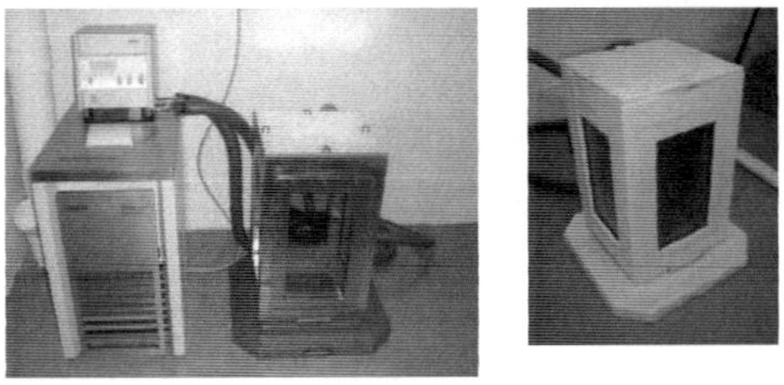

a) Cryothermostat relié au bain thermostaté (configuration haute température)

b) Bain thermostaté à la température de -16,4 °C (configuration basse température)

Fig.15. Bain thermostaté

Ces premiers tests ont été réalisés en circuit fermé, parce que le cryothermostat possède deux pompes de débits différents pour l'entrée et la sortie de fluide ce qui entraîne des débordements de fluide dans l'enceinte.

Le fonctionnement est possible sans apparition de condensation de vapeur d'eau sur le hublot pour des températures comprises entre + 15 °C et + 50 °C.

Ensuite la deuxième configuration, réservée aux basses températures a été testée. La température du bain est descendue jusqu'à - 16,4 °C, mais avec des temps prohibitifs et avec une condensation sur les hublots et un givrage de la vapeur d'eau sur le corps du bain thermostaté (figure 15 b).

Cette étape doit se poursuivre par une isolation thermique du bain thermostaté pour éviter le givrage de la vapeur d'eau et atteindre la température de – 10 °C en un temps relativement court

Pour permettre de faire fonctionner le bain normalement, en circuit ouvert, des pertes de charge et un système de maintien à niveau du liquide ont été installés.

3.3 Construction d'une cellule pour intercomparaisons et installation de celle-ci dans le bain thermostaté

D'un point de vue pratique, les étalonnages pour des intercomparaisons se font sur des faibles volumes de liquide. La cellule de mesure actuelle à un volume de 2500 ml, ce qui est trop important.

La construction d'une cellule de mesure d'un volume plus faible a été réalisée. Celle -ci est présentée sur la figure 16.

Fig. 16. Cellule pour inter-comparaison

La cellule à un diamètre intérieur de 50 mm et un volume de 300 ml.

La nouvelle cellule doit être suspendue au centre d'un système de déplacement micrométrique fixé sur la partie supérieure du bain thermostaté pour permettre les réglages optiques, notamment la mise au point de l'image sur la bille.

Le dessin du système de déplacement selon les directions X et Y est présenté sur la figure 17.

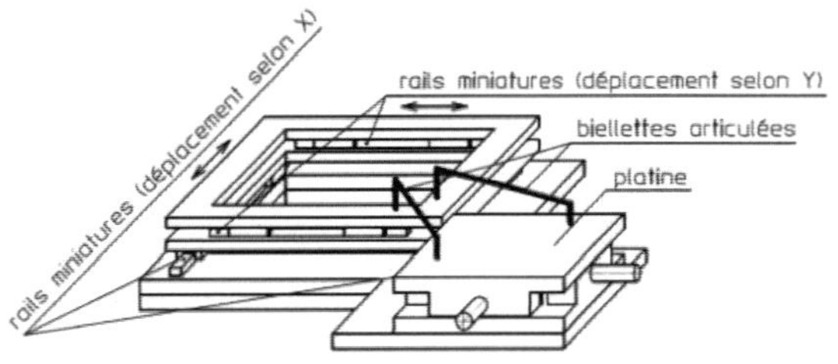

Fig. 17. Dessin en perspective du système de déplacement de la cellule

Deux rails parallèles permettent le déplacement selon la direction X. Deux autres disposés perpendiculairement permettent le déplacement selon Y.

Le système de déplacement a été construit et la cellule a été implantée dans le montage comme le montre la figure 18.

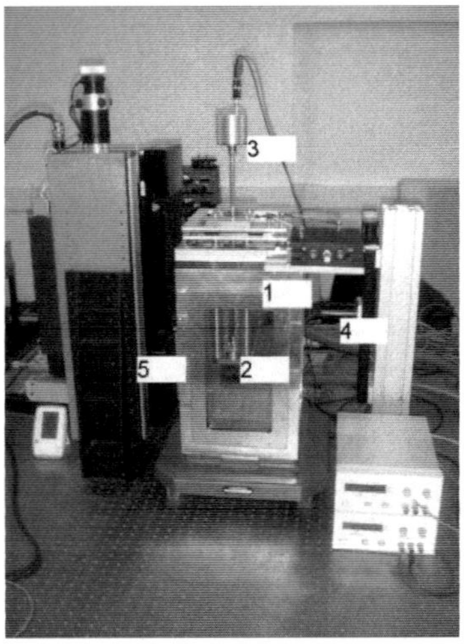

Fig. 18. Implémentation du bain dans le montage expérimentale

Sur cette photographie, à l'intérieur de ce bain thermostaté (1), on peut voir la cellule (2), le préhenseur (3). La diode laser avec son optique (4) avant son alignement à la caméra matricielle (5).

Après cet alignement, le faisceau laser éclaire la bille lors de son passage et l'ombre de la bille peut être enregistrée par la caméra. Un traitement de l'image ainsi formée permet de calculer la vitesse de la bille et d'en déduire la viscosité du fluide.

4 Conclusions

Ce travail doit se poursuivre par des mesures sur des fluides de différentes viscosités, notamment les faibles viscosités, aux températures normalisées, par exemple 15 °C ou 20 °C, mais aussi 40 °C pour les hydrocarbures.

L'isolation thermique du bain thermostaté doit se poursuivre pour examiner le fonctionnement à des basses températures jusqu'à – 10 °C.

La deuxième étape consiste à réaliser une cellule pressurisée jusqu'à 10 MPa pour mesurer des viscosités de liquides en fonction non seulement de la température mais aussi de la pression sur des étendues de mesure qui intéressent le transport des biocarburants.

Un autre intérêt des viscosimètres à chute de bille pour la mesure de viscosité aux faibles contraintes de cisaillement des fluides non newtoniens, pour la détermination du seuil de contrainte de cisaillement est montré dans différentes publications, comme par exemple celles-ci [25] [26] [27].

En parallèle à ces travaux une recherche débute sur l'utilisation du dispositif expérimental comme rhéomètre à chute de bille dans le cadre d'un programme de recherche européen financé par EURAMET qui se nomme: ENG59-NNL.

Ce programme d'une durée de 3 ans a débuté au 1 mai 2014. Ce programme de recherche présenté sur le site **www.eng59-rheology.eu** concerne la métrologie des fluides de forage des puits de pétrole.

Références bibliographiques

[1] E.Poitrat, Biocarburants, techniques de l'ingénieur, BE 8 550v2 (2009)
[2] A. L. Hantson, D. Thomas, Enjeux technologiques et écologiques majeurs des biocarburants, Congrès Français de Thermique, STF2010, Le Touquet (2010)
[3] S. Feng, A. L. Graham, P.T. Readon, J. Abbott, L. Mondy, Improving falling ball tests for viscosity determination, American society of mechanical engineers (2006)
[4] W.J. Milliken, M. Gottlieb, A.L. Graham, L.A. Mondy, R.L. Powel, The viscosity-volume fraction relation for suspensions of rod-like particles by falling-ball rheometry, Journal of Fluid Mechanics, **202**, pp 217-232 (1989)
[5] K. Fujii, Y. Fujita, N. Kuramoto, Y. Kurano, K. Fujii, A study on absolute measurement of viscosity by the falling ball method for a primary viscosity standard: Development of velocity measurement system for the falling ball. Thermophys Prop ISSN:0911-1743, **26**, p 430-432 (2005)
[6] Y. Fujita, N. Kuramoto, Y. Kurano, K. Fujii, A new projet at NMIJ for an absolute measurement of the viscosity by the falling ball method, 14th international

conference on the properties of water and steam in Kyoto (2004)
[7] Y. Fujita, progress of the absolute measurements of viscosity, CCM Working Group on Viscosity, BIPM, (2011)
[8] P. Ballereau, P. Pinot, T. Madec, M. Megharfi , Report on last improvements on falling ball viscometer, CCM Working Group on Viscosity, BIPM (2011)
[9] M. Brizard, Développement et étude d'un viscosimètre absolu à chute de bille, thèse de doctorat (2005)
[10] P. Ballereau, E. Mahé, P. Pinot, T. Madec, Density and viscosity of pure RME (rapeseed oil methyl ester) and SME (soybean oil methyl ester) at normal pressure, ENG09-Biofuel, annual meeting in Helsinki, January 31th (2011)
[11] T. Bohlin, On the drag on a rigid sphere moving in a viscous liquid inside a cylindrical tube, Trans. R. Inst. Tech. (Stockholm), **155**, pp 1-63 (1960)
[12] S. Candel, Mécanique des fluides, éditeur Dunod (1991)
[13] P. Chassaing, Mécanique des fluides, éléments d'un premier parcourt, deuxième édition, Cépadues-éditions (2000)
[14] I. L. Ryhming, Dynamique des fluids, deuxième édition, Presses polytechniques universitaires romandes (1991)
[15] H. Ha Minh, Les équations de Navier-Stokes: propriétés et application, 30ème colloque d'aérodynamique appliquée, Ecole centrale de Nantes (1993)
[16] P-L.Violet, Mécanique des fluides à masse volumique variable, éditeur Presses Pont et Chaussées (1997)
[17] J. Padet, Fluides en écoulement, méthodes et modèles, Editeur Masson (1991)
[18] G. G. Stokes, On the effect of the internal friction of fluids on the motion of a pendulum, Trans. Camb. Phi. Society, **9**, 8-106 (1851)
[19] H. Schlichting, Boundary-layer theory, seventh edition Mc Graw-Hill (1979)
[20] P. Chassaing, Mécanique des fluides, éléments d'un premier parcourt, deuxième édition, Cépadues-éditions (2000)
[21] E. Guyon, J-P. Hulin, L. Petit, Hydrodynamique physique, Editions du CNRS (1991)
[22] S. J. Liao, An analytic approximation of the drag coefficient for the viscous flow past a sphere, international Journal of Non-Linear Mechanics, **37**, 1-18 (2002)
[23] E. A. Brun, A. Martinot-Lagarde, J. Mathieu, Mécanique des fluides, tome 1, Dunod (1968)
[24] P. Bidault, Préhension en robotique, technique de l'ingénieurs, S 7 765 (2003)
[25] R.P. Chhabra, J.F. Richardson, Non-Newtonian flow and applied rheology, second edition, Elvesier (2008)
[26] M. Gottlieb, Zero-shear-rate viscosity measurements for polymer solutions by falling ball viscometry, Journal of Non-Newtonian Fluid Mechanics, **6**, 97-109 (1979)
[27] V. Subbaraman, R.A. Mashelkar, J. Ulbrecht, Extrapolation procedures for zero shear viscosity with a falling sphere viscometer, Rheol, Acta 10, 429-433 (1971).

Mini Six Sigma : Approches et outils pour l'amélioration des processus

Oumy TALL, Ingénieure en génie chimique, Chef de Service Formation/ Responsable métrologie
Sénégalaise Des Eaux, Tél : 00221338394150/00221776450410, Email : outa66@yahoo.fr/oumytall@sde.sn

RESUME:
La démarche que nous proposons désigne une méthode structurée de management visant une amélioration de la qualité et de l'efficacité des processus. Des approches d'analyses et des outils de base de la qualité nous permettent de: Définir, Mesurer, Analyser, Améliorer et Contrôler le processus. La réussite de cette démarche nécessite une implication de tous les collaborateurs au niveau des différentes structures de l'entreprise. L'étude que nous présentons, qui porte sur "l'analyse et l'amélioration du système de management de la qualité au niveau de la Sous Direction du Traitement des Eaux", représente notre contribution dans cette démarche. Pour ce faire nous avons effectué:
une analyse par approche processus des différentes activités de surveillance de la qualité des eaux
une analyse statistique des indicateurs et des dysfonctionnements du processus
une application de l'approche systématique de résolution de problèmes en groupe sur un des dysfontionnement qui fait intevenir le maximum d'acteurs. Ces leviers incontournables pour une démarche permanente d'amélioration continue nous ont permis, d'une part de vérifier la maîtrise du processus et d'autre part de déceler les différentes causes possibles des dysfonctionnements et de proposer des recommandations et des axes d'amélioration.

Mots clés: Définir, Mesurer, Analyser, Améliorer, Contrôler, amélioration processus.

1- Introduction

La mondialisation pousse les entreprises à s'engager dans des démarches Qualité Sécurité Environnement qui exigent une amélioration continue pour l'atteinte d'un niveau plus élevé d'efficacité et d'efficience des processus. La démarche 6 Sigma est une méthode d'amélioration des processus qui tend à réduire les causes de variabilité à l'origine des dysfonctionnements. Le cadre de notre étude, la Sénégalaise Des Eaux, première société de service public certifiée aux référentiels ISO, est dans cette dynamique.

Lors du déroulement des activités de contrôle de la qualité de l'eau, des dysfonctionnements apparaissent. Les actions menées sont-elles réellement des actions correctives ou préventives des causes, ou des symptômes des problèmes apparus? Existe-t-il des outils ou techniques qui permettent de déceler les causes réelles des dysfonctionnements et de les éradiquer ?

Cette étude représente notre contribution dans l'amélioration et l'optimisation du système de management du processus contrôle qualité de l'eau.

Son objectif est de réduire les dysfonctionnements, pour évoluer vers la satisfaction des clients. Pour mener à bien ce travail, nous avons procédé à une identification des différentes activités du processus, leurs interactions, et les risques de non maitrises afin de proposer des solutions. Nous avons aussi utilisé des outils de base de la qualité pour mettre en œuvre une méthodologie efficace d'amélioration du processus.

2- Approche théorique

La réussite d'une démarche d'amélioration de la qualité repose sur l'utilisation d'outils et de techniques développés visant à obtenir une meilleure satisfaction du client.

Les graphes sont des outils de contrôle continu d'un processus. Selon M. BRASSARD et D.RITTER [1] « ils sont utilisés pour surveiller, contrôler et améliorer les performances d'un processus dans le temps, en étudiant les variations et leurs sources. Ils aident à son amélioration, pour qu'il se fasse de façon constante et prévisible en vue d'un niveau de qualité supérieur, de coût réduit et d'une efficacité meilleure » ces méthodes statistiques sont très utilisées pour la maîtrise de la qualité.

L'efficacité d'un système de management de la qualité peut être mesurée par son aptitude et sa promptitude à résoudre les problèmes rencontrés.

Un problème est défini comme étant[2] « un écart entre une situation qui existe effectivement (situation actuelle) et une situation qui devrait exister (situation souhaitée). Une approche systématique est nécessaire pour le résoudre afin d'améliorer le niveau de qualité. »

La méthode de résolution de problème en groupe a pour objectif de traiter les problèmes avec efficacité afin de les supprimer en commençant par les plus importants. Dans ces groupes toutes les idées sont entendues, la participation, l'initiative, et la créativité de chacun apporte au groupe de travail une synergie nécessaire à la réussite de la démarche. « La qualité est l'affaire de tous mais aussi de chacun » [1] . Pour une meilleure efficacité, le groupe peut adopter une méthodologie simple avec un cadre de réflexion permettant, d'identifier le problème à traiter, de rechercher l'ensemble des causes, de trouver toutes les solutions envisageables et de choisir la solution la plus appropriée. Pour cela il faut un processus logique et cohérent avec des outils à chaque étape de la démarche. La réussite d'une démarche Six Sigma dépend donc de l'implication de tous les acteurs.

3- Methdologie

Nous avons procédé à l'exploitation des données du laboratoire sur une année, suivant une méthodologie d'analyse par :

APPROCHE PROCESSUS

- Cartographie du Processus Contrôle Qualité Eau
- Fiches d'analyse des différentes activités

(planification, prélèvement , surveillance physico chimique, bactériologique, assistance aux exploitations régionales)

APPROCHE STATISTIQUE

- Tableau de bord du Processus: Analyse par rapport aux objectifs :

Vérification de l'atteinte et détermination des causes de non atteinte.

Analyse par rapport aux limites de contrôle :

Détermination des sources de variation des différents indicateurs.

- Dysfonctionnements du Processus: Synthèse pour déceler les plus récurrents et proposer des solutions

APPOCHE SYSTEMATIQUE DE RESOLUTION DE PROBLEME

- Identification du problème: exemple Absence de chlore résiduel
- Recherche des causes : Brainstorming
- Diagramme d'affinité des causes
- Proposition de solutions
- Hiérarchisation des solutions

4- Resultats et discussions

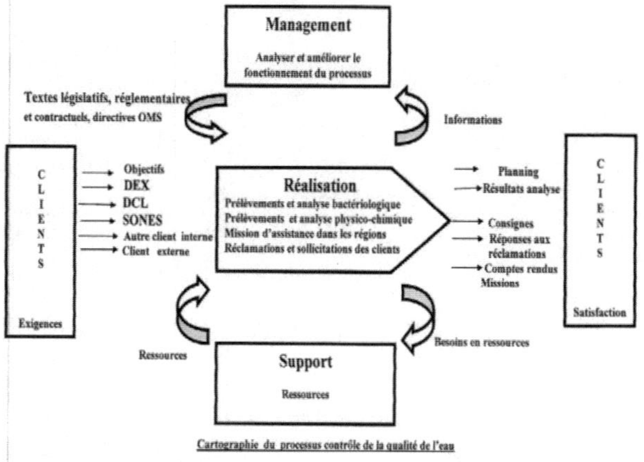

Fig. 1. Carthographie du processsus de contrôle de la qualité de l'eau

Nous avons procédé à une analyse des différents indicateurs du tableau de bord pour vérifier l'atteinte des objectifs, et déterminer les causes possibles de non atteinte. Mais aussi par rapport aux limites de contrôle pour détecter les sources de variation.

La fluctuation des données à l'intérieur des limites de contrôle supérieures et inférieures nous permet de caractériser le processus.

Les éléments statistiques ci dessous nous ont permis de tracer les cartes de contrôle ;
Obj = objectif annuel en %; M = moyenne annuelle en %; E = écart type; LCS = Limite Contrôle Supérieure = M + 3 E ; LCI = Limite de Contrôle Inférieure = M - 3 E ; LAS= Limite d'Alarme Supérieure = M + 2 E ; LAI= Limite d'alarme Inférieure = M - 2 E.

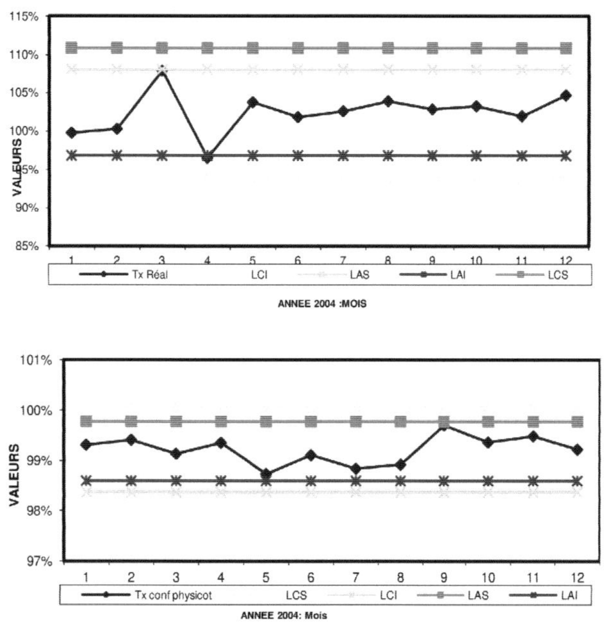

Fig. 3. Exemples de Graphes de contrôle du processus

L'analyse statistique des données de sortie du processus nous a permis de déceler les différentes sources possibles de variation des indicateurs.

Nous remarquons une fluctuation aléatoire due à des causes générales liées au système. Mais aussi une fluctuation non aléatoire due à des causes spéciales ; erreur humaine, événements non planifiés.

Par la suite nous avons, effectué une analyse statistique des dysfonctionnements enregistrés et choisit celui qui fait intervenir le maximum d'acteurs à savoir « une absence de chlore résiduel » pour procéder à une analyse par approche systématique de résolution de problème avec un groupe de travail composé de différents acteurs du processus.

Les travaux de groupe ont permis de tracer l'histogramme des causes du problème.

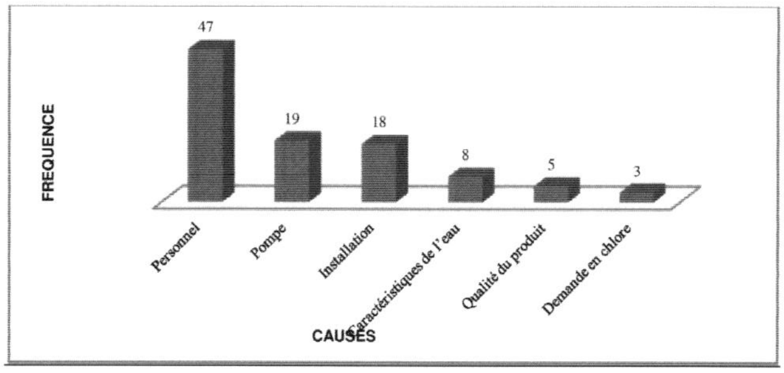

Fig. 5. Histogramme des causes

20% des causes (personnel, pompes, installation), produisent 80 % de l'effet (absence de chlore).

Sur la base de critères de choix associés à une pondération, nous avons classé les différentes solutions retenues par le groupe de travail:

S1 : formation et habilitation du personnel
S2 : surveillance du fonctionnement des pompes doseuses
S3 : suivi compteurs horaires des pompes doseuses
S4: gestion des stocks des pièces de rechange
S5: analyse fonctionnelle du besoin des exploitants

L'analyse par approche processus et les méthodes et outils de résolution des problèmes, nous ont permis d'identifier les causes des dysfonctionnements et de mettre en place des axes d'amélioration afin d'élimination les risques de non maitrise du processus:

Tableau 1. Quelques axes d'améliorations proposés aprés l'étude

Risques	Actions proposées après l'étude	Actions Réalisées
Non-respect du planning des missions	Organisation de l'activité assistance dans les régions	Renforcement des moyens. Mise en place d'indicateurs de nouveaux indicateurs.
Non-respect des consignes	Vérification taux de traitement (missions visites inopinées).	Mise en place de planning de visite inopinée. Contrôle des consignes.
Dépassement délai de réponse aux réclamations des clients	Permanence du service. disponibilité des techniciens du Labo. Suivi des actions	Mise en place d'indicateurs de suivi du délai de réponse aux réclamations des clients.
Formation des corresponds du laboratoire dans les régions	Etablir un plan de formation. Evaluation efficacité formation. Remise à niveau périodique.	Planning de formation. Evaluation des formations. Suivi électronique de la validité des cartes d'habilitation.
Rupture de stock de réactifs.	Gestion et suivi du matériel et des réactifs.	Installation d'un logiciel de gestion et de suivi du stock.

5 Conclusion et recommandations

La démarche " mini six sigma" que nous avons utilisée dans cette étude, nous a permis, de définir les objectifs et l'étendue du processus, de mesurer et d'analyser les données recueillies, et de proposer des solutions d'amélioration du processus en réduisant les causes de variabilité des dysfonctionnements.

Sa réussite est obtenue grâce à l'implication de tous les acteurs qui interviennent dans le contrôle de la qualité de l'eau.

L'étude que nous avons menée nous a permis de proposer, en plus des axes d'améliorations, un certain nombre de recommandations pour l'amélioration du système de management de la qualité :

-L'analyse des risques de non maitrise et la mise en place de plan d'amélioration comprenant des indicateurs d'efficacité du processus.
-L'analyse orientée vers les tendances, pour déceler les différentes causes possibles de variation des indicateurs
-L'utilisation des Méthodes et Outils de Résolution de problèmes pour apporter des solutions durables aux dysfonctionnements du processus.
-La mise en place d'une procédure de gestion des réclamations, avec une vérification de l'efficacité des actions correctives mise en place
-Le développement de la relation client / fournisseur interne pour mieux faire ressortir l'interaction entre les différentes activités du processus contrôle de la qualité de l'eau distribuée dans toutes les régions.

Références

1. Michel BRASSAR et Diane RITTER, Guide de poche des outils pour une amélioration continue et une planification efficace.
2. Aboubacry BARO, Méthodes et outils de résolution de problèmes, Institut Supérieur de Management.
3. Michel CATTAN, Nathalie IDRISSI, Patrick KNOCKAER Maîtriser les processus de l'entreprise
4. Oumy TALL, 2004 « Analyse et Amélioration du système de management de la qualité : Sous Direction du Traitement des Eaux », mémoire Diplôme d'Etudes Supérieures Spécialisées en management par la qualité totale, Institut Supérieur de Management (I.S.M), Dakar, 2005.

Mise en place de la fonction métrologie dans un systéme multi-référentiel: Qualité – Sécurité - Environnement

Oumy TALL, Ingénieure en génie chimique, Chef de Service Formation/ Responsable métrologie
Sénégalaise Des Eaux, Tél : 00221338394150/00221776450410, Email : outa66@yahoo.fr/oumytall@sde.sn

Résumé :
L'entreprise effectue des mesures pour, des besoins économiques, des essais, la production, ou le contrôle. Ces mesures peuvent fortement contribuer à la qualité des produits fabriqués ou des services.
Les produits doivent satisfaire aux attentes exprimées des clients, donc être conformes à des exigences (normes, spécifications internes). C'est pour toutes ces raisons que l'entreprise doit mettre en place une fonction métrologie pour coordonner la gestion et le suivi des équipements de mesure de contrôle et d'essai. Cet article présente l'expérience capitalisé d'un responsable métrologique au sein d'une entreprise certifié qualité sécurité environnement. Il décrit le processus de mise en place de la fonction métrologie.

Mots clés: **Mesure, Résultat, fiabilité, traçabilité, fonction métrologique**

Introduction

Le processus de mesure est un ensemble d'opérations effectuées pour déterminer la valeur d'une quantité. [1]. Les opérations de mesure sont effectuées tout au long de la chaîne de production, distribution, et d'approvisionnement des produits. Les résultats de mesure servent à prendre des décisions dont les conséquences peuvent être d'ordes, économiques, techniques, environnementales et sociales.

La métrologie c'est un moyen de communication entre les fournisseurs de résultats de mesures et d'essai et les utilisateurs de ces résultats. Cette science de la mesure se présente sous 03 aspects :

-la métrologie scientifique dont son niveau de développement dépend des besoins industriels du pays. Elle est appliquée au commerce, à la protection de l'environnement, au domaine de la santé, à la sécurité, et à certaines opérations fiscales ou douanières.

-la métrologie légale se rapportant aux activités qui résultent d'exigences réglementaires et qui s'appliquent aux mesurages, aux unités de mesures, aux instruments de mesure et aux méthodes de mesures, et sont effectuées par des organismes compétents (VIML) [1]

la métrologie industrielle, c'est l'ensemble des activités qui contribuent à garantir la qualité des mesures effectuées dans l'industrie et dans les activités de service

1- Métrologie- Qualité -Normalisation

Les référentiels de management de la qualité exigent: la maîtrise des processus de mesure afin de garantir la fiabilité et la traçabilité des résultats de mesure.
Des exigences liées au systéme de mesure sont spécifiées dans les trois réferentiels, qualité ISO 9001(§7.6) Maîtrise des dispositifs de surveillance et de mesure, sécurité ISO 14001: (§4.5.1) Surveillances et mesurage, et environnement
OSHAS 18001:(§4.5.1) Mesure et surveillance des performances
L'analyse des besoins des entreprises permettent de statuer sur le choix des moyens de mesures avec toutes les spécification techniques nécessaires.
Du mesurande au résultat l'efficacité de la mesure passe par la maitrise du processus et de ces 5 paramétres d'influences: la Matière (produit, emballage), le Milieu (Géographie, ambiance), la

Méthodes(Mode opératoire , reporting), le Matériel (Outils, machines, dispositif de transport, la Main d'œuvre (Personnel interne, sous-traitance).

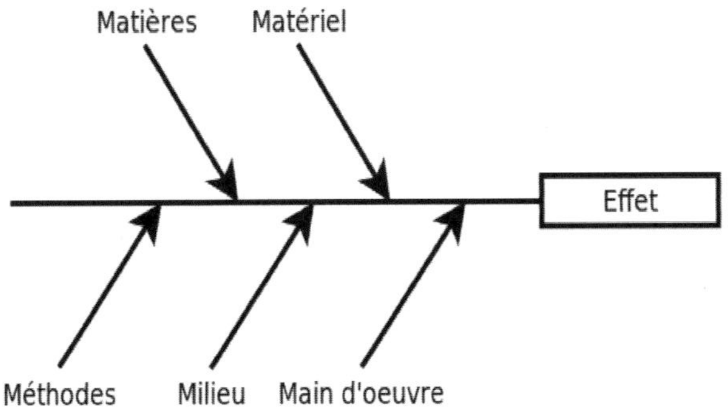

Fig. 1. Diagramme Ishikawa du processus de mesure

Le personnel effectuant les mesures doit être qualifié. Les moyens de mesures sont souvent complexes et nécessitent une formation spécifique. Un bon métrologue doit être curieux, méthodique, ordonner, avoir l'aptitude à douter et le sens de l'observation. Une application rigoureuse du § 7.6 de la norme ISO 9001 permet de garantir la traçabilité des mesures aux étalons nationaux. Le suivi périodique des moyens de mesure est une solution de surveillance du processus .

Nous pouvons citer 3 types de documents, les normes, les guides et les fascicules de documentation. Les documents de base en métrologie sont, la norme ISO 9001 (§7.6), le Vocabulaire International de Métrologie, (VIM), le Guide Universel de la Métrologie (GUM), et la norme ISO 10012. La maîtrise des dispositifs de surveillance et de mesure fait l'objet du § 7.6 de la norme ISO 9001, qui renvoie à ISO 10012 pour les conseils d'application. Cette dernière introduit les notions de confirmation et de fonction métrologie.

2 – Fonction métrologie dans l'entreprise

La fonction métrologie doit être définie par l'organisme. La direction doit garantir la disponibilité des ressources nécessaires pour établir et entretenir cette fonction afin d'assurer la fiabilité de toutes les mesures ayant un impact sur la qualité des produits et des services. Une entreprise certifiée aux trois reférentiels Qualité Sécurité Environnement dispose d'une organisation métrologique lui permettatant d'étre en conformité par rapport aux exigences, pour la satisfaction du client.

Elle a en charge la responsabilité administrative et technique de la mise en œuvre du système de management de la mesure[3]. Elle a pour objectif de garantir la qualité des mesures effectuées dans l'entreprise à tous les stades d'élaboration d'un produit.

Elle peut être assurer en 5 grandes étapes:

-L'analyse des besoins métrologiques. C'est un ensemble d'actions à effectuer en préparation des opérations de vérification/étalonnage, pour déterminer quels sont les instruments de mesure qui contribuent à garantir la qualité des produits ou des services.

-L'organisation de la métrologie. Elle permet de décliner la politique de l'entreprise en matière de vérification, les moyens, et les périodicités.

-La mise en place avec l'élaboration des procédures et la formation du personnel

-La gestion des équipements de mesure. Dans cette partie on valide les spécifications techniques des besoin, des commandes et des conditions de réception et de stockage des équipements (neuf ou en retour de réparation).

-La traçabilité et le raccordement aux étalons nationaux. Elle doit être assurer lors de la réalisation des opérations de vérifications périodiques des moyens de mesure de l'entreprise

3 – Application dans un systeme multiréférentiel

La Sénégalaise Des Eaux est la première société d'eau d'Afrique à être certifié Qualité Sécurité Environnement. Cette certification traduit la prise en compte de la protection des hommes et de l'environnement en plus de la satisfaction clientèle et l'amélioration permanente des performances. Les audites de suivie et de renouvellement permettent d'améliorer en permanence la qualité du service, le niveau de sécurité, et la maitrise des impactes environnementaux.

Au sein de l'entreprise et dans toutes les régions nous pouvons recenser des équipements de mesure de contrôle et d'essai dans trois domaines de compétences:
- Surveillance de la qualité physico chimique et bactériologique de l'eau (matériels de laboratoire)
-Mesures physiques, électriques et /ou mécaniques (production et la maintenance des ouvrages hydrauliques)
-Mesures de débits (compteurs d'eau).

Tous les équipements de mesure appartenant à l'entreprise, ou présents sur les installations qu'elle exploite sont classés dans l'une des deux catégories suivantes :
- les équipements qui sont indispensables pour garantir et démontrer la conformité aux exigences sur lesquelles elle s'est engagée, sont dénommés « équipements de mesure gérés ».
- les équipements qui ne correspondent pas à la définition ci-dessus mais qui fournissent simplement des indications analogiques ou numériques au personnel d'exploitation sont dénommés « équipements de mesure indicatifs du fonctionnement ».
La mise en œuvre du système management qualité, a fait émerger le rôle de la fonction métrologie dans la société. Sa mise en place a suivi plusieurs étapes:

3-1.Description du processus de mesure:

Nous avons tracé:
-La matrice de correspondance entre le processus maitrise des équipements de mesure et les autres processus pour déterminer leur degrés d'interaction (Forte F; Moyenne M; Faible;f)
- la matrice de sélection des équipements de contrôle, de mesure et d'essai : pour déterminer la criticité sur le produit, le service client, sur la sécurité des agents, des installations et sur l'environnement
-la cartographie du processus de mesure : afin de ressortir les interfaces avec les autres processus.

3-2.Mise en place des documents:

Rédaction des procédures et instrutions de travail tels que: outils de décision sur un équipement à gérer, état des mesurages, procédure de gestion, Inventaire des équipements, fiche de vie, planning d'intervention, mode opératoire de vérifivation et d'étalonnage, procédure de maintenance et de gestion des équipements non conformes.

La procédure a pour objet de définir les règles de gestion et de maintenance des équipements de mesure de contrôle et d'essai, utilisés pour garantir la conformité aux exigences spécifiées des prestations fournies ou des produits livrés au client, et celles liées à l'hygiène l'environnement et la sécurité au travail.

4-3. Réalisation des opérations de vérifications / étalonnage

Elles sont réalisées par des correspondants métrologies qui sont nommés pour chaque domaine de compétences (équipements de laboratoires, électromécaniques et compteurs). Ils sont chargés de la coordination de toutes les opérations mensuelles de vérification, l'exploitation des résultats et la rédaction des rapports de vérification. Ils calculent les indicateurs, renseignent le tableau de bord, les fiches de vies et étiquettent les équipements conformes. Les équipements non conformes suivent l'instruction de travail établie à cet effet.

En fin il suit l'avancement des travaux sur les équipements mis en réparation s'assure du bon fonctionnement d'un appareil en retour de réparation avant d'entreprendre sa qualification. Les enrégistrements de toutes les opérations sont conservés.

Des équipements sont mise en place pour la protection individuelle (EPI) et collective (EPC) des collaborateurs.

Des régles de gestions des déchets et des rejets sont établies et suivies lors des vérifications des équipements.

3-4. Traçabilité et raccordement

La traçabilité et le raccordement des étalons sont assurés par des laboratoires accrédités sur le plan national ou international et suivant un planning établit à cet effet.

3-5. Surveillance du processus

Toutes les données de sorties du processus de mesure sont consolidées par le Responsanble métrologie qui analyse les tendances observées avant transmission au Responsable du processus. Des actions correctives ou préventives, des plans d'amélioration sont décidés et validés en comité de direction pour l'amélioration du processus de mesure.

CONCLUSION

La mise en œuvre du système de management qualité a fait émerger le rôle de la fonction métrologie dans l'entreprise. L'introduction et l'organisation de la fonction métrologie a permis de garantir une qualité de service, un fonctionnement optimum des installations et le respect des exigences réglementaires en matière d'environnement et de sécurité. Elle constitue ainsi un outil de satisfaction des exigences clients.

Références

1. ISO 9001:Systéme de management de la qualité. Exgigences
2.VIM : 1993 Vocabulaire international des termes fondamentaux et généraux de métrologie,
3.ISO 10012. Systéme de management de la mesure- Exigences pour les processus et les équipement de mesure.

La traçabilité des faibles forces dans le futur SI

N-E. Khelifa*, P. Averlant+ et M. Himbert*

Laboratoire Commun de Métrologie LNE-Cnam
* Cnam, 61 rue du Landy- Case 2LAB10, F-93210, La Plaine Saint-Denis, France
+ LNE, 1 rue Gaston Boissier, F-75015 Paris, France

Abstract. L'unité de force est raccordée au kilogramme (unité de masse du Système International d'unités) et à son prototype international par l'intermédiaire de machines à poids morts utilisant des masses étalonnées. Cependant les forces inférieures à une dizaine de micronewtons, omniprésentes dans la nature et dans certains dispositifs, ne peuvent être mesurées avec une traçabilité au SI. La détermination de ces forces et de l'incertitude associée a des implications aussi bien pour la science fondamentale que pour les applications. Aujourd'hui, de nombreux secteurs émergents en micro-nano technologie et en biotechnologie commencent à produire et à utiliser des systèmes mettant en œuvre de faibles forces qui requièrent des résultats traçables. La révision du SI est prévue pour 2018 : elle consiste à relier les définitions du kilogramme, de l'ampère, du kelvin et de la mole à des valeurs numériques de certaines constantes fondamentales ; elle ouvre des perspectives pour la mesure des faibles forces. Dans cet article, nous présentons l'état de l'art du domaine, en particulier le développement d'un capteur de force utilisant un laser solide monolithique à cristal photoélastique. La force à mesurer, appliquée sur le cristal, induit une biréfringence dans le laser qui va se manifester par l'apparition d'un écart entre les fréquences associées aux deux composantes de polarisation du mode laser oscillant. Cet écart entre les deux fréquences est, dans la limite d'élasticité du cristal, proportionnel à la force appliquée, et peut être exploité pour la mesure.

Keywords: Système International d'unités (SI), laser solide, biréfringence, faible force, masse étalon, newton.

1. Introduction

La force, grandeur dérivée de la masse, est par conséquent traçable au kilogramme étalon. Durant les dernières années, de nombreux travaux ont été menés pour mettre en œuvre différentes techniques pour la mesure de forces avec une haute exactitude et notamment pour celles dont l'intensité est en dessous de 10 µN. Les premiers capteurs optiques dits « passifs » utilisant des fibres optiques intégrant des MEMS (Micro-Electro-Mechanical System), ou des réseaux de Bragg, se sont avérées inadaptées en raison de la complexité de leur réponse [1-3]. D'autres développements prometteurs sont en cours : ils portent notamment sur l'utilisation de balances électrostatiques [4-6], de balances à compensation électromagnétique [7] ou de capteur optique « actif » basé sur l'effet photoélastique dans un laser solide [8-10].

Aujourd'hui, en effet, de nombreux dispositifs sont capables de mesurer ou de détecter des forces avec des résolutions bien meilleures que le nanonewton. Cependant, au niveau international, il n'existe aucune aptitude reconnue dans les laboratoires de métrologie (Calibration and Measurement Capabilities, « CMCs » au sens du BIPM) en matière de mesures et d'étalonnages pour des forces en dessous de 0,1N [11]. Entre 0,1 N et 10 µN les mesures de forces sont réalisées avec un raccordement traçable aux unités de base du système international d'unités (SI) par l'utilisation de masses étalons, sans qu'il soit réellement utile d'identifier et de valider des capacités de mesures spécifiques (CMC).

* Correspondance: naceur.khelifa@cnam.fr

En revanche les mesures de force en dessous de 10 µN sont réalisées sans aucune traçabilité au SI. Aujourd'hui, des capteurs de forces relativement compacts, destinés aux mesures de forces (en compression et en traction) en dessous du newton commencent à apparaître sur le marché, mais leur étendue reste proche du newton. En dessous, des balances peuvent être utilisées, mais leur encombrement reste un grand inconvénient.

Les récents développements dans différents domaines des nanotechnologies montrent de plus en plus l'importance des capteurs de forces miniatures mais également de leur raccordement au SI. De ce fait, les industriels présents sur le marché de la mesure des faibles forces deviennent très prudents dès qu'il est question de l'étalonnage de leurs dispositifs et des incertitudes qui leurs sont associées. En effet, la reproductibilité des expériences impliquant des mesures de faibles forces est difficile à vérifier en utilisant des instruments différents.

L'objectif de cet article est d'identifier les techniques déjà mises en œuvre ainsi que les possibilités qui sont susceptibles d'être utilisées dans des dispositifs de mesures traçables des faibles forces, et les artefacts pouvant être utilisés pour assurer le transfert des références primaires vers les dispositifs nécessitant un étalonnage.

Les possibilités d'étalonnage des forces en dessous du newton dans différents laboratoires de métrologie ainsi qu'un aperçu des travaux dans le domaine des faibles forces sont donnés dans la section 2. De brefs rappels théoriques de la biréfringence induite dans un laser solide par une contrainte mécanique et son incidence sur le mode laser oscillant sont l'objet de la section 3.

La section 4 présente le dispositif expérimental du capteur photoélastique de force développé au Laboratoire Commun de Métrologie LNE-Cnam, ainsi que des résultats expérimentaux concernant la sensibilité de ce type de capteur. L'apport de ces travaux et les perspectives autour du défi instrumental pour la réalisation de références primaires mais aussi des dispositifs de transfert pour rendre traçable les mesures de faibles forces sont résumées dans la section 5.

2. La place des faibles forces

Le développement d'un artefact de transfert pour fournir une traçabilité des mesures de force dans la gamme du millinewton au micronewton est justifié par les besoins croissants dans l'industrie (indentation instrumentée; systèmes micro électro mécaniques MEMS) ...) mais aussi par le développement de certains secteurs émergents, notamment pour les dispositifs miniaturisés conçus pour manipuler des objets fragiles.

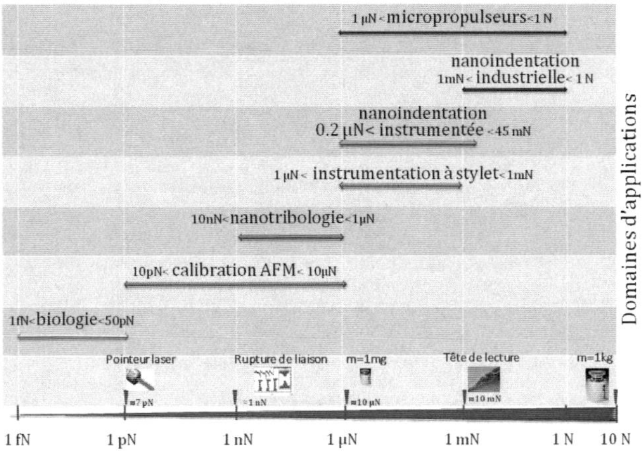

Fig. 1. Aperçu de quelques domaines utilisant des faibles forces.

La figure 1 donne quelques plages de force et leurs domaines d'utilisation avec, comme simple repérage, les ordres de grandeurs de la force associée à certains dispositifs simples.

3. Etat de l'art.

Au niveau international les CMC des laboratoires nationaux de métrologie ne recensent aucune possibilité en dessous de 0,1 N pour les forces.

Le tableau 1 donne les valeurs des forces minimales dans les CMC d'un certains nombre de laboratoire Européens, rassemblées (novembre 2014) à partir de la base de données des comparaisons clés du Bureau International des Poids et Mesures (BIPM). Les incertitudes relatives associées à ces valeurs minimales sont comprises entre 10^{-1} et 10^{-4}.

3.1. Force engendrée à l'aide de poids mort

Les dispositifs de mesure les plus courants dans les laboratoires de métrologie des masses reposent sur l'utilisation de balances à compensation et de séries de masses étalons raccordées au SI (kilogramme international). Ces moyens sont exploités dans le domaine des forces car la méthode la plus intuitive pour produire une force est celle qui consiste à utiliser une masse étalon dans le champ gravitationnel de la Terre.

Tab. 1. Forces minimales (CMC) raccordées au SI par quelques laboratoires de métrologie.

National Metrology Institute	Approval date	Instrument or Artefact	Instrument or Method	Minimum value of Measurand (N)	Expanded Uncertainty (%)	Coverage facteur of E.U	Level of confidence (%)
LNE- FR	11/10/2005	Force measuring device	Deadweight	5	0.0025	2	95
METAS - CH	02/07/2008	//	//	2.5	0.002	2	95
NPL- UK	?	//	//	1.5	0.008	2	95
INRIM- IT	03/01/2007	//	//	1	0.005	2	95
SP- SE	?	//	//	1	0.01	2	95
PTB- DE	03/01/2007	//	//	0.5	0.002	2	95
DFM- DK	11/10/2005	//	//	0.1	0.01	2	95

Mass and Related Quantities: Force (Tension & Compression)
Calibration and Measurement Capabilities (CMCs): BIPM key comparison database, Nov. 2014.

Une force appelée « poids mort » ou poids de la masse étalon est ainsi engendrée. Elle est donnée, en tenant compte de la poussée d'Archimède, par :

$$F_{pm} = \mathrm{m_e}\left(1 - {}^{\rho_a}/_{\rho_e}\right) \mathrm{g_l} \quad (1)$$

m_e est la masse de l'étalon utilisé et ρ_e sa masse volumique. ρ_a et g_l représentent respectivement la masse volumique de l'air ambiant et l'accélération locale de la gravitation.

La relation (1) conduit, pour une masse étalon de 100 mg dans le champ de gravitation du laboratoire, à un poids mort de $9{,}8094 \times 10^{-4}$ N avec une incertitude de l'ordre de 10 nN [12].

En termes d'étalons de masse, la plus petite valeur nominale de masse figurant dans les CMCs des laboratoires nationaux de métrologie est de 1 mg, dans les laboratoires cités dans le tableau 1, mais également dans tous les autres. En termes de poids mort, une telle masse étalon correspond à une force de l'ordre de 10 µN.

Il faut signaler que des micro-masses étalons ayant des valeurs nominales entre 900 µg et100 µg ont été réalisées au LNE [13-14] et sont utilisées comme références pour des étalonnages. Depuis, d'autres laboratoires se sont lancés dans la réalisation de ce type d'étalons (NPL-UK, PTB-DE, NIM-RO, METAS-CH, ...).

La méthode fondée sur l'utilisation des étalons de masses est utilisée dans les machines à poids morts (figure 2) pour la traçabilité de la force ; elle couvre la plage allant du newton au méganewton. Dans son principe, cette technique peut être utilisée pour des poids morts plus faibles sans aucune difficulté scientifique ou technologique jusqu'à une dizaine de micronewtons. Cependant, elle devient relativement difficile à mettre en œuvre en dessous de cette limite en raison des petites dimensions et des formes géométriques des micro-masses étalons introduisant une incertitude relativement élevée pour la mesure du poids. Nous verrons par la suite que les faibles poids morts sont utilisables comme artefacts de transfert en association avec des balances à grande résolution.

3.2. Mesure de forces

Au niveau national (LNE), les possibilités accréditées par le COFRAC selon la norme ISO 17025 couvrent le domaine de 1 N à 9 MN.

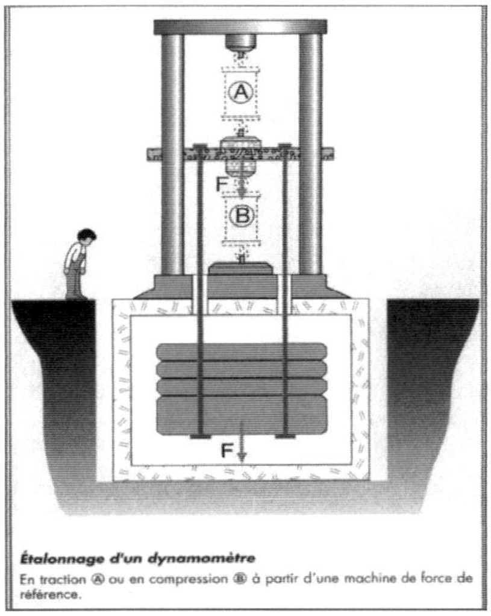

Fig. 2. Machine de force à poids morts [15].

Le LNE peut envisager de faire évoluer ses CMC revendiquées, en fonction des besoins exprimés d'industriels, pour descendre jusqu'à 10 µN par la technique des poids morts. Cette possibilité pourrait être rapidement mise en oeuvre compte tenu de la compétence de l'organisme pour le développement de nouvelles méthodes ou nouveaux moyens d'étalonnage, compétence reconnue par l'organisme français d'accréditation (COFRAC).
En effet le département "forces et grandeurs associées" du Laboratoire Commun de Métrologie, qui délivre actuellement des certificats d'étalonnage au delà de 1 N, est capable d'étendre ce type d'étalonnage vers le bas, par l'utilisation d'une masse étalon de 1 mg avec une incertitude de 0.6 µg, jusqu'à 10 µN. L'incertitude sur la force ainsi engendrée est alors d'une dizaine de nanonewtons. Ces moyens permettraient d'étalonner des capteurs de force en laboratoire, eux-mêmes utilisés pour faire des mesures tracables sur site. Il peut s'agir de capteur à jauges de déformation ou de balances de grande résolution, sensibles à la force qui leur est appliquée.
Cependant les bonnes pratiques recommandent l'étalonnage des capteurs de force sur le lieu de leur utilisation. Comme il est simple à l'utilisateur d'acquérir des étalons de masse dans la gamme correspondante et de calculer les forces engendrées, le développement des CMC reste peu utile à ce jour pour l'étendue de 1 N à 10 µN. En revanche la problématique persiste pour le domaine des forces inférieures à 10 µN.

4. Les principaux dispositifs électromécaniques dédiés aux mesures de faibles forces.

4.1. Etalons primaires

Quelques laboratoires dans le monde cherchent à développer des références de faibles forces basées sur des dispositifs électromécaniques (NIST, NPL, PTB, KRISS-KR).
Depuis plus d'une dizaine d'années, le National Institute of Standards and Technology (NIST), aux Etats-Unis, travaille sur un projet de "balance nanoforce" pour couvrir la gamme de force allant de 1nN à 1 µN et une incertitude relative de l'ordre de 0,1 % pour une force de quelques nanonewtons [16-18]. Cette balance électrostatique est fondée sur les mesures de tension électrique, de capacité et de déplacement traçables au SI avec de grandes exactitudes. Il faut noter que ce laboratoire développe également une "balance du watt" dédiée au raccordement d'un étalon de masse à la constante de Planck dans la perspective de la révision de l'actuel SI.

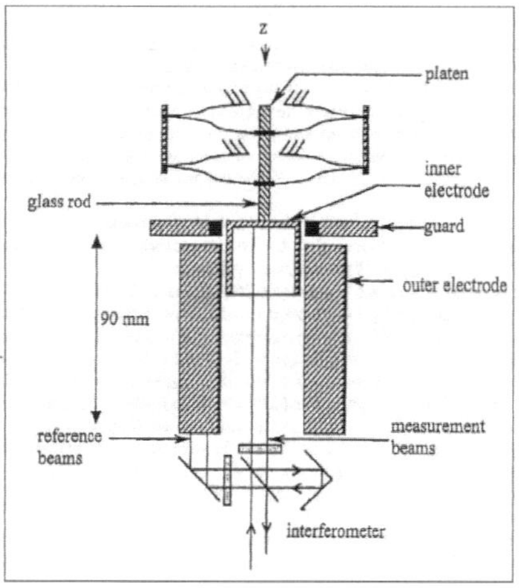

Fig. 3a. Schéma de principe de la balance électrostatique (NIST) [17]

Le condensateur est constitué de deux électrodes concentriques. L'électrode interne, mobile selon l'axe vertical, est guidée par une suspension à éléments flexibles.

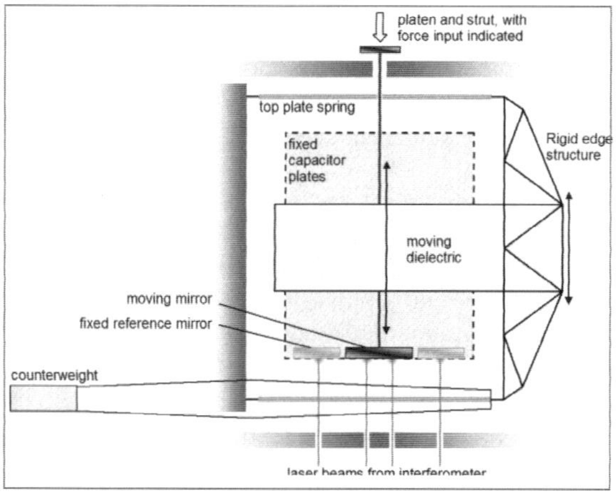

Fig.3b. Balance électrostatique (NPL) [19]

Les résultats les plus récents [18-19] font état des principales limitations liées d'une part, à la raideur du système de suspension et d'autre part, à la sensibilité du système et à la géométrie du condensateur. Les figures 3a et 3b donnent des schémas de principe d'une balance électrostatique. Une force verticale appliquée à la platine déplace l'élément de flexion dans la même direction. Ce déplacement, mesuré par un interféromètre différentiel à miroir plan, est converti par un système de commande en une tension de contre-réaction. La force de contre-réaction est alors produite par la différence de potentiel à travers les plaques du condensateur orienté verticalement.
La force électrique ainsi générée, en réponse à la charge le long de l'axe de la balance, est donnée en fonction des grandeurs électriques par:

$$F_e = \frac{1}{2}\frac{\mathrm{dC}}{\mathrm{dz}} \mathrm{V}^2$$

où dC est la variation de capacité mesurée pour dz donné du chevauchement des électrodes et V le potentiel électrique appliqué.

Ce type de balance joue le rôle d'un étalon primaire de force. Il nécessite un artefact de transfert de la référence donnée par la balance de faible forces (LFB) vers l'instrument cible à étalonner.
Le National Physical Laboratory (NPL-UK) a également conçu une « Low Force Balance » qui fonctionne sur le même principe. Celle-ci utilise un condensateur plan à quatre électrodes permettant de choisir la direction de la force exercée sur une plaque diélectrique suspendue au système de guidage en fonction des tensions appliquées (diélectrique mobile). La configuration choisie permet un étalonnage aussi bien en poussée qu'en traction. La dynamique attendue correspond à un domaine de forces comprises entre 10 µN et 1 nN avec une résolution de quelques dizaines de piconewtons [19]. L'intérêt de ce projet est qu'il relie un domaine non traçable à ce jour à un domaine traçable avec la méthode des poids morts. Il a également l'avantage de réaliser des efforts de traction.
Enfin, le KRISS, laboratoire de métrologie de la Corée du Sud, a développé un dispositif électrostatique qui comporte comme au NIST un condensateur coaxial. Le système de suspension repose sur l'utilisation de lames flexibles assurant la compensation de la masse suspendue [20]. La sensibilité de ce dispositif est de l'ordre de 1µN.

4.2. Étalons de transfert

Le Physikalisch Technische Bundesanstalt (PTB-DE), dispose de différentes balances électromagnétiques (étalons de transfert) pour une gamme de forces plus élevées. Le prototype du dispositif comporte un ensemble aimant-bobine, conçu pour couvrir le domaine des forces comprises entre 100 µN et 0.1N [21]. Son utilisation reste conditionnée à son raccordement au SI par l'intermédiaire de masses étalons. Enfin, le PTB cherche à réaliser des artefacts de transfert de forces fondés sur l'utilisation de MEMS (Micro Electro Mechanical Systems) [22].

Pour la mesure traçable de raideur de pointe d'AFM, le KRISS a développé un dispositif basé autour d'une microbalance à compensation électromagnétique commerciale préalablement étalonnée au moyen d'étalons de masse [25]. La pointe est fixée sur une platine de translation verticale dont on peut mesurer précisément le déplacement et l'extrémité libre de la pointe est amenée en appui sur une petite sphère placée sur le plateau d'une microbalance.

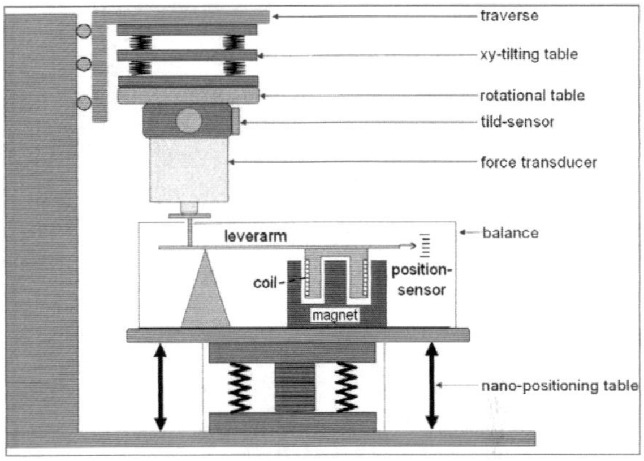

Fig. 3. Schéma de principe de la machine de force dans la gamme de 100 µN–100 mN, développée au PTB [21]

La force d'appui de la pointe sur la sphère engendre une réaction du système de compensation électromagnétique de la microbalance qui donne une indication en masse. Celle-ci est directement convertible en force en la multipliant soit parla valeur conventionnelle, soit par une valeur déterminée localement de l'accélération de la pesanteur. Des raideurs de l'ordre de 0,07 Nm^{-1} pour des forces appliquées de l'ordre de 500 nN ont été mesurées avec une incertitude relative de 1%. Le schéma ci-après présente le principe de ce montage.

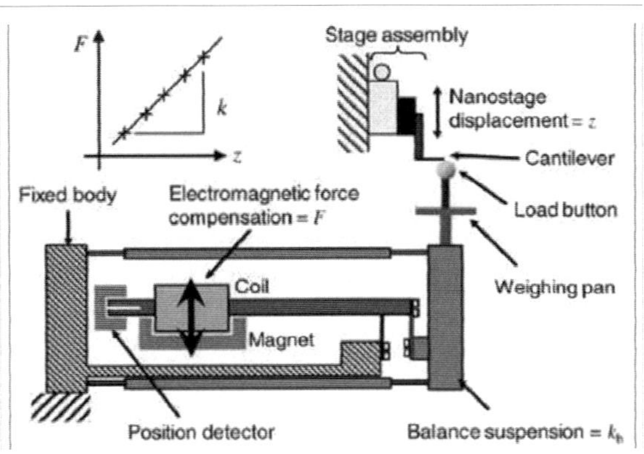

Fig. 5. Schéma de principe du dispositif du KRISS [24]

L'autre voie consiste à utiliser une balance électromagnétique fondée sur le principe d'une balance du watt. La mesure de la force inconnue est réalisée en utilisant la force de Laplace raccordée au préalable à un poids mort pour équilibrer la balance. Des études préliminaires ont été menées au LCM à l'aide d'un système prototype analogue à celui de la balance du watt. Les premiers tests portant sur l'étude de la sensibilité de cette balance sont très encourageants.

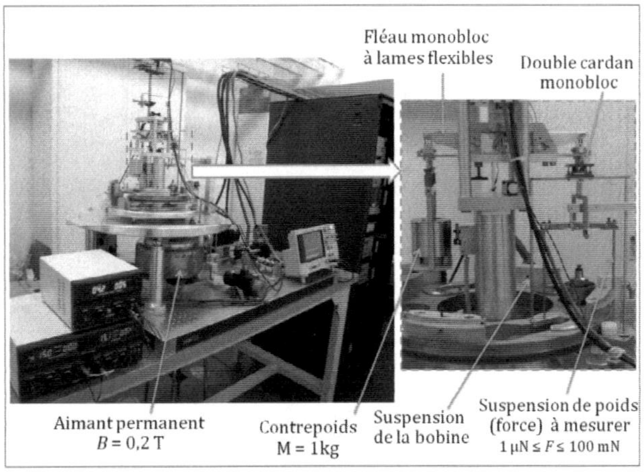

Fig. 4. Prototype de balance électromagnétique de force du Laboratoire Commun de Métrologie [25].

5. Dispositif à capteur élastique

5.1. Effet photoélastique dans un laser solide.

La biréfringence induite dans le milieu amplificateur d'un laser solide monolithique, lorsque ce dernier est soumis à une contrainte mécanique, se manifeste par des indices de réfraction différents selon que la polarisation de l'onde qui traverse le cristal est dans la direction d'application de la force ou dans la direction orthogonale. Cette biréfringence est d'autant plus importante lorsque la force appliquée F_{ext} est parallèle à l'un des deux axes de contraintes principales (photoélasticité à deux dimensions). Dans ce cas, les directions principales de l'ellipsoïde des indices coïncident avec celles des contraintes.

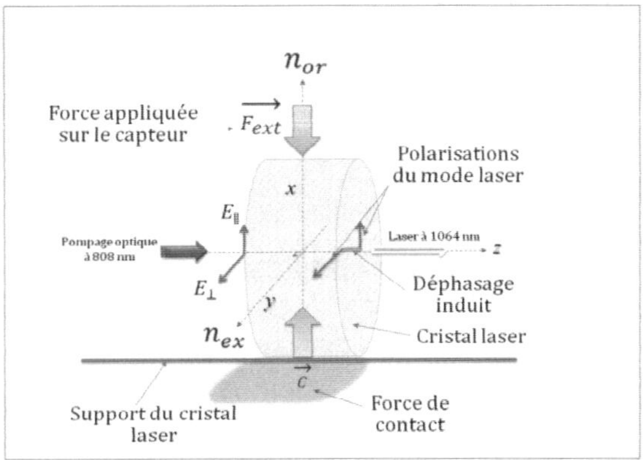

Fig. 5. Orientation et axes principaux du barreau à Nd-YAG.

L'expression de la biréfringence induite dans le milieu laser, représentée par la relation de contrainte optique, est donnée par la loi classique de Wertheim [26] :

$$\Delta n = n_o - n_e = C_{PE}^{(\lambda_q)}(\sigma_{\perp} - \sigma_{\parallel}) \qquad (2)$$

Ou, $\sigma_{\parallel}$ et $\sigma_{\perp}$ sont les contraintes principales induites au centre du milieu laser selon les directions parallèle et orthogonale à la force extérieure. $C_{PE}^{(\lambda_q)}$, est la constante de photoélasticité du cristal laser (Nd-YAG). Cette constante dépend faiblement de la longueur d'onde λ_q associée au mode laser longitudinal d'ordre q.

Dans le cas ou la force extérieure est dans un plan diamétral du barreau (figure 5), contenant les deux directions de contraintes principales, la conversion de cette dernière en contraintes internes s'écrit [27] :

$$\sigma_{\perp} - \sigma_{\parallel} = \frac{G}{\ell\, d} F_{ext} \qquad (2)$$

ℓ et d, sont respectivement la longueur et le diamètre du laser solide monolithique à Nd-YAG ; G est un facteur de forme, dont la valeur dépend des conditions d'alignements géométriques du barreau Nd-YAG par rapport au faisceau laser utilisé pour pomper optiquement le milieu laser.

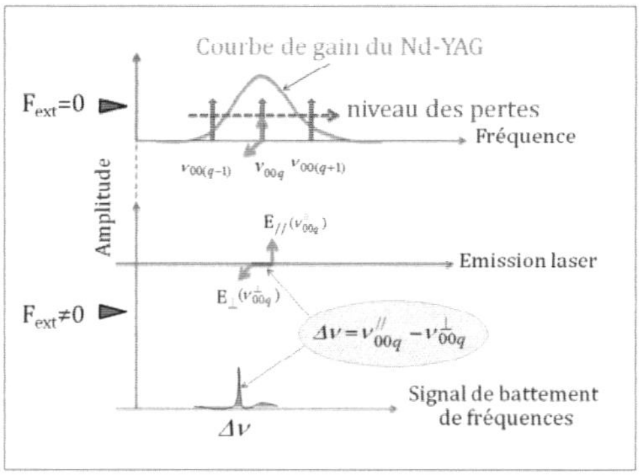

Fig. 6. Effet de la force appliquée sur les composantes de polarisations du mode laser

L'effet de la biréfringence sur le mode laser oscillant correspond à l'apparition d'un déphasage entre les deux polarisations orthogonales du mode laser. Comme indiqué sur la Figure 6, ce déphasage correspond à l'écart entre les fréquences des deux composantes de polarisations orthogonales du mode laser oscillant, donné par :

$$\Delta\nu = (\nu_{\perp} - \nu_{\parallel}) = \frac{c}{n\,\lambda_q}(\Delta n)$$

où n est l'indice de réfraction du Nd-YAG en absence de toute contrainte et c la vitesse de la lumière dans le vide.

Cet écart en fréquence s'exprime en fonction de la force extérieure par la relation suivante :

Cet écart en fréquence s'exprime alors en fonction de la force extérieure par la relation suivante :

$$\Delta\nu = G\, C_{PE}^{(\lambda_q)} \frac{\nu_q}{n\,\ell\, d} F_{ext} \qquad (3)$$

$\nu_q = c/\lambda_q$ est la fréquence d'émission du laser.

Dans le cas idéal, le faisceau de pompe doit être de faibles dimensions transverses par rapport au diamètre du laser Nd-YAG et centré sur l'axe de révolution de ce dernier.
Cette double condition devient relativement critique et par conséquent difficile à réaliser lorsqu'on utilise des lasers monolithiques miniatures.
En considérant les configurations des deux capteurs déjà étudiés et les valeurs des différentes constantes, la sensibilité théorique $\Delta\nu/F_{ext}$, s'exprime simplement par [12] :

* $S = \frac{492}{\ell d}$ pour les capteurs tels que $(\ell \times d) \geq 16\ mm^2$

* $S = \frac{369}{\ell\,\mathrm{d}}$ pour les capteurs tels que $(\ell \times d) \geq 6\ mm^2$

Pour des raisons de commodité, les grandeurs ℓ et *d,* dans les expressions précédentes de *S,* sont exprimées en mm pour avoir une sensibilité en MHz × N^{-1}.

5.2. Dispositif expérimental

Le schéma de principe de l'expérience et les éléments essentiels du dispositif sont indiqués sur la figure 7. Le cristal laser est monté sur un bloc en aluminium dont la température est stabilisée autour de 18 °C à mieux que 0.02 °C à l'aide d'une boucle d'asservissement de type P.I.D. utilisant un élément Peltier et une thermistance.

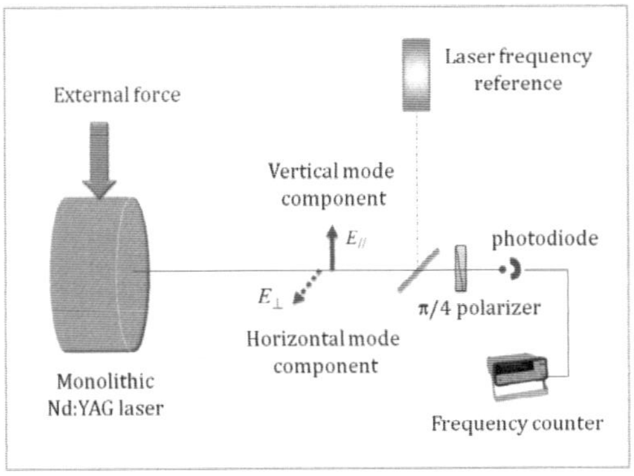

Fig. 7. Schéma de principe d'un capteur photoélastique de force.

L'expérience montre que le contrôle de la température du montage et sa rigidité mécanique sont essentiels pour la stabilité du signal de battement de fréquences et par conséquent pour la répétabilité des mesures. En effet, la fréquence d'émission d'un laser solide est très sensible aux variations de la température du milieu amplificateur mais aussi aux vibrations mécaniques. L'application de la force se fait par une série successive de déposes-retraits d'une masse étalon (poids dans le champ de pesanteur) sur la partie supérieure du cristal laser. La figure 8 montre une photographie du dispositif expérimental. On y distingue, à gauche le système optomécanique de la diode laser à 808 nm utilisée pour réaliser le pompage optique du laser Nd-YAG et à droite le détecteur rapide.

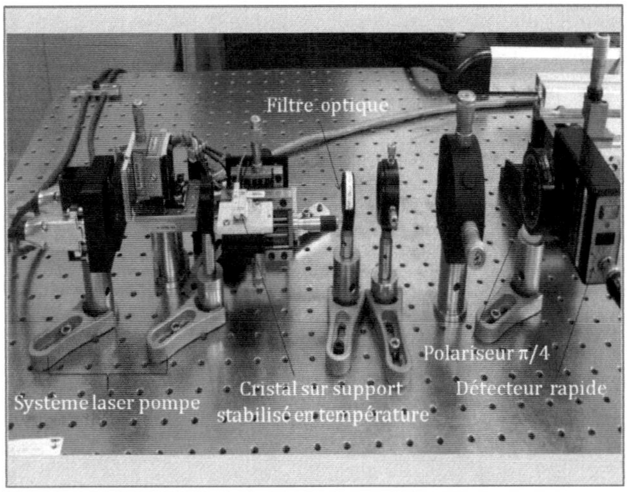

Fig. 8. Capteur photoélastique de force : photographie

5.3. Réponse et sensibilité du capteur photoélastique.

Pour caractériser le capteur sur une plage de chargement, des masses étalons du laboratoire ont été utilisées. Dans le cas de petites masses, ces dernières sont posées directement sur le barreau laser. L'incertitude de répétabilité associée à chaque mesure est évaluée à partir d'une série de mesurages avec le même poids mort pour environ une dizaine de déposes-retraits de l'étalon de masse. Les courbes de la figure 9 donnent, pour les deux capteurs utilisés, l'écart en fréquence entre les deux composantes de polarisations du mode laser lorsque ces capteurs sont sous la contrainte d'une masse comprise entre 0 et 2 g.
L'utilisation de masses plus élevées (500 g) est tout à fait envisageable en restant dans la limite d'élasticité du YAG.
Les courbes en trait plein de la figure 9 correspondent aux ajustements linéaires des valeurs expérimentales obtenues avec chacun des deux capteurs laser utilisés au laboratoire. Les résultats montrent que la réponse de ce type de capteur est quasi-linéaire dans la gamme des faibles forces (domaine d'élasticité du cristal Nd-YAG).

Pour les deux capteurs étudiés, les sensibilités expérimentales sont :

$S_1 = (0{,}558 \pm 0{,}008)\ \mathrm{MHz} \times \mathrm{g}^{-1}$ pour le capteur de dimensions $(2 \times 3)\ mm$

$\mathrm{S}_2 = (0{,}297 \pm 0{,}012)\ \mathrm{MHz} \times \mathrm{g}^{-1}$ pour celui de dimensions $(4 \times 4)\ mm$.

Une série de mesures a été effectuée avec le capteur (2x3) mm lorsqu'il est sous l'action d'une masse étalon donnée.
Le tableau 2 donne les valeurs des fréquences du signal de battement et la répétabilité observées lorsque ce dernier est successivement chargé ou non par des masses de 1 g puis de 100 mg. La valeur du champ local de pesanteur, mesurée au laboratoire, est : $g_\ell = 9{,}80939\ (1 \times 10^{-5})\ \mathrm{ms}^{-2}$

Les poids morts associés aux masses étalons de 1 g et 0,1 g sont donnés par l'expression (1) avec une incertitude inférieure à 50 nN [12].

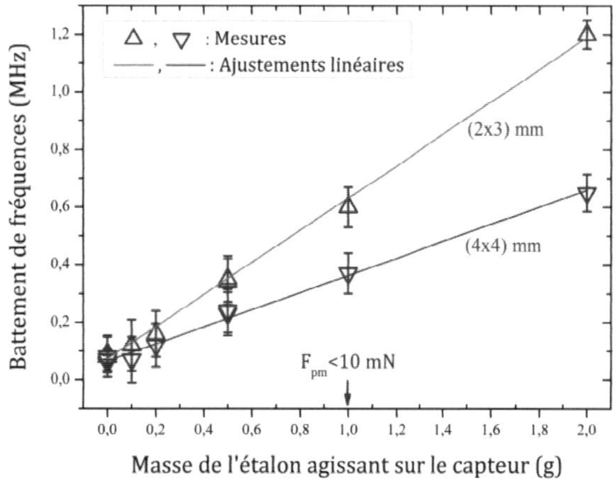

Fig. 9. Réponses du capteur photoélastique de force avec deux configurations géométriques de l'élément sensible à laser Nd-YAG.

Tab. 2. Battements de fréquences observés avec le capteur (2x3) mm chargé successivement par deux masses étalons.

Masse m_e [g]	$\Delta\nu^{(\mathrm{Fext=0})}$ [MHz]	$\Delta\nu^{(\mathrm{Fext\neq0})}$ [MHz]
1	0,065 (0,050)	0,630 (0,050)
0,1	0,065 (0,055)	0,13 (0,055)

La force appliquée sur le cristal est déterminée à partir des mesures des battements de fréquences $\Delta\nu^{(\mathrm{Fext=0})}$ (capteur non chargé), $\Delta\nu^{(\mathrm{Fext\neq0})}$ (capteur chargé) et de la valeur expérimentale de la sensibilité. Elle est calculée à partir de la relation suivante:

$$F_{exp} = \frac{\Delta\nu^{(\mathrm{Fext\neq0})} \quad \Delta\nu^{(\mathrm{Fext=0})}}{S_{\mathrm{exp}}}$$

Dans la plage des contraintes considérées, l'effet d'hystérésis est quasi-nul et par conséquent les battements de fréquences $\Delta\nu^{(\mathrm{Fext\neq0})}$ et $\Delta\nu^{(\mathrm{Fext=0})}$ sont faiblement corrélés. Dans le tableau 3, sont données les valeurs des poids morts selon la relation (1) et celles obtenues à l'aide du capteur photoélastique (2x3) mm.

Tab. 3. Poids local et poids morts mesurés avec le capteur.

m_e [g]	F_{pm} [mN]	F_{exp} [mN]	$\lvert F_{exp} - F_{pm}\rvert / F_{exp}$
1	9,808	9,933	1,2 %
0,1	0,9808	0,967	1,5 %

Pour ces capteurs de faible dimension, des difficultés techniques apparaissent lorsqu'il s'agit de charger ce dernier avec des petites masses. D'ailleurs, comme le montre le tableau 3, l'écart relatif du poids mesuré à celui donné par la relation (1) augmente légèrement.

La principale limitation de ce dispositif est associée à la reproductibilité de la méthode d'application de la contrainte sur le cristal laser. La présence d'un offset engendré par des contraintes résiduelles, pouvant varier au cours du temps, nécessite d'établir à chaque série de mesure un point de référence. Néanmoins la grande plage de linéarité de ce type de capteur et son faible temps de réponse constituent des atouts décisifs. Il est intéressant à miniaturiser pour, d'une part augmenter la sensibilité et atteindre des forces plus faibles et, d'autre part, effectuer le raccorder sur d'autres références que des étalons de masses. L'utilisation de ce capteur de force comme moyen de transfert dans les comparaisons inter-laboratoires est tout à fait envisageable dans la mesure où il peut couvrir une étendue qui présente des recouvrements avec celles correspondant pour d'autres dispositifs.

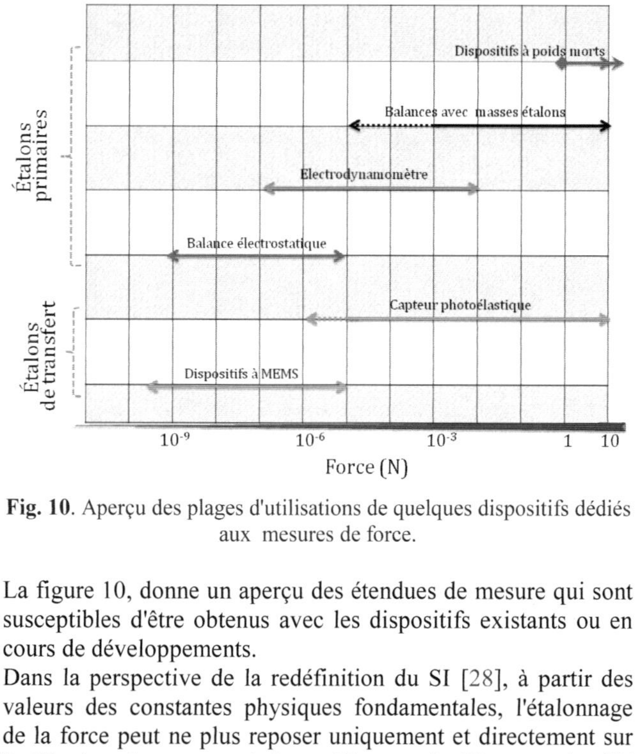

Fig. 10. Aperçu des plages d'utilisations de quelques dispositifs dédiés aux mesures de force.

La figure 10, donne un aperçu des étendues de mesure qui sont susceptibles d'être obtenus avec les dispositifs existants ou en cours de développements.

Dans la perspective de la redéfinition du SI [28], à partir des valeurs des constantes physiques fondamentales, l'étalonnage de la force peut ne plus reposer uniquement et directement sur l'utilisation des masses étalons. C'est particulièrement justifié dans le domaine des faibles forces, en raison des incertitudes engendrées avec l'utilisation des étalons de masses en dessous de 1 mg. L'approche consistant à utiliser la force électrostatique pour générer un moyen traçable, à partir des mesures de grandeurs électriques, est particulièrement prometteuse si des évolutions techniques sont apportées. L'autre approche consiste à développer directement des étalons de transfert susceptibles d'être miniaturisés, comme les capteurs de force fondés sur l'utilisation des MEMS et des cristaux photoélastiques. Une fois finalisés, de tels dispositifs peuvent constituer l'ossature d'une chaîne de traçabilité des mesures de faibles forces.

6. Conclusion

Les travaux entrepris par de nombreux laboratoires de métrologie témoignent d'une réelle diversité d'approches expérimentales pour rendre traçables au SI les mesures de faibles forces. Elles montrent l'utilité de disposer d'artefacts de transfert de la référence de force vers les systèmes à étalonner. Les études de sensibilité du capteur photoélastique , réalisées avec deux tailles différentes de l'élément sensible, ont permis d'identifier les différents paramètres d'influence pouvant affecter les caractéristiques de ce type de capteur de force. Elles ont permis d'établir que la miniaturisation du capteur facilite le traitement du signal de battement de fréquences et permet d'augmenter de façon significative la sensibilité pour étendre la plage de mesure vers le bas. Cependant, les limitations liées aux alignements optiques et à la dégradation de la reproductibilité des mesures prouvent que, au delà de la simple diminution des dimensions de l'élément sensible, une miniaturisation réussie doit intégrer l'élément sensible du capteur et les autres éléments optomécaniques dans une configuration compacte, qui serait d'ailleurs utilisable dans des installations de volume réduit.

Références

1. Barlow A.J. Payne D.N: The Stress-optic Effect in Optical Fibers; IEEE J. Quantum Electron.19, pp.834-839 (1983). http://dx.doi.org/10.1109/JQE.1983.1071934

2. Ni, X., Wang M., Chen X., Ge Y. and Rong H: An optical fibre MEMS pressure sensor using dual-wavelength interrogation; Meas. Sci. Technol. 17, pp.2401-2404 (2006). http://dx.doi.org/10.1088/0957-0233/17/9/005

3. Dao D.V., Nakamura K., Bui T.T. and Sugiyama S.: Micro/ nano - mechanical sensors and actuators based on SOI-MEMS technology; Adv. Nat. Sci: Nanosci. Nanotechnol. 1 013001 pp. 1-10 (2010). http://dx.doi.org/10.1088/2043-6254/1/1/013001

4. R.K. Leach, S.Oldfield, S.A. Awan, J. Bmackburn, J.M. Williams; Design of a bi-directional electrostatic actuator for realising nanonewton to micronewton forces; NPL report DEPC-EM 001 (2004).[21]

5. G. L. Miller, J. E. Griffith, E. R. Wagner and D. A. Grigg; A rocking beam electrostatic balance for the measurement of small forces; Rev. Sci. Instrum. 62, pp.705-709 (1991). http://dx.doi.org/10.1063/1.1142071

6. Jon R. Pratt, Jon A. Kramar; SI realization of small forces using an electrostatic force balance; xviii IMEKO world Congress, 17-22 september, Rio de Janeiro, Brazil (2006).

7. C. Diethold, M. Kühnel, F. Hilbrunner, T. Fröhlich, E. Manske; Determination of force to displacement curves using a nanopositioning system based on electromagnetic force compensated balances; Measurement, Vol.51, pp.343–348 (2014). http://dx.doi.org/10.1016/j.measurement.2014.02.034

8. W. Holzapfel and W. Settgast; Force to frequency conversion by intracavity photoelastic modulation; Appl. Opt. 28, pp. 4585-4594 (1989). doi: 10.1364/AO.28.004585

9. W.Holzapfel, S. Neuschaefer-Rube, M. Kobusch; High-resolution, very broadband force measurement by solid-state laser transducers; Measurement 28, pp.277- 291 (2000). doi:10.1016/S0263-2241(00)00042-7

10. N-E. Khelifa ; Micro force Measurement by an Optical Method;Proc. of the 20th International Metrology Symposium, Croatia (2008).

11.WEB site of the BIPM. http://kcdb.bipm.org/appendixC/search.asp?sservice=M/Force.4.3

12. N. Khélifa and M. Himbert; Sensitivity of miniaturized photoelastic transducer for small force sensing; Sensors & Transducers, 184(1), pp.19–25 (2015). http://www.sensorsportal.com/HTML/DIGEST/P_2581.htm

13. T. Madec, G. Mann, P-A Meury and T. Rabault; Micro-mass standards to calibrate the sensitivity of mass comparators; Metrologia, Volume 44, n° 5, pp.266–274 (2007). http://dx.doi.org/10.1088/0026-1394/44/5/002

14. T. Madec, G. Mann, P-A Meury, N. Khelifa; Extension de la dissémination de l'unité de masse entre 1 mg et 100 µg; Revue française de métrologie, n° 27, pp.29-38 (2011). http://dx.doi.org/10.1051/rfm/2011011

15. Étalons et unités de mesure- Les bases de la métrologie en France: mise en pratique du Système International d'unités; BNM & AFNOR, pp. 27 (1996).

16. J.R. Pratt, D.B. Newell, E.R. Williams, D.T. Smith, J.A. Krammar; Towards a traceable nanoscale force standard; Proc. of the 2nd Euspen international conference- Turin-Italy, 27-31 May (2001).

17. J. R. Pratt, D.B. Newell, J.A.Krammar; A flexure balance with adjustable restoring torque for nanonewton measurement; Vdi-Berichte NR. 1685, pp.77-82 (2002).

18. J.R. Pratt, D.T.Smith, D.B. Newell, J.A. Kramar, E. Whitenton; Progress toward Système International d'Unités traceable force metrology for nanomechanics; J. mater. Res., Vol. 19, n°1 (2004).

19. Ch.W. Jones, R. K. Leach; Review of Low Force Transfer Artefact Technologies, National Physical Laboratory, NPL, Report ENG 5 (2008).

20. In-Mook Choi, Dong-June Choi, Soo Hyun Kim; Double force compensation method to enhance the performance of a null balance force sensor; Jpn. J. Appl. Phys, vol 41, pp. 3987-3993 (2002).

21. Christian Schlegel, Oliver Slanina, Günther Haucke, Rolf Kumme; Construction of a standard force machine for the range of 100 µN 200mN; Measurement 45, pp.2388–2392(2012)

doi:10.1016/j.measurement.2011.11.022

22. S. Gao, Z. K. Zhang, Y. Wu and K. Herrman; Development of a Multifunctional Microelectromechanical Nano-Force Actuator for Calibration of the Spring Constant of an AFM Cantilever; Proceedings of the 9th Euspen International Conference, San Sebastian, 2-5 July, pp.267-270 (2009).

23. Min-Seok Kim, Jae-Hyuk Choi, Jong-Ho Kim and Yon-Kyu Park; SI-traceable determination of spring constants of various atomic force microscope cantilevers with a small uncertainty of 1%; Meas. Sci. Technol. 18, pp.3351–3358 (2007).

24. Min-Seok Kim, Jon R Pratt, Uwe Brand and Christopher W Jones; Report on the first international comparison of small force facilities: a pilot study at the micronewton level; Metrologia, Vol.49, n°1, pp.70-81 (2012).

25. P. Pinot; communication à la journée organisée par le GT2 du Club nanoMétrologie: thématique "Métrologie des très faibles masses et très faibles forces", Paris (2015).

26. M. G. Wertheim; Ann. Chim. Phys. 40, pp.156–221 (1854).

27. M. M. Frocht; Phtoelasticity, 8th edition, John Wiley and sons, London, pp.144- 349 (1941).

28. P. Richard and J.Ullrich; Joint CCM and CCU roadmap towards the redefinition of the SI in 2018, Approved by the CIPM on 13 November 2013.

Evaluation de la gestion des équipements dans les laboratoires du Sénégal avec la check list SLIPTA, au regard des exigences de la norme ISO 15 189

Diagne R[1], Lo S[2], Dia ML[3], Gning B[4], Diop M[5], Ka R[1], Sow AI[3].

1: Direction des Laboraoires du Sénégal, UFR Santé de Thiès
2: UFR Santé, Université Gaston Berger de Saint-Louis
3: Direction des Laboraoires du Sénégal, Faculté de Médecine, Pharmacie, Odontologie de Dakar
4: Direction des Laboraoires du Sénégal, Institut Pasteur de Dakar
5: Cabinet Humanity Progress

Résumé : Le respect des exigences de la norme ISO 15189 dans la gestion des équipements a été évalué dans les laboratoires du Sénégal. La check list SLIPTA élaborée par l'OMS a été utilisée. Notre étude a porté sur 127 laboratoires et la rubrique équipement était notée sur 30 points. Parmi eux, 64 ont obtenu entre 0 et 10 points, 57 ont obtenu entre 11 et 20 points, et 6 entre 21 et 30. Pour 23 % des laboratoires, les équipements sont installés et placés conformément au manuel d'utilisation du fabricant, les nouveaux équipements et les méthodes sont validés dans 18 % des laboratoires. Les spécifications et les besoins de maintenance des équipements sont régulièrement communiqués à la hiérarchie dans 34 % des laboratoires. Les données sur les inventaires de tous les équipements sont disponibles dans moins de 1% des laboratoires. Un étalonnage régulier des équipements est réalisé dans 11 % des laboratoires. Il est impératif que le volet équipement soit pris en compte au sein des laboratoires du Sénégal , en incluant la métrologie afin de renforcer la fiabilité des résultats de laboratoires et par conséquent d'assurer de meilleurs diagnostics et donc une meilleure santé de nos populations.

Mots clés : équipements, laboratoires, évaluation, SLIPTA

1 Introduction

Les services de laboratoire constituent un élément fondamental des services de santé. Les examens de biologie médicale constituent un élément de plus en plus décisif dans le diagnostic, le traitement, le pronostic, la prévention et l'épidémiologie des maladies. A ce titre, des tests de laboratoires précis, fiables et effectués en temps voulu sont une composante essentielle de la prévention et de la prise en charge efficace de la maladie.

La meilleure garantie que les biologistes et les techniciens de laboratoire peuvent apporter à la fiabilité des résultats qu'ils fournissent repose sur un système d'assurance qualité étayé par la pratique d'un contrôle de qualité rigoureux.

La Biologie Médicale étant une science expérimentale, les résultats des analyses sont soumis à des erreurs qu'il appartient au Biologiste de déceler pour qu'elles ne constituent pas un préjudice dans le soin du patient.

Un niveau bas de qualité dans les tests de laboratoire a un impact négatif sur sur la santé des populations. [1-4],

En 2009, le comité régional de l'OMS a lancé le programme de préparation graduelle des laboratoires en vue de leur accréditation.

L'initiative SLIPTA (Stepwise Improvement Process Towards Accreditation) est un processus graduel d'amélioration d'un laboratoire en vue de son accréditation selon les exigences de la norme ISO 15189. [5],

Le ministère de la santé du Sénégal a mis en place une Direction des laboratoires dans l'optique d'une meilleure organisation et d'un renforcement effectif du système des laboratoires .

Dans le cadre de la mise en conformité d'un système de management de la qualité, un laboratoire se doit de maitriser l'ensemble de ses équipements qui doivent etre étalonnés et /ou vérifiés régulièrement[6-7],

La Direction a comme priorité la mise en place de la démarche qualité et a réalisé une évalution des laboratoiresen utilisant le questionnaire SLIPTA.

La check list SLIPTA comporte 11 sections. Notre étude a porté sur la section 5 qui évalue la gestion des équipements.

L'objectif était de procéder à un audit qualité de départ des laboratoires du Senegal.

2 Matériels et méthodes

Les évaluateurs (15) ont été formés sur la check list SLIPTA. Ils ont ensuite réalisé des visites au niveau des laboratoires. Le personnel a été soumis au questionnaire SLIPTA élaboré par l'OMS, basé sur la norme ISO 15189, et qui vise l'accompagnement des laboratoires à la démarche qualité. L'étude s'est déroulée entre 2013 et 2014.

Le questionnaire comprend plusieurs chapitres dont le volet équipement, avec des aspects documentaires et des aspects techniques. [9],

La check list SLIPTA étant un outil qui fournit des niveaux graduels de la reconnaissance de la performance, des notes ont été attribuées à chaque laboratoire visité.

Les évaluateurs formés ont réalisé des visites au niveau des laboratoires et le personnel a été soumis au questionnaire SLIPTA élaboré par l'OMS, et qui vise l'accompagnement des laboratoires à la démarche qualité.

Les laboratoires ont ensuite été noté sur un total de 30 points et nous avons évalué des Laboratoires Nationaux, des Laboratoires d'Hôpitaux, des Laboratoires de Centre de Santé, des Laboratoires Régionaux et des Laboratoires Privés.

3 Résultats et discussions

Nous avons évalué 127 laboratoires dont 73 Laboratoires de Centres de Santé, 40 Laboratoires d'Hôpitaux et Nationaux, 11 Laboratoires Privés et 3 Laboratoires Régionaux.

Dans 23% des laboratoires les équipements sont installés et placés conformément au manuel d'utilisation du fabricant, avec un étiquetage unique. Nous avons noté ici que dans la majorité des cas les fournisseurs se chargent d'installer les équipements dans les laboratoires, ce qui est une forme de garantie dans le respect des normes d'installation.

Dans 37 % des laboratoires , les manuels d'utilisation du fabricant sont lisibles, compréhensibles et disponibles pour le personnel. Il faut cependant souligner que dans 63 % des laboratoires ces manuels sont soit rédigés dans une langue autre que le Français (la plupart du temps en anglais), soit ces manuels ne sont pas disponibles pour le personnel. Il est évident que lorsque le personnel ne comprend pas les instructions du fabricant, cela constitue un frein et un risque dans l'utilisation, la maintenance des équipements et les résultats des analyses.

La validation sur place des méthodes et des nouveaux équipements avec disponibilité des enregistrements qui documentent ces validations est réalisé par 18 % des laboratoires. Les laboratoires doivent démontrer que les méthodes d'analyse correspondent à l'usage pour lequel elles sont prévues. Ils doivent obtenir des critères objectifs de qualité destinés à la validation des dispositifs utilisés. [10-11], Un manque de formation aussi bien théorique que pratique sur la validation des méthodes est souvent à l'origine de cet écart observé.

Concernant la gestion des équipements défectueux, dans 66 % des cas ils ne sont pas convenablement étiquetés ni enlèvés du laboratoire. Lors de nos visites il a été constaté que de nombreux équipements non utilisés encombrent les paillasses des salles de manipulations. Etant donné que la plupart des laboratoires ne disposent pas d'assez d'espace, si de plus les locaux sont encombrés, cela influe négativement sur l'aménagement des zones de travail. L'opérateur ne bénéficiera donc pas de conditions optimales pour mener à bien son travail. Ces appareils défectueux sont très souvent couverts de poussières et donc responsables d'hygiène défectueuse au sein du laboratoire. Une situation pareille est source de démotivation du personnel. [12]

De plus ces équipements ne sont pas étiquetés correctement pour signaler leur non utilisation par un personnel non averti.

L'évaluation de la gestion des pannes d'équipements a montré que les procédures de sauvegarde en cas de panne d'équipements avec identification du laboratoire de sous traitance ne sont pas effectives dans 85% des laboratoires.

Des solutions pour assurer la continuité du service en cas de panne sont presque inexistantes. Cela suppose qu'en cas de panne, le laboratoire va improviser une solution alternative ou alors les échantillons des patients ne seront pas traités. De plus avec l'absence de sauvegarde, le laboratoire va courir le risque de perdre les données des patients.

Nous avons constaté que 82% des laboratoires ne réalisent pas un étalonnage régulier des équipements du laboratoire, incluant les pipettes, les centrifugeuses, les balances et les thermomètres. Pour asseoir la pertinence des décisions médicales, il est indispensable de maitriser les incertitudes, qui restent un excellent moyen d'accéder à une interprétation intelligente des résultats d'analyses.[13] La métrologie d'une manière générale constitue un problème crucial dans nos laboratoires. L'absence de resoources financières, de formation, et par conséquent de spécialistes en métrologie dans nos laboratoires pourrait expliquer cette situation observée.

L'évaluation de la disponibilité des données sur les inventaires des équipements a montré que le nom de l'équipement est noté dans 56 laboratoires, 21 laboratoires ont noté le contact détaillé du fabricant , 18 laboratoires ont notifié l'état de l'équipement à la réception (neuf, usagé ou reconditionné), 82 laboratoires n'ont pas enregistré le numéro de série, 89 n'ont pas enregistré la date d'achat de l'appareil, seul un laboratoire a noté la date prévisionnelle pour la mise hors service et 77 laboratoires n'ont pas noté la date de mise en service.

Le laboratoire devrait garder un inventaire écrit de tout son équipement. L'inventaire devrait être mis à jour avec les informations concernant chaque nouvel équipement, et les informations concernant le retrait du vieil équipement.

Des instructions concernant l'utilisation et l'entretien de l'équipement doivent être accessibles au personnel. Mais les informations relatives à l'entretien des équipements sont peu disponibles.

L'information sur le contrat d'entretien n'est disponible que dans 14% des laboratoires, 16% pour la prochaine date de maintenance. Les enregistrements de la performance du matériel et de sa maintenance ne sont disponibles que dans 26% des laboratoires, l'emplacement actuel de l'équipement est noté par 18 % des laboratoires et les décontaminations ne sont enregistrées que par 16,5% des laboratoires. Etant donné que les laboratoires utilisent des produits pathologiques pouvant être source de contaminations surtout infectieuses, il appartient au personnel du laboratoire de réaliser toutes les décontaminations nécessaires et de les enregistrer.

Le personnel chargé de la maintenance doit être protégé avec des preuves à l'appui des risques de contaminations éventuelles pouvant survenir lors du contact avec les équipements. [14-15]

L'autre information importante sur l'entretien des équipements est l'enregistrement de la dernière date de maintenance. Un effort a été noté au niveau de l'enregistrement puisque 40% des laboratoires ont enregistré leur dernière date de maintenance.

Concernant le suivi des réparations en cas de panne, seul 20% des laboratoires le font correctement ce suivi avec la vérification de la réparation et l'enregistrement de l'équipement comme étant en bon état de fonctionnement avant la remise en service.

Les pannes d'équipement sont rencontrées dans la plupart des laboratoires visités. Dans 67% des laboratoires, des interruptions dues aux pannes ont été observées durant l'année écoulée. Ces interruptions peuvent être à l'origine de résultats non fiables mais aussi d'interruptions du travail et donc de retards dans le rendu des résultats.

Nos résultats ont montré que les maintenances ne sont pas régulièrement réalisées de plus les enregistrements selon des procédures sont quasi absents. Seuls 11% des laboratoires réalisent la maintenance préventive avec des enregistrements selon les procédures. Pour la maintenance corrective, 14% des laboratoires maintiennent régulièrement les équipements par un personnel compétent et qualifié.

Les laboratoires sont très souvent confrontés au coût des contrats de maintenance proposés par les fournisseurs d'équipement. Il existe très peu d'école de formation à la maintenance des équipements au Sénégal et même en Afrique de l'Ouest. Cette situation pourrait expliquer le manque criard de mainenanciers et les problèmes rencontrés dans les laboratoires. Pour obtenir des résultats précis et fiables, il est nécessaire que les opérateurs connaissent en détail les procédures et pour cela il leur faut une mise à jour régulière de leurs connaissances[16].

Les pièces de rechange pour exécuter des réparations mineures sont disponibles dans 33% des laboratoires.

les commandes sont souvent faites dans des pays étrangers et par conséquent l'acquisition des pièces est souvent coûteuse, longue et difficile.

En vue de prévenir les pannes et de permettre une action curative rapide et efficace, 34% des laboratoires communiquent avec leur hiérarchie sur les besoins en maintenance.

Une communication rapide et efficace avec le fabricant influe fortement sur la riposte en cas de panne. Le contact détaillé de la personne à contacter chez le fabricant est disponible dans 46% des laboratoires.

La deuxième étape de notre étude a été d'attribuer des notes aux laboratoires. Le volet équipement dans la check list SLIPTA est noté sur un total de 30 points. Les graphiques suivants montrent les notes des laboratoires.

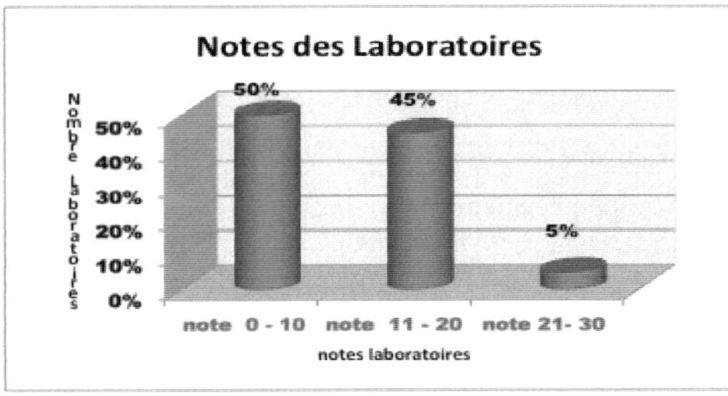

Figure 1: Distribution des notes obtenues par les Laboratoires du Sénégal lors de l'évaluation des équipements

Les notes obtenues par les laboratoires **(Figure1)** sont réparties entre 0 et 10 pour 50% des laboratoires, et entre 11 et 20 pour 45% des laboratoires. Seuls 5% des laboratoires ont entre 21 et 30 points. Ancun laboratoire n'a obtenu plus de 24 points.

Ces résultats montrent les problèmes que rencontrent les laboratoires dans la gestion des équipements. La plupart des laboratoires sont conscients des problèmes de maintenance qu'ils rencontrent surtout la maintenance corrective. Le coût élevé de ces maintenances est en bonne partie à l'origine de cette situation. De plus des lenteurs dans la formation du personnel en métrologie et dans la mise en place de la démarche qualité en général expliquent aussi ces résultats.

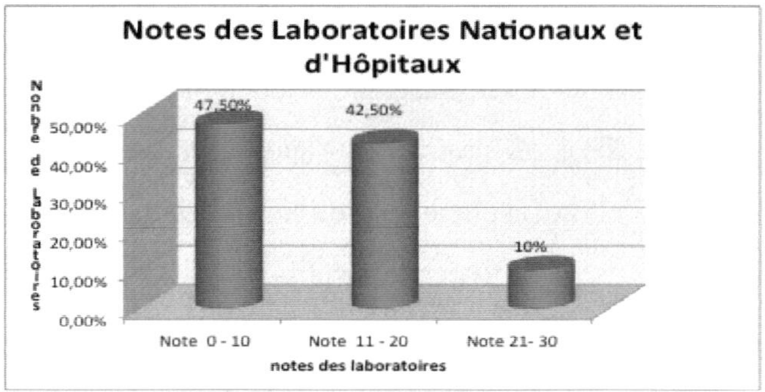

Figure 2: Distribution des notes obtenues des Laboratoires Nationaux et les Laboratoires d'Hôpitaux

L'analyse des notes des laboratoires d'hôpitaux et nationaux **(Figure 2)** nous montre des résultats légèrement meilleurs avec 10% des laboratoires qui ont des notes comprises entre 21 et 30. Les tendances sont presque les mêmes que pour les laboratoires pris globalement. Il faut noter que la meilleure note obtenue par ces laboratoires est 24 points. Cette note constitue le meilleur score que

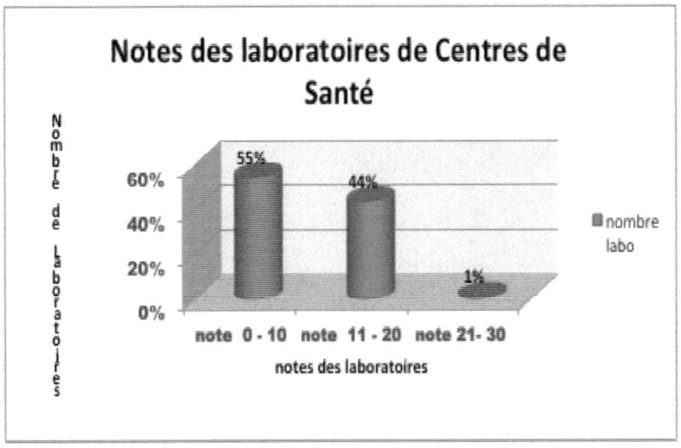

Figure 3 : Distribution des notes obtenues par les laboratoires de Centres de Santé

Les notes des laboratoires des centres de santé **(Figure 3)** donnent presque les mêmes résultats que les laboratoires pris dans leur globalité. Nous observons que 55 % ont des notes entre 0 et 10 points et 44 % ont entre 11 et 20 points. Ces laboratoires de Centre de Santé sont les plus nombreux (73 laboratoires). La meilleure note obtenue avec ces laboratoires de centre de santé est 21 points.

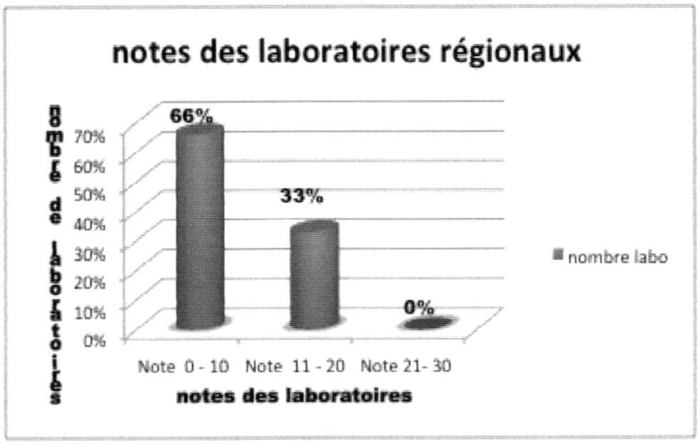

Figure 4 : Distribution des notes obtenues par les Laboratoires Régionaux

nous avons enregistré durant notre étude.

Les laboratoires régionaux **(Figure 4),** sont des laboratoires non hospitaliers, installés dans les régions, ils jouent le rôle de laboratoire de santé publique dans la région qui les abrite. Nous observons des notes un peu plus basses qu'avec les autres laboratoires: 2 laboratoires ont obtenu des notes comprises entre 0 et 10 et un laboratoire entre 11 et 20. Les notes de ces laboratoires régionaux n'ont pas dépassé 12 points.

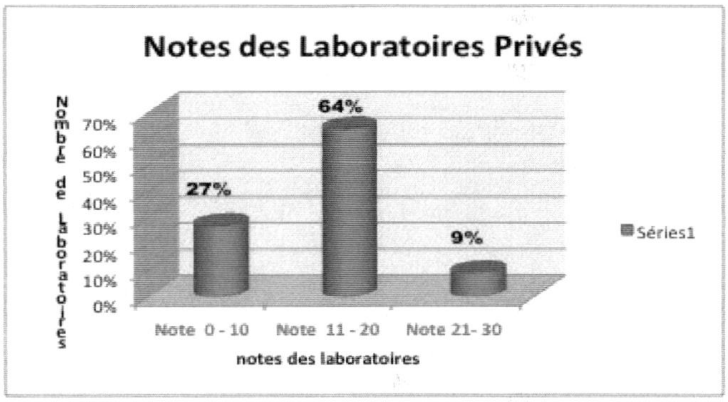

Figure 5: Distribution des notes obtenues par les Laboratoires Privés

Les notes des laboratoires privés **(Figure 5),** donnent une tendance meilleure car 64 % ont des notes comprises entre 11 et 20 points. Le pourcentage de laboratoires qui ont obtenu des notes comprises entre 0 et 10 points est ici plus faible que tous les autres laboratoires étudiés (27%) . Nous observons ausi que 9% des laboratoires ont obtenu des notes comprises entre 21 et 30 points.

Nous pouvons comprendre ici que les laboratoires privés ayant un peu plus de ressources financières ont la possibilité de contracter des programmes de maintenance avec les fournisseurs des équipements et peuvent aussi mettre en place la métrologie. Mais les ressources financières ne peuvent pas tout expliquer car la rédaction des procédures et l'enregistrement des actions réalisées dans la gestion des équipements ne demandent pas beaucoup de ressource financière.

Pour l'ensemble de ces laboratoires évalués, ces notes faibles qui ont été obtenues expliquent le nombre très bas de laboratoires d'analyses accrédités dans le pays. Très peu de laboratoires sont accrédités dans la région africaine. Une menée en 2014 sur 49 pays de l'afrique sub saharienne a montré que sur 37 pays n'avaient pas de laboratoire accrédité selon less normes ISO ou CLIA (Clinical Laboratory Improvement Amendements) [17]. L'afrique du sud habritant 91% de ces laboratoires accrédités. Sur 380 laboratoires accrédités 91% sont localisés en Afrique du sud. [18]

Cependant l'évaluation des laboratoires selon les critères SLIPTA de l'OMS permet d'observer un taux un peu plus élevé de laboratoires ayant le niveau de qualité minimum requis par l'OMS. [19]

Un examen des résultats des évaluations externes de la qualité du college of american pathologists (CAP) des laboratoires en Afrique a montré un taux d'échec de 1,63%.[20], ceci démontre le rôle important des évaluations à distance et des audits pour obtenir un niveau de qualité acceptable dans les laboratoires à ressources limitées.

4- Conclusion

L'essor des maladies transmissibles et non transmissibles a des effets catastrophiques sur la santé des individus, des familles et des communautés. Le cas des épidémies à virus Ebola qui sévissent actuellement en Afrique de l'ouest en est une parfaite illustration.

Notre étude a montré que la gestion des équipements en général pose problème au sein des laboratoires du Sénégal.

La métrologie et la validation des méthodes constituent de véritables obstacles que rencontrent ces laboratoires.

Les problèmes de maintenance des équipements aussi bien préventive que corrective et l'absence d'enregistrements de ces actions de maintenance empêchent les laboratoires d'atteindre les niveaux de qualité recommandés.

Le manque de resoources de ces laboratoires et les défauts de formations aussi bien théoriques que pratiques sur la maintenance des équipements, la métrologie et la validation des méthodes sont en grande partie à l'origine de ce constat.

Très peu d'école de formation en maintenance des équipements et en métrologie existent en Afrique de l'ouest.

Pour remédier à cette situation, des lignes de conduite et les procédures pour la maintenance doivent être décrites dans des documents appropriés. Tous les dégâts, dysfonctionnements, modifications ou réparation de l'équipement doivent être enregistrés.

Conserver de bons registres permettra une évaluation minutieuse des problèmes qui surviennent.

Les programmes de maintenance doivent inclure la sélection de l'équipement, la maintenance préventive et les procédures de dépannage et de réparation.

Un inventaire complet et exact de tout l'équipement du laboratoire doit etre réalisé , les documents fournis par le fabricant sur l'utilisation, la maintenance et le dépannage et les registres des activités de maintenance préventive et de réparation.

Le renforcement de la formation initiale et continue est aussi un axe incontounable pour relever le défi.

Pour apporter aux cliniciens des preuves tangibles et scientifiques de leurs diagnostics, nous devons mettre en place une organisation cohérente, transparente qui va permettre de maitriser l'ensemble des équipements des laboratoires.

Une telle avancée aura pour finalité une meilleure maitrise et une bonne prise en charge des maladies à potentiel épidémiques et des problèmes de santé publique.

5- Références

1- Kébé L, évaluation de la démarche qualité dans les laboratoires d'analyses biomédicales du Sénégal, thèse de Pharmacie, Université Cheikh Anta Diop de Dakar, année 2011, 104 pages.

2 -Urdea M, Penny LA, Olmsted SS, et al. Requirements for high impact diagnostics in the developping world. Nature. 2006; 444(suppl): 73-79.

3- Diémé O. Contribution à la démarche d'accréditation du laboratoire physico - chimique de SUNEOR établissement industriel de Dakar selon la norme ISO/CEI 17025, mémoire de fin d'études en Master Management de la qualité, sécurité, environnement, année 2012, 111 pages

4- Petti CA, Polage CR, QuinnTC, et Al. Laboratory medicine in Africa: a barrier to effective health care. Clin Infect Dis. 2006;42:377-382.

5- Norme internationale ISO 15189 : 2012 , Laboratoires de biologie médicale – Exigences concernant la qualité et la compétence.

6- norme internationale ISO 9001 : 2008, Systèmes de management de la qualité - exigences

7- Pinet C. l'ISO 9001 facile. Réussir sa démarche de certification, Lexitis editions, Mars 2011, 239 pages.

8- Norme internationale ISO 17025 : 2005 , prescriptions générales concernant la compétence des laboratoires d'étalonnages et d'essais . Suisse, Geneve.

9- WHO guide for the stepwise laboratory improvementprocess towards acceditation in the African Region (SLIPTA), 2015

10- Vassault A, Grafmeyer D, Graeve J, Cohen R, Beaudonnet A, J Bienvenu. Analayses de Biologie médicale: spécifications et normes d'acceptabilité à l'usage de la validation de techniques. Vol 57, n 6, 1999.

11- Cornaglia G, Courcol R, Hermann J L, European Manual of Clinical Microbiology ,1ère édition, ESCMID, April 2012, p 64 – 65

12- WHO, « Laboratory Quality Management System », training toolkit, 2009.Lyon , France.

13- Laurent JL, Gaumont B. De l'incertitude à la précaution: le role de la métrologie, annales des mines –responsabilité et environnement 2010/1 n°57, page 104

14- OMS, "manuel de sécurité biologique en laboratoire" , troisième édition, année 2005, 219 pages.

15- Agence de santé publique du Canada, lignes directrices en matière de biosécurité en laboratoire, 2004

16- OMS , manuel d'entretien et de maintenance des appareils de laboratoire , 2é édition, Genève 2008, p 121

17-centers for medicare and medicaid services , clinical laboratories Improvement Amendements (CLIA).

Washington, DC. Available at: http: //www.cms.gov/clia/.

18- Lee F.Schroeder, Amukele T, MD.Medical Laboratories in Sub-Saharan Africa that meet international quality standards. Am J Clin Pathol 2014 ;141 :791-795

19 - Elbireer AM, Jackson JB, SendagireH, et al. The good, the bad, and the unknown : quality of clinical laboratories in Kampala, Uganda. *PloS One*.2013 ;8 :e 64661

20- Amukele TK, Michael K, Hanes M, et al. external quality assurance performance of clinical research laboratories in sub-saharan Africa .Am J Clin Pathol. 2012 ; 138(5) :720-723

Les cellules de travail dynamiques dans les réseaux d'entreprise.

S. Gamache et G. Abdul-Nour
Université du Québec à Trois-Rivières, Trois-Rivières, Qc., Canada

Résumé. L'optimisation de la performance des réseaux est un enjeu de plus en plus crucial pour les petites et moyennes entreprises. Le dynamisme du marché et l'incertitude de la demande obligent à concilier productivité et flexibilité. Il a été prouvé à maintes reprises que les cellules dynamiques permettaient de rallier ces deux objectifs. Le pont n'a toutefois pas été fait entre les entreprises réseaux et l'utilisation des DCMS. La revue de littérature a permis de mettre en lumière des éléments inhérents aux deux concepts. Un design expérimental suivi d'une modélisation à l'aide d'un logiciel de simulation à événements discrets a permis d'étudier un cas réel et conclure sur l'effet de l'utilisation des cellules dynamiques sur la performance des réseaux. D'autres facteurs tels que la variation de la demande en termes de volume et du mix-produit, la conception modulaire et la fiabilité des fournisseurs et leurs effets seront considérés dans cette étude.

Mots clés : Cellules dynamiques, DCMS, PME, Entreprises réseaux, DOE, Design Expérimental, Simulation

1 Introduction

La mondialisation semble pour certaines organisations être synonyme d'un bénéfice majeur alors que pour d'autres, elle constitue un défi colossal. La chute des barrières internationales tant au niveau commercial que manufacturier crée une structure mondiale où la compétitivité et la productivité sont la clé pour la survie des entreprises locales (De Loecker et Goldberg, 2014).

Le transfert des ressources en Chine et l'importation de masse de nombreux produits à moindre coût affectent les entreprises québécoises. Pour se relever, la solution est l'augmentation de sa productivité. Toutefois, la hausse des produits sur mesure, les changements rapides et imprévisibles des consommateurs, la requête du prix le plus bas, la durée de vie des marchandises qui diminue continuellement et le développement incessant de la technologie obligent à concilier productivité et flexibilité.

Les PME (Petites et moyennes entreprises) au Québec ont cet avantage. Leur petite taille donne souvent lieu à une agilité que l'on ne retrouve pas dans les grandes entreprises (TheOpenGroup, 2014). Il faut alors trouver un moyen d'intégrer cet avantage et d'en faire sa prérogative majeure.

D'un autre côté, une entreprise ne travaille pas seule. Elle fait partie intégrante d'un réseau de fournisseurs et clients (appelé chaîne d'approvisionnement) qui doit, tout comme elle, se démarquer tant au niveau de l'efficacité que de la flexibilité. Il est dans l'avantage de tout le réseau de se développer mutuellement afin de mettre la main sur le marché mondial (Poulin et al., 1994).

De nombreux auteurs ont étudié l'effet des différents systèmes de production sur l'efficacité interne d'une entreprise. Entre autres, les cellules de production dynamiques (DCMS) représentent une méthode d'amélioration de l'efficacité et la flexibilité qui fait couler de plus en plus d'encre.

D'autres chercheurs ont évalué l'impact de nombreux facteurs sur la performance des réseaux. Toutefois, aucun pont n'a été fait entre l'utilisation des cellules dynamiques et la performance des entreprises réseaux.

L'efficacité interne des entreprises a un impact évident sur l'ensemble des activités d'un réseau. L'objectif principal de cette recherche sera de déterminer l'effet de l'utilisation des systèmes de production en cellules dynamiques sur la productivité et la flexibilité des entreprises réseaux. La revue de littérature permettra de déterminer où la communauté scientifique se situe au niveau des connaissances dans ce domaine. Une méthodologie alliant le design expérimental et la simulation par événements discrets permettra d'étudier un cas réel dans des nouvelles conditions expérimentales.

Dans les pages suivantes, il sera possible de mieux comprendre le comportement des entreprises réseaux dans des situations où les conditions de production et environnementales sont perpétuellement perturbées.

2 Revue de littérature

Dans le contexte de mondialisation actuel, l'efficacité des entreprises est incontournable. De nombreuses entreprises travaillent individuellement pour des objectifs personnels singuliers sans tenir compte des activités se déroulant en amont et en aval. Les entreprises doivent être conscientes des conséquences que peuvent engendrer leurs propres pratiques au sein du bien-être de leur réseau. Dans un monde aussi concurrentiel, il est important de prendre en compte les effets de sa participation dans un réseau et les impacts de ses actions individuelles. Il faut que l'entreprise soit consciente qu'il est nécessaire d'avoir une intégration horizontale et verticale dans le réseau. Il doit y avoir une cohérence est des objectifs commun avec l'ensemble du réseau.

Chaque PME recherche l'efficacité et la flexibilité. Le réseau peut aider à bonifier ces deux exigences. L'idée est de voir comment il sera possible d'améliorer cette productivité tout en demeurant le plus flexible possible. Le système des cellules de production dynamiques a été élaboré en 1995 par Rheault et al. Ce système est l'un des sujets de recherche très prisés par les auteurs intéressés à améliorer la productivité et la flexibilité des entreprises manufacturières. Bien que certains auteurs ne soient pas tout à fait convaincus de leur nécessité (Darkov et Naydenov, 2011), d'autres affirment que ce système a réellement su faire ses preuves dans de nombreux contextes (Drolet et al., 2008).

Face à cette réalité où efficacité et flexibilité doivent être maximisées simultanément, il est naturel de se demander comment il sera possible de le faire. La première question que l'on se pose est donc la suivante :

Comment est-il possible de régler les problèmes d'efficacité dans les réseaux tout en conservant une flexibilité concurrentielle?

En considérant une situation où les cellules dynamiques sont effectivement efficaces comparativement aux autres modes de production tels les *Job shop* et les cellules classiques, il convient de se demander si l'utilisation des cellules de travail dynamiques pourraient permettre d'améliorer cette efficacité.

Évidemment, il faut comprendre que ce n'est pas tous les profils d'entreprise qui demandent l'utilisation des cellules dynamiques. Certains auteurs ont d'ailleurs abordé ce sujet (Drolet et al. 2008). Dépendamment de nombreux facteurs, il peut devenir plus intéressant d'opter pour une production par produit (très efficace, mais peu flexible) ou à l'inverse, pour une production en ateliers (très flexible, mais peu efficace).

L'objectif principal de cette recherche sera de déterminer l'effet de l'utilisation des cellules dynamiques sur l'efficacité et la flexibilité des entreprises réseaux. L'efficacité sera déterminée par le nombre d'encours et la quantité de commandes sortantes. La flexibilité sera mesurée par le temps de réaction de l'entreprise pour répondre à la demande. Un réseau où la demande est variable tant en termes de quantité que du mix-produit sera considéré.

D'autres objectifs tels que la détermination des conditions de réussite pour l'implantation des cellules dynamiques dans le contexte réseau seront analysés. Les structures modulaires sont un exemple de facteur qu'il sera intéressant de vérifier. Le développement d'indicateurs de performance des réseaux sera un autre point à l'étude. L'étude permettra enfin de vérifier s'il existe la possibilité d'établir un pont entre le profil des entreprises et l'utilisation potentielle des cellules dynamiques dans les réseaux.

Essentiellement, cette recherche tentera de résoudre les problèmes d'efficacité dans les réseaux des PME québécoises. Les résultats obtenus lors de cette étude auront des conséquences signifiantes dans la réalité des entreprises et permettront également de s'hasarder à prévoir l'utilisation des méthodes étudiées sur le plan pratique.

Une exploration de la littérature permet de faire le point sur l'état des connaissances actuelles. Jusqu'à aujourd'hui, aucun lien n'a été fait entre l'utilisation des cellules dynamiques et la performance des entreprises travaillant en réseau. Cette section sera présentée en deux parties. La première partie traitera des cellules dynamiques dans les entreprises manufacturières alors que la seconde tentera d'inventorier les systèmes de mesure de la performance dans les chaînes d'approvisionnement. L'idée sera de voir les liens qui peuvent exister entre les deux principes et voir s'il est possible de les mettre en parallèle pour une utilisation plus pratique.

Cellules de production dynamiques (DCMS)

Rheault et al. (1995) ont démontré qu'un environnement turbulent brise le paradigme où un aménagement linéaire est optimal. Dans le but de répondre rapidement au client, le DCMS est la nouvelle solution. L'article propose un modèle mathématique qui permet de modifier régulièrement la configuration du plancher de production en fonction de la demande. Les auteurs tentent via ce modèle de minimiser le coût total de production.

DCMS Modèles mathématiques

À la suite de Rheault et al., plusieurs auteurs se sont concentrés sur l'élaboration de modèles mathématiques toujours plus complets et distinctifs.

Le modèle de Rheault et al. (1995) est repris par, entre autres, Safaei et Tavakkoli-Moghaddam (2009). Les auteurs proposent de combiner la formation de cellules manufacturières et la planification de la production directement dans le modèle. L'objectif de la recherche est d'optimiser la formation de cellules sur plusieurs périodes et la planification de la production dans un DCMS. En 2011, Ghotboddini et al. (2011) proposent également d'inclure le regroupement des pièces et des machines et l'assignation de la main d'œuvre. L'objectif de leur recherche est de minimiser les coûts marginaux et de maximiser le taux d'utilisation de la main d'œuvre. Dans la même année, Li, Hu et Murata (2011) incluent l'incertitude dans le modèle mathématique. Les auteurs recherchent alors l'horizon de planification "optimale" qui permettra de maximiser l'effet positif de l'utilisation des cellules dynamiques.

Kia et al. (2012) proposent un modèle qui permet de déterminer une configuration optimale des cellules en incluant de nombreuses variables telles que les gammes de fabrication alternatives, le volume des pièces produites, le fractionnement des lots, l'aménagement intra et intercellulaire, etc. Soolaki (2012) propose d'ajouter l'effet de l'assignation des travailleurs par rapport à leurs compétences. Les auteurs soulignent l'importance de la planification de la production dans la minimisation du coût total de production.

Paydar et al. (2013) reprennent la majorité des idées déjà présentées et incluent la satisfaction de la demande, la grandeur des cellules, la disponibilité des machines et plus encore. Soolaki (2013) ajoute la robustesse dans le modèle en considérant l'aspect de l'incertitude. Dans cette même idée, Tavakkoli-Moghaddam et al. (2014) proposent un nouveau modèle qui ajoute l'incertitude au niveau du temps d'opération des pièces.

D'un modèle à l'autre, certains éléments demeurent constants. Il s'agit du caractère financier. L'idée est toujours d'améliorer sa productivité ainsi que sa flexibilité au moindre coût possible. La planification des activités devient indissociable de la reconfiguration des cellules et la robustesse devient de plus en plus essentielle à considérer.

Comparaison des Systèmes de Production

Darkov, et Naydenov (2011) défendent la supériorité des systèmes de production en cellules virtuelles (VCMS) par rapport aux autres systèmes de production. Le système de production peut sembler préférable à utiliser dépendamment du contexte manufacturier, mais le manque de données statistiques n'a pas permis de prouver cette hypothèse de supériorité.

Drolet, Marcoux et Abdul-Nour (2008) ont étudié l'effet du système de production sur la performance d'une entreprise dans plusieurs contextes de production. Les conclusions du rapport démontrent que les cellules dynamiques (DC) surpassent les *Job shop* (JS) et les cellules classiques (CC) sur presque tous les plans, principalement dans les environnements turbulents où on fabrique une variété de produits en petites quantités.

Entreprises Réseaux

L'idée de créer des ententes et partenariats d'affaires selon Poulin, Montreuil et Gauvin (1994) est principalement de se développer mutuellement et générer des bénéfices communs. Ces alliances stratégiques ont pour caractéristique de permettre aux entreprises concernées de réaliser des économies d'échelle, maîtriser la complexité des processus et des marchés, réagir plus vite au changement et augmenter sa flexibilité. Maintenant, les décideurs ne se concentrent plus uniquement sur la performance interne d'une entreprise mais également sur l'efficacité globale du réseau tout entier. Il devient alors important d'évaluer et mesurer cette performance de manière représentative (Beamon, 1999; Gunasekaran et Kobu, 2007; Tan et al., 2007; McCormack et al., 2008; Martin et Patterson, 2009; Anvari et al., 2011; Shepherd et Günter, 2011).

Ip, Chan et Lam (2011) élaborent un modèle mathématique qui permet de mesurer la performance et la stabilité des chaînes d'approvisionnement via la fiabilité du produit, la satisfaction de l'employé, la satisfaction du client, la livraison à temps, la croissance des profits et l'efficacité opérationnelle. Yoon et al. (2002) abordent la nécessité du transfert de connaissance et des données pour améliorer la performance du réseau. Kearney et Abdulnour (2004) ont rappelé l'importance d'une bonne communication, de l'augmentation du niveau de qualité ainsi que de l'acquisition de l'expertise externe par le biais de l'échange de connaissances et de savoir-faire au sein du réseau.

D'autre part, différents outils ont été élaborés pour optimiser la performance des chaînes d'entreprises. Feng et Zhang (2013) étudient l'impact de la conception modulaire sur l'efficacité des réseaux d'entreprises. Les conclusions ont prouvé que la conception modulaire améliore toujours l'efficacité d'un réseau si le partage d'information est suffisant. De leur côté, Anvari et al. (2011) abordent la relation entre la performance des réseaux d'entreprises et le *lean manufacturing*. La planification, la gestion des ressources humaines, la production et la livraison sont des processus inhérents à un réseau ainsi qu'au *lean*. Les mesures de performance sont également un outils essentiel dans l'implantation du *lean*.

Zhang et Qi (2013) ont étudié la relation entre les configurations des chaînes d'approvisionnement (*lean*, agile, *leagile* ou traditionnelle) et les pratiques des entreprises. Les résultats démontrent qu'une configuration *leagile* permet de rendre les pratiques de la personnalisation de masse plus bénéfiques pour la performance des entreprises.

Purvis et al. (2014) élaborent une nouvelle taxonomie qui relie dynamiquement la configuration du réseau (*lean*, agile, *leagile*) et la durée de vie des produits, la variation du mix-produit et du volume de production ainsi que la durée de vie du réseau. Christopher et Ryals (2014) abordent l'importance du client dans le réseau tout entier ainsi que celle du développement mutuel des entreprises dans la chaîne d'approvisionnement.

À la lumière de toutes ces considérations, Bulsara et al. (2014) ont établi une revue de littérature qui a pour but de fournir systèmes de mesure de performance des chaînes d'approvisionnement. (SCPMS). Les 5 caractéristiques principales qui ressortent, après avoir regroupé 89 articles, sont les ressources, les extrants, la flexibilité, l'innovation et finalement, la technologie de l'information

3 Expérimentation

Un design expérimental suivi d'une simulation à événements discrets a permis d'étudier le système. Un réseau d'entreprises d'assemblage mécanique a été utilisé comme cas à l'étude dans le but de modéliser le système et valider les résultats de cette recherche.
À la suite de la revue de littérature, sept facteurs ont été sélectionnés dans le but de vérifier leur influence respective sur les réponses. Il s'agit de la fiabilité des fournisseurs (A), l'interdisciplinarité (B), le volume de demande (C), la conception modulaire (D), le système d'alimentation (E), le système de production (F) ainsi que le nombre d'employés (G). À la figure suivante, il est possible de voir la structure de l'expérimentation à l'étude.

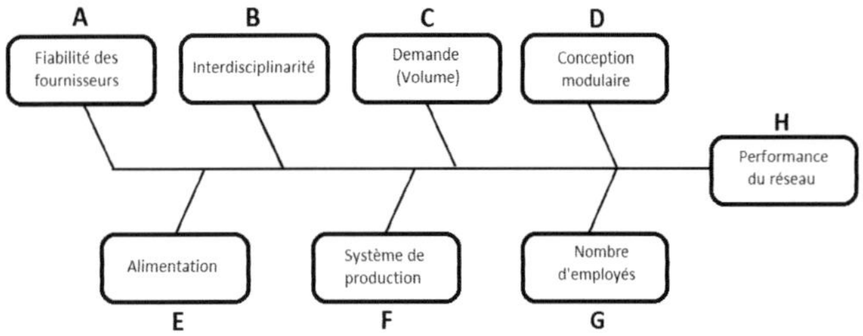

Fig. 1. Variables indépendantes à l'étude

L'analyse de la variance a permis de déterminer statistiquement la signifiance des relations entre les facteurs et la réponse. La méthodologie offre une meilleure compréhension du processus étudié et les variations causées par les différents paramètres. La table 1 démontre les différents niveaux des facteurs étudiés.

Table 1. Facteurs et niveaux étudiés

	Niveau		
Variable	0	1	2
Livraison à temps	0,9	0,95	0,99
Interdisciplinarité	Non	-	Oui
Demande (Volume)	0,5	1	1,5
Structure modulaire	Aucun	2e niveau BOM	1er niveau BOM
Alimentation	Bac	Kanban	Ressource de plus au montage
Type de production	Fixe	Équipe	Cellule
Nombre d'employés	-1	=	1

Un plan Taguchi L18 a été utilisé pour l'expérience. Ceci a permis de détecter de la manière la plus optimale possible l'effet des facteurs les plus significatifs. Les expériences ont été exécutées à l'aide du logiciel de simulation Rockwell Arena. Cinq réplications de chaque expérience ont été faites dans le but de maximiser la rigueur et la fiabilité des conclusions statistiques.

4 Résultats et discussions

Trois réponses ont été choisies parmi celles trouvées dans la littérature pour représenter les mesures de performance du sujet d'étude. Il s'agit du temps de réaction, du nombre d'encours et les ventes totales. Le temps de réaction a été déterminé comme le moment entre l'entrée de la commande jusqu'à l'expédition du produit fini. Le nombre d'encours est représenté en nombre de commandes-client dans le système et les ventes sont mesurées à partir des entités sortant du modèle.

Après l'analyse du plan d'expériences complété, les résultats ont démontré avec un degré de confiance de 95% que le facteur le plus significatif était le volume de la demande. Deux autres plans ont par la suite été montés en fixant la demande à un volume de 1 fois et 1.5 fois supérieur au volume réel de l'entreprise.

Dans ces deux cas, le design expérimental a démontré que le temps de réaction était considérablement réduit si les employés sont interdisciplinaires, il y a une structure modulaire de premier ou deuxième niveau, on utilise le système de production en cellules dynamiques, il y a une ressource de plus au montage (pas d'alimentation indirecte) et le nombre d'employé est égal ou supérieur au nombre actuel. Le tableau 2 indique les résultats de l'analyse de la variance du temps de réaction par rapport aux sept facteurs d'intérêt.

Table 2. ANOVA de l'effet des facteurs sur le temps de réaction

Source	DL	Seq SS	Adj MS	F	P
Interdisciplinarité	1	31871	31871	16,42	0,000
Structure Modulaire	2	138261	69131	35,61	0,000
Type de production	2	35566	17783	9,16	0,000
Alimentation	2	38143	19072	9,82	0,000
Nombre d'employés	2	18595	9298	4,79	0,011
Livraison à temps	2	11230	5615	2,89	0,061
Erreur	78	151413	1941		
Total	89	425077			

Le nombre d'encours suit les mêmes résultats, sauf au niveau du nombre d'employés. L'analyse de la variance n'a pas démontré que ce facteur était significatif sur le nombre d'encours.

Pour le nombre d'entités sortant, l'ANOVA ne démontre pas de différences significatives au niveau du type de production et du système d'alimentation. Il démontre toutefois une maximisation des ventes si le nombre d'employés est égal ou supérieur au nombre actuel et que la fiabilité des fournisseurs est à un niveau de 95% ou 99%. Le tableau 3 résume l'optimisation des mesures de performance choisies.

Table 3. Représentation des niveaux optimaux en fonction du délai de réaction

Délai de réaction (Minimisation)	Niveau optimal
Interdisciplinarité	Toutes
Structure Modulaire	1er et 2e niveau
Type de production	Cellules
Alimentation	Ress. + au montage
Nombre Employés	= et +1
Livraison à Temps	90%, 95% et 99%

Table 4. Représentation des niveaux optimaux en fonction du nombre d'encours

Nombre d'encours (Minimisation)	Niveau optimal
Interdisciplinarité	Toutes
Structure Modulaire	1er et 2e niveau
Type de production	Cellules
Alimentation	Ress. + au montage
Nombre Employés	= et +1
Livraison à Temps	90%, 95% et 99%

Table 5. Représentation des niveaux optimaux en fonction du nombre d'entités sortant

Nombre d'entités sortant (Maximisation)	Niveau optimal
Interdisciplinarité	Toutes
Structure Modulaire	1er et 2e niveau
Type de production	Fixe, Équipe, Cellules
Alimentation	Kanban, Bac, Ress. + au montage
Nombre Employés	= et +1
Livraison à Temps	95% et 99%

Globalement, dans les conditions étudiées, si on désire optimiser à la fois le délai de réaction, le nombre d'encours et le nombre d'entités sortant, il convient d'avoir des employés multidisciplinaires, la présence d'une structure modulaire au premier ou deuxième niveau, une production en cellules dynamiques, un nombre d'employés égal ou supérieur à celui actuel et une fiabilité des fournisseurs à 95% ou 99%.

Il est à noter que le niveau « Ress. + au montage » a été jugé comme avantageux pour les trois réponses mesurées. Dans le cas réel, le responsable de l'alimentation n'est pas dédié à temps plein à l'alimentation. Ses autres tâches consistent à exécuter la réception de la marchandise et la redistribution dans d'autres départements. Le niveau « Ress. + au montage » ne prend pas ce détail en compte. Lorsqu'il est actif, il fournit une capacité à temps plein supplémentaire au système. Lorsqu'il est inactif, il y a la moitié de la capacité de cette ressource qui est inutilisée puisque ses tâches ne sont pas représentées dans le modèle.

L'intérêt des cellules dynamiques repose sur la variabilité subie par les entreprises tant en termes de volume qu'au niveau du mix-produit. Dans le cas actuel, les expériences ont montré que les cellules dynamiques sont particulièrement intéressantes à un niveau de demande élevé. Lorsque le niveau est similaire à celui actuellement dans l'entreprise, il n'y a pas de différence significative entre une production fixe et une production en cellules dynamiques. Les plus gros avantages se font surtout sentir au niveau du délai de réaction et du nombre de commandes en cours dans le système. On peut expliquer ce phénomène par le chevauchement des opérations et l'ordonnancement qui est fait en fonction du temps d'entrée de la commande dans le système. Ces deux outils de planification ont pour conséquences de réduire considérablement le temps qu'une commande passe dans le système, en comparaison à un système de production fixe qui doit absolument effectuer toutes les tâches en série.

Dans le cas d'étude actuel, la variabilité du mix-produit est représentée par la présence d'une structure modulaire. Dans le cas où une entreprise ne fonctionne qu'en commandes personnalisées et qu'aucune standardisation n'est possible, il n'y aurait aucune conception modulaire possible. Du coup, l'absence d'une structure modulaire peut être considérée comme une variabilité très grande. Une structure modulaire de deuxième niveau de la nomenclature indique qu'il commence à y avoir une certaine standardisation au niveau de certaines composantes. La structure au premier niveau indique que les produits ont été standardisés jusqu'aux sous-assemblages et que, dans ce contexte, il y a peu de variabilité. Il faut toutefois mentionner qu'une structure modulaire implique nécessairement une variabilité puisqu'en son absence, on opterait davantage pour une production continue. On comprendra alors avec les résultats obtenus qu'une production en cellules dynamiques sera intéressantes où il y a un minimum de standardisation, qu'elle soit au deuxième ou au premier niveau de la nomenclature.

5 Conclusion

L'amélioration de la performance des réseaux est une question importante pour les petites et moyennes entreprises si elles désirent survivre à la compétition mondiale. Le dynamisme du marché et l'incertitude oblige à concilier productivité et flexibilité. Les auteurs ont prouvé que les cellules dynamiques peuvent rallier ces deux objectifs. Néanmoins, aucun pont n'a été fait entre les chaînes d'approvisionnement et l'utilisation des DCMS. La revue de littérature a permis de souligner les éléments inhérents aux deux concepts.

Un design expérimental suivi par une simulation Monte-Carlo a permis d'étudier un cas réel et conclure sur les effets de l'utilisation des DCMS sur la performance des réseaux. La simulation démontre que l'interdisciplinarité, la présence d'une structure modulaire, une production en cellules dynamiques, un nombre d'employés suffisant et une fiabilité des fournisseurs d'au moins 95% permettent d'optimiser le temps de réaction, le nombre d'encours et les ventes totales. Plusieurs facteurs ont pu être négligés dans cette recherche comme l'horizon de planification, la présence de plusieurs produits différents, l'étude d'un réseau plus élaboré, le système de communication, la sous-traitance et autres. L'étude de ces facteurs et autres mesures de performance ouvriraient la porte à des études éventuelles.

Références

1. Ali, R. M., Deif, A. M. (2014) Dynamic lean assessment for takt time implementation Proceedings *of the 47th CIRP Conference on Manufacturing Systems*, *Volume* 17, pp. 577–581

2. Anvari, A. and al. (2011) Performance measurement system through supply chain management to lean manufacturing. *World Applied Sciences Journal*, *Volume* 14, No. 2, pp. 285-292

3. Beamon, B. M. (1999) Measuring supply chain performance. *International Journal of Operations & Production Management*, *Volume* 19 No. 3, pp.275 - 292

4. Bulsara, H. P., Qureshi, M. N., Patel, H. (2014) Supply chain performance measurement - An exploratory study. *International Journal of Logistics Systems and Management*, *Volume* 18, No. 2, pp.231–249.

5. Christopher, M.; Ryals, L. J. (2014) The supply chain becomes the demand chain. *Journal of Business Logistics*, *Volume* 35, No. 1, pp. 29–35

6. Darkov, I., Naydenov, P. (2011). Factors that influence the success of the practical implementation of virtual cellular manufacturing system. *Societal studies*, *Volume* 3, No. 1, pp.95-106

7. De Loecker, J. and P. K. Goldberg (2014). Firm performance in a global market. *Annual Review of Economics*, *Volume* 6, pp. 201-227

8. Drolet, J., Marcoux, Y., Abdulnour, G. (2008). Simulation-based performance comparison between dynamic cells, classical cells and job shops: a case study. *International Journal of Production Research*, *Volume* 46, No.2, p.509-536

9. Feng, T., Zhang, F. (2013) The Impact of Modular Assembly on Supply Chain Efficiency. *Production and Operations Management*, *Volume* 23, Issue 11, pages 1985–2001

10. Ghotboddini, M. M., Rabbani, M., Rahimian, H. (2011) A comprehensive dynamic cell formation design: Benders' decomposition approach. *Expert Systems with Applications*, *Volume* 38, Issue 3, pp. 2478–2488

11. Gunasekaran, A., Kobu, B. (2007) Performance measures and metrics in logistics and supply chain management: A review of recent literature (1995-2004) for research and applications. *International Journal of Production Research*, *Volume* 45, No. 12, pp. 2819-2840

12. Ip, W. H., Chan, S. L., Lam, C. Y. (2011) Modeling supply chain performance and stability. *Industrial Management & Data Systems*, *Volume* 111, No. 8, pp.1332 - 1354

13. Kearney, S., Abdul-Nour, G. (2004) SME and quality performance in networking environment. *Computers & Industrial Engineering*, *Volume* 46, No. 4, pp. 905–909

14. Kia, R. et al. (2012) Solving a group layout design model of a dynamic cellular manufacturing system with alternative process routings, lot splitting and flexible reconfiguration by simulated annealing. *Computers & Operations Research*, *Volume* 39, No. 11, pp. 2642–2658

15. Li, W., Hu, L., Murata, T. (2011) Production planning in dynamic cellular manufacturing system using optimization of cell reconfiguration planning time horizon with uncertain demand. IEEE *International Conference on Automation and Logistics (ICAL)*, 15-16 août 2011, pp.466-470

16. Martin, P.R., Patterson, J.W. (2009) On measuring company performance within a supply chain. *International Journal of Production Research*, *Volume* 47, No. 9, pp. 2449-

2460
17. McCormack, K. and al. (2008) Supply chain maturity and performance in Brazil. *Supply Chain Management*, *Volume* 13, No. 4, pp. 272-282
18. Paydar, M. M., Saidi-Mehrabad, M., Kia, R. (2013) Designing a new integrated model for dynamic cellular manufacturing systems with production planning and intra-cell layout. *International Journal of Applied Decision Sciences (IJADS)*, *Volume* 6, No. 2
19. Purvis, L., Gosling, J., Naim, M. M. (2014) The development of a lean, agile and leagile supply network taxonomy based on differing types of flexibility. *International Journal of Production Economics*, *Volume* 151, pp. 100–111
20. Rheault M., Drolet J. R., Abdulnour G. (1996). Les Cellules Dynamiques: Un Concept pour PME. *3e Congrès International Francophone de la PME (CIFPME 96)*, 23-25 octobre 1996, Université du Québec à Trois-Rivières, pp 955-968
21. Rheault, M., Drolet, J. R., Abdulnour, G. (1995). Physically reconfigurable virtual cells: A dynamic model for a highly dynamic environment. *Proceedings of the 17th International Conference on Computers and Industrial Engineering*, *Volume* 29, No.1-4, p.221-225
22. Rheault, M., Drolet, J. R., Abdulnour, G. (1996). Dynamic Cellular Manufacturing System (DCMS). *Proceedings of the 19th International Conference on Computers and Industrial Engineering*, *Volume* 31, Issues 1-2, P.143-146
23. Safaei, N., Tavakkoli-Moghaddam, R. (2009). Integrated multi-period cell formation and subcontracting production planning in dynamic cellular manufacturing systems. *International Journal of Production Economics*, *Volume* 120, No. 2, Pages 301–314
24. Saxena, L. K., Jain, P. K. (2011) Dynamic cellular manufacturing systems design - A comprehensive model. *The International Journal of Advanced Manufacturing Technology*, *Volume* 53, No. 1-4, pp 11-34
25. Shepherd, C., Günter, H. (2011) Measuring supply chain performance: Current research and future directions. *International Journal of Productivity and Performance Management*, *Volume* 55, No. 3/4, pp. 242-258
26. Soolaki, M. (2012) A multi-objective integrated cellular manufacturing systems design with production planning, worker assignment and dynamic system reconfiguration. *International Journal of Industrial and Systems Engineering*, *Volume* 12, No. 3, pp.280-300
27. Soolaki, M., Izadi, A. (2013) A robust optimisation model for manufacturing cell design problem under uncertainty. *International Journal of Services and Operations Management*, *Volume* 15, No.2, pp.238 - 258
28. Tan, Y., Ma, S. H., Gong, F. M. (2007) Empirical study on impact of logistics operations capability on supply chain performance. *International Conference on Wireless Communications, Networking and Mobile Computing*, 21-25 septembre 2007, pp. 4760-4766
29. Tavakkoli-Moghaddam, R., Sakhaii, M., Vatani, B. (2014) A robust model for a dynamic cellular manufacturing system with production planning. *International Journal of Engineering, Transactions A: Basics*, *Volume* 27, No. 4, pp. 587-598
30. Yamchello, H. T. and al. (2014) A review of the critical success factors in the adoption of lean production system by small and medium sized enterprises. *Applied Mechanics and Materials*, *Volume* 564, Chapter 8: Industrial Engineering, pp. 627-631
31. Yoon, T. and al. (2002) Knowledge fusion among the virtual production enterprises within the technology information infrastructure environment. *IEEE Internation Engineering Management Conference*, *Volume* 1, pp. 35-40
32. Zhang, M., Qi, Y. (2013) Impact of supply chain strategy on mass customisation implementation and effectiveness: Evidence from China. *International Journal of Information and Decision Sciences*, *Volume* 5, No.4, pp.393 - 413
33. Poulin D., Montreuil B. and Gauvin S. (1994). *L'entreprise réseau: bâtir aujourd'hui l'organisation de demain.* Montréal, Publi-Relais, p.335
Sushil et Stohr E. A. (2013) *The Flexible Enterprise (Flexible Systems Management)* (Édition 2013). Springer, p.374
34. Tompkins J. A., White J. A., Bozer Y. A. and Tanchoco J. M. A. (2010). *Facilities Planning.* (4ème édition) Wiley, p.864
Industrie Canada (2012) "Recherche et statistique sur la PME", [En ligne], consulté le 06-12-2014 <https://www.ic.gc.ca/eic/site/061.nsf/fra/01278.html>
35. Houtart F. (2007) "Les effets de la mondialisation", [En ligne], consulté le 06-12-2014 <http://www.cetri.be/spip.php?article79>
36. Hulten, C. R. (2001). Total factor productivity. A short biography. In *New developments in productivity analysis* (pp. 1-54). University of Chicago Press, [En ligne], consulté le 06-12-2014 <http://www.nber.org/ chapters/c10122.pdf>
37. Perny P., Spanjarrd O., (2005) Optimisation robuste. *Universite Paris 6*, [En ligne], consulté le 06-12-2014 <https://www-master.ufr-info-p6.jussieu.fr/2005/IMG/pdf /rhad6.pdf>
38. The Open Group (2014), Maximizing the Value of Cloud for Small-Medium Enterprises: Key SME Characteristics (Business and IT), [En ligne], consulté le 06-12-2014 <http://www. opengroup.org/cloud/cloud/cloud_sme /characteristics.htm>

« Estimation des incertitudes de mesures 3D liées aux outils logiciels»

Charfadine Nimane Mahamat *, Stéphane Raynaud **, Youssouf Mandiang ***
* Institut National Supérieur des Sciences et Technique d'Abéché(INSTA), Tchad (machanimane@yahoo.fr/charfadine01@gmail.com)
** Centre Technique de L'innovation MECA3D- Laboratoire MIP2-Métrologie Numérisation Qualité, INSA de Lyon, France, stéphane.raynaud@insa-lyon.fr
*** Laboratoire d'Energétique Appliquée (LEA), Ecole Supérieure Polytechnique (ESP) de Dakar, BP 5085 Université Cheikh Anta Diop (UCAD), Sénégal

Résumé : Les moyens de mesures 3D se sont largement multipliés ces derniers années, dans les laboratoires de métrologie, dans les ateliers de production et sur les chantiers de construction métalliques. Les incertitudes de mesures sont fonction de nombreux facteurs. Nous allons nous intéresser à l'influence des moyens de mesure et surtout à l'influence du logiciel utilisé par le contrôleur. Le triptyque machine, homme, logiciel peut produire des résultats assez éloignés des valeurs vraies!. Après plusieurs études et expériences, nous avons constaté que l'incertitude de mesure dépend beaucoup de ce que font les utilisateurs avec le logiciel de moyens de mesure 3D et les spécifications géométriques à contrôler ». Pour prendre en compte ce facteur d'incertitude dans les résultats de mesure au préalable il faut s'assurer que les exigences aux normes sont respectées dans les outils logiciels et que les contrôleurs l'utilise correctement. Pour ce faire nous réalisons des tests R et R à l'aide d'un inter comparaison de résultats de mesures à l'aide d'un étalon numérique (CAO et nuages des points théoriques) testé avec différents logiciel et ceci permet de s'affranchir de l'incertitude machine.
Mots clés : Contrôle 3D, logiciel, cotation, Incertitude, moyens de mesure 3D.

Abstract: The means of 3D measurements have greatly multiplied in recent years in metrology laboratorys, workshops and production on metal construction sites. The measurement uncertaintys are based on many factors. We will look at the influence of the measurement means and especially the influence of the software used by the controller. Machine triptych, man, software can produce enough away from true values results!. After several studies and experiments, we found that the measurement uncertainty depends a lot on what users are doing with the 3D measurement means software and geometric specifications to control. " To account for this uncertainty in the measurement results first make sure that the requirements are complied with the standards in the software tools and the controllers used properly. To do this we perform tests of physical and virtual measurements using an inter measures of comparison results with a digital standard (CAD clouds and theoretical points) tested various software and this enables to overcome the uncertainty machine.
Keywords: 3D control, software, trading, uncertainty, 3D measuring means.

.

1 Introduction

La métrologie tridimensionnelle a permis initialement de se rendre compte des défauts géométriques des produits mécaniques. Au fur et à mesure des évolutions technologiques matériels et logiciels, les moyens sont de plus en plus de bonne qualité. Néanmoins la partie plus difficile à maitriser pour le contrôleur est l'outil logiciel en adaptant au mieux le contrôle des spécifications des produits. De ce fait l'un des problèmes majeurs pour de nombreuses industries et laboratoires utilisant des moyens 3D est l'estimation des incertitudes de mesures pour chacune des spécifications géométriques mesurées. Très peu de rapport de contrôle 3D font apparaitre les incertitudes de mesures estimées. Seulement les incertitudes des points mesurés sont définis par le constructeur et contrôlées lors de la vérification d'une machine.

Les machines à mesurer tridimensionnelles (MMT) se sont largement répandues, dans les laboratoires de métrologie et dans les ateliers, Les logiciels associés à ces machines ont grandement progressé, permettant de travailler à partir des définitions numériques des pièces à contrôler. Pour autant, la fiabilité des mesures reste délicate à quantifier et les calculs d'incertitudes ne sont pas faits dans les règles de l'art ou prennent trop de temps!

2 Contexte

L'objectif de ces travaux est de proposer une méthodologie et un outil pragmatique d'estimation des incertitudes de mesures. Pour un tel outil, il faut:

- explicitement spécifier le domaine d'application déclaré du logiciel,

- respecter les exigences relatives aux logiciels d'évaluation des incertitudes selon la norme XP ISO/TS 15530-4.

La déclaration doit inclure les spécifications suivantes qui sont les sources principales des incertitudes:

- le type de machines à mesurer tridimensionnelles (MMT) pour lesquelles le logiciel est applicable,

- tous les accessoires MMT autorisés,

-les erreurs MMT prises en compte,

- les conditions environnementales considérées pour la MMT et la pièce,

- les types de palpeurs applicables et accessoires, les éléments associés possibles,

- le tolérancement géométrique à contrôler,

-les modes opératoires et stratégies de mesurage pris en compte,

- les effets liés à l'opérateur,

- tout autre facteur d'influence..

Détermination de l'incertitude de mesure spécifique d'une spécification.

Il convient que les paramètres du mesurage simulés, qui sont importants d'un point de vue métrologique, soient aussi similaires que possible à ceux du mesurage réel. L'incertitude type d'un résultat de mesure y est composée:
- de l'incertitude Usim déterminée par la simulation,
- des incertitudes Ui issues des grandeurs d'influence non prises en compte dans la simulation et évaluées par d'autres moyens appropriés. L'incertitude type combinée, U, est alors calculée (en supposant la non-corrélation des Ui) à l'aide de l'équation suivante:

$$U = \sqrt{u_{sim}^{2\,2} + \sum u_i^2}$$

2.1 Cycle de Mesure

Un cycle de mesures réelles comprend l'analyse des specifications du CAO, le maniement des pièces. La position et l'orientation des pièces mesurées sont laissées à la discrétion de l'utilisateur dans la plage couverte par l'évaluation de l'incertitude.

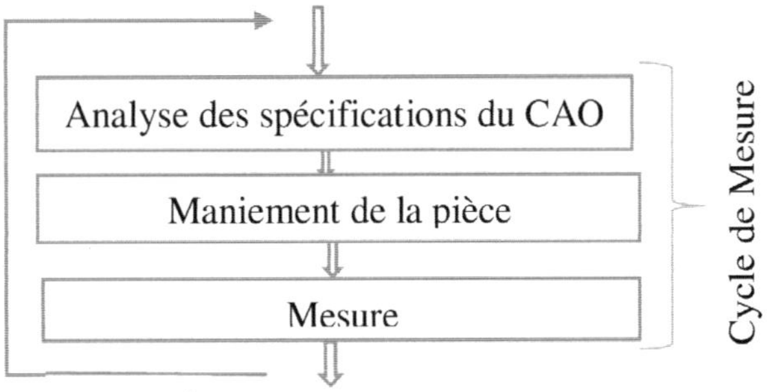

Figure 1: Mode opératoire de mesure

2.3 Calcul de l'incertitude

Dans un certificat d'étalonnage ou un rapport de mesure, le résultat de mesure, y, et son incertitude élargie, U, doivent être exprimés sous la forme y ± U, où U est déterminé avec un coefficient k = 2 pour une probabilité d'élargissement approximative de 95 %.

Lors de la réalisation des mesures, quatre facteurs d'incertitudes fondamentaux doivent être pris en compte. Ils sont décrits par les incertitudes-types suivantes :

- Incertitude-type associée à l'incertitude de l'étalonnage de la pièce étalonnée indiquée dans le certificat d'étalonnage U_{cal},
- Incertitude-type associée au mode opératoire de mesure tel qu'évalué par l'évaluation de l'incertitude U_p,
- Incertitude-type associée à l'erreur de justesse de l'évaluation du processus de mesure utilisant la pièce étalonnée U_b ;
- Incertitude-type associée aux variations dans la fabrication des produits et dans le matériau U_w (dues à la variation du coefficient de dilatation, des erreurs de forme, de la rugosité, de l'élasticité et de la plasticité).

L'incertitude de mesure élargie U, de tout paramètre mesuré est calculée à partir de ces incertitudes-types comme suit :

$$U = k\times\sqrt{u_{cal}^2 + u_p^2 + u_b^2 + u_w^2}$$

3. Partie expérimentale

Les mesures ont été réalisées dans le cadre de développement d'un outil d'aide aux calculs des incertitudes de processus tridimensionnel.
Elles ont porté sur deux parties:

- Une partie concerne des mesures physiques sur une pièce test (étalon) par les différents moyens de mesures 3D (machine-homme-logiciel), les mesures physiques elles sont toutes faites dans les mêmes conditions: température 20°c, hygrométrie contrôlée et le même opérateur.
- Une deuxième partie concerne la détermination des éléments et des cotations, définis sur le CAO, à partir des nuages de points, en utilisant les moyens de mesures 3D (homme-logiciel).

3.1 Inter comparaison des logiciels des Machines à Mesurer Tridimensionnel par des mesures physiques sur une pièce test

Objectif:

L'objectif de cette inter-comparaison est de chercher les influences des logiciels dans les calculs des incertitudes de mesures de processus tridimensionnel.

Procédures de mesure:

On a une pièce étalon (test) qui a plusieurs cotations (tolérances géométriques) à vérifier, on fait des mesures sur les différentes machines MMTs du Laboratoire MIP2-Métrologie Numérisation

Qualité, INSA de Lyon, en suivant une même procédure avec les différents logiciels.

machine	logiciel
Tri-mesure Manuelle	Metrolog XG 6
ZEISS CN	Metrolog XG 13
Mitutoyo CN	Cosmos 2.0
Mahr K-Mess	Cosmos 2.4
LK Nikon	CMM Manager

Tableau 1 : Moyens de mesures

3.2 Méthode d'association:

On a utilisé le critère de moindres carrés pour tous les calculs d'éléments associés, qui a l'avantage par rapport aux autres critères de donner un résultat fiable et robuste quel que soit le nombre de points et quelle que soit l'étendue de la surface mesurée, définie par une fonction W de la façon suivante:

$$w = \sum_{i=1}^{n} e_i^2$$

$$W = \sum_{i=1}^{n} \left(\xi i - \left(To \otimes P \vec{n}\, i \right) \right)^2$$

$$w = \sum_{i=1}^{n} (\xi i - (u.a_i + v.b_i + w.c_i + \alpha.L_i + \beta.M_i + \gamma.N_i))^2$$

W est une fonction à 6 variables W=f(u,v,w,α,β,γ).

On obtient 6 équations linéaires à l'aide des dérivées partielles par rapport aux 6 inconnues:

$$\frac{\partial w}{\partial u} = 0;\ \frac{\partial w}{\partial v} = 0;\ \frac{\partial w}{\partial w} = 0;\ \frac{\partial w}{\partial \alpha} = 0;\ \frac{\partial w}{\partial \beta} = 0;\ \frac{\partial w}{\partial \gamma} = 0$$

La connaissance de u, v, w, α, β, γ permet ensuite de calculer dans le repère local lié à la surface nominale, la nouvelle position des points théoriques définissant la position initiale de l'élément géométrique nominal et de connaître enfin dans le repère de calcul (ou repère machine), la situation de l'élément géométrique associé (optimisé) à l'ensemble des points palpés.

Les éléments et cotations à vérifier dans ces expériences : Plan, Angle, Distance, Diamètre, Rectitude, Circularité, Cylindricité, Planéité, Localisation, sont représentés (figure 2) sur le dessin du CAO.

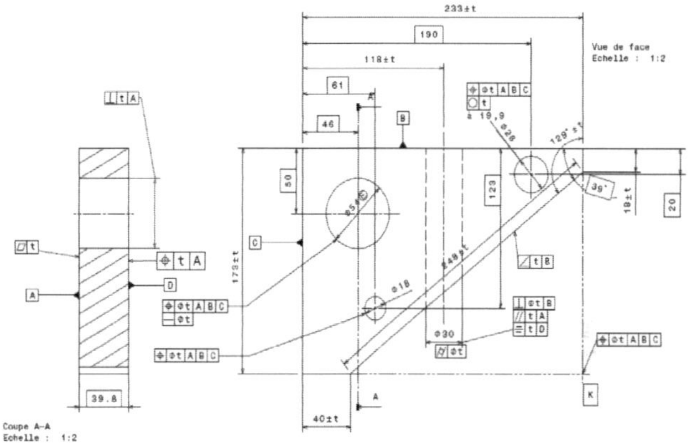

Figure 2: CAO de la piéce test (étalon)

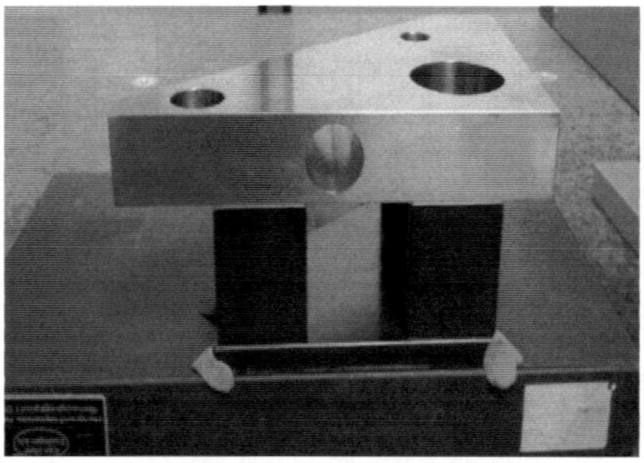

Figure 3 : piéce test (étalon)

Figure 4 :Representation des éléments associés

3.3 Résultats de mesures physiques

Ces résultats issus de mesures des éléments géométriques et cotations à vérifier définis sur le CAO de la pièce étalon, on a choisi de présenter dans ces résultats: angle de plans (129°), distance entre deux points (165mm), la planéité de la pièce et la circularité du cercle de diamètre (54mm). Les résultats sont obtenus en utilisant le critère de moindre carrés, chaque élément spécification à vérifier est mesuré trois(3) fois sur chaque machine-logiciel, et on fait une comparaison entre les valeurs mesurées et la valeur nominale de l'élément.

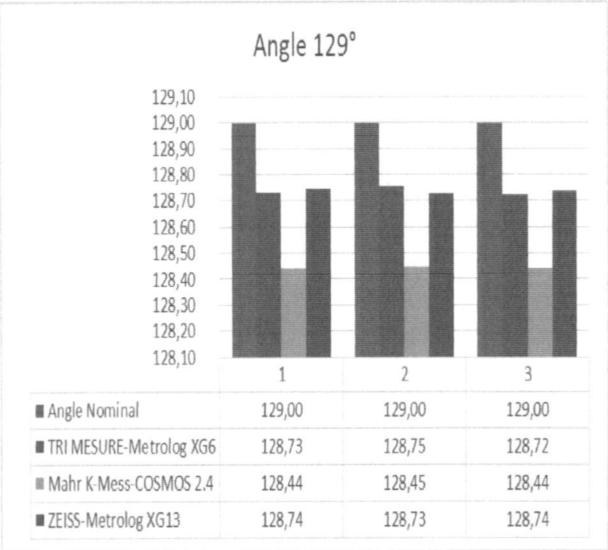

Figure 5: Angle 129°

La figure 5, présente des résultats de mesure d'un angle de plans de 129°, obtenus par la répétabilité de mesures, les écarts (en degré) sont présentés dans le tableau 2.

Mesure(en degré)	Metrolog XG6	COSMOS 2.4	Metrolog XG13
1	-0,27	-0,56	- 0,26
2	- 0,25	-0,56	- 0,27
3	- 0,28	-0,56	-0,26

Tableau 1: Ecarts (en degré) entre la valeur vraie de l'angle et les valeurs mesurées.

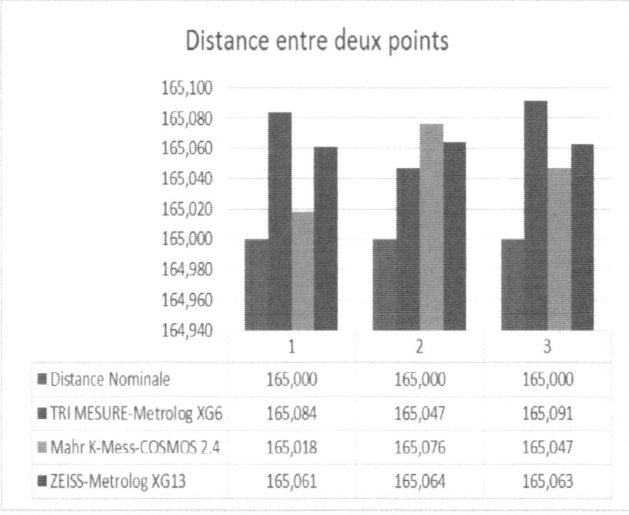

Figure 6 : Distance entre deux points

Cet histogramme illustre une comparaison entre la valeur vraie de la distance (165mm) entre deux points et les valeurs évaluées des différents logiciels.

Mesure(en mm)	Metrolog XG6	COSMOS 2.4	Metrolog XG13
1	0,084	0,061	0,084
2	0,047	0,076	0,064
3	0,091	0,047	0,063

Tableau 3: Ecarts entre la valeur vraie de la distance entre deux points et les valeurs mesurées

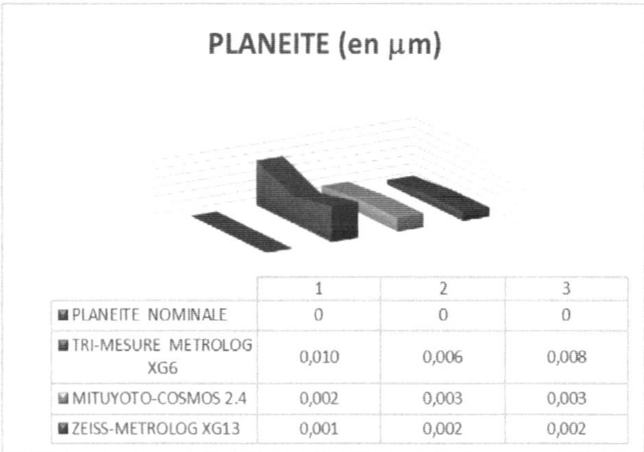

Figure 6: planiété de la piéce étalon

La figure 6 représente les planéités évaluées (étendue des points) de la pièce expérimentale.

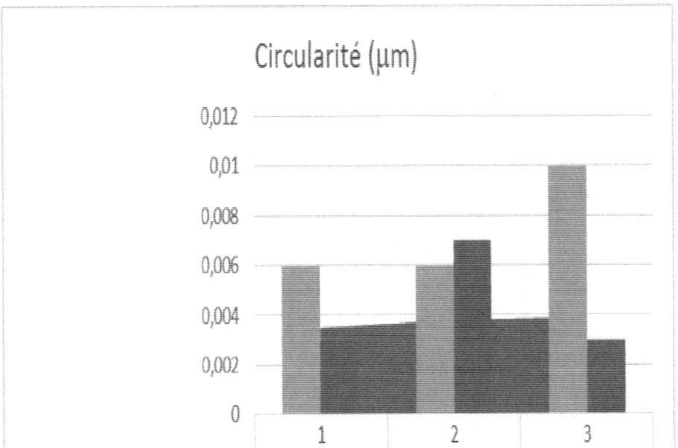

	1	2	3
TRI MESURE-METROLOG XG6	0,004	0,004	0,004
CIRCULARITE NOMINALE	0	0	0
MITUYOTO-COSMOS 2.4	0,006	0,006	0,010
ZEISS-METROLOG XG13	0,003	0,007	0,003

Figure 7: Circularité du cercle de diamètre 54mm

Cette figure montre la circularité (en µm) du cercle de diamètre 54mm, évaluée par chacun des logiciels, par rapport à une planéité nominale supposée zéro(0).

Conclusion

Les résultats des différentes mesures physiques nous montrent, il y a des écarts non négligeables entre les valeurs nominales et mesurées, mais il faut faire l'évaluation des spécifications à l'aide des nuages des points.

4. Inter comparaison de logiciels des machines à mesurer tridimensionnelles par des nuages de points de pièces palpées.

Objectif:

L'objectif de cette partie des expériences est de chercher l'influence due à la partie logicielle dans les résultats de mesures de moyens 3D ,en utilisant les nuages des points, il s'agit de mesurer des écarts de taille, d'orientation et de position, et d'éléments tolérances de référentiel tels qu'ils sont définis sur le dessin (Figure 8),

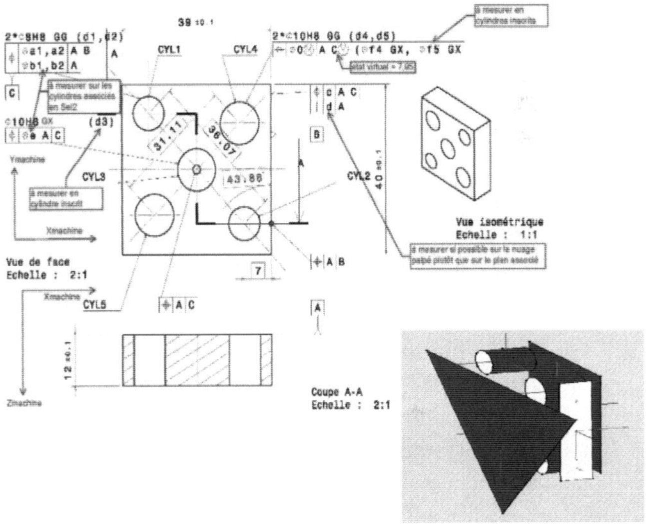

Figure 8: Dessin de la pièce

4.1 Méthode d'association

– **Logiciels utilisés :**

logiciel	Version
Metrolog	XG 4
Metrolog	XG 6
Metrolog	XG 13
Metrolog	XG 14
Cosmos	2.4

Tableau 3: logiciels utilisés

On a utilisé une macro sous Excel pour la conversion au format logiciel des points PNT qui constituent chacune des 120 pièces (figure 8) à construire. Nous allons prendre quelques-unes des 120 pièces pour ces expériences.

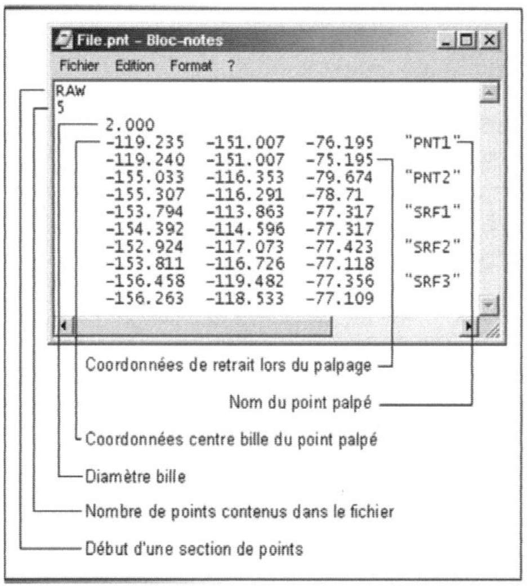

Figure 9:Type de fichier PNT

– **Procédure :**

Elle consiste à:

- Identification des nuages de points constituant chaque élément de la pièce à réaliser,
- Construction des plans,
- Construction des droites,
- Définition des repères,
- Evaluation des éléments.

Figure 10 : Nuages de points

On a fait un programme d'exécution de la même procédure pour tous les logiciels en utilisant le critère de moindres carrés, pour l'évaluation des éléments des pièces. On exécute le programme trois (3) fois sur chacune des pièces, et on calcule la moyenne.

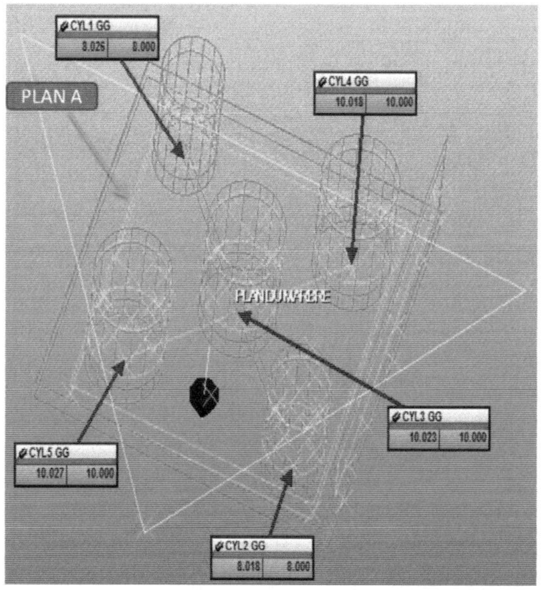

Figure 11 : Représentation des éléments associés

La figure 11 présente les éléments associés, elle est constituée de trois (3) cylindres de diamètre 10mm, deux (2) de diamètre 8mm et trois plans.

4.2 Résultats des mesures des nuages de points

Dans ces résultats on présente l'évaluation des spécifications à partir des nuages de points de quelques pièces, les nous montrent des écarts entre les valeurs nominales et mesurées sur chaque pièce et aussi entre les valeurs mesurées de logiciels.

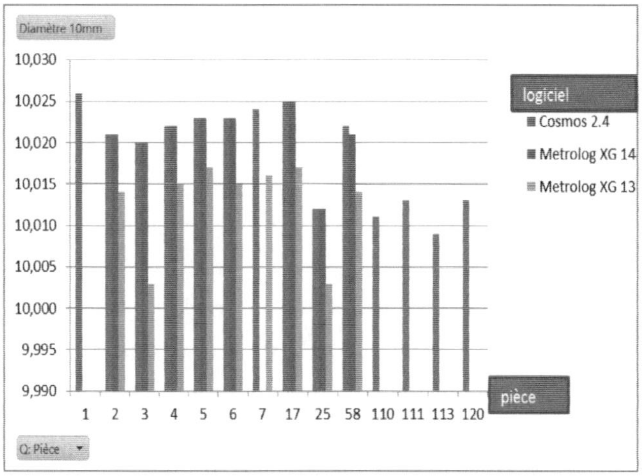

Figure 12: Diamètre 10mm

La figure 12 illustre les résultats de moyennes de mesures des cylindres de diamètre 10mm de pièces.

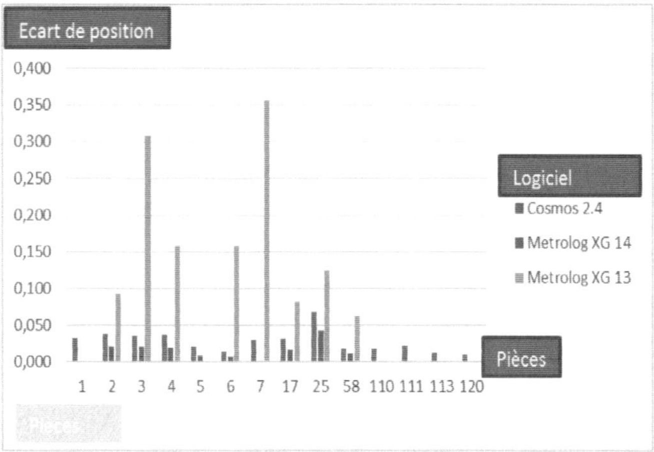

Figure 13: Ecarts de position

La figure 13 évaluation des écarts de position du cylindre de diamètre 8mm, de différentes pièces par rapport au plan A (figure11).

Discussion et Conclusion

Nous avons montré par des expérimentations des mesures physiques et à l'aide des nuages de points, les écarts des spécifications entre les valeurs nominales et évaluées par les moyens de mesures 3D, les logiciels de contrôle 3D ne sont pas développés en respectant les normes ISO, c'est pourquoi on évalue des écarts entre les deux valeurs dans les processus tridimensionnels, les résultats que nous obtenu confirment, l'importance de développer un outil d'aide aux calculs des incertitudes des processus tridimensionnels, qui va permettre de tenir en compte aux contrôleurs, les influences dues aux outils logiciels: Compensation, exploitation statistique, Exploitation de graphes; mesure. Les éditeurs des logiciels ne donnent pas les algorithmes utilisés dans le logiciel, alors que le contrôleur doit faire le choix de critère d'associés le mieux adapté à la spécification.

Les limites logicielles ne nous ont pas permis d'évaluer certaines spécifications dans l'art, le développement d'un outil pragmatique est essentiel, en regroupant les ingénieurs méthodes, les éditeurs des logiciels et les métrologues utilisateurs des moyens de mesures 3D.

Références

[1] ISO/TS 23165,2006, Spécification géométrique des produits (GPS) — Lignes directrices pour l'estimation de l'incertitude d'essai des machines à mesurer tridimensionnelles (MMT),

[2] XP ISO/TS 15530-4, Spécification géométrique des produits (GPS) Machines à mesurer tridimensionnelles (MMT) : Technique pour la détermination de l'incertitude de mesure Partie 4 : Évaluation de l'incertitude de mesure spécifique d'une tâche à l'aide de simulations, JUILLET 2008

[3] NF EN ISO 15530-3, Décembre 2011 : Spécification géométrique des produits (GPS) Machines à mesurer tridimensionnelles (MMT) : Technique pour la détermination de l'incertitude de mesure Partie 3 : Utilisation de pièces étalonnées ou d'étalons de mesure,

[4] Spécification géométrique des produits (GPS), Essais de réception et de vérification périodique des machines à mesurer tridimensionnelles (MMT) NF EN ISO 10360-1 Mars 2001 Partie 1 : Vocabulaire

[5] NF EN ISO 10360-5, Novembre 2010, Partie 5 : MMT utilisant des systèmes de palpage à stylet simple et à stylets multiples,

[6] NF EN ISO 10360-6, Février 2002, Spécification géométrique des produits (GPS), Partie 6 : Estimation des erreurs dans le calcul des éléments associés Gaussiens,

[7] NF EN ISO 10360-2, Janvier 2010, Spécification géométrique des produits (GPS), Partie 2 : MMT utilisées pour les mesures de dimensions linéaires,

[8] Iso 1101:1983, Dessins Techniques-Tolérancement géométrique-Tolérancement de forme, orientation, position et battement-généralités, définitions, symboles, indications sur les dessins,

[9] Contrôle tridimensionnel, Edition 2009, S.RAYNAUD,

[10] Métrologie avec les normes ISO, volume 5, 2011, Bernard Anselmentti,

[11] Résumé de métrologie dimensionnelle IUT Nancy-Brabois Dpt QLIO à Lunéville Cyril Domptail,

[12] Thèse, ABDELHAK Nafi, 2011, Vérification et diagnostic des Machines Mesurer Tridimensionnelles avec découplage machine et palpeur,

[12] Thèse, Gabriel CLOITRE, Octobre 2012, Contribution à la connaissance et à la modélisation des paramètres influant sur la capabilité des procèdes de mesure tridimensionnels,

[13] 9éme Congrès français de Mécanique, Marseille 24-28 août 2009, A. Jalid, Hariri, J.P Senelaer, A. ELGHARAD,

[14] Thèse, François HENNEBELLE, 05 décembre 2007, Détermination des incertitudes de mesures sur machines à mesurer tridimensionnelles application aux engrenages,

[15] Contrôle des machines à mesurer, Jean-Paul MATHIEN, LNE, Avril 2005,

[16] Thèse, Boukar Abdelhakim, pilotage des usinages tridimensionnels, 22 janvier 2013,

[17] Logiciels des machines à mesurer tridimensionnelles, Pierre BOURDET, Avril 2005,

[18] Guide de reference pour le calcul des incertitudes de mesure sur machine a mesurer tridimensionnelle, C.WadelPage, 16/02/2006 ,

[19] Etude chaines de cotes et cotation, ISO, Chapitre 9,S.RAYNAUD 2013,

[20] Les normes ISO de tolérancement GPS, une fracture dans le processus d'apprentissage, Frédéric CHARPENTIER, Jean-Marc PRENEL, Avril 2009,

[21] Évaluation des données de mesure-Guide pour l'expression de l'incertitude de mesure, , JCGM 100:2008(F),

[22] DAVID Janisek, Cours de Géne logiciel, les différentes paradigmes de programmation,

[23] FD E 11-157,Spécification géométrique des produits (GPS),Machines à mesurer tridimensionnelles,Guide pour l'élaboration d'un cahier des charges, Décembre 1997.

Mesures en vue de l'étude de la relation entre la densité de poussière accumulée à la surface des modules PV et la dégradation de leurs caractéristiques de performance

Ababacar Ndiaye [a,b,*], Cheikh M. F. Kébé [b], Boudy Ould Bilal [b,d], Abdérafi Charki [c], Vincent Sambou [b], Papa A. Ndiaye [b]

[a] Université Assane Seck de Ziguinchor, UFR – Sciences et Technologies, Département de Physique, BP 523 Ziguinchor, Sénégal.
[b] Centre International de Formation et de Recherche en Energie Solaire (CIFRES), Ecole Supérieure Polytechnique-UCAD, BP 5085 Dakar-Fann, Sénégal.
[c] Université d'Angers-ISTIA-LASQUO, 62 Avenue Notre Dame du Lac 49000 Angers, France.
[d] Ecole des Mines de Mauritanie (EMiM), BP 5259, Nouakchott, Mauritanie.

Résumé. Une des contraintes majeures liées aux conditions de fonctionnement des systèmes photovoltaïques en milieu sahélien, en plus des fortes températures, est relative aux dépôts d'aerosols particuliérement la poussière sur la surface des modules. En effet, la zone sahélienne est caractérisée par de fréquents et permanents épisodes de tempête de sable qui impactent sur son fort potentiel solaire. Cependant, les avis restent encore partagés sur l'impact significatif de la poussiere sur la production des modules photovoltaïques. Ce papier est consacré à l'étude de la corrélation entre la densité de poussière en dépôt à la surface des modules photovoltaïques de technologie en silicium cristallin et leur impact sur leurs performances electriques. Cette étude menée sur deux modules respectivement de technologie mono et polycristalline, porte sur la tension en circuit-ouvert (V_{co}), le courant de court-circuit (I_{cc}), le facteur de forme (FF) et plus particulièrement la puissance maximale (P_{max}). Ce papier présente la méthodologie et l'étude expérimentale mises en oeuvre pour mesurer les paramètres d'environnement (Ensoleillement, température, humidité), la densité de poussière et les caractéristiques de performance (Icc, Vco, FF et Pmax). Enfin, les résultats sur la corrélation entre la densité de poussière et chacune des caractéristiques sont présentés.

Mots clefs: Photovoltaïque, Dégradation, Poussière, corrélation

1. Introduction

L'accumulation des particules de poussière sur la surface du module PV peut affecter grandement sa performance surtout dans les zones désertiques. Cependant, les régions désertiques sont les plus adaptées à la production d'électricité photovoltaïque en raison de la disponibilité abondante du rayonnement solaire tout au long de l'année. Aujourd'hui, l'idée de mettre en place de vastes champs photovoltaïques dans les pays sahéliens en vue de l'exportation de l'énergie produite vers d'autres pays est en cours de discussion [1]. L'accumulation de poussière sur la surface du panneau PV dépend de différents paramètres comme l'inclinaison du module PV, le type d'installation, l'humidité.

Hottel et Woertz ont été parmi les premiers à travailler sur l'impact de la poussière sur les systèmes solaires [2]. Ils ont enregistré une dégradation maximale des performances de 4,7%, avec une perte moyenne de rayonnement solaire incident inférieure à 1%. Une autre étude de l'accumulation de la poussière sur un système photovoltaïque installé dans un village près de Riyad a montré une réduction de 32% de la performance au bout de huit mois sans que les modules ne soient nettoyés [3]. Une réduction de la puissance photovoltaïque de 17% sur des modules installés dans la ville de Koweït city a été notée après six jours sans nettoyage des modules [4]. En outre, l'étude a également indiqué que l'influence de la poussière sur les performances PV serait plus élevée pendant les saisons sèches de l'année. Dans une autre étude sur les effets de la poussière sur le module photovoltaïque à Palo Alto, en Californie, il a été montré que l'accumulation de la poussière sur les modules photovoltaïques a provoqué une réduction de 2% du courant de court-circuit par rapport à celui des modules propres [5,6]. Shaharin et al. ont trouvé que la réduction de la puissance due au dépôt de la poussière sur le module PV peut aller jusqu'à 18% [7].

La perte de puissance due à la poussière est fonction du type de poussière, du temps écoulé depuis la dernière pluie et du calendrier de nettoyage [8]. Detrick et al. avancent que la perte moyenne annuelle de puissance d'un module photovoltaïque varie de 1% à 4% [9]. Dans les zones où les pluies sont fréquentes, il a été montré que la pluie pouvait nettoyer les modules PV à un point de restauration de la performance à 1% de perte sur la pleine puissance [10]. Dans une étude plus récente effectuée en Crète, la perte moyenne annuelle de puissance due à la poussière était de 5,86%, avec 4 % à 5% pendant l'hivernage et 6 % à 7% en été [11]. Une étude a été réalisée sur des systèmes photovoltaïques installés en Egypte en comparant l'énergie produite par un module propre et un module qui a été exposé à la poussière pendant une période d'une année et un module qui a été exposé à la poussière mais nettoyé tous les deux mois. Les résultats ont montré que le module resté une année sans être nettoyé produit une énergie inférieure de 35% à celle du module propre. Le module nettoyé tous les deux mois produit une énergie inférieure à 25% par rapport au module propre **[12]**.

Pour un utilisateur d'un système photovoltaïque, il serait intéressant de savoir à quelle fréquence le module doit être nettoyé. Dans le cas où le nettoyage fréquent n'est pas possible, il est important de connaître la perte de performance due à la poussière pour en tenir compte. L'étude sur les effets de la poussière sur les modules PV aiderait également dans le choix de la technologie, du type et de l'emplacement des modules. L'étude de la corrélation entre la dégradation et la densité de poussière déposée à la surface des modules PV permettra de répondre à la problématique relative à la fréquence de nettoyage à préconiser.

2. Matériels et méthodes

2.1. Méthodologie

L'étude de la corrélation entre la densité de poussière et la variation des caractéristiques de performance a porté sur deux modules à l'état neuf, du même constructeur mais de technologies différentes.

Les deux modules neufs, après avoir été bien nettoyés sont caractérisés avant d'être exposés sous ensoleillement naturel dans les mêmes conditions (ensoleillement, température, humidité). Les mesures sont réalisées par pas d'une semaine pendant six semaines d'exposition. Pendant toute la semaine, les paramètres moyens d'environnement tels que la vitesse du vent, l'ensoleillement, la température ambiante et l'humidité sont mesurés.

A la fin de chaque semaine, les caractéristiques de performance des modules sont mesurées dans les conditions standards de test avec l'analyseur de modules PV (IV-400).

La densité de poussière en dépôt sur chaque module est également déterminée par une méthode que nous présentons dans la section suivante.

Ainsi, la valeur nominale de chaque paramètre est déterminée en prenant comme référence la valeur du paramètre mesurée sur le module propre au début de l'expérience. Cette valeur normalisée qui traduit la variation du paramètre est corrélée avec la densité de poussière déposée sur chaque module. Le résumé des différentes étapes de la méthodologie adoptée est présenté par Fig.1.

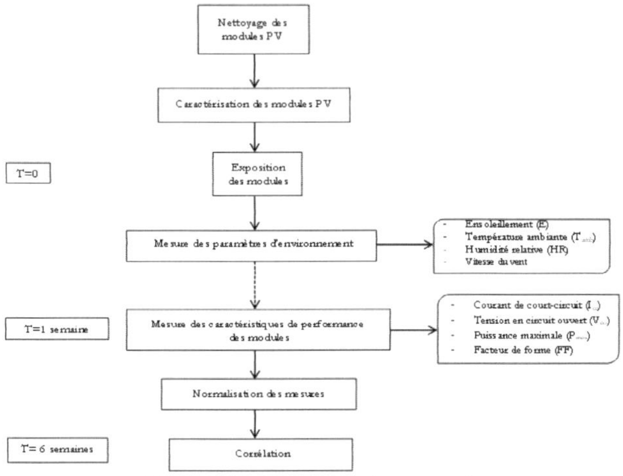

Fig. 1. La méthodologie proposée.

2.2. Détermination de la densité de poussière

Pour mesurer la densité de poussière en dépôt sur les modules, deux options sont possibles. La première consiste à mesurer le poids du module nettoyé au début de l'expérience et celui du module avec les dépôts de poussière à la fin de l'expérience. La différence entre ces deux mesures correspond au poids total de la poussière qui s'est déposée à la surface du module. Le rapport entre le poids de la poussière ainsi obtenu et la surface du module donne la densité des dépôts de poussière **[13]**. Cependant cette technique nécessite une exposition de longue durée qui permettrait de collecter une quantité de poussière significative mesurable relativement au poids du module.

Nous avons opté pour la deuxième méthode qui consiste à utiliser deux lamelles de verre de 67 grammes exposées côte à côte de chaque module et avec la même inclinaison que celui-ci. Les lamelles sont identiques avec une surface de 10 cm^2 soit 10cm x 10cm. A la fin de chaque semaine, les lamelles sont pesées avec une balance de haute précision. Le poids de la poussière déposée sur le module est obtenu à partir du poids total de la lamelle avec le dépôt de poussière et du poids de la lamelle propre. Ainsi, on peut déterminer la densité de poussière déposée par centimètre carré (cm^2).

2.3. Présentation de la plateforme expérimentale

Les spécifications techniques des deux modules utilisées dans le cadre de cette étude sont données dans le Tableau 1.

L'utilisation des modules monocristallins et polycristallins permet également d'étudier la corrélation en fonction de la technologie.

Pour la détermination de la densité de poussière, une balance Kern de haute précision dont les caractéristiques sont données au Tableau 2 été utilisée. Elle dispose d'un couvercle qui permet d'éviter des pertes durant la pesée des lamelles de collecte de la poussière.

Modules	Technologie	Fabriquant	Référence	Paramètres	Valeurs
1	Monocristallin	Tenesol	TE55-36P	P_{max} (W)	55
				V_{max} (V)	17,79
				I_{max} (A)	3,1
				V_{co} (V)	22
				I_{cc} (A)	3,3
				FF (%)	75
2	Polycristallin	Lorentz	LC50-12M	P_{max} (W)	50
				V_{max} (V)	17,1
				I_{max} (A)	2,9
				V_{co} (V)	21,7
				I_{cc} (A)	3,2
				FF (%)	72

Tableau 1. Spécifications techniques des modules.

Fabricant	Référence	Plage	Précision	Résolution	Spécificités
Kern	Kern ABS / ABJ	1 mg – 220 g	1 mg	0,1 mg	Tarage automatique

Tableau 2. Caractéristiques de la balance utilisée pour la pesée des dépôts de poussière.

Fig.2 présente la plateforme expérimentale comportant les deux modules et les lamelles de collecte exposés.

Fig.2. Plateforme expérimentale.

Chaque module est associé à deux lamelles de verre pour la collecte de la poussière. Une cellule de référence est installée sur la plateforme pour la mesure de l'ensoleillement global incident à la surface des modules. L'analyseur de modules PV « IV-400 » est utilisé pour mesurer les caractéristiques de performance des modules.

2.4. Paramètres caractéristiques de la période de mesure

L'expérience dédiée à l'étude de la corrélation entre la densité de poussière et la variation des caractéristiques de performance des modules polycristallins et monocristallins a duré six semaines.
Les principaux paramètres d'environnement mesurés pendant cette période sont présentés au tableau 3.

Pour une telle étude, il est nécessaire de déterminer les paramètres d'environnement de la période de mesure pour l'interprétation des résultats de la corrélation.

N° Semaine	Vitesse du vent ($m.s^{-1}$)			Température ambiante (°C)			Humidité relative (%)			Ensoleillement ($W.m^{-2}$)	
	moy	max	min	moy	max	min	moy	max	min	moy	max
1	1,2	4,7	0,2	25,19	37,7	20	73,8	98,9	24,3	632	710
2	1,58	4,9	0,02	26,89	36,1	22,3	70,3	91,4	27,2	710	721
3	1,98	5,3	0,02	27,3	34	23,5	70,8	90	39,8	702	735
4	2,13	5,2	0,1	28	35	24	73	91	35	812	820
5	1,8	4,8	0,3	27	34	23	68	87	40	708	790
6	1,6	4,9	0,02	23	34	27	72	90	39	835	937

Tableau 3. Paramètres d'environnement sur la période.

3. Resultats et discussions

3.1. Evaluation de la densité de poussière

La quantité de poussière déposée sur chaque lamelle est déterminée à la fin de chaque semaine. La quantité déposée sur chaque module est donnée par la moyenne des dépôts sur les deux lamelles de dix centimètres carrés (10 cm^2) qui lui sont associées.
Nous faisons l'hypothèse que la répartition de la poussière sur la surface du module est homogène.
La Figure suivante (Fig.3) présente l'évolution de la densité de poussière en surface durant la période pour chaque module.

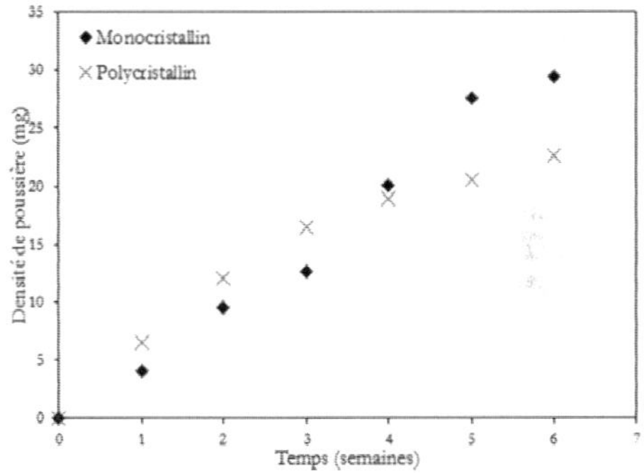

Fig.3. Variation de la densité de poussière pendant six semaines.

L'accumulation de la poussière induit l'augmentation dans le temps de sa densité à la surface des modules. L'évolution de cette densité est fortement dépendante des paramètres environnementaux tels que la vitesse du vent, la température ambiante, l'humidité.
La corrélation entre la densité de poussière et la variation des caractéristiques des modules photovoltaïques est étudiée par la suite.

3.2. Variation des caractéristiques de performance avec la densité de poussière

Pour l'étude de la variation des caractéristiques de performance en fonction de la densité, les valeurs normalisées sont considérées. Pour chaque paramètre, la valeur correspondant au module propre avant le début de l'expérience est prise comme référence dans la normalisation. La valeur normalisée correspond au rapport entre la valeur relative au module avec un dépôt de poussière et la valeur relative au module propre.

Toutes les mesures sont réalisées dans les conditions standards de test à partir de l'analyseur.

La variation normalisée des différentes caractéristiques de performance des modules des deux technologies est présentée sur les figures suivantes (Fig.4, Fig.5, Fig.6, Fig.7).

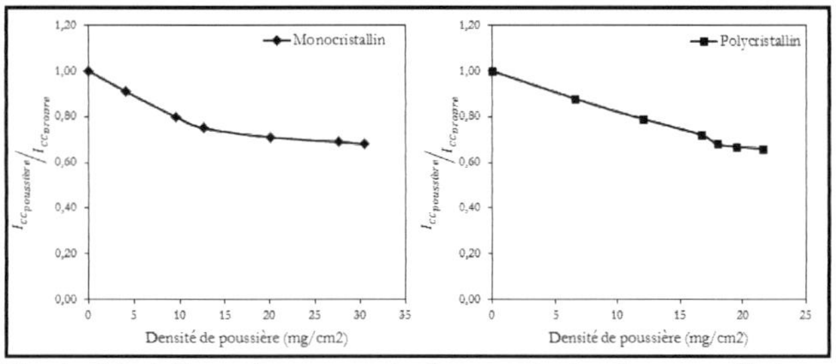

Fig.4. Variation du courant de court-circuit normalisé en fonction de la densité de poussière.

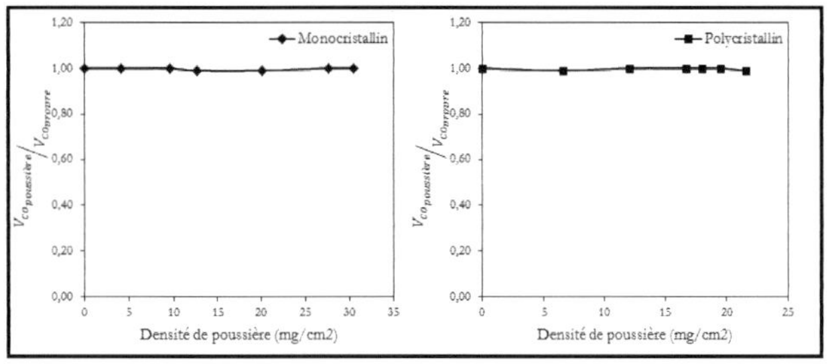

Fig.5. Variation de la tension en circuit ouvert normalisée en fonction de la densité de poussière.

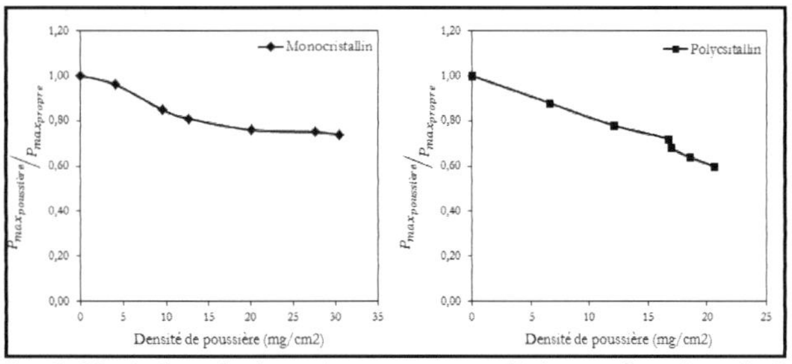

Fig.6. Variation de la puissance normalisée en fonction de la densité de poussière.

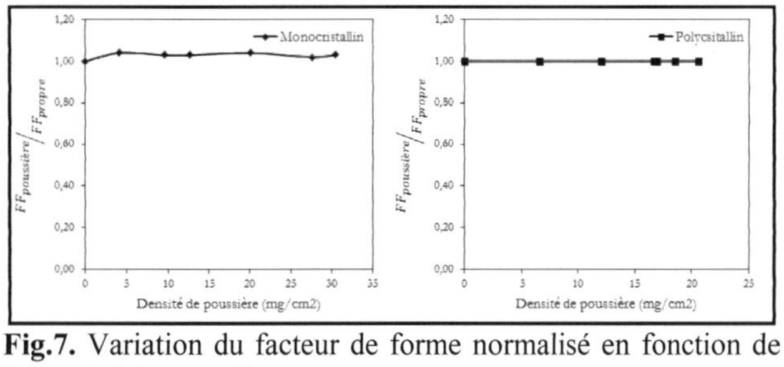

Fig.7. Variation du facteur de forme normalisé en fonction de la densité de poussière.

On remarque que les valeurs normalisées du courant de court-circuit et de la puissance diminuent avec la densité de poussière pour les deux technologies. Cette baisse traduit l'influence de la densité de poussière sur le rendement des modules photovoltaïques. On note que cette baisse évolue assez rapidement, en six semaines d'exposition sans nettoyage des modules :

- Le courant de court-circuit a diminué de 30% pour le monocristallin et 34% pour le polycristallin par rapport au module propre pour une densité de poussière respectivement de 30,5mg/cm^2 et 21,6mg/cm^2.
- La puissance maximale présente une baisse de 26% pour le monocristallin et 40% pour le polycristallin par rapport au module propre pour les mêmes densités de poussière.

La tension en circuit ouvert et le facteur de forme restent constants malgré l'augmentation de la densité de poussière pour les deux technologies.

Ce résultat relatif à la tension en circuit ouvert est en phase avec ceux de **[10, 14]** selon lesquels celle-ci n'est pas dégradée par l'accumulation de la poussière.

Nous allons dans la suite, étudier les relations qui permettent de lier ces variations avec la densité de poussière.

3.3. Relation entre la densité de poussière déposée à la surface des modules et la dégradation de leurs caractéristiques

Nous avons étudié les corrélations les plus appropriées entre la variation des caractéristiques de performance des modules et la densité de poussière. La corrélation a été étudiée pour tous les paramètres par les régressions exponentielle et polynomiale.

Les Figures 8, 9, 10 et 11 présentent les différentes corrélations correspondant à chaque caractéristique et à chaque technologie.

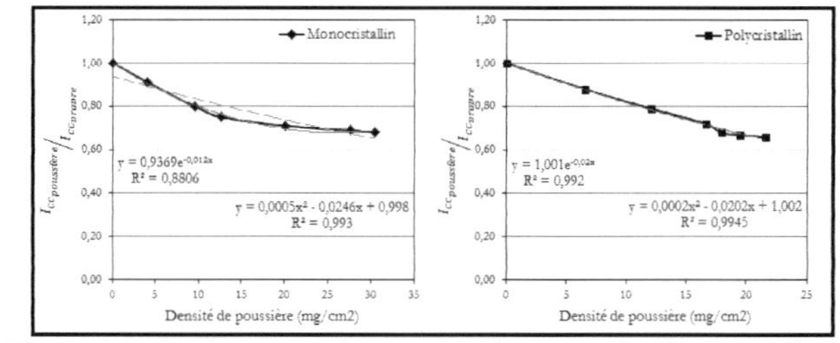

Fig.8. Corrélation entre le courant de court-circuit normalisé et la densité de poussière.

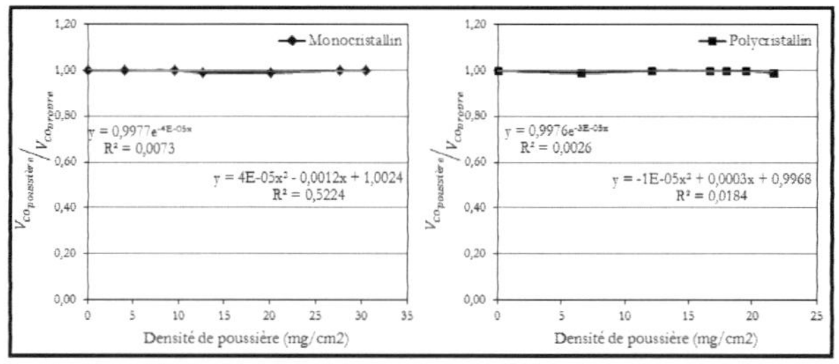

Fig.9. Corrélation entre la tension en circuit ouvert normalisée et la densité de poussière.

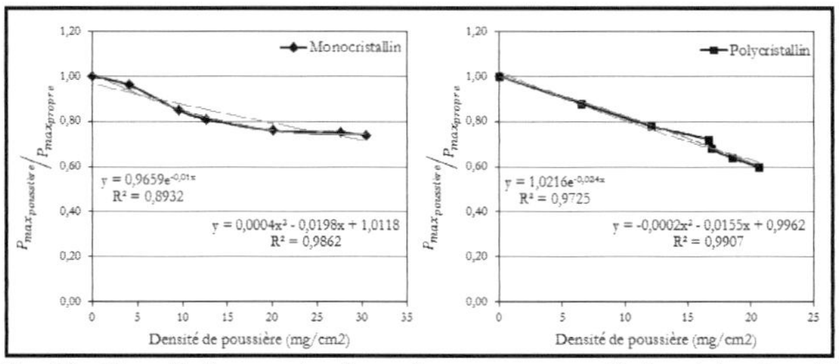

Fig.10. Corrélation entre la puissance normalisée et la densité de poussière.

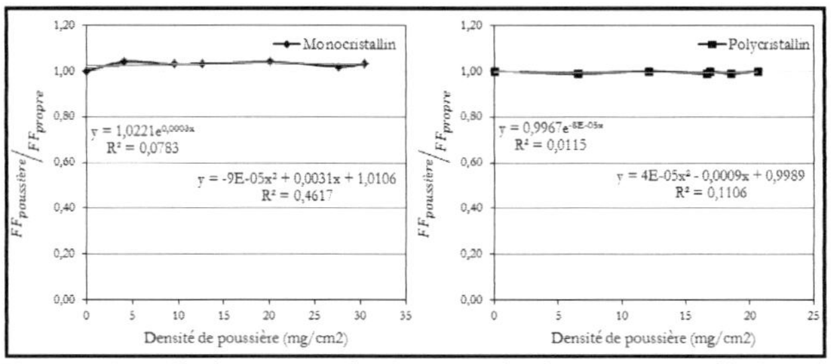

Fig.11. Corrélation entre le facteur de forme normalisé et la densité de poussière par les régressions exponentielle et polynomiale.

L'objectif est de déterminer la régression qui traduit le mieux la relation entre le paramètre en question et la densité de poussière.

Les courbes présentées dans les Figures (Fig.8 à Fig.11) montrent la droite de régression, son équation et le coefficient de détermination correspondant à chaque caractéristique pour chaque technologie. Le Tableau 4 résume les principaux résultats de cette étude.

Régression	Coefficient de détermination (R^2)							
	Monocristallin				Polycristallin			
	$\frac{I_{cc_{poussière}}}{I_{cc_{propre}}}$	$\frac{V_{co_{poussière}}}{V_{co_{propre}}}$	$\frac{P_{max_{poussière}}}{P_{max_{propre}}}$	$\frac{FF_{poussière}}{FF_{propre}}$	$\frac{I_{cc_{poussière}}}{I_{cc_{propre}}}$	$\frac{V_{co_{poussière}}}{V_{co_{propre}}}$	$\frac{P_{max_{poussière}}}{P_{max_{propre}}}$	$\frac{FF_{poussière}}{FF_{propre}}$
Exponentielle	0,880	0,007	0,893	0,078	0,992	0,002	0,972	0,011
Polynomiale	0,993	0,522	0,986	0,461	0,995	0,018	0,990	0,110

Tableau 4. Coefficients de détermination des régressions exponentielle et polynomiale.

L'étude expérimentale permet de proposer une relation entre la variation des caractéristiques et la densité de poussière.

Le courant de court-circuit et la puissance qui sont les deux caractéristiques dont les variations sont plus sensibles au dépôt de poussière présentent des coefficients de détermination très proches de un pour la régression polynomiale comme le montre le Tableau 4.

La tension en circuit ouvert et le facteur de forme présentent de faibles coefficients de corrélation pour les deux régressions.

Cependant l'étude expérimentale précédente [12] sur l'impact de la poussière qui a porté sur une année d'exposition des modules sans nettoyage avait montré que le facteur de forme pouvait être dégradé jusqu'à un maximum de 18% par rapport au module propre. Ainsi, nous pouvons penser que les six semaines d'exposition sont trop courtes pour pouvoir détecter une variation du facteur de forme.

4. Conclusion

Ce papier a porté sur l'étude expérimentale de la corrélation entre la variation des caractéristiques de performance des modules photovoltaïques et la densité de poussière. Il propose une méthode de détermination de la densité de poussière tenant compte de la distribution homogène de la poussière sur la surface des modules étudiés.

L'étude de la corrélation a montré que la variation du courant de court-circuit et de la puissance maximale en fonction de la densité de poussière suit une loi de régression polynomiale avec un très bon coefficient de détermination (0,99%) pour les deux technologies.

L'étude réalisée dans ce papier constitue une contribution dans un objectif de définition de la périodicité de nettoyage des modules photovoltaïques dans la zone d'étude.

References

1. EPIA: European Photovoltaic Industry Association, *Global Market Outlook for Photovoltaics until 2015*, 2011.

2. M.C. Hottel, B.B. Woertz, Performance of flat plate solar heat collectors, *ASME Trans.*, vol. **64**, pp. 91-104, 1942.

3. A. Salim, F. Huraib, N. Eugenio, PV power-study of system options and optimization, *In Proceedings of the 8th European PV Solar Energy Conference*, Florence, Italy, 1988.

4. F. Wakim, Introduction of PV power generation to Kuwait, Kuwait *Institute for Scientific Researchers*, Kuwait City, 1981.

5. J.K. Kaldellis, M. Kapsali, Simulating the dust effect on the energy performance of photovoltaic generators based on experimental measurements, *Energy* **36** (2011), 5154-5161, 2011.

6. G.B. Katz, Effect of Dust on Solar Panels, *www.gregorybkatz.com/Home/effect-of-dust-on-solar-panels*, 2011.

7. A.S. Shaharin, H.H. Haizatul, H.N.L. Nik Siti, S.I.R. Mohd, Effects of Dust on the Performance of PV Panels, *World Academy of Science, Engineering and Technology* **58**, 2011.

8. E. Kymakis, S. Kalykakis, T.M. Papazoglou, Performance Analysis of a Grid Connected Photovoltaic Park on the Island of Crete, *Energy Conversion and Management*, Vol. **50**, No. 3, pp. 433–438, 2009.

9. A. Detrick, A. Kimber, L. Mitchell, Performance Evaluation Standards for Photovoltaic Modules and Systems, *Proceedings of the 31st IEEE Photovoltaics Specialists Conference*, pp. 1581-1586, ISBN 0-7803-8707-4, Lake Buena Vista, USA, January 2005.

10. A. Ndiaye, C.M.F. Kébé, P. A. Ndiaye, A. Charki, A. Kobi, V. Sambou, Impact of dust on the PV modules characteristics after an exposition year in Sahelian environment: the case of Senegal, *International Journal of Physical Sciences – academicjournals*, Vol. **8(21)**, pp. 1166-1173, 2013.

11. E. Kymakis, S. Kalykakis, T.M. Papazoglou, Performance Analysis of a Grid Connected Photovoltaic Park on the Island of Crete, *Energy Conversion and Management*, Vol. **50**, No. 3, pp. 433–438, 2009.

12. M. Ibrahim, B. Zinsser, H .El-Sherif, E. Hamouda, G. Makrides, G.E. Georghiou, M. Schubert, J.H. Werner, Advanced Photovoltaic Test Park in Egypt for Investigating the Performance of Different Module and Cell Technologies, *Proceedings of the 24th Symposium Photovoltaic Solar Energy*, Staffelstien, Germany, March 2009.

13. M.S. El-Shobokshy, F.M. Hussein, Effect of dust with different physical properties on the performance of photovoltaic cells, *Solar energy*, Vol. **51**, n°6, pp. 505-511, 1993.

14. A. Ndiaye, C.M.F. Kébé, A. Charki, P.A. Ndiaye, V. Sambou, A. Kobi, Degradation evaluation of crystalline-silicon photovoltaic modules after a few operation years in a tropical environment, *Solar Energy - Elsevier ScienceDirect*, Vol. **103** (2014), pp. 70-77, 2014.

Evaluation de covariances à l'aide de bilans d'incertitudes

Title : Covariance Evaluation with Assessments of Uncertainties

Christophe Dubois[1], Laurent Leblond[2] et Jean-Michel Pou[1]

Résumé : Il est d'usage d'analyser un processus de mesure en établissant un bilan d'incertitude, c'est à dire en listant toutes les causes d'incertitude ou du moins le plus grand nombre. L'incertitude est alors déduite en sommant en variance ces incertitude-types suivant les recommandations du GUM (JCGM 100 2008). Dans cette étape, la prise en compte des covariances entre les causes d'incertitude est souvent négligée car difficile à évaluer. L'objet de cet article est de montrer comment les bilans d'incertitudes des différents processus de mesures peuvent raisonnablement permettre d'obtenir un ordre de grandeur des covariances lorsque leurs estimations expérimentales ne sont pas envisageables. Il propose une simplification de l'expression de la covariance en s'appuyant sur un modèle de décomposition des erreurs en fonction de leurs opportunités de variations dans le processus de mesure (variation L.O. - low Opportunity - et H.O. - High Opportunity -)

Abstract : It is the practice to analyze a measurement process by establishing an Assessment of Uncertainty, that is to say by listing all sources of uncertainty or at least the greater number. The uncertainty is then deducted by summing variance uncertainties kind following the recommendations of the GUM (JCGM 100 2008). In this step, the inclusion of covariance between the causes of uncertainty is often overlooked as difficult to assess. The purpose of this article is to show how the Assessments of Uncertainties of different measurement process can reasonably be expected to obtain an order of magnitude of covariance when their experimental estimates are not feasible. It offers a simplification of the expression of the covariance based on a decomposition model of the errors according to their opportunities variations in the measurement process (variation L.O. - low Opportunity - and H.O. - High Opportunity -).

Mots-clés : Covariance, Bilan d'incertitude, Principe de L.O. dcomposition.
Keywords : Covariance, Assessments of Uncertainties, Principle of L.O. decomposition.

1 Problématique et notations

Un mesurande est associé à une variable aléatoire relle X de carré intégrable sur un espace de probabilité. Chaque réalisation de cette variable est une valeur auquel un processus de mesure donne accès. Ce processus de mesure de X est caractérisé par une moyenne $\mu_X = \mathbb{E}(X)$ et une incertitude-type $\sigma_X = \sqrt{\mathbb{V}(X)}$ éventuellement dépendante de μ_X. Le lecteur trouvera en annexe les rappels sur les propriétés calculatoires des opérateurs espérance $\mathbb{E}$ et variance $\mathbb{V}$ sur un ensemble de variables aléatoires.

Une grandeur d'intérêt Y est en générale dépendante de k **grandeurs** $\underline{X} = (X_1, ..., X_k)$ mesurées par des processus distincts ou non, ces processus étant soumis à un ensemble de **facteurs influents**. On suppose que le **modèle de mesure** f est connue avec une éventuelle erreur de modélisation ϵ ($\mu_\epsilon = 0$) indépendante de X_i pour tout i de 1 à k :

$$Y = f(\underline{X}) + \epsilon \qquad (1)$$

[1]Delta Mu, Centre d'affaires du Zénith, Le trident E – 48 rue Sarliève, 63800 Cournon d'Auvergne. E-mail : cdubois@deltamu.fr ; jmpou@deltamu.fr
[2]PSA Peugeot Citroën, C.T. de Vélizy A, 2, route de Gisy, 78943 Vélizy-Villacoublay Cedex. E-mail : laurent.leblond1@mpsa.com

L'expression des quantités μ_Y et σ_Y en fonction des μ_{X_i} et σ_{X_i} peut s'avérer analytiquement difficile dès que le modèle de mesure n'est pas linéaire. Une solution traditionnelle (JCGM 100, 2008) est d'effectuer un développement limité à l'ordre 1 de f au voisinage de $\mu_{\underline{X}} = (\mu_{X_1}, ..., \mu_{X_k})$:

$$f(\underline{X}) \approx f(\mu_{\underline{X}}) + \frac{\partial f}{dX_1}(\mu_{\underline{X}})(X - \mu_{X_1}) + ... + \frac{\partial f}{dX_n}(\mu_{\underline{X}})(X - \mu_{X_k}) \tag{2}$$

Avec cette approximation, par un calcul d'espérance et de variance :

$$\mu_Y \approx f(\mu_{\underline{X}}) \tag{3}$$

$$\sigma_Y^2 \approx \sum_{i=1}^{k} \left(\frac{\partial f}{dX_i}(\mu_{\underline{X}}) \sigma_{X_i} \right)^2 + \sum_{\substack{i,j=1 \\ i \neq j}}^{k} \frac{\partial f}{dX_i}(\mu_{\underline{X}}) . \frac{\partial f}{dX_j}(\mu_{\underline{X}}) . \sigma_{X_i, X_j} + \sigma_\epsilon^2 \tag{4}$$

Pour évaluer cette dernière expression il faut notamment estimer $\sigma_{X_i,X_j} = \mathbb{C}ov(X_i, X_j)$. Une covariance exprime les variations simultanées des erreurs de mesures de deux grandeurs. Elle est positive lorsque les écarts entre les variables et leurs moyennes ont tendance à être de mêmes signes, négative dans le cas contraire.

La raison de cette co-variation est à chercher dans les causes d'erreurs de mesures communes à X_i et X_j. Ce sont les facteurs influents sur les processus de mesures de ces grandeurs, dont on dira qu'ils ont une faible opportunité de varier au moment des mesures de X_i et X_j, qui sont à l'origine de cette co-variation. De telles influences sont dites L.O. pour **Low Opportunity** en opposition aux influences H.O. pour **High Opportunity** qui, elles, induisent une variabilité à chaque nouvelle mesure des grandeurs (Dubois, 2013).

Pour s'en convaincre, considérons la surface d'une plaque rectangulaire déterminée à l'aide du même processus de mesure de la longueur L et de la largeur l de cette plaque. Nous supposons que seule la température ambiante T, via un coefficient de dilatation λ constant, est un facteur influent L.O. sur le processus de mesure d'une distance D entre deux points éloignés réellement de D_0 lorsque la température est de 20°C :

$$D = D_0(1 + \lambda(T - 20)) + E_D^{HO} \tag{5}$$

Par hypothèse, l'erreur E_D^{HO} de moyenne nulle, indépendante de T et additive, exprime l'influence H.O. des autres facteurs agissants sur le processus de mesure de D. L'erreur systématique (constante réelle) est notée $e_D^{sys} = \lambda D_0 (\mu_T - 20)$ et l'erreur L.O. de moyenne nulle est notée $E_D^{LO}(T) = \lambda D_0 (T - \mu_T)$.

Par définition, en posant $\lambda_T = 1 + \lambda(\mu_T - 20)$, on a $\mu_D = D_0 + e_D^{sys} = D_0 \lambda_T$ et l'erreur de mesure de D additionne les erreurs systématiques, H.O. et L.O. indépendamment :

$$E_D^m(T) = e_D^{sys} + E_D^{LO}(T) + E_D^{HO} \tag{6}$$

Lorsque ce processus de mesure est appliqué successivement à L et l, il est raisonnable de supposer que T est invariante et que E_L^{HO} et E_l^{HO} sont indépendantes :

$$L = L_0 + e_L^{sys} + E_L^{LO}(T) + E_L^{HO} \tag{7}$$

$$l = l_0 + e_l^{sys} + E_l^{LO}(T) + E_l^{HO} \tag{8}$$

Comme la même température alatoire intervient dans les expressions ci-dessus, la covariance entre les erreurs de mesures $E_L^m(T)$ et $E_l^m(T)$ est non nulle. En effet, par hypothèses d'indépendances et bilinéarité de la covariance (Saporta, 2006), on a :

$$\sigma_{L,l} = \mathbb{C}ov\left(E_L^m(T), E_l^m(T)\right) = \mathbb{C}ov\left(E_L^{LO}(T), E_l^{LO}(T)\right) = L_0 l_0 \lambda^2 \sigma_T^2 \tag{9}$$

Aussi, $\sigma_{L,l} = \sqrt{\mathbb{V}(E_L^{LO}(T))\mathbb{V}(E_l^{LO}(T))}$ et la détermination d'une covariance se ramène ici à la détermination de variances.

Bien que la norme NF ISO/CEI Guide 98-3 (2014) propose de négliger les covariances en tenant compte de considérations physiques sur la mesure effectuée (en supposant par exemple que la température n'est pas un facteur aléatoire dans l'exemple précédent), il n'est pas toujours possible de s'en affranchir. L'objet de cet article est de présenter une généralisation du constat précédent et de montrer comment les bilans d'incertitudes des différents processus de mesures des grandeurs X_i peuvent raisonnablement permettre d'obtenir une évaluation des covariances lorsque leurs estimations expérimentales ne sont pas envisageables.

Si des mesures de longueur et de largeur $(L_j^{mes}, l_j^{mes})_{j=1\ldots n}$ sont reproduites à des températures distinctes n fois ($n > 1$), ces valeurs peuvent être considérées comme des réalisations de variables indépendantes identiquement distribuées et dans ces conditions on a les estimations suivantes avec $D = L$ ou l :

$$\hat{\mu}_D = \bar{D}^{mes} = \frac{1}{n}\sum_{j=1}^{n} D_j^{mes} \quad et \quad \hat{\sigma}_D = \sqrt{\frac{1}{n-1}\sum_{j=1}^{n}\left(D_j^{mes} - \bar{D}^{mes}\right)^2} \tag{10}$$

$$\hat{\sigma}_{L,l} = \frac{1}{n-1}\sum_{j=1}^{n}(L_j^{mes} - \bar{L}^{mes})(l_j^{mes} - \bar{l}^{mes}) \tag{11}$$

Cependant, en pratique, cette situation est rarement envisageable et il faut prendre soin de ne pas la confondre avec des mesures répétées où la température est invariante par hypothèse. Les estimations précédentes ne sont plus valables parce que deux mesures successives de longueur (respectivement de largeur) sont liées par les modèles (7) (respectivement (8)) et sont donc corrélés. Par exemple, la formule (11) estime alors $\mathbb{C}ov\left(E_L^{HO}(T), E_l^{HO}(T)\right)$ qui est nulle par hypothèse. On est donc dans la même impossibilité d'estimation expérimentale de la covariance entre L et l que lorsqu'on ne dispose que d'une seule valeur mesurée de longueur et de largeur.

Conventionnellement, un résultat de mesure de distance est défini comme un intervalle ayant 95% de chance de contenir la vraie valeur D_0. Dans la situation fréquente d'une seule mesure (T^{mes}, D^{mes}) et sous hypothèse de normalité de la loi de D, cet intervalle nécessite une estimation a priori $\hat{\sigma}_D$ de l'incertitude-type σ_D et s'exprime sous la forme :

$$\left[\frac{D^{mes} - 2\hat{\sigma}_D}{1 + \lambda\left(T^{mes} - 20\right)}; \frac{D^{mes} + 2\hat{\sigma}_D}{1 + \lambda\left(T^{mes} - 20\right)}\right] \tag{12}$$

C'est dans l'expression d'un résultat de mesure de surface que l'incertitude-type a priori σ_T devient en plus nécessaire pour tenir compte de la covariance. La surface $S = l \times L \approx \mu_L \mu_l + \mu_L(l - \mu_l) + \mu_l(L - \mu_L)$ approximée selon (2) est alors telle que :

$$\mu_S \approx \mu_L \mu_l = (L_0 + e_L^{sys})(l_0 + e_l^{sys}) = L_0 l_0 \lambda_T^2 \tag{13}$$

$$\sigma_S^2 \approx \mu_l^2 \sigma_L^2 + \mu_L^2 \sigma_l^2 + 2\mu_L \mu_l \sigma_{L,l} = L_0^2 l_0^2 \lambda_T^2 \left(\frac{\sigma_L^2}{L_0^2} + \frac{\sigma_l^2}{l_0^2} + 2\lambda^2 \sigma_T^2\right) \tag{14}$$

Il est intéressant de comparer l'approximation de μ_S avec son calcul exact à partir de l'espérance de S conditionnellement à T ($\mathbb{E}(S/T) = L_0 l_0 (1+\lambda(T-20))^2$) :

$$\mu_S = \mathbb{E}(S) = \mathbb{E}(\mathbb{E}(S/T)) = L_0 l_0 \lambda_T^2 + L_0 l_0 \lambda^2 \sigma_T^2 \tag{15}$$

Le terme de covariance entre L et l intervient dans cette expression. Il est souvent négligeable dans la plupart des cas pratiques puisque λ est faible. Une expression exacte de σ_S^2 qui dépend du moment d'ordre 4 de T peut également être obtenue (cf. annexe). Le résultat de mesure de surface sous approximation normale et lorsqu'une seule mesure ($T^{mes}, L^{mes}, l^{mes}$) est réalisée, se présente alors sous la forme :

$$\left[\frac{L^{mes}l^{mes} - 2\hat{\sigma}_S}{(1+\lambda(T^{mes}-20))^2}; \frac{L^{mes}l^{mes} + 2\hat{\sigma}_S}{(1+\lambda(T^{mes}-20))^2}\right] \tag{16}$$

avec $\hat{\sigma}_S^2 = (l^{mes}\hat{\sigma}_L)^2 + (L^{mes}\hat{\sigma}_l)^2 + 2L^{mes}l^{mes}\hat{\sigma}_{L,l}$.

2 Expression d'une covariance

Chaque grandeur mesurée X_i est la somme d'une valeur réelle $x_{i,0}$ et d'une erreur de mesure $E_{X_i}^m$ qui se décompose en une somme d'erreurs dues aux m facteurs influents pris en compte pour analyser les processus de mesures. En supposant que $E_{i,l} = 0$ si le facteur influent l n'intervient pas dans le processus de mesure de X_i, on a :

$$X_i = x_{i,0} + E_{X_i}^m = x_{i,0} + \sum_{l=1}^{m} E_{i,l} \tag{17}$$

Par hypothèse, les erreurs $(E_{i,l})_{l=1...m}$ sont indépendantes mais pas les $(E_{X_i}^m)_{i=1...k}$.

Les éléments constitutifs ordinaires d'un **bilan d'incertitudes** du processus de mesure de X_i sont les erreurs systématiques $(e_{i,l}^{sys} = \mathbb{E}(E_{i,l}))_{l=1...m}$ et les incertitude-types $(\sigma_{i,l} = \sqrt{\mathbb{V}(E_{i,l})})_{l=1...m}$.

L'erreur de mesure systématique $e_{X_i}^{sys} = \mathbb{E}(E_{X_i}^m)$ et l'incertitude-type $\sigma_{X_i} = \sqrt{\mathbb{V}(E_{X_i}^m)}$ de la grandeur X_i s'expriment alors ainsi :

$$e_{X_i}^{sys} = \sum_{l=1}^{m} e_{i,l}^{sys} \quad et \quad \sigma_{X_i}^2 = \sum_{l=1}^{m} \sigma_{i,l}^2 \tag{18}$$

Aussi, en notant $w_{i,l} = \frac{\sigma_{i,l}^2}{\sigma_{X_i}^2}$ le **poids** du facteur influent l sur X_i : $\sum_{l=1}^{m} w_{i,l} = 1$.

Principe de L.O.-décomposition

*Les erreurs $(E_{i,l})_{i=1...k,l=1...m}$ sont dites **L.O.-décomposables** s'il existe des effets aléatoires $(\Delta_l^{LO})_{l=1...m}$ indépendants et des réels $(\lambda_{i,l})_{i=1...k,l=1...m}$ dits **coefficients d'influences L.O.** tels que $\left(E_{i,l}^{HO} = E_{i,l} - e_{i,l}^{sys} - \lambda_{i,l}\Delta_l^{LO}\right)_{i=1...k}$ sont deux à deux indépendantes et indépendantes de Δ_l^{LO} pour tout l de 1 à m.*

Le principe de L.O.-décomposition est au cœur de la simplification de l'expression d'une covariance. Il signifie que pour tout facteur influent l sur X_i, l'erreur $E_{i,l}$ se décompose en une erreur systématique $e_{i,l}^{sys}$, une **erreur L.O.** $E_{i,l}^{LO} = \lambda_{i,l}\Delta_l^{LO}$ de moyenne nulle et une **erreur H.O.** $E_{i,l}^{HO}$ de moyenne nulle, ces erreurs vérifiant les hypothèses d'indépendances usuelles.

Lorsque le facteur influent l n'intervient pas dans le processus de mesure de X_i, $\lambda_{i,l} = 0$ par convention, et :

$$E_{i,l} = e_{i,l}^{sys} + \lambda_{i,l}\Delta_l^{LO} + E_{i,l}^{HO} \tag{19}$$

La particularité d'une telle décomposition tient au fait que pour un facteur influent l sur X_i, les deux erreurs L.O. réduites $\frac{E_{i,l}^{LO}}{\sqrt{\mathbb{V}(E_{i,l}^{LO})}}$ et $\frac{E_{j,l}^{LO}}{\sqrt{\mathbb{V}(E_{j,l}^{LO})}}$ pour $i \neq j$ sont supposées totalement corrélées (leur covariance est égale à ± 1). L'exemple d'une mesure de longueur et de largeur étudié au chapitre précédent illustre ce principe.

Le modèle représentant le processus de mesure de X_i s'écrit alors, avec $E_{X_i}^{HO} = \sum_{l=1}^{m} E_{i,l}^{HO}$ et des erreurs indépendantes :

$$X_i = \; x_{i,0} + e_{X_i}^{sys} + \sum_{l=1}^{m} \lambda_{i,l}\Delta_l^{LO} + E_{X_i}^{HO} \tag{20}$$

La **part de variance L.O.** du facteur influent l sur X_i, nulle par convention si $\lambda_{i,l} = 0$, est définie par :

$$\gamma_{i,l} = \frac{\mathbb{V}(E_{i,l}^{LO})}{\mathbb{V}(E_{i,l})} = \frac{\lambda_{i,l}^2 \mathbb{V}(\Delta_l^{LO})}{\sigma_{i,l}^2} \in [0,1] \tag{21}$$

C'est l'évaluation de cette part qui complètera les bilans d'incertitudes pour chaque facteur influent. Le calcul suivant, où sont utilisées les indépendances et la bilinéarité d'une covariance, montre que la covariance entre X_i et X_j est le produit des incertitude-types de chacune des variables pondérée par un coefficient dépendant notamment des parts de variances L.O. et des poids :

$$\sigma_{X_i,X_j} = \mathbb{C}ov\left(E_{X_i}^m, E_{X_j}^m\right) = \sum_{u=1}^{m} \lambda_{i,u} \sum_{v=1}^{m} \lambda_{j,v} \mathbb{C}ov\left(\Delta_u^{LO}, \Delta_v^{LO}\right) = \sum_{l=1}^{m} \lambda_{i,l}\lambda_{j,l}\mathbb{V}(\Delta_l^{LO})$$

$$= \sigma_{X_i}\sigma_{X_j} \sum_{l=1}^{m} sgn(\lambda_{i,l}\lambda_{j,l}) \sqrt{\gamma_{i,l}\gamma_{j,l}} \sqrt{w_{i,l} w_{j,l}} \tag{22}$$

Dans cette expression, $sgn\left(\lambda_{i,l}\lambda_{j,l}\right) = 1$ si le facteur influent l agit de la même manière sur X_i et X_j et $sgn\left(\lambda_{i,l}\lambda_{j,l}\right) = -1$ sinon, ce l'on notera $\pm_l^{i,j}$.

Hypothèse d'égalité des parts de variances L.O. :

Les parts relatives d'incertitude L.O. induites par chaque facteur influent sont les mêmes pour toutes les grandeurs sur lesquelles il intervient. Autrement dit, pour tout l de 1 à m, les $\left(\gamma_{i,l}\right)_{i=1...k}$ non nuls sont égaux et notés $\gamma_l > 0$.

Cette hypothèse simplificatrice exprime l'idée qu'une influence L.O. réduit de la même manière la part de variation des facteurs sur lesquels il intervient au moment des mesures. Elle sera souvent supposée en pratique car, même si les processus de mesures sur lesquels le facteur influent agit sont différents, les parts de variances L.O. ne sont que des estimations d'ordres de grandeurs et, sauf cas avérés, il est raisonnable de ne pas multiplier des a priori aux justifications hasardeuses. Dans ces conditions, la formule suivante permet d'évaluer aisément une covariance :

$$\sigma_{X_i,X_j} = \sigma_{X_i}\sigma_{X_j} \sum_{l=1}^{m} \pm_l^{i,j} \; \gamma_l \sqrt{w_{i,l} w_{j,l}} \tag{23}$$

Evidemment, les principes et hypothèses sont toujours critiquables, souvent à juste titre, mais il ne faut pas oublier que l'objectif de bilans d'incertitudes, ne serait-ce que pour l'évaluation des incertitude-types, est d'avoir une appréhension de phénomènes qui peuvent être difficilement quantifiables faute de modélisations précises. Aussi, comme l'illustre les exemples suivants, la formule (23) à l'avantage d'une application aisée pour évaluer une covariance.

3 Deux exemples d'application

Ces exemples simples à caractère pédagogique ont pour objet de présenter la mise en œuvre pratique de l'évaluation de covariances. Le premier concerne la mesure de l'épaisseur d'une pièce et le second la mesure d'un courant électrique.

3.1 Moyenne de deux mesures de l'épaisseur d'une pièce

La grandeur d'intérêt est ici la moyenne en deux points de mesures différents d'un mesurande correspondant à l'épaisseur d'une pièce de $\mu_X = 10\ mm$. La mesure est effectuée sur un marbre avec un comparateur (cf. Figure 1). Une cale étalon de L = 10 mm est utilisée comme référence pour le comparateur.

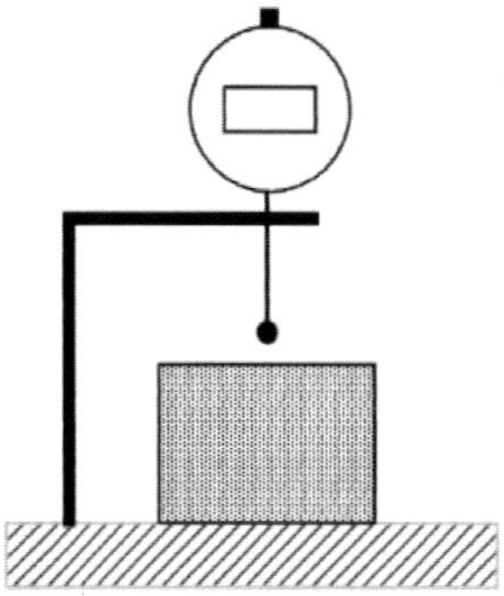

Figure 1: Mesure d'une épaisseur avec un comparateur

En notant X_a (respectivement X_b) l'épaisseur de la pièce au point a (respectivement b), la grandeur d'intérêt $\bar{X}$ est donc :

$$\bar{X} = \frac{X_a + X_b}{2} \tag{24}$$

Les sources d'incertitudes suivantes, supposées indépendantes, sont retenues ici pour une mesure d'épaisseur :

1. *Répétabilité* : répétabilité du processus de mesure obtenue expérimentalement.
2. *Résolution* : résolution du comparateur de $0,001\ mm$ déjà contenu dans la répétabilité.
3. *Étalon* : incertitude d'étalonnage de la cale étalon utilisée comme référence.
4. *Opérateur* : incertitude liée à la méconnaissance de l'opérateur effectuant une mesure et obtenue expérimentalement.
5. *Pièce* : la pièce n'est pas parfaitement plane et une estimation de sa planéité est donnée par un rayon de tolérance de 1 μm.

À partir de ces informations, on construit le tableau suivant où la partie de gauche correspond au bilan des incertitudes de mesure classique (JCGM 100, 2008) et où la partie de droite est un complément qui est présenté ci-après. Pour rester dans les notations conventionnelle, l'incertitude-type de chaque facteur influent l est notée u_l au lieu de σ_l.

Bilan d'incertitudes classique						**Complément**	
N°	*Source (l)*	*Type*	*Demi-étendue (μm)*	*Div.*	u_l (μm)	*Poids (w_l)*	*Part L.O. (γ_l)*
1	Répétabilité	A	-	-	**0,70**	24%	0%
3	Etalon	B	$0,14 + 2.10^{-6}$L	2	**0,08**	0%	Négligeable
4	Opérateur	A	-	-	**1,10**	59%	100%
5	Pièce	B	1	$\sqrt{3}$	**0,58**	17%	0%

On en déduit l'incertitude-type composée (somme quadratique des u_l) sur une mesure d'épaisseur X :

$$u_X = \sqrt{\sum_l u_l^2} \simeq 1,429\ \mu m \tag{25}$$

L'incertitude-type de la moyenne des deux mesures d'épaisseur peut ici se calculer de manière exacte (cf. annexe) en tenant compte de la covariance σ_{X_a,X_b} entre X_a et X_b, variables qui ne sont pas indépendantes, notamment par le fait que le même opérateur effectue les deux mesures :

$$u_{\bar{X}} = \sqrt{\frac{u_{X_a}^2 + u_{X_b}^2 + 2\sigma_{X_a X_b}}{4}} \tag{26}$$

Lorsque la covariance n'est pas prise en compte, tout se passe comme si les mesures étaient supposées indépendantes et on obtiendrait :

$$u_{\bar{X}}^{sans\ covariance} = \frac{u_X}{\sqrt{2}} \simeq 1,011\ \mu m \tag{27}$$

La méthode présentée au chapitre 2 permet d'estimer σ_{X_a,X_b} en complétant le bilan d'incertitudes classique dans lequel on retrouve les informations pour appliquer (23).

- La première colonne contient le poids $w_l = \frac{u_l^2}{\sum_{k=1}^{m} u_k^2}$ de chaque source d'incertitude l dans l'incertitude totale.
- La seconde colonne contient γ_l, la part L.O. du facteur influent l (cf. (21)).

La détermination de la part L.O. s'effectue par des a priori métier sur le processus de mesure. Ainsi, dans cet exemple, les erreurs de mesures de l'épaisseur dues à la Répétabilité et à la Pièce sont indépendantes entre les deux mesures, la part L.O. de chacune de ces influences est donc nulle. Par contre, le même opérateur effectuant les deux mesures, l'effet Opérateur ne s'exprime pas entre les deux résultats, sa part L.O. est donc $\gamma_{Op.} = 1$ (100%). Enfin, le poids de l'Étalon étant jugé négligeable, la part L.O. de cette influence n'est pas prise en compte, ce qui simplifie la présentation du calcul.

Comme, par hypothèse, l'opérateur (seule influence L.O.) agit de manière similaire entre les deux mesures, $\pm^{a,b}_{Op.} = 1$ et l'application de (23) donne alors :

$$\sigma_{X_a,X_b} = u_{X_a} u_{X_b}\, \gamma_{Op.} \sqrt{w_{Op.} w_{Op.}} = 1,21\ \mu m^2 \tag{28}$$

L'incertitude-type sur la moyenne $\bar{X}$ s'en déduit par (26) :

$$u_{\bar{X}} = \frac{u_X}{\sqrt{2}} + \sqrt{\frac{\sigma_{X_a,X_b}}{2}} \simeq 1,788\ \mu m \tag{29}$$

Ce résultat montre à quel point l'incertitude peut être sous-estimée lorsqu'on ignore une covariance. En désignant par $E_{a,op}$ (respectivement $E_{b,op}$) l'erreur de mesure due à l'opérateur sur le point a (respectivement b), le coefficient de corrélation entre ces deux erreurs est égale à 1 par hypothèse :

$$r_{E_{a,Op.},E_{b,Op.}} = \frac{\sigma_{E_{a,Op.},E_{b,Op.}}}{u_{E_{a,Op.}} u_{E_{b,Op.}}} = 1 \tag{30}$$

Comme $u_{E_{a,Op}} = \sqrt{w_{op}}.u_{X_a}$, $u_{E_{b,Op}} = \sqrt{w_{op}}.u_{X_b}$ et $\sigma_{X_a,X_b} = \sigma_{E_{a,Op.},E_{b,Op.}}$, on retrouve le résultat (29) en utilisant la corrélation totale (30). C'est de cette façon que le G.U.M. (JCGM 100, 2008 - §5.2.2) présente le calcul dans ce cas particulier. L'exemple suivant présente un cas où la corrélation n'est pas totale, cas pour lequel le G.U.M. ne propose qu'une estimation expérimentale pour évaluer la covariance, ce qui n'est malheureusement pas toujours possible.

3.2 Mesure d'un courant électrique

La grandeur d'intérêt est ici l'intensité d'un courant électrique. La mesure est effectuée à l'aide d'un shunt et d'un voltmètre numérique (cf. Figure 2). L'intensité du courant est voisine de $\mu_I = 10\ A$, le shunt a une valeur nominale de $\mu_R = 0,01\ \Omega$. La mesure est effectuée à $\mu_T = 20°C\ (\pm 3°C)$.

En notant V la tension mesurée et R la résistance du shunt, l'intensité I du courant est obtenue par la relation :

$$I = \frac{V}{R} \tag{31}$$

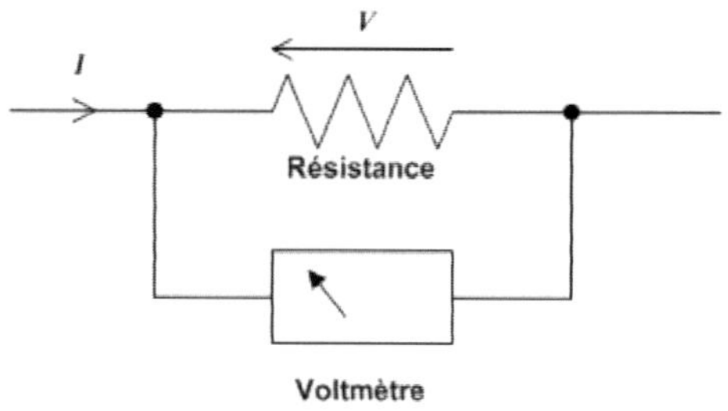

Figure 2: Mesure d'un courant électrique avec un shunt et un voltmètre numérique

L'application de la loi de propagation selon les recommandations du GUM donne alors l'incertitude-type de l'intensité du courant (où $\mu_V = \mu_R \mu_I = 0,1\ V$ et $\underline{\mu} = (\mu_V, \mu_R)$) :

$$u_I^2 \approx \left(\frac{\partial I}{dV}(\underline{\mu}).u_V\right)^2 + \left(\frac{\partial I}{dR}(\underline{\mu}).u_R\right)^2 + 2.\frac{\partial I}{dV}(\underline{\mu}).\frac{\partial I}{dR}(\underline{\mu}).\sigma_{V,R} \tag{32}$$

$$avec\ \frac{\partial I}{dV}(\underline{\mu}) = \frac{1}{\mu_R} = 100\ \Omega^{-1}\ et\ \frac{\partial I}{dR}(\underline{\mu}) = -\frac{\mu_V}{\mu_R^2} = -1000\ A.\Omega^{-1}$$

Cet exemple présente le cas où les mesures de la tension et de la résistance sont corrélées par une même influence : la température.

Les sources d'incertitudes, supposées indépendantes et retenues pour la mesure de tension sont les suivantes :

1. *Répétabilité* : répétabilité du processus de mesure obtenue expérimentalement.
2. *Résolution* : résolution du voltmètre de $0,01\ mV$ déjà contenu dans la répétabilité.
3. *Constructeur V* : caractéristiques techniques constructeur du voltmètre $(0,1\ mV)$.
4. *Température V* : sensibilité à la température ($4.10^{-5}\ V/°C$)

Les sources d'incertitudes, supposées indépendantes et retenues pour la résistance sont les suivantes :

1. *Constructeur R* : caractéristiques techniques constructeur du shunt ($6\ \mu\Omega$).
2. *Température R* : sensibilité à la température ($8.10^{-7}\ \Omega/°C$)

À partir de ces informations, on construit, comme dans l'exemple précédent, les tableaux suivants avec les informations complémentaires discutées ci-après.

Bilan d'incertitudes classique *Voltmètre* — **Complément**

N°	*Source (l)*	*Type*	*Demi-étendue*	*Div.*	$u_{V,l}$ (μV)	*Poids* ($w_{V,l}$)	*Part L.O.* (γ_l)
V1	Répétabilité	A	-	-	**90**	45%	0%
V3	Constructeur	B	$0,1\ mV$	2	**50**	14%	0%
V4	Température	B	$0,04\ mV/°C$ (3°C)	$\sqrt{2}$	**85**	41%	85%

Bilan d'incertitudes classique *Résistance* — **Complément**

N°	*Source (l)*	*Type*	*Demi-étendue*	*Div.*	$u_{R,l}$ ($\mu\Omega$)	*Poids* ($w_{R,l}$)	*Part L.O.* (γ_l)
R3	Constructeur	B	$6\ \mu\Omega$	2	**3**	76%	0%
R4	Température	B	$0,8\ \mu\Omega/°C$ (3°C)	$\sqrt{2}$	**1,7**	24%	85%

On en déduit l'incertitude-type composée sur la tension et la résistance :

$$u_V \simeq 133,5.10^{-6} V \quad et \quad u_R \simeq 3,45\ .10^{-6}\Omega \tag{33}$$

Si l'on néglige le terme de covariance dans la formule (32) qui pourtant existe du fait de la température ambiante au moment de la mesure, on obtiendrait le résultat :

$$u_I^{sans\ covariance} \approx \sqrt{\left(\frac{\partial I}{dV}(\underline{\mu}).u_V\right)^2 + \left(\frac{\partial I}{dR}(\underline{\mu}).u_R\right)^2} \simeq 13,8\ mA \tag{34}$$

Les bilans d'incertitudes sont complétés comme dans l'exemple précédent pour estimer la covariance. Lors de la mesure, la résistance et le voltmètre sont soumis à peu près à la même température. Cette notion d'à peu près peut être quantifiée par les considérations métier suivantes sur le processus de mesure : les écarts variables de température entre le voltmètre et la résistance sont de 1°C sur une étendue de variation possible de 6°C, aussi, la part L.O. est choisie telle que : $\gamma_T \simeq \frac{5}{6} \simeq 85\%$.

Le signe $\pm_T^{V,R}$ peut être déduit du sens de variation des facteurs en fonction de la température. Nous considérons que l'erreur du voltmètre et la résistance augmentent avec la température. Comme les variations sont dans le même sens : $\pm_T^{V,R} = 1$. Si les variations avaient été en sens contraire (par exemple augmentation de la résistance et diminution de l'erreur du voltmètre avec la température) on aurait eu $\pm_T^{V,R} = -1$. Par conséquent avec les notations conventionnelles ($w_{V,T} = 41\%$ et $w_{R,T} = 24\%$) on a une approximation de la covariance par application de (23) :

$$\sigma_{V,R} = u_V u_R \; \gamma_T \sqrt{w_{V,T} w_{R,T}} \simeq 1,23.10^{-10} \; V^2\Omega^2 \tag{35}$$

On en déduit l'incertitude-type sur l'intensité du courant par (32) :

$$u_I \simeq 14,7 \; mA \tag{36}$$

L'impact de la covariance est de 6,5% sur l'évaluation de l'incertitude-type d'intensité du courant alors qu'elle est induite par une influence de la température pesant 40% dans l'incertitude de la tension et 24% dans celle de la résistance. Ce résultat, qui n'était pas nécessairement intuitif, est obtenu avec une analyse et des calculs simples.

4 Conclusion

L'application de la loi de propagation dans le cadre de l'évaluation des incertitudes de mesures impose de prendre en considération les éventuelles covariances entre les erreurs de mesures sur les grandeurs d'entrée. Les évaluations de type A des différentes covariances peuvent vite devenir difficiles à réaliser compte tenu du nombre de mesures d'un mesurande parfaitement stable dont il faut disposer. Le G.U.M propose donc d'estimer un coefficient de corrélation entre les erreurs de mesure, coefficient à partir duquel il est possible de calculer une covariance. La méthode que propose cet article permet, en définitive, de déterminer ce coefficient de corrélation en s'appuyant sur une analyse physique des conditions de la mesure. Comme nous l'avons démontré, la prise en compte du caractère L.O./H.O. des différents facteurs d'incertitude et les causes communes d'incertitude entre les grandeurs d'entrée suffisent, sous certaines hypothèses, à estimer les covariances. Comme les deux exemples proposés l'ont montré, ces évaluations-là (part L.O./H.O. et causes communes) étant facilement accessibles, le métrologue trouve avec cette méthode une solution simple pour prendre en compte tous les termes de la loi de propagation et ainsi améliorer la connaissance des incertitudes de son processus.

5 Bibliographie

[1] JCGM 100 (2008), Évaluation des données de mesure – Guide pour l'expression de l'incertitude de mesure (Evaluation of measurement data – Guide to the expression of uncertainty in measurement).

[2] NF ISO/CEI Guide 98-3 (2014), Guide pour l'expression de l'incertitude de mesure.

[3] C. Dubois (2013) Covariance dans le processus d'étalonnage – 16th International Congress of Metrology, EDP Sciences.

[4] G. Saporta (2006) Probabilités, Analyse des Données et Statistiques – 2ème édition révisée et augmentée, Paris, Editions Technip.

6 Annexe

Une variable aléatoire réelle X sur un espace de probabilité $(\Omega, \mathcal{T}, \mathbb{P})$ fixé est une application de Ω dans $\mathbb{R}$ telle que pour tout intervalle $]a, b[\subseteq \mathbb{R}$, $X^{-1}(]a, b[) \in \mathcal{T}$. Elle admet une densité $f_X : \mathbb{R} \to \mathbb{R}_+$ si, de plus :

$$\mathbb{P}(X \in [a, b]) = \int_a^b f_X(t)dt \tag{37}$$

Lorsqu'elle existe, l'espérance de X est définie par :

$$\mathbb{E}(X) = \int X \mathrm{d}\mathbb{P} = \int t f_X(t)\mathrm{d}t \tag{38}$$

La variable aléatoire réelle X est dite de carré intégrable si X^2 admet une espérance (X admet alors également une espérance).

Nous rappelons ci-dessous les formules usuelles de calcul d'espérance, de variance et de covariance d'une somme et d'un produit de variables aléatoires de carré intégrables (i.e. admettant une variance) non nécessairement indépendantes. Nous renvoyons le lecteur à Saporta (2006) pour la définition d'indépendance entre deux variables aléatoires réelles X et Y ainsi qu'à la définition d'espérance conditionnelle $\mathbb{E}(Y/X)$.

Soient X, Y et Z des variables aléatoires de carré intégrables. Par définition :

- $\mathbb{V}(X) = \mathbb{E}((X - \mathbb{E}(X))^2)$
- $\mathbb{C}ov(X, Y) = \mathbb{E}((X - \mathbb{E}(X))(Y - \mathbb{E}(Y))) = \mathbb{C}ov(Y, X)$

En conséquence, pour $a \in \mathbb{R}$:

- $\mathbb{E}(Y) = \mathbb{E}(\mathbb{E}(Y/X))$, $\quad \mathbb{V}(Y) = \mathbb{C}ov(Y, Y) = \mathbb{V}(\mathbb{E}(Y/X)) + \mathbb{E}(\mathbb{V}(Y/X))$
- $\mathbb{E}(X^2) = \mathbb{V}(X) + \mathbb{E}(X)^2$, $\quad \mathbb{V}(X^2) = \mathbb{E}(X^4) - \mathbb{E}(X)^4 - \mathbb{V}(X)^2 - 2\,\mathbb{V}(X)\mathbb{E}(X^2)$
- $\mathbb{E}(X + Y) = \mathbb{E}(X) + \mathbb{E}(Y)$, $\quad \mathbb{V}(X + Y) = \mathbb{V}(X) + \mathbb{V}(Y) + 2\,\mathbb{C}ov(X, Y)$
- $\mathbb{E}(aX) = a\,\mathbb{E}(X)$, $\quad \mathbb{V}(aX) = a^2\,\mathbb{V}(X)$
- $\mathbb{E}(XY) = \mathbb{E}(X)\mathbb{E}(Y) + \mathbb{C}ov(X, Y)$
- $\mathbb{V}(XY) = \mathbb{V}(X)\mathbb{E}(Y)^2 + \mathbb{V}(Y)\mathbb{E}(X)^2 + \mathbb{V}(X)\mathbb{V}(Y)$
  $$+\mathbb{C}ov(X^2, Y^2) - \mathbb{C}ov(X, Y)^2 - 2\,\mathbb{E}(X)\mathbb{E}(Y)\mathbb{C}ov(X, Y)$$
- $\mathbb{C}ov(X + Y, Z) = \mathbb{C}ov(X, Z) + \mathbb{C}ov(Y, Z)$

- $\mathbb{C}ov(aX, Z) = a\ \mathbb{C}ov(X, Z)$
- $\mathbb{C}ov(X+Y, XY) = \mathbb{V}(X)\mathbb{E}(Y) + \mathbb{V}(Y)\mathbb{E}(X)$
  $+\mathbb{C}ov(X^2, Y) + \mathbb{C}ov(Y^2, X) - (\mathbb{E}(X) + \mathbb{E}(Y))\mathbb{C}ov(X, Y)$

Lorsque X et Y sont indépendantes, $\mathbb{C}ov(X, Y) = 0$ et :

- $\mathbb{V}(X+Y) = \mathbb{V}(X) + \mathbb{V}(Y)$
- $\mathbb{E}(XY) = \mathbb{E}(X)\mathbb{E}(Y)$
- $\mathbb{V}(XY) = \mathbb{V}(X)\mathbb{E}(Y)^2 + \mathbb{V}(Y)\mathbb{E}(X)^2 + \mathbb{V}(X)\mathbb{V}(Y)$

Dans l'exemple d'un calcul de surface $S = l \times L$ avec $D = L$ ou l :

- $D = D_0(1 + \lambda\,(T - 20)) + E_D^{HO}$
- $\mu_D = D_0\lambda_T$
- $\sigma_D^2 = D_0^2\lambda^2\sigma_T^2 + \sigma^2_{E_D^{HO}}$
- $S = L_0 l_0(1 + \lambda\,(T - 20))^2 + (1 + \lambda\,(T - 20))(L_0 E_l^{HO} + l_0 E_L^{HO}) + E_l^{HO} E_L^{HO}$
- $\mathbb{E}(S/T) = L_0 l_0 (1 + \lambda(T - 20))^2 = L_0 l_0(\lambda_T^2 + \lambda^2(T - \mu_T)^2 + 2\lambda\lambda_T(T - \mu_T))$
- $\mathbb{V}(S/T) = (1 + \lambda(T - 20))^2(L_0^2\sigma_l^2 + l_0^2\sigma_L^2 - 2L_0^2 l_0^2\lambda^2\sigma_T^2)$
  $+(\sigma_L^2 - L_0^2\lambda^2\sigma_T^2)(\sigma_l^2 - l_0^2\lambda^2\sigma_T^2)$
- $\mathbb{V}(\mathbb{E}(S/T)) = L_0^2 l_0^2(\lambda^4\mathbb{E}((T - \mu_T)^4) - \lambda^4\sigma_T^4 + 4\lambda^2\lambda_T^2\sigma_T^2)$
- $\mathbb{E}(\mathbb{V}(S/T) = L_0^2 l_0^2\lambda_T^2\left(\frac{\sigma_l^2}{l_0^2} + \frac{\sigma_L^2}{L_0^2} - 2\lambda^2\sigma_T^2\right) - L_0^2 l_0^2\lambda^4\sigma_T^4 + \sigma_L^2\sigma_l^2$
- $\sigma_S^2 = \mathbb{V}(S) = \mathbb{V}(\mathbb{E}(S/T)) + \mathbb{E}(\mathbb{V}(S/T)$
  $= L_0^2 l_0^2\lambda_T^2\left(\frac{\sigma_l^2}{l_0^2} + \frac{\sigma_L^2}{L_0^2} + 2\lambda^2\sigma_T^2\right) + L_0^2 l_0^2\lambda^4(\mathbb{E}((T - \mu_T)^4) - 2\sigma_T^4) + \sigma_L^2\sigma_l^2$

Développement et caractérisation d'une photodiode ZnO/Ge pour les mesures de rayonnements optiques dans le proche infrarouge

Z. Ben Achour*, M. Hammami, O. Touayar***

*: Institut National des Sciences Appliqués et de Technologies, Université de Carthage, INSAT BP 676 Centre Urbain Nord 1080 Tunis Cedex, Tunisie.
**: Faculté des Sciences de Tunis, Université El Manar, Compus Universitaire Farhat Hachad, Tunis, Tunisie.

Résumé

Les travaux de recherche de l'équipe de Métrologie des rayonnements optiques et pyrométriques de l'INSAT englobent entre autre le développement de détecteur servant aux mesures de rayonnements optiques dans le domaine visible et infrarouge. Dans le présent travail, nous présentons l'étude et la réalisation d'un nouveau type de détecteur pour les mesures de rayonnements proche Infrarouge soit donc une photodiode Ge/ZnO à base de jonction en Germanium et de couche mince d'oxyde de Zinc. Nous avons par la suite caractérisé optiquement et électriquement la photodiode ainsi réalisée pour laquelle nous avons élaboré un diagramme des bandes d'énergie. Les résultats obtenus nous ont permis de constater une amélioration des caractéristiques optiques et électriques de la photodiode ainsi réalisée par rapport à celles à base de Germanium simple réalisées dans notre laboratoire. Le diagramme des bandes d'énergie proposé explique le phénomène de transport de porteurs de charges pour notre structure et est en harmonie avec les résultats expérimentaux obtenus.

Mots clés

Photodiode, Oxyde de Zinc, Réflectivité, Résistance série, Résistance shunt, Mesures radiométriques.

Introduction

Des travaux de recherche menés au sein de l'équipe de recherche de mesures radiométriques et pyrométriques de L'INSAT, ont permis de réaliser par implantation ionique des jonctions NP à partir de substrat de Ge type P ainsi que la réalisation de photodiodes au germanium poreux [1-3]. Ces travaux ont montré une amélioration de l'absorption de la lumière incidente par rapport aux photodiodes commercialisées à base uniquement de jonction au germanium. Nous cherchons dans le présent travail à étudier l'influence apportée par une couche mince de ZnO déposée par dessus une jonction Ge réalisée par implantation ionique. En effet, les couches minces de ZnO en plus de leurs caractères transparents dans le proche infrarouge, elles forment d'excellents candidats pour les électrodes transparentes et les couches antireflet [4,3]. Ces propriétés optiques et électriques des couches minces de ZnO leurs permettent de diminuer la réflectivité des substrats sur lesquels elles sont déposées [6]. Dans la première partie de ce travail nous présentons les résultats de la caractérisation électrique et optique des jonctions à base de germanium uniquement. Dans la deuxième partie on s'intéresse au développement et à la caractérisation optique et électrique du nouveau type de photodiode Ge/GeZnO que nous avons développé. Ces photodiodes sont à base de jonction Germanium réalisée par implantation ionique où nous avons déposé par dessus une couche mince d'oxyde de zinc par la technique Spary pyrolisis [4,7,8]. Nous proposerons par la suite un diagramme des bandes d'énergie de la structure ainsi réalisée.

1. Caractérisation des jonctions NP au Germanium:

Les jonctions utilisées sont des jonctions NP au germanium réalisées par implantation ionique à partir de substrat de Ge type P polymiroir. Ce substrat de type P est initialement dopé Galium, d'orientation (1,0,0), de résistivité inférieur à 1 Ω cm et d'épaisseur 300 μm. Ces substrats présente une reflectivité de l'ordre de l'ordre de 33% environ pour la plage de longueur d'onde allant de 800 nm à 2000nm [1,2]. L'implantation ionique est réalisée par l'implanteur ionique installé à l'Institut de Microélectronique de Barcelone. Elle est réalisée avec une énergie du faisceau ionisant de 150 keV pour des doses d'impuretés de Phosphore égale à 1.10^{-15} at/cm^2 [1,9,10]. Les jonctions ainsi réalisées présentent une profondeur de jonction de quelques 0,4 μm.

1.1. Caractérisation électrique des jonctions au germanium:

La caractéristique I-V montre les processus internes qui régissent le fonctionnement de la cellule. Elle représente aussi les grandeurs macroscopiques en l'occurrence Rs, Rsh , Iph et le courant diodique ce qui reflète les phénomènes de transport des porteurs charges à l'intérieur de la structure.

La caractéristique I-V sous éclairement est relevée sur un banc de mesure éclairé par une lampe spectrale et polarisé par une tension délivrée par une alimentation continue.

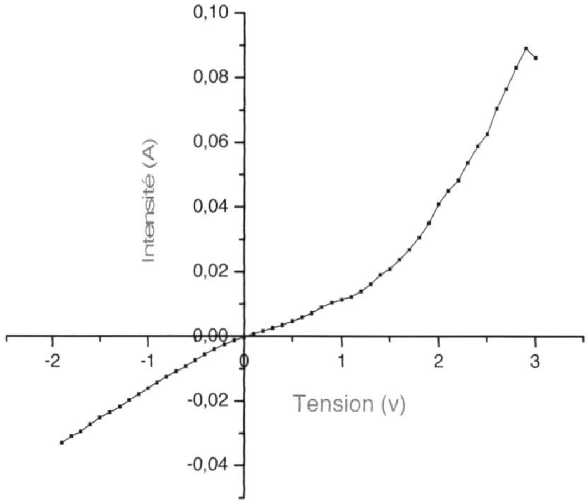

Fig. 1. Réponse I-V des jonctions au germanium

D'après la courbe de réponse I-V on en déduit le courant photonique correspondant aux jonctions au germanium I_{ph} = $-8{,}52.10^{-5}$ A. L'exploitation de cette caractéristique nous a aussi permis de déterminer les valeurs de la résistance série R_S = 1,08 Ω et de celle shunt R_{sh} = 94,98 Ω.

Dans le tableau suivant (Table. 1.) on synthétise les différents paramètres électriques des jonctions au germanium.

Table. 1. Paramètres électriques des jonctions au germanium

Tension seuil V_s	0,411 V
Courant photonique I_{ph}	$-8{,}52.10^{-5}$ A
Courant de saturation I_{sat}	$6{,}1.10^{-4}$ A
Résistance série R_s	1,08 Ω
Résistance shunt R_{sh}	94,98 Ω

La résistance série est de même ordre que celles des photodiodes commercialisées. Sa faible valeur reflète la qualité de l'état de la structure interne. En effet, l'implantation ionique est un processus de dopage ayant pour résultat une distribution uniforme des impuretés implantés. Par ailleurs, le traitement post-implantation permet de guérir des défauts apparus lors de l'implantation ce qui réduits les pièges des porteurs de charge et par conséquent la résistance série.
La résistance shunt comptabilisée au niveau des jonctions est inférieure à celles des photodiodes commercialisées qui ont une résistance shunt de quelques centaines d'ohms. En effet, cette résistance caractérise les pertes par recombinaison des porteurs dues aux défauts structurales du germanium. L'existence de fissures et de défauts de structure complexes en surface, devient également le siège de phénomène physique assimilable à une résistance parallèle Rsh [9, 10].

1.2. Caractérisation optiques des jonctions au germanium:

La détermination de la valeur de la réflectivité nous permet d'évaluer le niveau de perte par réflexion du flux lumineux incident à l'interface Germanium/Air du dispositif formant la photodiode que nous désirons réaliser.

Les mesures ont été effectuées au Laboratoire de Physique de la Matière Condensé (LPMC) de la Faculté des Sciences de Tunis avec un spectrophotomètre Perkin Elmer lambda 950 (Fig. 2.). L'intervalle spectrale s'étale de l'UV visible de 200 nm, jusqu'au proche infrarouge 2500 nm.

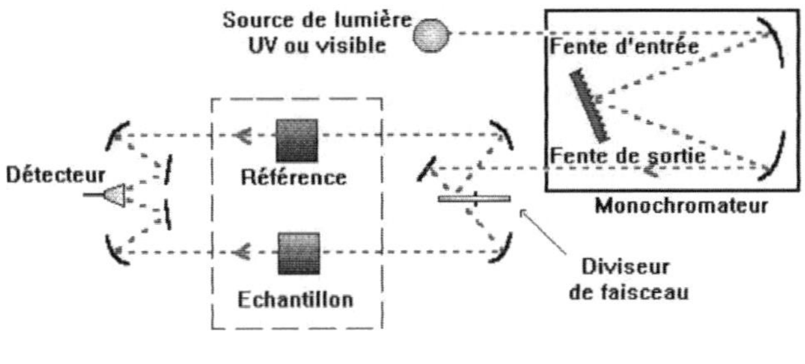

Fig. 2. Schéma de principe du spectromètre Perkin Elmer lambda 950

Sur la figure ci-dessous (Fig. 3.) nous représentons les résultats de la réflectivité des photodiodes à base de jonction au germanium seulement.

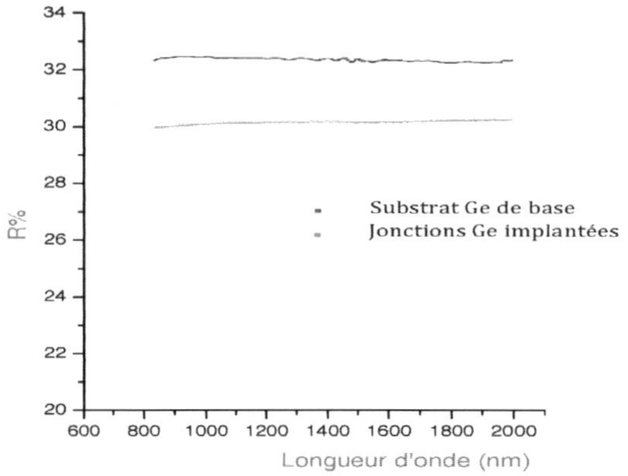

Fig. 3. Réflectivité des jonctions à base de germanium

La réflectivité des jonctions au germanium est de 30 % en moyenne sur la gamme de longueur d'onde allant de 800 nm à 2000 nm environ. Nous constatons par ailleurs, une légère réduction de la réflectivité de près de 3% en moyenne entre les jonctions au Germanium et celle des substrats de base. Cette réduction de la réflectivité est due d'une part à l'oxyde natif et d'autre part à l'oxydation du germanium lors du traitement post-implantation. En effet, l'implantation ionique engendre un désordre cristallographique au niveau de la matrice implanté, nécessitant ainsi un recuit qui permet de guérir les défauts induits par l'implantation, d'activer les impuretés implantées et d'homogénéiser la couche dopée. L'analyse des résultats trouvés nous permet d'en déduire qu'après l'optimisation des conditions de fabrication des jonctions, il serait impératif d'introduire des couches antireflets dans la structure des photodiodes au germanium. Ces couches permettront d'une part de réduire la réflectivité et d'autre part de stabiliser chimiquement la surface du germanium et préserver ses caractéristiques physico-chimiques.

2. Dépôt du ZnO sur les jonctions Ge et caractérisation:

Les couches minces de ZnO sont déposées par la technique Spray Pyrolisis sous ambiance inerte à partir d'une solution d'acétate de zinc 0,1M dopé à l'Aluminium à 3%. La température de dépôt est 460°C pour une durée optimale de 60 mn [4]. Le choix de cette durée et de cette température permet l'obtention de couches de ZnO transparentes à 90% dans la plage allant de 500 nm à 2500 nm. Les couches minces de ZnO ainsi réalisées ont une résistivité égale à 3.10^{-3} Ω.cm et une orientation cristallographique préférentielle (0,0,2) [4]. L'épaisseur de ces films fins est de quelques 1 μm environ et leurs gaps est de l'ordre de 3,21 eV [4].

La figure suivante (Fig. 4.) représente une coupe en tranche de la structure formant la photodiode Ge/ZnO ainsi réalisée.

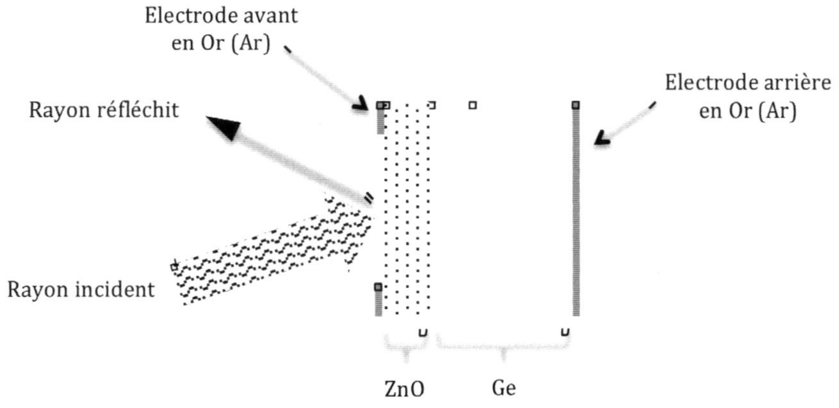

Fig. 4. : Structure de la photodiode ZnOGe

2.1. Caractérisation optique de la structure Ge/ZnO:

On s'intéresse dans cette partie à l'étude de la réflectivité de la nouvelle structure ainsi réalisée soit la Ge/ZnO et ce dans la plage de longueur d'onde 800 à 2000 nm. Les résultats de cette étude menée sur le même spectromètre utilisé précédemment, sont représentés sur la figure suivante (Fig. 5.):

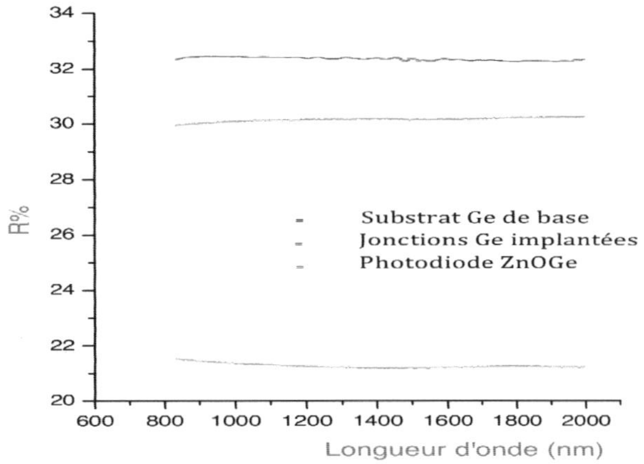

Fig. 5. Réflectivité de la photodiode ZnOGe

Nous constatons bien que les couches de ZnO apportent une réduction nette de la réflectivité des jonctions Ge. En effet, la réflectivité passe de 30% à 21% en moyenne sur une plage de longueur d'onde allant de 800 à 2000 nm soit donc un gain de près de 9% pour l'absorption du flux lumineux. Ce gain est du d'une part au caractère antireflet des couches minces de ZnO déposées sur les jonctions Ge. D'autre part, les couches minces de ZnO sont des couches cristallines lorsqu'elles sont déposées sur une surface polymiroir ne présentant aucune rugosité elles forment des lames à faces parallèles. Par conséquent, tout rayonnement lumineux incident est confiné en partie dans le ZnO ce qui augmente l'absorption par la jonction Ge.

2.2. Caractérisation Electrique de la structure Ge/ZnO:

Pour cette partie nous avons adopté la même démarche décrite précédemment. Sur la figure (Fig. 6.) nous avons représenté les relevés de la caractéristique I-V de la photodiode Ge/ZnO.

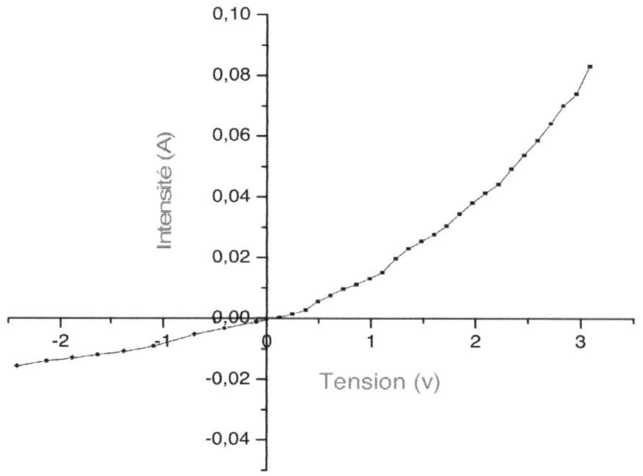

Fig. 6. Réponse I-V de la photodiode ZnOGe

D'après cette caractéristique, on peut déduire que la structure de la photodiode au germanium munie d'une couche mince de ZnO sur sa face avant, présente une résistance série Rs et une résistance shunt Rsh, plus élevées que la photodiode à base de jonction au germanium seulement. En effet, la pente $\Delta I/\Delta V$ $(V \longrightarrow 0)$ diminue nettement, ce qui entraine ainsi une diminution des courants de fuite et une augmentation notable de la résistance shunt.

Lorsque la photodiode au germanium est munie d'une couche mince de ZnO, on remarque une nette amélioration de sa réponse en courant suite à la variation de la tension ce qui s'explique par les nouvelles valeurs des résistances série et shunt qu'on a pu obtenir.

L'amélioration de la caractéristique I-V après introduction de la couche de ZnO dans la structure de la photodiode est due aux caractéristiques optiques et électriques de cette couche. En effet, son aspect antireflet permet de confiner énergétiquement le flux lumineux ce qui améliore l'absorption de la photodiode et par conséquent sa réponse. Le courant photonique déterminé à partir de la caractéristique I-V sous éclairement est de l'ordre de $-1{,}22.10^{-5}$ A

L'augmentation considérable de la résistance shunt de 94,98 Ω jusqu'à 12,915 kΩ suite à la déposition de la couche mince de ZnO est due à la passivation des liaisons pendantes du germanium ainsi que l'oxyde natif. Ceci entraine donc une réduction des puits quantiques et des imperfections dans lesquels sont piégés les porteurs de charges notamment en surface. Outre cela, les couches minces de ZnO sont des électrodes transparentes permettant ainsi de récupérer les charges créées en surface. Ceci a donc pour conséquences de diminuer les vitesses de recombinaison des porteurs de charges et d'allonger leur durée de vie en surface.

Par ailleurs, on note une augmentation de la résistance série qui caractérise la résistance interne de la cellule de 1,08 jusqu'à 36 Ω. Cette variation est probablement du aux effets d'agitation thermique sur la structure interne de la jonction suite au recuit lors du dépôt de la couche ZnO. Nous pouvons aussi attribuer cette augmentation à la barrière de potentiel qui se crée à l'interface ZnO/Ge. En effet, le gap du Germanium est de 0,66 eV [1] et celui de la couche ZnO déposée de l'ordre de 3,21 eV [4].

Les paramètres caractéristiques de la photodiode ZnOGe sont regroupés dans le tableau suivant (Table. 2.) :

Table. 2. Paramètres électriques de la photodiode ZnOGe

Tension seuil V_s	0,471 V
Courant photonique I_{ph}	$-1{,}22.10^{-5}$ A
Courant de saturation I_{sat}	8.10^{-4} A
Résistance série R_s	36 Ω
Résistance shunt R_{sh}	12,915 kΩ

3. Diagramme des bandes d'énergie:

Afin de mieux comprendre le processus de conversion des porteurs de charges et de mieux interpréter l'amélioration apportée par le dépôt des couches minces ZnO sur les photodiodes au germanium, nous proposons un diagramme des bandes d'énergie de la structure ZnOGe ainsi réalisée. Le modèle physique du schéma des bandes d'énergie que nous proposons est un modèle expliquant les mécanismes de la conduction électrique au sein de notre photodiode et tenant compte des différentes couches et leurs propriétés physiques.

Notre structure étudiée est une hétérojonction où deux semiconducteurs de natures différentes sont mis en contact. Lorsque les deux semi-conducteurs sont mis en contact, ils échangent des électrons de manière à aligner leurs niveaux de Fermi. Cet échange se fait au voisinage de la jonction et fait apparaître une charge d'espace à laquelle est associée une barrière de potentiel V_d qui arrête la diffusion des porteurs et définit l'état d'équilibre.

$$V_d = V_2 - V_1 = \phi_1 - \phi_2 \quad (1)$$

où: $\phi_1$et ϕ_2 les potentiels des deux semiconducteurs et $e\phi_1, e\phi_2$les travaux de sorties correspondants.

La condition $\phi_2 > \phi_1$ entraîne $V_d < 0$, il s'établit ainsi une différence de potentiel positive entre le semi-conducteur à faible travail de sortie et le semi-conducteur à fort travail de sortie.

Les différences de densité d'états et de dopage des semi-conducteurs entrainent des valeurs différentes des paramètres $e\phi_{F1}$et $e\phi_{F2}$, c'est-à-dire des valeurs différentes des énergies des bandes de conduction des régions neutres des deux semi-conducteurs.

Soit : $\Delta E_{c_n} = \Delta E_{c_1} - \Delta E_{c_2} = e(\phi_{F_1} - \phi_{F_2})$ (2) [11]

Enfin si la différence des énergies de gap de deux semi-conducteurs est différente de ΔE_{c_n}, le complément se traduit par une différence d'énergie des bandes de valence avec la conduction.

$$\Delta E_g = E_{g_2} - E_{g_1} = (E_{c_2} - E_{c_1}) - (E_{v_2} - E_{v_1})$$

Soit donc: $\Delta E_g = \Delta E_{c_n} - \Delta E_{v_n}$ (3)

La différence d'énergie des bandes de valence est par conséquent donnée par :

$$\Delta E_{v_n} = e(\phi_{F_2} - \phi_{F_1}) - \Delta E_g$$

or $\Delta E_{c_n} = e(\phi_{F_2} - \phi_{F_1}) = e[(\phi_2 - \chi_2) - (\phi_1 - \chi_1)] = -eV_d - e(\chi_2 - \chi_1)$ (4)

d'où $\Delta E_{v_n} = -eV_d - [e(\chi_2 - \chi_1) + \Delta E_g]$ (5)

avec:

ΔE_{c_n}: la différence d'énergie des bandes de conduction

ΔE_{v_n}: la différence d'énergie des bandes de valence

ΔE_g: la différence des gaps des deux semiconducteurs

En raison de la continuité du potentiel, à l'interface V_1=V_2 ainsi donc les équations 4 et 5 deviennent au voisinage de la jonction :

$\Delta E_{c_n}(\text{à } l'interface) = -e(\chi_2 - \chi_1)$ (6)

$\Delta E_{v_n}(\text{à}l'interface) = -[e(\chi_2 - \chi_1) + \Delta E_g]$ (7)

3.1. Hétéro-jonction n-n : Oxyde de zinc-Germanium

Notre hétéro-structure correspond à une jonction de l'oxyde de zinc sur le front de type n de la photodiode du germanium poly-miroir où $e\phi_{ZnO} > e\phi_{Ge}$.

Ainsi donc, les électrons diffusent du germanium Ge vers l'oxyde de zinc ZnO et vice versa pour les trous. Le régime d'équilibre s'établit par diffusion des électrons du germanium vers le ZnO et vice versa pour les trous, donc les électrons sont repoussés de l'interface et les trous en sont attirés.

On a :

$E_{ZnO} = 3{,}33\ eV$ [4], $e\chi_{ZnO} = 4{,}1\ eV$ [11], $e\phi_{ZnO} = 5{,}33\ eV$ [12]

$E_{Ge} = 0{,}66\ eV$ [13], $e\chi_{Ge} = 4\ eV$ [13], $e\phi_{Ge} = 4{,}16\ eV$ [13].

d'où $eV_d = e(V_2 - V_1) = -(e\phi_{Ge} - e\phi_{ZnO}) = -1{,}17\ eV$

Au voisinage de la jonction on a donc:

$$-e(\chi_{Ge} - \chi_{ZnO}) = 0{,}1\ eV$$

$$\Delta E_g = E_{Ge} - E_{ZnO} = -2{,}67\ eV$$

$$-[\Delta E_g + e(\chi_{Ge} - \chi_{ZnO})] = 2{,}77\ eV$$

Par conséquent :

$$\Delta E_{c_n} = -[e(\phi_{Ge} - \phi_{ZnO}) - e(\chi_{Ge} - \chi_{ZnO})] = -1{,}27\ eV$$

$$\Delta E_{v_n} = -[\Delta E_g + e(\chi_{Ge} - \chi_{ZnO})] - eV_d = 3{,}94\ eV$$

Suite aux différentes explications suscitées on peut proposer comme diagramme d'énergie de la première partie de notre structure étudiée soit donc ZnO/front de la photodiode au germanium, le diagramme suivant :

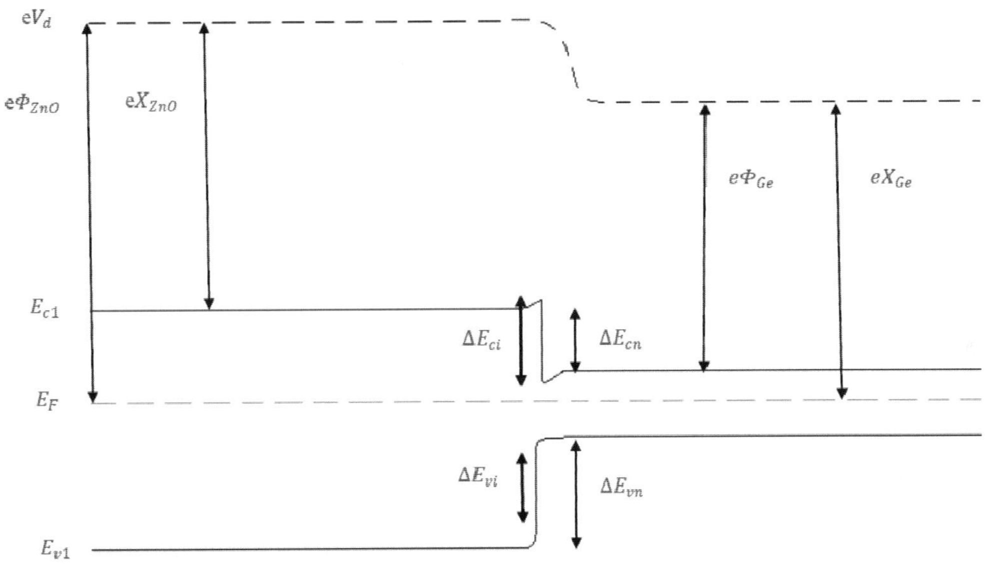

Fig. 7. Diagramme des bandes d'énergie de la structure ZnO/Germanium type n

Suite à la diffusion des électrons du Ge vers le ZnO et vice versa pour les trous, il apparaît une charge d'espace positive dans le Ge et négative dans le ZnO. Cette charge d'espace est de nature et d'extension spatiale tout à fait différents suivant le type de chaque semi-conducteur.

Dans le semi-conducteur ZnO la charge d'espace est négative (le ZnO est de type n), cette charge d'espace est du à une augmentation de la densité d'électron au voisinage de l'interface. D'où la charge d'espace dans le semi-conducteur ZnO est une charge d'accumulation et elle est localisée au voisinage immédiat de l'interface.

Pour le semi-conducteur Ge la charge d'espace est au contraire positive, il s'établit au voisinage de l'interface un régime de déplétion avec une certaine extension spatiale de la densité de charge.

3.1. Diagramme final de la photodiode ZnOGe

La structure de notre photodiode ZnOGe est constituée de deux parties. La première partie est une hétérojonction n-n d'oxyde de zinc et de germanium. La deuxième partie est une homojonction n-p au germanium qui formait la photodiode de base avant le dépôt de la couche ZnO.

En tenant compte de tous les paramètres caractéristiques de toutes les parties de la photodiode ZnOGe, nous proposons dans la figure 8 un diagramme des bandes d'énergie de cette structure.

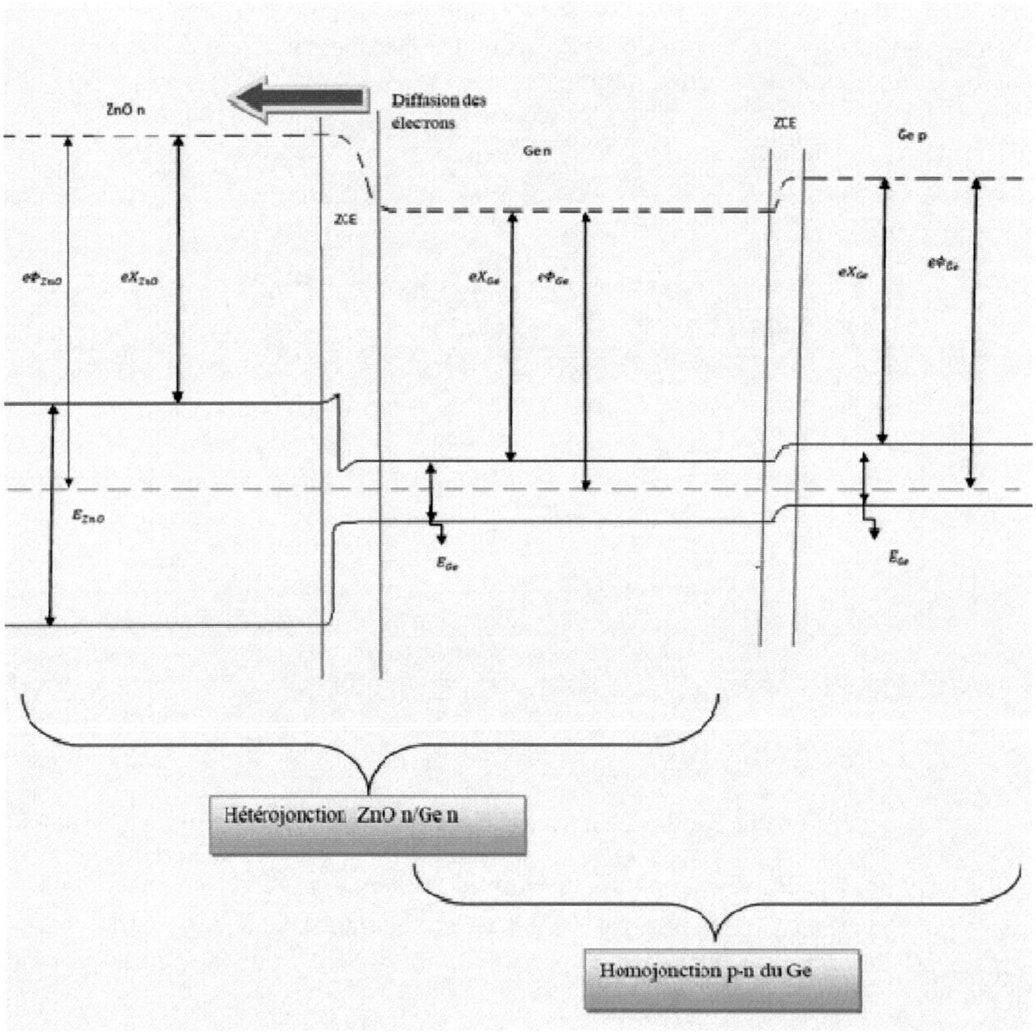

Fig. 8. Diagramme des bandes d'énergie de toute la photodiode ZnOGe

Le courant est toujours beaucoup plus important au niveau d'une forte discontinuité qu'à au niveau d'une pseudo-continuité.

Au niveau d'une forte discontinuité la barrière de potentiel est relativement étroite au voisinage du sommet de sorte que certains porteurs peuvent passer par effet Tunnel. Ce processus est un processus qu'on peut qualifie d'intra-bande [11].

Conclusion :

Les études optiques et électriques menées sur la photodiode ZnOGe, mettent en évidence l'amélioration significative des caractéristiques des jonctions germanium après introduction des couches mince de ZnO dopées aluminium dans la structure. En effet, nous avons noté une réduction de la réflectivité de 13 %. La nouvelle photodiode présente une réflectivité de quelques 21 % en moyenne sur la plage de longueur d'onde allant de 800 nm à 2000 nm. Nous avons aussi mis en évidence l'amélioration des caractéristiques électriques notamment la résistance shunt qui a grimpé de 95 Ω jusqu'à 12,915 kΩ suite à la déposition de la couche mince de ZnO. Néanmoins nous avons noté une légère augmentation de la résistance série qui est passé de 1.08 Ω à 36 Ω et qui reste comparable à celle des photodiodes commercialisées. Le diagramme des bandes d'énergie proposé explique le processus de transfert de porteurs de charge dans les différentes parties constituant notre structure ZnOGe et apporte quelques arguments physique supplémentaires à l'amélioration électrique observée. Nous chercherons dans des travaux ultérieurs à mener une caractérisation métrologique de la photodiode ainsi réalisée. Ceci permettra éventuellement de concevoir ce type de photodiode pour des applications radiométriques.

Bibliographie :

[1] : E. AKKARI, O. TOUAYAR, F.J del CAMPO, J.MONTSERRAT, Photodiode obtained by Phosphorus Ion Implantation, Int. J. Nanotechnology, Vol. 10, 553- 562 (2013).

[2] E. AKKARI, Z.BEN ACHOUR, S.AOUIDA, O.TOUAYAR, B.BESSAIS and J.BEN BRAHIM, Study and Characterization of Porous Germanium for Radiometric Measurements", Phys.Status Solidi C 6, N° 7, 1685-1688 (2009).

[3] E. AKKARI, Oualid TOUAYAR and Brahim BESSAIS, Reflectivity, Absorption and Structural Studies of Porous Germanium", Sensor LETTERS Vol 9, 2295-2298 (2011).

[4] : Z. Ben Achour, T. Ktari, B. Ouertani, O. Touayar, B. Bessais, J. Ben Brahim, Effect of doping level and spray time on zinc oxide thin films produced by spray pyrolysis for transparent electrodes applications, Sensors and Actuators A, 134, pp.447–451 (2007).

[5] : S. Major, S. Kumar, M. Bhatnagar, Appl. Phys. Lett. 49, 394 (1986).

[6] : Z. Ben Achour, O. Touayar, E. Akkari, J. Bastie, B. Bessais, J. Ben Brahim, Study and realization of a transfer detector based on porous silicon for radiometric measurements, Nuclear Instruments and Methods in Physics Research A, 579, pp.1117–1121 (2007).

[7] : F. Paraguay, W. Estrada, D.R. Acosta, Thin Solid Films 350, 192 (1999).

[8] : M. Amlouk, F. Touhari, S. Belgacem, N. Kamoun, R. Bennaceur, Phys. Status Solidi (a) 163, 73 (1997).

[9] : E. Simoen, A. Satta, A. D'Amore, T. Janssens, T. Clarysse, K. Martens, B. De Jaeger, A. Benedetti, I. Hoflijk, B. Borijs, M. Meuris, W. Vandercost, Materials Science in Semiconductor Processing 9, p634-639 (2006).

[10] : Th. Canneaux, D. Mathiot, J. P. Ponpon, S. Roques, S. Schmitt, Ch. Dubois, Materials Science and Engineering B 154-155, 68-71 (2008).

[11] : Henry Mathieu, Physique des semi-conducteurs et des composants électronique, Edition Masson, 300-334 (2009).

[12]: S. Yu. Davydov, V. A. Moshnikov, and A. A. Fedotov, Gas adsorption on Semiconducting Oxides : A change in the work Function , 2004.
[13]: Handbook of semiconductor Germanium technology/germanium Based from materials to devices (2004).